JOACHIM ROHDE

REDISCOVERING THE TEACHING OF
THE EVANGELISTS

THE NEW TESTAMENT LIBRARY

Advisory Editors

JOACHIM ROHDE

REDISCOVERING THE TEACHING OF THE EVANGELISTS

The Westminster Press
PHILADELPHIA

Translated by Dorothea M. Barton from the German
Die redaktionsgeschichtliche Methode
published 1966 by Furche-Verlag, Hamburg
(original edition, *Evangelische Verlagsanstalt*, Berlin)
with revisions and additional material from the author, 1968

STANDARD BOOK NO. 664–20856–8

LIBRARY OF CONGRESS CATALOG CARD NO. 69–14423

Published by The Westminster Press®
Philadelphia, Pennsylvania

PRINTED IN THE UNITED STATES OF AMERICA

CONTENTS

ABBREVIATIONS

ASNU	Acta Seminarii Neotestamentici Upsaliensis, Uppsala
AThANT	Abhandlungen zur Theologie des Alten und Neuen Testaments, Zürich
BhEvTh	Beihefte zur *Evangelischen Theologie*, Munich
BEvTh	Beiträge zur *Evangelischen Theologie*, Munich
BHTh	Beiträge zur historischen Theologie, Tübingen
BWANT	Beiträge zur Wissenschaft vom Alten und Neuen Testament, Stuttgart
BZ	*Biblische Zeitschrift*, Paderborn, New Series after 1957
BZNW	Beihefte zur Zeitschrift für die Neutestamentliche Wissenschaft, Giessen/Berlin
EvTh	*Evangelische Theologie*, Munich
FRLANT	Forschungen zur Religion und Literatur des Alten und Neuen Testaments, Göttingen
HNT	Handbuch zum Neuen Testament, Tübingen
KEKNT	Kritisch-exegetischer Kommentar über das Neue Testament (Meyer), Göttingen
KuD	*Kerygma und Dogma*, Göttingen or Berlin
NF	New Series
NovTest	*Novum Testamentum*, Leiden
NTA	Neutestamentliche Abhandlungen, Münster
NTF	Neutestamentliche Forschungen, Gütersloh
NTS	*New Testament Studies*, Cambridge
RGG	*Religion in Geschichte und Gegenwart*, Tübingen
RNT	Regensburger Neues Testament, Regensburg
SgVSThR	Sammlung gemeinverständlicher Vorträge und Schriften zur Theologie und Religionswissenschaft, Tübingen
StANT	Studien zum Alten und Neuen Testament, Munich
SupplNovTest	Supplementum Novum Testamentum, Leiden/Köln
ThBl	*Theologische Blätter*, Leipzig
ThF	Theologische Forschung, Hamburg/Bergstedt
ThHKNT	Theologischer Handkommentar zum Neuen Testament, Berlin

ThLZ	*Theologische Literaturzeitung*, Leipzig/Berlin
ThR	*Theologische Rundschau*, Tübingen, New Series after 1929
ThZ	*Theologische Zeitschrift*, Basel
TU	Texte und Untersuchungen zur Geschichte der altchristlichen Literatur, Berlin
WMANT	Wissenschaftliche Monographien zum Alten und Neuen Testament, Neukirchen
WR NtlR	Wissenschaft der Religion, Neutestamentliche Reihe, Berlin
WUNT	Wissenschaftliche Untersuchungen zum Neuen Testament, Tübingen
ZDPV	*Zeitschrift des Deutschen Palästinavereins, Wiesbaden*
ZKG	*Zeitschrift für Kirchengeschichte*, Stuttgart
ZkTh	*Zeitschrift für katholische Theologie*, Wien
ZNW	*Zeitschrift für die neutestamentliche Wissenschaft*, Giessen/Berlin
ZSTh	*Zeitschrift für systematische Theologie*, Berlin
ZThK	*Zeitschrift für Theologie und Kirche*, Tübingen

FOREWORD

THE INVESTIGATION presented here is for the most part drawn from the second half of a dissertation entitled 'Form Criticism and Redaction Criticism in Modern New Testament Study', which was submitted to the Theological Faculty of Humboldt University in Berlin in the autumn semester of 1962. The extent of the work made it necessary for me to omit a great deal when preparing the text for publication in the original German edition, and it was only possible to mention in passing some of the more recent publications on the subject.

Fortunately, however, the making of the English translation enabled me to take account of a number of recent studies which have appeared in the last five years; I hope that as a result the reader will find an account of the most significant work on redaction criticism in German scholarship to have been done so far.

I am grateful to Professor D. Fascher and Professor D.Dr Schneider for all their help and advice, and for their critical comments during the writing of this book. It is dedicated to my wife.

I

FROM LITERARY CRITICISM TO REDACTION CRITICISM

I

A. The relationship between literary and source criticism and form criticism

THE HISTORY OF the study of the synoptic gospels is not concerned only with its continual advance towards fresh and more precise knowledge and with attempts to explain the problems presented by the extensive agreement of the synoptic gospels and by the characteristic divergences between them. It is at the same time also the history of the changing methods used in the endeavour to obtain fresh knowledge.

The purpose of the investigation offered in this book is to give an account of the method employed in the use of redaction criticism and of its achievements. We must begin, however, with a brief outline of the origin of this method of research, which had as its precursors both literary and source criticism as well as form criticism.

Literary criticism and source criticism reached a climax towards the end of the nineteenth century and at the beginning of the twentieth. At that time it was believed that the problems arising from the divergences and the agreements between the synoptic gospels could be explained by the two-source theory. There were even hopes that it would be possible to determine the precise extent and wording of both sources. But the variety in results was as great as the number of attempts. The last and at the same time the most extreme attempt at source analysis is represented by the two comprehensive volumes of Emanuel Hirsch, *Die Frühgeschichte des Evangeliums* (I/II 1941, I 1951[2]). We must also place in the same category the attempt still to be found today to reconstruct a special source for Luke.[1]

---

[1] J. Jeremias, 'Perikopen-Umstellungen bei Lukas?', *NTS* 4, 1957/8, pp. 115–19; F. Rehkopf, *Die lukanische Sonderquelle*, Tübingen 1959; cf. also the studies made by Schürmann of Luke's account of the Last Supper.

Since the last century, one hypothesis after another has been propounded dealing with sources, strata and original documents of the synoptic gospels. Yet they have all ended in a blind alley. In the last resort, the search for better and for the best sources of the life of Jesus is nothing more than the heritage of rationalism, which is so difficult to extirpate. Yet the synoptic tradition cannot be completely explained in this way.[2] Just because the conclusions diverged so far from each other, they yielded a negative proof that the synoptic problem could not be solved by this means alone. Undoubtedly the two-source theory was an important step towards the solution of the problem, as is shown by its fundamental significance even in redaction criticism.[3] But its acceptance without qualification (or as the sole method) and the hair-splitting subtlety of literary criticism generally could only lead into error. In searching for sources of an official nature, this theory passed across the boundary to historical criticism and its attempts to separate the sources were, at any rate in part, to a large extent subjective constructions.[4] Consequently, the verdict of Karl Ludwig Schmidt on source analysis at the beginning of this century would seem to be correct: 'In this matter the persons—I mean those who took part in the research and had to work out with the greatest acumen and in every detail a hypothesis of this kind—suffered fruitless martyrdom, and the same may be said of the objects which they attempted to ascertain. . . . Nevertheless, these things had and still have a significance in that they were the means by which an inadequate method was pursued and had to be pursued *ad absurdum*.'[5]

Research into the synoptic tradition had perhaps reached a dead end with Bousset's book, *Kyrios Christos* (1913), and its excessive emphasis on the influence of the theology of the community. It is against this background that we must see the rise of the form-critical method. Bousset was certainly aware of the inadequacy of the literary

[2] See K. L. Schmidt, *Das Christuszeugnis der synoptischen Evangelien*, BhEvTh 2, 1936, pp. 10f.

[3] On this see H. Conzelmann, *The Theology of St Luke*, London 1960, pp. 9–17. For the source problem in the synoptists see also W. G. Kümmel, *Introduction to the New Testament*, London and New York 1966, pp. 42–60. A recent contribution from the English-speaking world is R. L. Lindsey, 'A modified Two-Document Theory of the Synoptic Dependence and Interdependence', *Nov Test* 6, 1963, pp. 239–63.

[4] E. Schick, *Formgeschichte und Synoptikerexegese*, Münster 1940, p. 5.

[5] K. L. Schmidt, 'Die Stellung der Evangelien in der allgemeinen Literaturgeschichte', in: *Eucharisterion für Gunkel II*, Göttingen 1923, pp. 125f.

criticism and source analysis practised before his time. He was already demanding a fresh method of research 'which must above all discuss the style critically and apply itself to the study of the laws of the oral tradition'.[6] Thus the development of form criticism is connected with the fact that the earlier methods had simply come to a standstill in the labyrinth of theories about sources and were not getting any further. Moreover, owing to the fact that no fresh studies could be published, the First World War enforced a creative 'pause in the discussion'.[7]

In the literary and source criticism which preceded form criticism, the evangelists and the authors of the sources postulated were thought to be authors in their own right; i.e., the synoptic gospels and their earlier stages were regarded as the literary achievements of individuals. Here, however, two things were overlooked: first, the evangelists were also at the same time the exponents of the Christian community, the unknown forerunners and the bearers of the earliest tradition; secondly (and this was forgotten much more often), before the tradition was fixed in writing it was essentially an oral tradition. It was therefore necessary not only to estimate correctly the nature of the transmission as community tradition (to be distinguished from community theology), but also to take full account of the importance of the oral tradition and of the laws of its transmission.[8]

Whereas the two-source theory attempted to explain how the gospel material took fixed literary form, the last process in the transmission, form criticism, in view of the excessive subtlety of literary criticism, posed the question what the material looked like before it received permanent literary form.[9] The chief object of its enquiry was thus to investigate the oral tradition of the material preceding the gospels; form criticism is therefore 'palaeontology of the gospels' (col. 638).

The individual persons, such as the authors of the gospel had been considered to be, began to move into the background and to fade away the moment the synoptic gospels began to be regarded as the outcome of a pre-literary work of collection, undertaken by the Christian communities. Within the synoptic gospels the individual

[6] W. Bousset, *Kyrios Christos*, Göttingen 1921[2], p. 33.
[7] H. J. Ebeling, *Das Messiasgeheimnis und die Botschaft des Markus-Evangelisten*, Berlin 1939, p. 48.
[8] Cf. W. Michaelis, *Einleitung in das Neue Testament*, Bern 1954[2], p. 81.
[9] K. L. Schmidt, in the article 'Formgeschichte', *RGG* II[2], col. 639.

stories were now considered to be the primary matter, and their framework, i.e. the sketch of Jesus' life in Mark and most of the chronological statements and many of the geographical ones, to be secondary.[10] In other words, a distinction began to be made between transmitting and redaction.

The two-source theory failed to explain many details of the agreements and divergencies between the synoptic gospels, above all the agreement of two synoptists against the third (for example, of Mark and Luke against Matthew) particularly since the size of the sayings-source, Q, remained hypothetical, because no unanimity could be reached over its extent. Form criticism also relaxed the literary rigidity of the sources, so that they became 'more fluid transitional stages',[11] and they were understood as strata rather than as compositions.[12] As regards the relationship between form criticism and literary criticism it may be said that the form-critical method does indeed presuppose literary criticism, but at the same time it sets legitimate limits to its analysis of sources. It does so by demanding knowledge of previous history in decisions about material which has been fixed in writing. It seeks to trace the fortunes of the material back to the historical conditions out of which the formation of the material arose,[13] to determine its so-called *Sitz im Leben*. By means of concentrating attention consistently on the individual passages, form criticism has 'cleared the way for a task suited to the manner by which the synoptic gospels came into being and liberated us from a merely logic-chopping, scissors-and-paste method of dealing with the sources'.[14] Hence form criticism is at the same time a reaction against and a correction of an excessive subtlety in source-analysis.[15]

B. *Basic features of form criticism*

The most important insights and presuppositions of the form-critical

[10] Cf. G. Bertram, 'Die Geschichte der synoptischen Tradition', *ThBl* 1 1922, col. 9.
[11] A. Jülicher/E. Fascher, *Einleitung in das Neue Testament*, Tübingen 1931[7], p. 349.
[12] M. Dibelius, *From Tradition to Gospel*, London 1934, p. 235; cf. E. Fascher, *Die Formgeschichtliche Methode*, Giessen 1924, p. 233. On the source Q see W. G. Kümmel, *op. cit.*, pp. 51–58, and now: J. M. Robinson, λόγοι σοφῶν, in *Zeit und Geschichte* (Bultmann Festschrift), Tübingen 1964, pp. 77–96.
[13] E. Schick, *op. cit.*, p. 10.   [14] A. Jülicher/E. Fascher, *op. cit.*, p. 349.
[15] E. Schick, *op. cit.*, p. 10. On the problem of form criticism, cf. also W. Marxsen, *Einleitung in das Neue Testament*, Gütersloh 1964[2], pp. 112–19, and W. G. Kümmel, *op. cit.*, pp. 29f.

method as applied to the synoptic gospels may perhaps be summarized in six statements:

(1) The synoptic gospels are not homogeneous compositions, but collections of small units.

(2) In the pre-literary stage only small units (single stories, short groups of sayings, single *logia*) were handed on in the oral tradition.

(3) When the small units have been detached from the framework of the synoptic gospels, definite characteristic genres can be recognized (short stories, paradigms, legends, etc). During their pre-literary oral transmission, the individual genres had a particular *Sitz im Leben* in the Christian community.

(4) The evangelists collected the small units and strung them together loosely to form their gospels, the first one being Mark, the creator of the genre 'gospel'. Matthew and Luke certainly used Mark, but in addition they also drew material from oral tradition (sayings-material from the source Q).

(5) The synoptic gospels are not biographies in the historical sense, but testimonies to the faith of primitive Christianity.

(6) The Easter faith of the community did not remain without influence on the accounts of Jesus' life. They have been fashioned under the influence of the community's theology. Bultmann and Bertram especially presuppose in addition an unfettered theological productivity on the part of the community.

The first fundamental works of the form-critical method of studying the synoptic gospels originated with Karl Ludwig Schmidt, Martin Dibelius, Rudolf Bultmann, Martin Albertz and Georg Bertram. They were conceived independently of each other and influenced each other only in so far as they did not appear simultaneously, but within the three years 1919–22; thus those which appeared last could just comment briefly on the first ones. The affinity of method makes it clear that this new manner of approach was as it were in the air. First Karl Ludwig Schmidt dissolved the gospel framework with his book *Der Rahmen der Geschichte Jesu* (1919) and pointed out that all the introductory statements of place and time surrounding the individual passages were only interlacing links, merely the framework of the story. This cleared the way for considering the individual items without regard to the conception of the gospels as a whole, and for the question of the stage in the tradition during its oral transmission before the material was fixed in writing.

Recently, however, J. Schreiber has shown that it is not enough to eliminate the details of time and place as the work of the evangelist because of their doubtful historical reliability. These very details must be investigated with a view to discovering the theology contained in them.[16]

Martin Dibelius' book, *From Tradition to Gospel* (*Die Formgeschichte des Evangeliums*), which set out this theme, gave a name to the new method and at the same time indicated the road to be pursued. Dibelius proceeded synthetically, i.e. he started from the *Sitz im Leben* of the individual passages and sought to explain the traditional material of the gospel and its forms by the needs of the Christian community. Bultmann, on the other hand, in his book *The History of the Synoptic Tradition* (1921) proceeded analytically; he began with the individual units and by means of a meticulously scrupulous analysis endeavoured to answer the question whether they had been changed, enlarged or altered in the tradition or whether they were genuine old material. Whilst Dibelius worked out his method on relatively few individual passages, Bultmann analysed considerably larger parts of the matter of the synoptic tradition. In its second edition (1933), Dibelius' book had increased to three times its size. The author had not only expanded the individual chapters, e.g. on paraenesis and on the comparison of individual genres with similar literary forms in the Jewish and Hellenistic environment; he also inserted additional chapters, a study of legends and legendary themes and an analysis of the passion story. Bultmann's book, too, was substantially enlarged in the second edition (1931) both by his submission of the whole traditional material of the synoptists to analysis, and by a discussion of criticism of the form-critical method.

Unlike the works of these three New Testament scholars, the works of Albertz and Bertram are concerned only with particular parts of the material of the synoptic tradition. Whereas Albertz examined the gospel controversies in *Die synoptischen Streitgespräche* (1921), Bertram's book is called *Die Leidensgeschichte Jesu und der Christuskult* (The Passion Story of Jesus and the Cult of Christ) (1922). The method by which Albertz proceeds is the precise opposite of that used by the other scholars. He does not go back from the existing material in the synoptic gospels to the stage of the pre-literary tradition; he starts with the 'original conversation' (in the controversies) between Jesus and his opponents, and he goes forward to the fixing of these events in writing in the synoptic gospels. This

[16] J. Schreiber, *Theologie des Vertrauens*, Gütersloh 1967, especially pp. 87–217.

provokes Bultmann's criticism that his book cannot be claimed as genuine form-critical research.[17] Bertram's examination of the passion narrative ought to be called a historical study of the cult rather than a form-critical study (the sub-title of his book).[18] For he traces the alterations which the passion narrative underwent through the influence of the Christian cult, and understands this story to be essentially a cultic legend: 'We must understand the passion narratives in our gospels with the cult of the primitive community in mind'.[19]

Next came a detailed description and a critical appreciation of these first form-critical works by Fascher: *Die formgeschichtliche Methode* (1924). In this book, the roots of the principles underlying the methods of form criticism are traced back to Herder and Lessing.[20] In spite of all the criticism which was devoted in the ensuing years to the form-critical method, its insights and results have nevertheless been accepted by German New Testament scholars. They have also been accepted increasingly by Scandinavian, English and American scholars and have not been without an echo in Roman Catholic research.[21]

The synoptic gospels have remained the chief sphere of the form-critical method, yet its work has not been confined to them. It has in fact also undertaken 'incursions into other New Testament writings' (Fascher). These include not only the Acts of the Apostles, but in particular those passages of the epistles which did not receive their form initially from the author of the epistle in question, but were in existence previously and had simply been incorporated by him into his writing. In particular, the epistle of James, which consists of loosely connected paraenetic passages, was a profitable subject for form-critical research, as were the domestic codes, the lists of virtues and vices, and the cultic and liturgical passages in the epistles of the New Testament and in the Revelation of St John the

[17] R. Bultmann, *The History of the Synoptic Tradition*, Oxford and New York 1963, p. 40, note 2.

[18] Cf. on this his article 'Die Bedeutung der kultgeschichtlichen Methode für die neutestamentliche Forschung', *ThBl* 2, 1923, cols. 25–36.

[19] G. Bertram, *Die Leidensgeschichte Jesu und der Christuskult*, Göttingen 1922, p. 2.

[20] E. Fascher, *op. cit.*, pp. 8–37. In the part of my dissertation which has not been printed this path has been briefly sketched, with special attention to the immediate precursors of the form-critical method (pp. 6–14). In addition, the results of the works of Schmidt, Dibelius, Bultmann, Albertz and Bertram and Fascher's critical appreciation are described in detail (pp. 14–55).

[21] Cf. for this pp. 76–227 in the unprinted version of my dissertation.

Divine.[22] It is only in the case of the Gospel of John that the form-critical method is not applicable to the same extent as to the other New Testament writings. No method has yet been found, in view of its peculiar nature, which could be applied to the Gospel of John in the same way as form criticism.[23] On the other hand, the situation is different with regard to the New Testament apocryphal work, and especially the writings of the Apostolic Fathers, because in them, too, traditional matter has been accepted and incorporated.[24]

The results of form-critical studies have often been described in various articles. Here only the most important accounts in the literature need be mentioned. The continuing influence of the form-critical method is seen not least in the fact that the second editions of the fundamental works on form criticism by Dibelius and Bultmann have appeared in recent years in fresh editions with appendices, or rather supplements.[25] In addition, Bultmann's study-report, 'Die Erforschung der synoptischen Evangelien' (1926), which treats of the results of the discussion aroused by the form-critical method, has been republished in new enlarged editions in 1930 and 1960 (ET 'The Study of the Synoptic Gospels' in *Form Criticism*, New York, 1934). The analogous report by Dibelius appeared in *ThR NF1*, 1929, pp. 185–216. In his article 'Zur Formgeschichte des Neuen Testaments (ausserhalb der Evangelien)' in *ThR NF3*, 1931, pp. 207–42, Dibelius endeavours to demonstrate how form criticism may be used for New Testament writings other than the synoptics. From the pen of Schniewind comes the article 'Zur Synoptikerexegese' in *ThR NF2*, 1930, pp. 129–89. A very detailed and instructive account by Gerhard Iber of this research, 'Zur Formgeschichte der Evangelien' in *ThR NF24*, 1957/58, pp. 283–338 shows not only how form-critical study has continued in Germany, but also how the stimulus of this method has been felt in other countries, especially in English-speaking areas. The response of Roman Catholicism to form criticism has been dealt with in the unprinted version of my dissertation on pp. 197–227.[26]

[22] On this see *op. cit.*, pp. 234–59.
[23] On this see *op. cit.*, pp. 228–34.
[24] The position in these has been sketched in my dissertation on pp. 259–70.
[25] M. Dibelius, *Die Formgeschichte des Evangeliums* (third revised edition, edited by Günther Bornkamm with an addendum by Gerhard Iber, Tübingen, 1959). The ET is of the second German edition, 1933. R. Bultmann, *Die Geschichte der synoptischen Tradition* (third edition, Göttingen 1957; fourth edition with a supplement in collaboration with P. Vielhauer, Göttingen 1959; reprint of the fourth edition, Berlin 1961). The ET, *The History of the Synoptic Tradition*, is of the fourth German edition.
[26] See in addition a recent Roman Catholic contribution: R. Schnackenburg, 'Zur formgeschichtlichen Methode in der Evangelienforschung', *ZkTh* 85, 1963, pp. 16–32.

C. *An account of redaction criticism*

Between the two world wars the form-critical method played an ever-increasing part in studies of the synoptic gospels and outside them as well. Criticism has indeed been repeatedly directed at its exaggerations, but its positive applications have been accepted and utilized and sometimes even extended. After 1945, research into the synoptics showed a trend similar to that after the First World War. The cessation of literary publications enforced by the war led to endeavours to pass beyond form criticism and to put fresh questions to the synoptic gospels. This opened up the possibility of emerging from a certain stagnation and attenuation of form criticism to an aesthetic consideration of the form of the text.[27]

Previously questions had been raised about the history of the *forms*; now it was the turn of the *redaction*; in other words, whereas previously attention had been concentrated on the *small units*, now the *gospels as a whole* began to be examined again. For it had been recognized that the evangelists were not only *collectors* and *transmitters* of traditional material. In their work as redactors they had also to some degree to be regarded as authors in their own right. They were seen to be men who by their methods, and particularly by arranging the material with a quite definite object in view and in quite definite contexts, were attempting to express their own theology, and more than that, the theology of a quite definite group and trend in primitive Christianity. Nevertheless, the resources for presenting the particular theology of each of the synoptists were modest and each had only a limited scope. Beside the grouping of the material under definite points of view and in definite contexts, it was a matter of selection, omission and inclusion of traditional material, and modifications of it, which, although slight, were yet very characteristic.[28]

The method of redaction criticism, with which we are here concerned, is in principle applicable only to the synoptic gospels, including the Acts of the Apostles, and not to the Epistles. An exception may at the most be made for the Epistle of James. In this case scholars are beginning to abandon the extensive lack of cohesion as

[27] Cf. G. Klein, *Die zwölf Apostel*, Göttingen 1961, p. 17.
[28] Cf. G. Bornkamm in the introduction to *Tradition and Interpretation in Matthew*, London and New York 1963, p. 11 and *ThLZ* 79, 1954, col. 341.

a principle of exegesis and to regard the Epistle as a theological whole.[29]

The first important figure was Bornkamm, who analysed the pericope of the Stilling of the Storm by means of redaction criticism.[30] He was at once followed by other scholars; nearly all of these belonged to the fresh university generation which extended his method of investigation to all the synoptic gospels and to the Acts of the Apostles. In addition to these there are already complete studies in redaction criticism, as well as several short articles, amongst them those of Conzelmann (*The Theology of St Luke*, 1960) and Marxsen (*Der Evangelist Markus*, 1956[1], 1959[2]). These outline the programme of redaction criticism in the same way as the works of Dibelius and Bultmann did for the method of form criticism. There are also several investigations into the Gospel of Matthew and Acts with a more restricted scope. It is in my opinion open to question whether the Swedish study, *The School of St Matthew*, by K. Stendahl can be regarded as a contribution to redaction-critical research. At any rate, Stendahl's conclusions have been received far more critically than the works in the German language. Common to them all is the fact that they are based on form criticism and have continued to build on its results.

However that may be, the redaction-critical method has meanwhile emerged from the stage of fundamental debate on the foundations and general outlines to that of taking a cross-section of the synoptic gospels. Examples of this are provided by the studies of G. Klein (*Die Zwölf Apostel*, 1961), J. Gnilka (*Die Verstockung Israels*, 1961), G. Baumbach (*Das Verständnis des Bösen in den synoptischen Evangelien*, 1963) and E. Grässer (*Das Problem der Parusieverzögerung in den synoptischen Evangelien und in der Apostelgeschichte*, 1957), while S. Schulz (in his investigation *Die Stunde der Botschaft*, 1967) attempts to sum up the whole contribution of previous work in redaction criticism to date.

The expression 'redaction criticism' was first coined by Marxsen in the *Monatsschrift für Pastoraltheologie* 1954, Heft 6, p. 254, where he discussed Conzelmann's book and problems of method. It is then

[29] On this see G. Braumann, 'Der theologische Hintergrund des Jakobusbriefes', *ThZ* 18, 1962, pp. 401–10: J. B. Souček, 'Zu den Problemen des Jakobusbriefes', *EvTh* 18, 1958, pp. 460–8.

[30] G. Bornkamm, 'Die Sturmstillung im Matthäusevangelium', in *Wort und Dienst, Jahrbuch der Theologischen Schule Bethel NF* 1, 1948, pp. 49–54; reprinted in G. Bornkamm, G. Barth and H. J. Held, *Tradition and Interpretation in Matthew*, 1963, pp. 52–57.

used regularly in his inaugural dissertation, which carries the sub-title 'Studien zur Redaktionsgeschichte des Evangeliums'. As a justification of this new term he states that the expression '*Form-geschichte*' (form criticism) ought strictly to have been '*Formgeschichte des synoptischen Traditionsstoffes*' (history of the form of the traditional material of the synoptists), whereas the method which he now designates as '*redaktionsgeschichtliche Forschung*' (redaction-critical study) ought really in view of this to be called *Formgeschichte der Evangelien* (the history of the form of the gospels). He is coining the fresh term only because the old concept '*Formgeschichte*' now has an established meaning and a change might cause confusion.[31] Haenchen would prefer to speak of 'composition criticism' (*Kompositionsgeschichte*) rather than 'redaction criticism', because source criticism imagined the redactor as one who assembled the sources willy-nilly with scissors and paste to form a gospel. But this is not what Marxsen is thinking of.[32]

We must begin with Bornkamm's first article. His introductory remarks make it evident how far he is building on the form-critical method. He attributes to form criticism the methodical elaboration of the insight that the gospels must be understood as *kerygma*, and not as biographies of Jesus of Nazareth; and that they cannot be fitted into any of the literary categories of antiquity, but that they are stamped and determined in every respect by faith in Jesus Christ, the Crucified and Risen One, both in their content and their form, as a whole and in detail. This has put an end to the fiction of the *Quest of the Historical Jesus*, as though it would ever be possible to distil out of the gospels a picture of the historical Jesus free from all the 'over-painting' added by faith. Faith in Jesus Christ as the Crucified and Risen One does not belong to a later stratum of the tradition; this faith is the place where tradition was born, out of which it has grown and through which it becomes intelligible. This faith explains the conscientiousness and faithfulness with regard to the tradition about Jesus, and also the peculiar freedom with which this tradition is modified in detail.[33] 'The evangelists do not hark back to some kind of church archives when they pass on the words and deeds of Jesus, but they draw them from the kerygma of the Church and serve this kerygma.'[34]

[31] W. Marxsen, *Der Evangelist Markus*, Göttingen 1956, p. 11.
[32] E. Haenchen, *Der Weg Jesu*, Berlin 1966, p. 24.
[33] Cf. G. Bornkamm, *op. cit.*, pp. 52ff. (references are to the English translation).
[34] *Op. cit.*, p. 52.

After these preparatory remarks, Bornkamm endeavours to illustrate the method of the evangelists in detail by the pericope of the Stilling of the Storm in Matthew. If we compare this with the accounts of the other synoptists we see that it does not stand in a biographical context, but as one of a series of healing miracles which are intended to set forth Jesus as the 'Messiah of deed', after the evangelist has shown him in the preceding Sermon on the Mount (chs. 5–7) as the 'Messiah of the word'. In Mark this vivid and full account has the character of a typical miracle story and for this reason Dibelius classifies it as a 'tale'.[35]

By contrast Matthew omits the story-telling details and makes the pericope serve a new theme, modifying its course. This theme appears from its context, for it is preceded by two sayings about discipleship: the first is Jesus' reply to the scribe who wishes to follow him, that foxes have holes and birds have nests, but the Son of Man has nowhere to lay his head (Matt. 8.19–20), and the second is the answer to the man who wants first to bury his father, where Jesus declares that the man must let the dead bury their dead and follow him. In both cases it is a matter of ἀκολουθεῖν, in the first a warning against unconsidered decision, in the second a summons to a radical resolve. ἀκολουθεῖν also occurs in the next pericope, that of the storm on the lake.[36]

In Bornkamm's exposition, these sayings about following give the incident of the stilling of the storm exemplary significance. Consequently Matthew does not merely hand on the story, but by placing it in a particular context is also its *earliest exegete*. As the first expositor of the tradition which also occurs in Mark he interprets the rough journey of the disciples with Jesus and the stilling of the storm as referring to discipleship, and thus to the little ship of the Church. The term of address in the disciples' cry to Jesus for help must also be noted. In Matthew it is κύριε, in Mark, on the contrary, διδάσκαλε and in Luke ἐπιστάτα; in the two other synoptists the term κύριος is only a human title of respect, but in Matthew it is a divine predicate of majesty, as it is in other passages in his gospel. It is thus a prayer

---

[35] *Op. cit.*, p. 54. Cf. also the article by E. Hilgert, 'Symbolismus und Heilsgeschichte in den Evangelien', in: *Oikonomia*, Cullmann-Festschrift, Hamburg-Bergstedt 1967, pp. 51–56. There the narratives of the Stilling of the Storm and the Gerasene demoniacs are investigated with a view to seeing the extent to which they reflect a salvation-historical approach. The author appeals to both Marxsen and Conzelmann.

[36] Bornkamm, *op. cit.*, p. 55.

and contains a confession of discipleship. Moreover, in Mark and Luke first the miracle is told, then the disciples are reproached for their lack of faith; but in Matthew the reproach to the disciples occurs first and only then is the storm stilled.[37] Jesus' term of address to the disciples, ὀλιγόπιστοι, a favourite expression of Matthew, turns the particular situation of the disciples into a typical situation of discipleship in general. The expression σεισμὸς μέγας is extremely unusual for a storm on a lake and is found elsewhere, and not only in Matthew, as the designation of apocalyptic horrors (Matt. 24.7; 27.54: Luke 21.11: Mark 13.8: Rev. 6.12; 11.13; 16.18 et passim). This makes the distress of the disciples on the lake the symbol of the discipleship of Jesus as a whole.[38]

Moreover, Bornkamm points out that the incident in Matthew is confirmed not by the disciples but by the people as a whole (ἄνθρωποι), who express their astonishment in the question in the concluding verse (Matt. 8.27). These ἄνθρωποι of the 'choral endings' are intended to stand for people who are encountered by this story in the preaching. Thus this pericope is turned from a description of discipleship in which the disciples experience trial and rescue, storm and security into a summons to this imitation and discipleship (p. 56).

In conclusion, Bornkamm declares that in this interpretation of the stilling of the storm he does not intend to attack the principles of form criticism, according to which the single pericopes are regarded as the primary data of the tradition. In the future, however, even greater care must be taken to enquire about the motives for the composition by the *individual* evangelists. It is true that they had worked to a large extent as collectors; yet it is important to ascertain the definite theological intentions revealed by the composition. By its connection with the sayings about discipleship, the stilling of the storm has become *kerygma* and a paradigm of the danger and glory of discipleship.[39]

[37] Op. cit., pp. 55f. On discipleship and the term ἀκολουθεῖν in Matthew (where it occurs 25 times, in Mark 18 times, in Luke 17 times), see G. Strecker, Der Weg der Gerechtigkeit, Göttingen 1962, p. 230, note 4.

[38] G. Bornkamm, op. cit., p. 56.

[39] Op. cit., p. 57. O. Glombitza uses the pericope of 'The Sign of Jonah' (NTS 8, 1961/2, pp. 359–66) to illustrate the different theological conceptions of Matthew and Luke expressed by their editorial work. The same method can be seen in the article by E. Haenchen, 'Die Komposition von Mark 8.27–9.1 und par.', Nov Test 6, 1963, pp. 81–109. By a comparative study of this section, Haenchen establishes that in Mark it is an invitation to martyrdom, in Luke to bear an everyday cross patiently, and in Matthew an indication of a change from the bearer of revelation to Satan in the figure of Peter (p. 109).

Undoubtedly these fresh insights point the way forward. Since then they have found increasing acceptance in the study of the synoptists. But a warning is needed for care in those cases in which the new method of investigation does not produce the hoped-for answers, in case the text is distorted by over-interpretation which reads ideas into it. But if that does not occur it is, in our opinion, altogether possible to make discoveries in the study of the synoptic gospels in matters beyond the scope of form criticism and its questions and answers.

D. *The chief concerns of redaction criticism*

Form criticism regarded the authors of the three synoptic gospels primarily as collectors and transmitters of the traditions handed down to them. Therefore it considered the question of the unity and the controlling ideas of the individual gospel writings to be only a marginal problem. Its main interest was in the material, its form, its *Sitz im Leben* and the history of its transmission. By its attempt to detach the old traditional material from the secondary framework, it arrived at a description of the gospels as composite works.[40]

After this preliminary, necessary one-sidedness of the form-critical method it was equally necessary for the pendulum to swing back. It was important, however, that it should not now swing too far in the opposite direction. After the emphasis given by form criticism to the individual traditions, attention had to be paid to the general conception and composition of the synoptic gospels without at the same time abandoning the methodology and the conclusions of form-critical work on the individual traditions.[41] The most important discovery of redaction criticism which goes beyond form criticism is that it is not the gospels as a whole which must be claimed as composite material but only their content, whilst the redaction of it, that is to say, its grouping, its composition and arrangement into a definite geographical and chronological framework with quite definite theological viewpoints, must be regarded as the work of the evangelist. This investigation of redaction criticism into the gospel as a whole led to the realization that the evangelists' choice of

[40] Cf. G. Iber, 'Zur Formgeschichte der Evangelien', *ThR NF* 24, 1957/8, p. 335.

[41] Cf. W. Trilling, *Das wahre Israel*, Leipzig 1959. See also the forward-looking remarks of J. Schniewind on the 'kerygma of the synoptic apostle' and the 'historical content' of this kerygma ('Zur Synoptikerexegese', *ThR NF* 2, 1930, p. 171).

material, the order in which they placed what they had collected, especially the arrangement of their compositions, and the alterations they made in the traditional matter, are all determined by their theology; in other words, the evangelists did their work as theologians and from theological viewpoints.[42]

Certain theological differences between the synoptic gospels were indeed already emphasized by Dibelius and Bultmann in their form-critical studies. But as this problem was only of secondary interest in their investigation, they did not pursue particular, more or less consistently and systematically planned themes through the individual synoptic gospels. 'The particular theology and theme of the first three Gospels goes deeper into the substance of them than is generally recognized, and modifies their message not insignificantly, even though over large areas their traditions are the same.'[43] Bornkamm and his pupil Held therefore employ for the evangelist Matthew the concept of an interpreter of the received tradition. This concept also appears in the title of their investigations.[44]

Various basic theological ideas in the individual gospels were presented through redaction-critical work on the synoptic gospels, partly in smaller articles in periodicals, partly in longer dissertations. Amongst the works on Matthew, those of Trilling and Strecker must be considered general redaction-critical outlines. In the same class, dealing with Mark, Marxsen's study *Der Evangelist Markus* examines the relationship between the imminent expectation and the pro-clamation of the gospel in the second gospel. J. M. Robinson's study *The Problem of History in Mark* also belongs to this class, though it has other methodological presuppositions. Johannes Schreiber questions both these books on the basis of the results achieved by W. Wrede and M. Kähler (see his *Theologie des Vertrauens*). Conzelmann's investigation of the Lucan historical work, *The Theology of St Luke*, endeavours to prove that Luke, when the parousia still did not appear, placed the epoch of Jesus' ministry in the centre of time by dividing up

---

[42] Cf. W. Grundmann, *Die Geschichte Jesu Christi*, Berlin 1959², p. 15. A. Suhl (*Die Funktion der alttestamentlichen Zitate und Anspielungen im Markusevangelium*, Gütersloh 1965) even argues that the term 'synoptic' can be used in redaction criticism only in a much weakened sense and can only indicate that certain complexes of tradition are held in common. The evangelists were very different and completely independent theologians (*op. cit.*, p. 9).

[43] G. Bornkamm, in *Tradition and Interpretation in Matthew*, p. 11.

[44] G. Bornkamm, 'Matthäus als Interpret der Herrenworte', *ThLZ* 1954, cols. 341 to 346; H. J. Held, 'Matthew as Interpreter of the Miracle Stories' in *Tradition and Interpretation in Matthew*, pp. 165–299.

salvation history into periods in order to solve the problems created by the delay of the parousia.

It is a striking fact that redaction-critical work has been decisively advanced above all by the work of beginners. Conzelmann's book consists of his dissertation and inaugural lecture, Marxsen's study is his inaugural dissertation, Trilling's studies are part of his dissertation and Strecker's treatise consists of his inaugural dissertation.

E. *The role of the evangelists in form criticism and redaction criticism*

Form criticism had undertaken to go behind the existing synoptic gospels and to investigate the stage of the oral tradition which preceded them. By contrast, the interest of redaction criticism is devoted to the existing written gospels, their historical background and their theological testimony.[45] The two investigations are certainly not opposed to each other, but they differ over the subject to which they each direct their attention. The point of contact between the two investigations lies in the fact that form criticism is also investigating the literary character of the gospel writings as a whole,[46] but, be it noted, merely the *literary* character. It is precisely here that redaction criticism goes beyond the form-critical investigation of the nature and classification of the traditional material according to genres. Form criticism did not investigate *primarily* the theological character and the theological conception of the existing written gospels; it did that only marginally.[47] Nor does redaction criticism pose the historical question how the events reported by the synoptists actually happened, but attempts to understand how the evangelists understood them and therefore described them.[48]

Marxsen points out that even the scholars who represented the two-document theory were already showing signs of posing the questions asked by redaction criticism, and mentions Wrede's well-known study of Mark's gospel, Wellhausen's study on Mark and his *Einleitung in die drei ersten Evangelien*; also the remark of Johannes Weiss: 'The task of the expositor of the gospels is a many-sided one.

[45] Cf. G. Iber, *op. cit.*, p. 337.
[46] See especially K. L. Schmidt, 'Stellung der Evangelien . . .' (in note 5), *op. cit.*, pp. 50–134.
[47] Cf. G. Iber, *op. cit.*, p. 337; W. Marxsen, 'Redaktionsgeschichtliche Erklärung der sogenannten Parabeltheorie des Markus', *ZThK* 52, 1955, p. 238.
[48] See W. Marxsen, *Der Evangelist Markus*, p. 12; also H. Conzelmann, *The Theology of St Luke*, p. 10.

His duty is first to understand the author, to realize what he wishes to tell his readers. . .'[49] These ideas, hinted at but not worked out more fully by the studies of literary criticism, were developed by redaction criticism into a further recognition. This was that the evangelists had done their work within the framework of what was possible for them and, in spite of their ties to tradition, had done it deliberately and of set purpose. Their redactional work was undertaken to serve a theological conception and particular theological themes.[50]

Bultmann was still maintaining that the composition of the gospels 'involves nothing in principle new, but only completes what was begun in the oral tradition'.[51] Consequently he regarded it as unnecessary to make an examination of every detail of the evangelists' work; for results could hardly be expected. Meanwhile Marxsen was asserting on the contrary: 'The very conclusions of form criticism contradict this statement. Here the diversities of the "forms" and—thus in their context—the diverse *Sitze im Leben* of the individual tradition are displayed. Now this means that the traditional material itself is not a catalyst! . . . It is far from being self-evident that the whole of this disparate material finally flowed into the unity of the gospel.'[52] According to Marxsen, the whole variety of the forms and purposes of the individual traditions is derived from the original unity preceding the stablization in writing of the synoptic gospels, namely from the unity of the image of Jesus Christ, and this total image is recorded in each single piece of the tradition. To this unity of the total image of Jesus' life we must go on to add the unity created by the evangelist, first of all by Mark; this is expressed in the methodically composed work of a gospel.[53]

Form criticism had made it a matter of principle to regard the gospels from an anti-individualistic point of view. Hence it traced back to the anonymous community not only the tradition but also the formulation, the shaping and even the re-shaping, and it considered the stablization in writing merely as the completion and conclusion of the anonymous stage of the tradition. Marxsen was right in emphasizing, contrary to form criticism, that this anony-

[49] J. Weiss, *Die Schriften des Neuen Testaments*, Vol. 1 (1906), p. 62, quoted from W. Marxsen, *op. cit.*, p. 11, note 2; see also G. Klein, *Die zwölf Apostel*, p. 16, note 34.
[50] Cf. G. Iber, *op. cit.*, p. 337.
[51] R. Bultmann, *History of the Synoptic Tradition*, p. 321.
[52] W. Marxsen, *op. cit.*, p. 8.
[53] Cf. W. Marxsen, *op. cit.*, p. 9.

mous verbal transmission would necessarily have led gradually to the '*disintegration*' of the tradition. But the redaction countered this natural development. Therefore it must be ascribed to an author in his own right who pursued a definite object in his labours. The existence of an author in his own right must at all costs be stressed, even if the extent and delimitation of his sources, his share in shaping them, his name, his home, his fortunes could never be established with complete certainty.[54] 'If . . . the anti-individualistic consideration of the gospels is raised to the status of a dogma it is impossible to catch sight of the evangelists themselves.'[55]

Redaction criticism does not dispute the fact that the evangelists worked up anonymous traditions, but it does not attribute this work to a large number of oral transmitters, but just to an individual author in his own right. Marxsen emphasizes this authorship first in Mark, because he had had at his disposal, except for the passion-narrative and smaller collections, only an anonymous tradition. He was the first to introduce the element of the individual into the formulation and shaping of the tradition and therefore his contribution in shaping it himself is greater than that of Matthew and Luke, who would already have been able to find support from precursors.[56]

The form-critical thesis that in the synoptic gospels we have only what had been handed down, and that the first task is to extract the tradition which the collector had to hand,[57] is challenged by Marxsen. He maintains the thesis on which the redaction-critical method is based, namely that we have in the synoptic gospels what the *evangelists* have handed down, i.e. merely the tradition deposited in the gospels. It is not the individual tradition which must be reconstructed but the world of the evangelist, if we are to come nearer to the individual tradition. In opposition to form criticism, Marxsen declares that we must not attempt to by-pass the evangelist in the search for the traditional material of the synoptists, but that a double task must be performed, namely to extract the redaction as well as the tradition.[58]

[54] *Op. cit.*, p. 9; see also C. Maurer, 'Knecht Gottes und Sohn Gottes im Passions-bericht des Markusevangeliums', *ZThK* 50, 1953, p. 34.

[55] W. Marxsen, *op. cit.*, p. 9. J. Schneider also agrees with this: 'Der Beitrag der Urgemeinde zur Jesusüberlieferung im Lichte der neuesten Forschung', *ThLZ* 87, 1962, col. 405.

[56] W. Marxsen, *op. cit.*, p. 9.

[57] Thus M. Dibelius, 'Zur Formgeschichte der Evangelien', *ThR NF* 1, 1929, p. 210.

[58] W. Marxsen, *op. cit.*, p. 10.

'Form-criticism which by-passes the authors of the gospels hangs somehow in the air.'[59]

Form criticism followed K. L. Schmidt in limiting the 'framework' of the story of Jesus to the topographical and chronological statements and regarded as unprofitable historically and pragmatically the redactional terms used by Mark to connect the sayings of Jesus and the individual pericopes. Redaction criticism, on the other hand, takes a wider view of the significance of the framework and regards it as the *real* achievement of the author of the gospel. In addition to the itinerary, redaction criticism reckons as part of the framework the connecting links between the scenes and the modifications in the text in so far as these can be discovered by a comparison of the synoptics. Redaction criticism does not seek to demolish this framework historically in order to have the individual traditions in full view, but endeavours to interrogate it for its own *Sitz im Leben* over and above that of the individual tradition.[60]

Their 'circular' quality is characteristic of both redaction criticism and form criticism. In form-critical research Dibelius had reconstructed the history of the synoptic tradition synthetically from the views of the community and their needs. Bultmann, on the other hand, started with the analysis of passages from the tradition.[61] That is, Dibelius had asked which genres were possible and probable in the sociological context of primitive Christian life, and, conversely, whether the types he had worked out gave evidence of particular conditions of life and cult.[62] Redaction-critical study also attempts, not constructively like Dibelius, but analytically like Bultmann, to draw inferences from the form of the gospels as a whole about the conception of the author and the situation of his community. It also looks beyond this, by throwing more and more light on the two historical factors of the evangelist and his community for the explanation why the history of the redaction of the synoptic material led to this particular form of the gospel.[63]

Most of the scholars who use the redaction-critical method start with the two-source theory and try to grasp the specific theology of the individual evangelist by comparing the synoptists. In contrast,

[59] *Op. cit.*, p. 11.
[60] *Op. cit.*, p. 12. See also especially J. Schreiber, *Theologie des Vertrauens*, Gütersloh 1967, p. 11.
[61] R. Bultmann, *History of the Synoptic Tradition*, p. 5.
[62] M. Dibelius, *From Tradition to Gospel*, pp. 7ff.
[63] W. Marxsen, *op. cit.*, p. 14.

Eduard Schweizer in his examination of Mark's theology starts with the vocabulary of the redactional sections (e.g. κηρύσσειν, διδάσκειν, θεραπεύειν) and in this way reaches very interesting conclusions.[64] We must refer once again to one last point. When the theological nature of the redaction has been recognized, it follows that attention must be paid to the context within which the pericope occurs, especially since the position of a pericope in its context is frequently the earliest commentary on it.[65]

That means that in distinguishing between tradition and redaction it is important to note what traditions the evangelist takes up and how he arranges them to provide connections and make statements. Even the tradition is in the first place part of the redaction, insofar as the redaction determined what traditions were taken up. It is therefore insufficient to allot to the redactor the occasional marginal verse as he connected the different traditions. It is also necessary to ask what the evangelist wanted to say to his own day with the tradition incorporated in his gospel.[66]

Schreiber even goes so far as to say in his investigation of the gospel of Mark that anyone who attempts to separate tradition and redaction without noting the whole of the gospel of Mark has not even seen the basis of the gospel account, far less made a careful investigation of the tradition available to Mark. He has blinded himself by using the concepts of modern history without reflecting on them first.[67]

Finally, Iber's verdict on the relationship between form criticism and redaction criticism may be quoted: 'The contribution of the evangelist is not exhausted when he has collected the stories and sayings of Jesus current in the community. His work is more important and more impressive than this; it is a considered and astonishingly consistent literary composition and theological conception. This shows the limit of what form criticism can contribute to the understanding of the synoptic gospels and of what its judgment on them decisively corrects and supplements. The form-critical manner of regarding the gospels retains without any qualifications its importance for the interpretation of the synoptic gospels. But it is only a first step. It must be followed by a second one which deals with the

[64] See E. Schweizer's article, 'Anmerkungen zur Theologie des Markus', in *Neotestamentica et Patristica* (SupplNovTest VI), Leiden 1962, pp. 35–46.

[65] W. Grundmann, *Geschichte Jesu Christi*, p. 15.

[66] Cf. also J. Schreiber, *op. cit.*, p. 11.

[67] *Op. cit.*, p. 13.

work of the evangelists and the statements of the gospels as complete entities. It is to the credit of redaction-critical works that they have demonstrated the necessity for this second step and shown the way to carry it out.'[68]

2. DETERMINING THE *Sitz im Leben* OF THE PRESENT SYNOPTIC GOSPELS

Amongst form-critical scholars, Jeremias followed Dodd in distinguishing between an original historical context and a *Sitz im Leben*[69]. He originally spoke of a twofold *Sitz im Leben*, meaning by the first *Sitz im Leben* the situation in which a parable arose. In more recent editions of his book on the parables, however, he has rightly made a change in his terminology as the term '*Sitz im Leben*' may not be used for the situation in which a parable arises, since the proper content of the term is not appropriate here, as Bultmann[70] and Schürmann[71] have stressed.

Jeremias designates the 'life' of these parables in the primitive church before they were fixed in writing, when Jesus' sayings were proclaimed in the mission, preached at the meeting of the community and taught during the instruction, as the *Sitz im Leben*. In this situation between the cross and the expected parousia, the community collected the sayings (and parables) and expanded and allegorized them under different material perspectives. Many parables ought to be taken out of the *Sitz im Leben* and the thought of the primitive Church and an attempt should be made to fit them again into their original situation in Jesus' life.[72]

In its method, Haenchen's study of the discourse about the Pharisees in Matt. 23 displays points of contact with Jeremias' exegesis of the parables. Haenchen proceeds from the point of view of form criticism as well as from that of redaction criticism. He considers that in the case of this discourse the original historical context is not the life of Jesus, but the situation of hostility between the Jewish-Christian community of Jerusalem and the Jews before the catastrophe of AD 70.[73] The admonitions in vv.

---

[68] G. Iber, *op. cit.*, p. 338.
[69] J. Jeremias, *The Parables of Jesus*, London and New York, 1963, p. 23.
[70] R. Bultmann, *op. cit.*, p. 5.
[71] H. Schürmann, 'Die vorösterlichen Anfänge der Logientradition', in *Der historische Jesus und der kerygmatische Christus*, Berlin 1960, p. 351.
[72] J. Jeremias, *The Parables of Jesus*, 1963, p. 23.
[73] E. Haenchen, 'Matthäus 23', *ZThK* 48, 1951, p. 51.

8–10 belong among his words of Christian prophets in the name of the exalted Lord which have the same validity as the sayings of the earthly Jesus,[74] out of which Matthew has read an exhortation to Christian humility.[75] Verse 13, too, containing the first woe, is not concerned with the situation of Jesus, but with the situation of the Christian community which was being impeded in its mission by the representatives of Judaism (p. 47). The further question as to the *Sitz im Leben* of these sayings in the composition of Matthew's gospel is not posed by Haenchen, although he certainly agrees with the approach of the method of redaction criticism.[76]

Redaction criticism distinguishes another *Sitz im Leben* from that of the original material. That is the *Sitz* of the three synoptic gospels in the history of the primitive Church. Thus redaction criticism investigates the evangelist and his community, the one in which he is standing and for whom he is writing, unlike form criticism, which enquires about the *Sitz im Leben* of the individual pericopes. It is therefore especially concerned with the situation in the time of the evangelist, his community and its problems, and how they are overcome.[77] 'The redaction-critical investigation will not indeed give us any information about the historical Jesus, but it can convey to us a picture of the thought and life, of the strength and the expectation of the faith of the young community of Christians in which the evangelist was standing' (p. 271). 'What the situation was actually like is of interest only insofar as the question refers to the situation of the primitive community in which the gospels originated.'[78] This produces a threefold task for synoptic research: 'to extract the redaction, to extract the tradition, to extract what has been transmitted as a historical entity by itself'.[79]

Here we may insert a short note on E. Hirsch and his theory of how the synoptic gospels came into being and what was their origin. We certainly do not wish to agree even remotely with this source-theory, which is as

[74] *Ibid.*, p. 43, F. Neugebauer disputes firmly and radically that the prophetic sayings inspired by the spirit could have become logia of Jesus. For the primitive Christian communities were not led by prophets, but by apostles (F. Neugebauer, 'Geistsprüche und Jesuslogien', *ZNW* 53, 1962, pp. 218–28, especially pp. 227f.).

[75] E. Haenchen, *op. cit.*, p. 45.

[76] In order to guard against a possible misunderstanding it must be stated that we ought strictly speaking to have used the terms *Sitz im Leben* and *Sitz im Leben* of the gospel; but since Haenchen traces Matt. 23 back not to Jesus' sayings, but to utterances of Christian prophets against Judaism, the former *Sitz im Leben* is not the life of Jesus, but that of the community.

[77] W. Marxsen, 'Parabeltheorie des Markus' (see note 47), p. 258.

[78] W. Marxsen, *Der Evangelist Markus*, p. 12.

[79] W. Grundmann, *Das Evangelium nach Markus*, Berlin 1959, p. 23.

complicated as it is improbable. But in my opinion attention must nevertheless be drawn just once to that point in Hirsch's method of approach which shows a certain affinity to the establishment by redaction criticism of a *Sitz im Leben* for the gospel. We are referring to the attempt by Hirsch to seek and to find for each of the sources of the synoptic gospels postulated by him a definite historical place and a definite time in the history of the primitive Church. This attempt has not in fact succeeded in the main, because his whole source-theory is composed of fantastic and improbable hypotheses. Nevertheless, we do not want to reject the method of approach used by Hirsch, but only the results and conclusions deduced from it.

Marxsen in particular has devoted some notes on method worked out in more detail to the problem of the *Sitz im Leben* of the gospels. He calls it the third *Sitz im Leben*. With this definition he is concerned with the community in which the gospels originated. Marxsen explains that the community must not be assumed without qualification to be limited as to its place, though we must also allow for the possibility that this can be determined precisely. It is more a question both of a sociological factor, its points of view, its period, possibly also its make-up, and also of an individualistic trait, the definite interest and the conception of the particular evangelist.[80] This third *Sitz im Leben*, too, must be regarded as having altogether a character of its own, yet not so complicated as the second one. We have in the three synoptic gospels definite 'fixed points'. By watching the development from one gospel to the next we may derive a very vivid picture of the history of the primitive Church.[81]

In order to achieve this object Marxsen endeavours to look first for the pattern of Mark. For this purpose tradition and redaction must be separated from each other by going back behind Mark and then the pattern itself must be made intelligible and explained. Marxsen's method here is like that of Dibelius. After this, it is necessary to compare the two 'great gospels', Matthew and Luke, in order to penetrate behind their altered pattern as well. Finally, an attempt may be made to grasp what is peculiar to Mark from the development of the tradition in Matthew and Luke. By this means conclusions of significance for Mark itself could be drawn from the development of the tradition which extends beyond Mark (p. 16).

[80] Cf. also A. Kuby, 'Zur Konzeption des Markus-Evangeliums', *ZNW* 49, 1958, pp. 52–64. Maurer says that the evangelists as redactors must be understood to be individual figures and account must be taken of their particular characteristics (see his article 'Knecht Gottes . . .', *op. cit.*, pp. 1–38).
[81] W. Marxsen, *Evangelist Markus*, p. 13.

We shall begin by investigating the establishment of the *Sitz im Leben* in primitive Christianity for the existing synoptic gospels in some of the redaction-critical works published so far. We shall start with Mark's gospel, which redaction criticism also recognizes as the earliest one. Lohmeyer had already named the district of Galilee as the location of its author.[82] Marxsen thinks that he can deduce from the existing local traditions that the place in which the gospel of Mark originated is not to be sought in Rome, as the tradition of the early Church had it, but in Galilee.[83] The existing Galilee tradition was no historical memory for the evangelist, but he wanted his editorial work to indicate where he himself was (p. 54). Mark's leading motif in his gospel is one of place, namely Galilee (p. 69). The use of the concept of Galilee in Mark raises the question whether his whole gospel is not oriented to Galilee and whether a community in Galilee is not standing behind it.[84]

Marxsen assumes that at the beginning of the year 66, when the Jewish War had broken out and the original community had fled from Jerusalem to Pella, the expectation of the parousia was much intensified (p. 70). Its announcement by an oracle had ensued, traces of which still exist in Mark 14.28 and 16.7 (pp. 57f., also pp. 115f.). The shaping of Mark has been determined by two ideas; the parousia which was awaited in Galilee and the orientation of Jesus' ministry to Galilee (p. 60). For his coming again was expected in the same place at which his first coming took place. Marxsen deduces from Mark 13 that Mark wrote his gospel in Galilee in the community which had moved out of Jerusalem. In this connection Galilee must be taken in an altogether wider sense, including the town of Pella (pp. 54, 70, 75). This also supplies a fresh explanation for the allegedly lacking conclusion of Mark. Mark 16.7 is not to be explained as pointing to the expected appearances of the Risen One in Galilee, but to the parousia imminently expected by Mark (p. 54). Because this parousia had not yet taken place, Mark could not report the fulfilment of the promise of 16.7, and therefore his conception required his gospel to end after 16.8.[85] Marxsen is, however, to be asked whether according to Mark 13 the expectation of the end was in

[82] E. Lohmeyer, *Das Evangelium des Markus*, Göttingen 1959[15], p. 72; cf. *id.*, *Galiläa und Jerusalem*, Göttingen 1936, p. 97.
[83] W. Marxsen, *op. cit.*, p. 41. So, too, his *Einleitung*, p. 128.
[84] *Ibid.*, p. 70, also in *Einleitung* . . ., p. 124.
[85] *Ibid.*, p. 77. This point has recently been criticized by J. Schreiber in an article. On this problem cf. also W. Marxsen, *Einleitung*, pp. 125-7.

fact as fervid in this gospel as he supposes. Mark 9.1 shows that only a few of the generation still living were to experience the parousia.[86]

The theological position of the earliest gospel is described by Marxsen as the situation of early Christianity, when there were threats on the one hand of a process of disintegration by 'fragmentation' in the tradition which Mark had encountered, and on the other of a gnosticizing of the preaching of Paul, who had hardly carried enough weight to oppose the tendency to mythologizing and to prevent the loss of the connection with history (p. 147). Thus Mark combines the two roots of the earliest Christian preaching, the Pauline kerygma and the synoptic tradition. In so doing he stands 'as a theologian of an altogether distinctive stamp between Paul and the anonymous tradition on the one hand and the later gospels on the other'.[87]

Schreiber assigns the christology of Mark to the Gentile-Christian Hellenistic type of the Pauline sphere. The heterogeneous traditional material of Mark's gospel has been welded by the Christ myth into a unity, into the book of secret epiphanies. Although Schreiber rejects Marxsen's particular Galilee theory, he suggests the origin of Mark's gospel before 70 in Tyre, Sidon or the Decapolis. Karnetzki, on the other hand, does not assign the whole gospel of Mark to that part of Syria adjacent to Galilee, but only the last revision but one, the Galilean redaction assumed by Bussmann, which is said to have been used only by Mark and Matthew, but not by Luke.[88]

Trilling has determined a *Sitz im Leben* for the gospel of Matthew.

[86] See also E. Haenchen, *Der Weg Jesu*, p. 24, note 26; also, especially J. Schreiber, *op. cit.*, pp. 126–45.

[87] *Ibid.*, p. 147. Cf. on this also S. Schulz, 'Markus und das Alte Testament', *ZThK* 58, 1961, pp. 184f., 188f.; also E. Schweizer, 'Anmerkungen zur Theologie des Markus', *op. cit.*, pp. 35–46. He writes in this article (pp. 43f.): It follows from the redactional passages in Mark and Paul that we have in Mark on the whole acceptance of tradition with little editing, in Paul on the contrary only very little acceptance of tradition (Phil. 2; I Cor. 15). The chief concern of the redactional additions of Paul is to emphasize the cross and resurrection and the confession of Jesus' eternal divine Sonship. Paul does not consider the historical Jesus important, but only the limiting framework of his historical life. In Mark, on the contrary, the editorial sections revolved particularly round the concept of teaching and understanding, and described the activities of the earthly Jesus between his baptism and crucifixion.

[88] J. Schreiber, 'Die Christologie des Markusevangeliums', *ZThK* 58, 1961, p. 183, especially note 2 (cf. note 85 above); see also M. Karnetzki, 'Die galiläische Redaktion im Markusevangelium', *ZNW* 52, 1961, especially p. 240, and *id.*, 'Die letzte Redaktion des Markusevangeliums', in: *Zwischenstation*, Kupisch-Festschrift, Munich 1963, pp. 161–74.

He thinks he can identify as the background of this gospel more clearly than of any other the image of a church which might be compared, for example, with the picture conveyed by the epistles to the Corinthians of the church there. Even without raising the question of the period and place of this church, this evidence for a historical figure has inestimable value. In spite of its fragmentary nature, the image presents outlines which are in some measure firm.[89] This church's external form, which can easily be grasped, enables order and office, authority and commission to be discerned, and the discourse about the community in Matt. 18 enables us to see an image of a church which for depth and sobriety is without an equal in the literature of primitive Christianity. Indications of the external form of the church are less visible, but in compensation the features of the inner image which this church has of itself are all the more impressive (p. 189).

The aggressive attitude taken up towards the Jews and the didactic revision of the tradition directed to its own members have contributed to the significant expression of this church's understanding of itself: it understands itself to be the true Israel (p. 190). But we must not overlook the dark passages in Matthew's image of the church. The shady side of the real conditions forms a painful contrast to this church's lofty consciousness of its vocation. The state of affairs is not all for the best in the church; weeds are rampant amongst the wheat; there are charlatans, seducers, false prophets, and scandals in many forms, malice and sin in its own ranks, even treachery, uncharitableness and hate (Matt. 24.10–12; 13.24–30) (p. 190). Other passages, too, point to the phenomena of a routine Christianity with lukewarmness, weariness, flagging of the first ardour and loss of the first love, with a relaxation of the radical claims and close affinity with wordly ways of life. It is a picture of a relatively mature development of a church which has already settled down and established itself in the world. This internal threat is confronted with forceful trenchancy by the imperative, based on the indicative (Matt. 5.13f.; 48). It is understood quite seriously that the church is not living in a short interim period, but definitely in the world and that it must prove its vocation there.[90]

Trilling finds support on the one hand in the studies of Kilpatrick[91]

---

[89] W. Trilling, *Das wahre Israel*, p. 189.
[90] *Ibid.*, p. 191; cf. on this, W. Marxsen, *Einleitung* . . ., p. 133.
[91] G. D. Kilpatrick, *The Origins of the Gospel According to St Matthew*, Oxford 1948.

and Stendahl;[92] on the other hand, he advances even further along his own line. He is right in accepting Kilpatrick's point of view that the liturgical life of the church exerted a strong influence on the shaping of the material. In this matter, according to Kilpatrick, the public worship of the synagogue with scripture reading and exposition influenced Christian worship. Before the gospel of Matthew was composed as a revised gospel-book for the worship of the church, individual writings had been read and explained for more than two decades in Matthew's church. Traces of this practice have survived. Trilling adds the statement that the influence of the life of public worship can undoubtedly be noticed in the gospel of Matthew and expresses itself amongst other ways in the tendency towards a solemn elevated style in the terminology and in the stereotyped repetition of strongly stamped formulae. But Kilpatrick's attempts to apply this point of view to the whole of Matthew's gospel and to raise it to the only or, at any rate, the principal criterion are, in Trilling's view, inadequate.[93]

Trilling agrees more fully with Stendahl's approach. Stendahl considers the *Sitz im Leben* to be not public worship and the sermon (stressed by Dibelius as well as Kilpatrick), but the task of teaching, training and instruction. He regards the purpose of this 'school' to be the education of superintendents and catechists and accordingly he explains the gospel of Matthew as the textbook for this group.[94] Stendahl takes a view directly opposed to that of Dibelius about where the *Sitz im Leben* is to be found.[95] But he restricts his investigation to the quotations from the Old Testament, in particular the pronounced 'reflective quotations' in Matthew.[96] Thus Trilling is able to raise the valid objection that the basis for such far-reaching assertions is too small. Even if his explanation of the unsolved problem of the 'reflective quotations' were the best which we have today, it is

---

[92] K. Stendahl, *The School of St Matthew*, Uppsala 1954.

[93] W. Trilling, *op. cit.*, p. 196.

[94] See K. Stendahl, *op. cit.*, p. 35; W. Trilling, *op. cit.*, p. 196; cf. on this also W. Marxsen, *Einleitung*, p. 136.

[95] See K. Stendahl, *op. cit.*, pp. 13–19.

[96] A study worked out with the greatest preciseness about the influence of the Old Testament on the synoptic tradition is available in the unprinted dissertation of M. Karnetzki, *Die alttestamentlichen Zitate in der synoptischen Tradition* (Tübingen 1955). Karnetzki examines (from the form-critical point of view) not only the 'reflective quotations' from the Old Testament, but all the Old Testament echoes. He attempts not only to determine a *Sitz im Leben* for them, but also to sketch a historical development of the use of the Old Testament in the separate earlier and later strata of the synoptic tradition.

very doubtful whether it would be possible to indicate so precisely the bearers and the purpose of this theological task.[97]

When all is taken into account, then, a generally satisfactory answer to the question about the *Sitz im Leben* has not yet been found. The investigation always results in a complex impression and the individual elements cannot all be brought under one denominator, especially when a smooth solution is desired. But even if all the differentiated separate answers do not conform to the facts of the case, they still point to a *Sitz im Leben* in a local church. Such a local church must therefore be accepted as a *Sitz im Leben*; a church with a many-sided life, the forms of whose inner life are diverse.[98]

Trilling thinks that for the *Sitz im Leben* 'a complete church, with its many-sided expressions of life, can most readily be assumed. In a local church of this kind the traditional material was collected, handed on and recast to meet the most varied needs. In the same church the final shape of the gospel seems to have originated as a witness to their faith and to have been intended for their own use. This last process seems to be the work of a single man, and in fact that of a very learned and sensitive professional theologian, who produced the finished result out of many years' labour on the traditional material. Thus the gospel of Matthew would be from the most varied points of view a genuine "book of the church", and this is what it has remained throughout all its history until today' (p. 199).

The question of the circle of its readers, closely connected with that of the *Sitz im Leben*, cannot be answered unequivocally, since it is possible to identify traits both of Jewish and of Gentile Christians. It is altogether a mistake to pose a question which demands a decision between the two movements. We must allow for the fact that when the final redaction of Matthew's gospel took place, this church was made up in a different way, and that the distinctions between Gentile and Jewish Christianity hardly, if at all, played a part. Hence it is only possible to ascertain how the church was composed in the intermediate period of the transmission and to see that the milieu of this process was of a Jewish-Christian complexion.[99]

[97] Trilling, *op. cit.*, pp. 196f.; for a criticism cf. also Iber, *op. cit.*, p. 315. G. Strecker in his inaugural lecture examined the 'reflective quotations' of Matthew in order to use them for drawing conclusions on the mother-tongue of the evangelist and his theological views (*Weg der Gerechtigkeit*, pp. 49–85).

[98] W. Trilling, *op. cit.*, p. 197.

[99] *Ibid.*, p. 200. N. A. Dahl ('Die Passionsgeschichte bei Matthaeus', *NTS* 2, 1956, p. 24) points out that the passion according to Matthew depends on a definite church milieu as its *Sitz im Leben*.

'The book would in that case be evidence for a historical process in which the strictly Jewish-Christian traditions were taken up and preserved, though extremist doctrines were rejected and a lapse into the Jewish-Christian heresy was averted. The church of Matthew must be regarded as a place in which a Christianity developed relatively independently within the main body of the Church, a Christianity which has been refined to an astonishing degree of universality. The circle of readers and the last author testify to an attitude of mind which can be called neither typically Gentile Christian nor typically Jewish Christian.'[100]

As its geographical setting, Trilling names a Jewish milieu with longstanding, tenacious and embittered controversies with Pharisaic Judaism.[101] But he does not express an opinion on the probable historical situation of the origin of the first gospel.[102]

We move on now to Conzelmann's views on the *Sitz im Leben* of Luke's gospel. We must introduce them by saying that the concept *Sitz im Leben* as a designation of the historical setting of the Lucan gospel does not occur in his terminology, though it certainly does as subject-matter. For he states it to be the aim of his studies to enquire into the whole of the literary composition, which is a self-contained scheme.[103] Conzelmann regards the historical situation in which Luke's gospel came into being as 'the situation in which the Church finds herself by the delay of the parousia and her existence in secular history, and Luke tries to come to terms with the situation by his account of historical events' (p. 14).

As regards method Conzelmann bases himself on the two-source theory and starts from the assumption that Luke used Mark's gospel. By comparing the presentation of Luke and Mark in their conceptions as well as in detail, he attempts to determine the independent share of Luke in shaping the material taken over from Mark. To this

---

[100] W. Trilling, *op. cit.*, p. 200; cf. on the other hand, N. A. Dahl, *op. cit.*, p. 28.
[101] W. Trilling, *op. cit.*, p. 198.
[102] E. Käsemann places Matthew's gospel in the border country of Palestine and Syria. The evangelist is in fact writing for Gentile Christians, but largely out of a Jewish-Christian tradition. The period preceding the gospel had been filled with extremely violent theological tensions (E. Käsemann, 'Die Anfänge christlicher Theologie', *ZThK* 57, 1960, p. 163). J. Gnilka assumes as a background not only a revised Jewish-Christian tradition, but also a Jewish-Christian milieu. He thinks that Matthew is engaged in a discussion with unbelieving Pharisaic Judaism (J. Gnilka, 'Die Kirche des Matthäus und die Gemeinde von Qumran', *BZ NF* 7, 1963, p. 43).
[103] H. Conzelmann, *The Theology of St Luke*, p. 9.

extent he is writing a redaction criticism of the gospel of Luke and the whole of the Lucan historical work. Conzelmann sees in the differences between Luke and Mark Luke's particular theology of history, which is determined quite strongly by the fact of the postponement of the parousia. Luke explains this fact by the idea of the divine plan and makes the exhortation follow from the thought of the suddenness of the irruption of the parousia, which is still to be awaited (pp. 131f.). The fading away of the imminent expectation brought with it a new meaning for the suddenness of the irruption. It is intended to emphasize the necessity for constant readiness *in spite of* the long wait (p. 132, note 1).

The situation of the Church in the Acts of the Apostles is determined by persecution. The ethic for martyrs to be seen in it has the purpose of rendering endurance possible (p. 210). The Church and its history is not yet for Luke a factor in salvation in the sense of being an object of faith, but only a means of conveying the message, not an independent factor in the saving events (p. 225). The themes aimed at the moulding of daily life are already taking a more prominent place and in doing so are beginning to show up the independence of the ethical element. There is a connection between the delay of the parousia and the increase of paraenesis, which is expressed in the summons to be prepared. The eschaton is no longer a direct summons, but merely a conception which influences ethics only indirectly by means of the idea of judgment (p. 232).

Thus Conzelmann makes no direct statements about a *Sitz im Leben* for the gospel of Luke. He establishes neither a place of origin nor a direct period for its coming into being. He describes only the internal condition of the church represented by Luke, by displaying the theology of salvation history expressed in the gospel and in Acts. But it is to be assumed that on account of the statements which Conzelmann makes about the persecution of the Church and the problem of loyalty to the Roman state in the Lucan historical work, he would fix the reign of Domitian as the period of its origin and its birthplace as an area lying at any rate outside Palestine, possibly Asia Minor, but still more probably Rome.

II

PRECURSORS OF REDACTION CRITICISM

A. *Form criticism*

BULTMANN, IN AN addendum to the third edition of his study *Die Erforschung der synoptischen Evangelien*, has attempted to demonstrate the genealogical connection between form criticism and redaction criticism in the following statement: 'In recent years form-critical work has been endorsed by the fact that it has served and is still serving as a postulate for a progressive task.'[1] But we must not overlook in this addendum the fact that Bultmann sees himself only as an observer of the results of redaction criticism. He himself is no longer involved in working them out.

He stresses that hitherto the task of considering the gospels as complete entities and of grasping the theological motives actuating them has not been altogether overlooked, '. . . but it has latterly moved into the centre of interest. The work on this task has only just begun. . . . It can indeed be said that such studies lead on beyond form criticism, but by postulating it they are at the same time an endorsement of it' (p. 53). In another passage he speaks of positive continuation of form-critical work by redaction-critical studies.[2]

There is, of course, no point in arguing whether form criticism or redaction criticism came first; both methods can claim descent from Wrede's study of the Messianic secret. A warning against too one-sided an interest of form criticism in oral tradition, given by E. von Dobschütz, is, however, in order. The earlier oral tradition cannot be assessed properly without an understanding of the procedure of the evangelists in recording the tradition in writing.[3]

The question of the precursors of the redaction-critical method thus also involves the problem of its connection with form criticism. It is not

[1] R. Bultmann, *Die Erforschung der synoptischen Evangelien*, Berlin 1960³, pp. 52f.
[2] R. Bultmann, *History of the Synoptic Tradition*, pp. 381f.
[3] E. von Dobschütz, 'Zur Erzählkunst des Markus', *ZNW* 27, 1928, p. 193.

only a case of the two methods following each other in time without an inner connection; there is also a continuity throughout in the history of research. Form criticism must by no means be underestimated as the necessary postulate of redaction criticism. Nor is it mere chance that the beginnings of a redaction critical view of the gospels in the works of Wrede and Wellhausen mentioned by Marxsen (*Der Evangelist Markus*, p. 11), could not prove fruitful in advance of the form-critical method.[4] We can only agree with the following remark by G. Klein: 'It is not in spite of, but because of the postulate of form-critical studies that it is possible and necessary today to place in the forefront the question of the theological conceptions of the synoptic authors. Without this postulate, the question could not even be raised to any purpose' (p. 16).

The significance of William Wrede for redaction-critical scholarship is stressed very strongly in most recent investigations. This is especially true of J. Schreiber's book, *Theologie des Vertrauens*. Wrede's results, with a number of modifications, virtually serve there as a basis for a comprehensive redaction-critical investigation and to set the gospel in its context in the history of religions. The investigations of Wilhelm Bousset and Rudolf Bultmann are also cited for determining this latter context.[5]

We shall first look for instances in which there were traces of progress towards redaction criticism in form-critical studies before redaction criticism. Dibelius already pointed out in the second edition of his *Formgeschichte des Evangeliums* (1933, ET *From Tradition to Gospel*) that even before Mark, Jesus' sayings on the same or kindred themes had been gathered together as instruction for the community.[6] He drew this conclusion from his observation in Mark (in the disputes and in the chapter of parables), and even more in Matthew and Luke, that we have collections of stories and logia of Jesus with quite definite themes. This led Dibelius then to the final conclusion, taken over by redaction criticism, that a significant connection between the sections of the tradition had been brought about by their interpretation, in that the evangelist had placed a series of incidents in a particular perspective.[7]

[4] Cf. G. Klein, *op. cit.*, p. 16.
[5] See, too, the articles by: S. Schulz, 'Die Bedeutung des Markus für die Theologiegeschichte des Urchristentums'; by G. Strecker, 'Zur Messiasgeheimnistheorie im Markusevangelium'; U. Luz, 'Das Geheimnismotiv und die markinische Christologie'; and E. Schweizer, 'Zur Frage der Messiasgeheimnistheorie bei Markus'.
[6] M. Dibelius, *From Tradition to Gospel*, p. 222.
[7] *Ibid.*, p. 225. Similar ideas also appear in Cullmann, when he describes the arrangement of the material to be attributed to the evangelist as a commentary on the significance of the individual narrative (O. Cullmann, *Peter. Disciple, Apostle,*

It is obvious that Dibelius himself was not yet at all aware of the significance of this idea, for he assigns to the authors of the synoptic gospels only the role of collectors and transmitters, whose function would have consisted in handing on, grouping and revising the material reaching them. Only to a quite small extent could they be regarded as authors in their own right.[8] Haenchen rejects this view firmly and calls it 'harmful prejudice'; by contrast, he states: 'Matthew in particular showed himself to be an author of high quality when he composed the great discourses which go far beyond what existed before his time in the shape of attempts to arrange the material in accordance with its subject-matter'.[9]

Where can we find in other form-critical studies some germinal traces which later became fruitful in redaction criticism, but now no longer as isolated principles of method but within a self-contained conception of methodology?

Lohmeyer is not acknowledged as belonging to the form-critical school to the same extent as other New Testament scholars. Yet he was one of the first in the German language area, as far as we can see, to devote himself to the significance of the framework of the story of Jesus. After the destruction of this framework by K. L. Schmidt, attention was naturally concentrated on the individual sections, whilst the framework was neglected. Conzelmann calls Lohmeyer's decision to undertake the examination of the framework a necessary second stage in the work on the history of the tradition.[10] It was precisely by detaching this framework from the rest of the original traditional material that it became possible to see the framework itself as an entity *sui generis* and to interpret it as such. Lohmeyer took the first significant step forward here by his study *Galiläa und Jerusalem* (cf. *ibid.*, p. 10). The works of the English scholars, Grant, Dodd and R. H. Lightfoot, point in roughly the same direction.[11]

In Lohmeyer's book,[12] which is a preliminary study for his commentary on Mark, his object is to examine the relationship of the

---

Martyr, London and Philadelphia 1962[2], p. 181; see also p. 182 about the evangelist's placing of the passage Matt. 16.17–19 in the context of the gospel).

[8] M. Dibelius, *op. cit.*, p. 225.

[9] E. Haenchen, 'Matthäus 23', *loc. cit.*, p. 27.

[10] Conzelmann, *op. cit.*, p. 10.

[11] Cf. *ibid.*, p. 10; also Iber, *op. cit.*, p. 336; and further W. Schmauch, 'Die Komposition des Matthäus-Evangeliums in ihrer Bedeutung für seine Interpretation', in . . . *zu achten aufs Wort*, Berlin 1967, p. 67.

[12] E. Lohmeyer, *Galiläa und Jerusalem*.

accounts of the appearances of the Risen One in Galilee on the one hand, and in Jerusalem on the other. He attempts to prove that the difference between these two has a theological stamp and is based on the disagreement between the Christian communities in Galilee and Jerusalem.[13] Grundmann has taken up this idea and formulates it thus: 'The differences between Acts 1 and the Pauline traditions, as well as those between the appearances in Jerusalem and those in Galilee, point to problems in the history of the primitive Christian Church. They are not in the first place differences in the tradition, but between those who transmitted it' (p. 367). Lohmeyer derives his thesis from the following considerations: on the one hand Galilee had become, after the destruction of Jerusalem, the new centre of the Jewish people and of their faith, and when the teaching started at the settlement at Jamnia it had stepped into the place of Jerusalem.[14] On the other hand, at the time when the synoptic gospels were composed, Galilee was considered to be a *terra christiana*, and the people of Galilee to be a *populus christianus*, as we see from the statement of the maid in the pericope about Peter's denial (Mark 14.70 par. Luke 22.59; cf. Matt. 26.69, 73) (p. 28).

Lohmeyer also compares with each other the geographical statements, i.e. the significance of the places Galilee and Jerusalem in the gospels. From this the following situation emerges: in Mark, Jerusalem is the city of deadly enmity to Jesus, the city of sin and death. 'The outline of Jesus' life in the gospel of Mark rests on the distinct theological idea that God had chosen for his eschatological work and gospel the despised Galilee. This outline is not created by Mark, but existed in the community's tradition' (Mark 14.28; 16.7) (p. 34). Matthew, in 4.12–17, removed the curse of pagan impurity from Galilee (p. 37), but at the same time quietly reduced the excessive weight attached to Galilee in Mark (p. 39). In John, on the other hand, Jerusalem stands much more definitely and emphatically in the centre of Jesus' activity (p. 39), for the reason that Golgotha stands at the centre of it (p. 41). In his gospel, Galilee is the land of concealment: the land, as it were, in keeping with Jesus' ministry (p. 40). Luke, again, has reduced the role of Galilee in Mark, but has created in Samaria a fresh theatre for Jesus' activity (p. 42). He distributed Jesus' ministry equally between the three theatres of Galilee, Samaria and Jerusalem (p. 46).

13 Cf. W. Grundmann, *Geschichte Jesu Christi*, p. 368.
14 E. Lohmeyer, *op. cit.*, p. 26.

Lohmeyer's opinion is based on the fact that the accounts of the appearance of the Risen One are set in Galilee as well as Jerusalem. The missionary charge of Matt. 28.16–20 shows that the tradition preserved by Matthew later regarded Galilee as the mother country of Christ's manifestation and of the primitive Christian faith (p. 17). For Luke, who knows only of appearances in Jerusalem, this city is merely the historically given, not theologically necessary place of Jesus' appearance, whereas for Paul the place is altogether immaterial (p. 24). Lohmeyer thinks that in the appearances in Galilee and Jerusalem two different theological trends are clearly distinguished (p. 23). 'The juxtaposition of the Galilean and Jerusalem appearances is based on the juxtaposition of this twofold conception' (p. 46).

From what he has noted, Lohmeyer draws the conclusion that the primitive community in Palestine had two centres: one in Galilee, owing to the origin and activity of Jesus and his kindred; the other in Jerusalem, owing to the activity of his disciples (p. 58). Furthermore, there was a juxtaposition of differing theological ideas: the natural kindred of the Son of Man in Galilee were contrasted with the bearers of the spirit of the Messiah in Jerusalem (p. 96). Lohmeyer even ventures to assert that Galilee clung to faith in the Son of Man and the confession Κύριος Ἰησοῦς, and Jerusalem to faith in the Messiah and the confession Χριστὸς Ἰησοῦς (p. 97). 'This prepares the way for a solution of the problem of the actual juxtaposition. First, different traditions are speaking through them; the one proves the existence of an early Christianity rooted in Galilee, the other that of an early Christianity gathered in Jerusalem' (p. 97).

Bultmann challenged this division of the early Palestinian community by Lohmeyer with very convincing arguments. He leaves open the possibility of different trends in the Palestinian community, and also the existence of a Galilean community; but he disputes the fact that this community had the importance which Lohmeyer attributes to it. For Paul takes account only of a Jerusalem community, led first by the twelve apostles, then by the Lord's brother James, thus by people who all came from Galilee and represented the Galilean tradition. In any case, it seems impossible to consider the two titles 'Messiah' and 'Son of Man' as the expressions of two different theological views of Jesus and hence as distinguishing marks of two different communities or trends. After adducing quotations from late Jewish apocalyptic literature (Ethiopian Enoch, IV Ezra,

Syrian Baruch) he writes: 'Both [titles] alike denote the eschatological salvation-bringer. The ancient title "Messiah", once expressing Israelitic national hope, was no longer confined to this narrower meaning but could just as well be transferred to the heavenly salvation-bringer awaited by the apocalyptists, as the salvation brought by the latter could, vice versa, take on nationalistic traits.'[15] Thus nothing in the synoptic tradition indicates 'that the varying titles "Messiah" and "Son of Man" express varying conceptions of Jesus' person. Moreover, Paul, who does not use the apocalyptic title "Son of Man", clearly does not use the term Christ . . . in the sense of the nationalistic hope, but in that of apocalypticism' (p. 53).

Without entering here on a detailed discussion, we do not think that Lohmeyer's theses are consistent with the actual facts. They have been originated from forced interpretations of the text and interpolations into it. It seems to us doubtful whether it is at all possible to speak of an original community in Galilee, especially since nothing can be gathered about its existence directly from the New Testament writings, unless the gospel of Mark, by virtue of its orientation towards Galilee, is interpreted as evidence of an early Galilean Christianity at the time when the gospel came into being (thus Marxsen). It is simply mentioned in Acts 9.31 that the church throughout all (ἐκκλησία καθ' ὅλης) Judaea, Galilee and Samaria had peace (after the persecution which began with the stoning of Stephen). But this formulation looks as if it were merely enumerating in summary fashion the three main areas of Jesus' ministry by the names used in the gospel, that is to say, in the first part of the Lucan historical work. We are not able to attribute any historical value to this summary list in Acts 9.31, especially since in Acts 8.1 it is merely stated that the Christians of the original community were scattered throughout Judaea and Samaria in consequence of the persecution which set in with the stoning of Stephen. In the latter passage there is no mention of Galilee. On the contrary, it appears from Acts 11.19 that the Jewish Christians, probably Hellenists, who had fled from Jerusalem, passed along the Mediterranean coast through Phoenicia as far as Antioch, and that the second centre of primitive Christianity came into being there (Acts 11.22, 25, 27).

In summing up Lohmeyer's work, we emphasize that in it we rate positively and as a contribution towards the future of redaction criticism, *the fact* that he made the attempt to survey as an entity in its own right the framework of Jesus' story which had been broken up and analysed by form criticism, and to interpret it; but we must

[15] R. Bultmann, *Theology of the New Testament* I, London and New York 1968[5], pp. 52f.

regret *the manner* in which he did so. The fundamental distinction between his investigation and the procedure of redaction criticism consists in the fact that he tries to interpret only the framework detached from the individual pericopes, and not to examine the composition and the theological conception of the individual gospels as we have them. Redaction criticism, on the other hand, endeavours to understand the gospels in their entirety against the background of a definite theological situation in the church, and thereby to determine their 'third *Sitz im Leben*'.[16] 'Its interest lies in the gospels in their written form, in their historical background and in their theological testimony.'[17]

In other form-critical studies, too, there are hints of a redaction-critical approach to the gospels. The difference between these hints and redaction criticism proper lies in the fact that in form criticism only a few separate observations were made, which were then systematically collected and utilized by redaction criticism. We can identify the same procedure, too, in the case of the precursors of form criticism.[18]

The first point made by the precursors of redaction criticism amongst the form critics was to emphasize the fact that the evangelists were not only collectors and transmitters, but also authors in their own right. In particular they drew attention again and again to the gospel of Matthew. But questions were also asked about the well-planned composition by the authors of the other two synoptic gospels, who can thus be understood to be the mouthpiece of the Christian Church as a whole, or of particular groups of communities. We will justify this statement by several characteristic examples.

In an essay 'Der historische Jesus als geschichtswissenschaftliches und theologisches Problem' (The historical Jesus as a problem for the historian and the theologian), N. A. Dahl makes the demand that the gospels as we have them should first be studied and interpreted as literary wholes. This demand is to be understood as an antithesis to the previous form-critical analysis of the synoptic material and its dissection into individual pericopes in order to be able to set the different earlier and later traditions in relief against each other.[19]

[16] W. Marxsen, *Evangelist Markus*, p. 12.
[17] G. Iber, *op. cit.*, p. 337.
[18] On this see E. Fascher, *op. cit.*, pp. 8–48 and the unprinted version of my dissertation, pp. 5–14.
[19] N. A. Dahl, 'Der historische Jesus als geschichtswissenschaftliches und theologisches Problem', *Kerygma und Dogma* I, Berlin 1956, p. 120.

When this has been done, a study of the history of the traditions of the small and smallest units must be made (p. 120).

The statements of Michaelis point in the same direction. They, too, arise out of the rejection of particular assertions of form criticism. He disputes that the synoptic gospels are made up of very small units. In that case the authors of accounts like the gospels [the assumed precursors of our gospels] would have been faced with the quite insoluble problem of creating a well arranged whole out of fragments.[20] Michaelis does indeed concede with Dibelius the unliterary quality of the synoptic gospels, but in opposition to Dibelius' view he emphasizes that they are in a certain respect the achievements of authors. Both characteristics, their unliterary quality on the one hand and their quality as the achievement of authors on the other, must not be treated too much as in opposition (p. 23).

The statements made by Dahl and Michaelis refer to all three synoptists. Other authors illustrate similar points from individual synoptic gospels. In this matter the gospel of Matthew always stands in the foreground. But in Mark and Luke, too, a general theological conception is assumed to be the principle of the shaping and the arrangement. Writers are unanimous in holding the view that Matthew's gospel in particular is controlled by a definite technique of composition.

Fascher calls attention to the fact that in the case of Matthew we are not concerned with a work of mere collection, but with the author's pronounced individuality in diction, in intention and in the colour of his tone and thoughts.[21] Procksch emphasizes the fact that the gospel of Matthew is drawn up according to a clear plan which reveals very vigorous methodical thought. In the centre of the gospel there stand five main sections which are in each case brought to an end with a discourse.[22] 'Matthew has the sharply-defined nature of an author with a forcible point of view and will-power, and with an unusual talent to shape and arrange material available to him. Similarly Mark must also be esteemed as a character who has given his gospel a special stamp' (p. 74). He rejects the hypothesis that the evangelists could merely be copyists and compilers and wants appreciation to be shown of their personal share in their enterprise in

[20] W. Michaelis, op. cit., p. 22.

[21] A. Jülicher/E. Fascher, op. cit., p. 294; similarly Michaelis, op. cit., p. 37, on the composition of the discourses in Matthew.

[22] O. Procksch, Petrus und Johannes bei Markus und Matthäus, Gütersloh 1920, p. 62.

which, beside special knowledge and a special point of view, a special faith is included (p. 74).

Soiron understands the synoptic gospels as testimonies of faith which are intended to express the meaning of Jesus' mission through the manner of their composition.[23] The three laws of construction controlling their accounts are enumeration, classification and combination by means of catchwords (p. 12). Here enumeration means that sayings and stories taken from Jesus' life are arranged in definite groups according to particular numbers (p. 12). By classification (according to theme), analogous material is combined to form discourses or groups of tales (p. 17). Finally, the catchword is used where no classifications linked the discourses or stories together, but merely the use of the same word or the external association of sentences or words (p. 22). In another place, Soiron had already examined the technique of the three first evangelists in their compositions to see how they had fitted the sayings of Jesus into the composition of their gospels.[24] He makes the important suggestion that the tendency of the gospels is to shape a life which is formed through the gospels. They had already completed their formation in the primitive community, which was the life of a definite fellowship.[25] We consider that this last suggestion gives a lead into the future, because it contains the presupposition (albeit implicit) that the gospels as wholes had a *Sitz im Leben* in the community.

The remarks which point forward to the work of redaction criticism are not confined to the gospel of Matthew, but are present also in individual studies of the gospel of Mark. Thus Riesenfeld considers the arrangement in this gospel, namely that the first main section as far as 8.26 has for its subject 'The Son of Man and Israel', and the second one up to 10.52 'The Messiah as teacher and judge', to be the result of previous theological reflection by the evangelist or his predecessors.[26]

In his study of Mark 13, Busch claims that our first concern cannot be the question of the authenticity of Jesus' sayings in this chapter, as this would be for the time being unprofitable; the road must lead away from the problem of authenticity to the sole concern of

---

[23] T. Soiron, *Das Evangelium als Lebensform des Menschen*, Munich/Rome 1925, p. 5.

[24] *Id., Die Logia Jesu*, Münster 1916, pp. 23–144.

[25] *Id., Das Evangelium als Lebensform* . . ., p. 29.

[26] H. Riesenfeld, 'Tradition und Redaktion im Markusevangelium', in *Neutestamentliche Studien für Bultmann*, Berlin 1954, p. 160.

ascertaining how the question of truth is dealt with in the gospels.[27] Hence the real aim must be to understand the evangelist, for the individual sayings (in Mark 13) acquired their meaning from their context (p. 36). Hence we must raise the problem of the construction of the whole gospel in connection with the disclosure of the Messianic secret, in accordance with the understanding of the evangelist, leaving aside the problem of authenticity and the historical Jesus (p. 37). For even if the evangelist has not rendered Jesus' sayings absolutely correctly, this rendering of them must in itself be taken seriously because he had seen a meaning in the context which he had produced (p. 38).

The study by the Roman Catholic Franciscan, W. Hillmann, *Aufbau und Deutung der synoptischen Leidensberichte* (Construction and Interpretation of the Synoptic Accounts of the Passion) deserves detailed description. The sub-title of this work, 'A contribution to the technique of the composition and to the interpretation of the meaning of the three earlier gospels', already shows us that in terms of method the approach to the study is leading towards redaction criticism. Hillmann endeavours to show that the gospels are composed according to a definite plan.[28] In his opinion, this method of composition appears in the selection and arrangement, partly also in the shaping of the individual traditions (p. 2). It is more important here than in the form-critical research of Dibelius to determine the purpose of the individual evangelists; in this way, the relative independence of each one will stand out. We can already read off some of the history of the tradition from the shifting of the centre of gravity in the individual gospels (p. 6).

'In a comparison of the synoptic gospels, far too little attention has been paid to this because since so much of the material was the same, the *special* line taken in the gospel was not sufficiently recognized and emphasized. But this is what matters, for only by this means do the gospels reveal the real content which the evangelist himself has contributed' (p. 7).

It is not sufficient to survey the general scheme of the synoptists, which in the last analysis is the same in all three. The composition of the individual groups must be examined to see how the evangelist has formed them. We do not get very much further if we classify the

---

[27] F. Busch, *Zum Verständnis der synoptischen Eschatologie*, Gütersloh 1938, p. 35.
[28] W. Hillmann, *Aufbau und Deutung der synoptischen Leidensberichte*, Munich 1951, p. 2.

individual traditions into genres (p. 8). Hillmann follows Büchsel in emphasizing that in the case of each of the synoptists we must pay attention to the general understanding of Jesus, his sayings, his story, his person, etc. (p. 8). In the account of the passion also, each evangelist has created a formal composition peculiar to himself by means of special materials and omissions of tradition (p. 11). From this we can infer the specific meaning and the leading idea which coloured their views of Jesus' life (p. 12).

We need not describe here how Hillmann carried out the plan of his study. His results are too problematical in several respects for this: for instance, when he thinks he can demonstrate in Matthew a pattern of threes and sevens, in Mark a pattern of twos and in Luke one of fours. Such matters of form by themselves do not take us any further. We can only value his approach decisively and positively in terms of method.

Hillmann also fits the individual gospels in their entirety into the history of primitive Christianity, but he definitely rejects the thesis of form criticism that a *Sitz im Leben* can be determined for the individual passages (p. 260). Hence he is trying to discover the so-called third *Sitz im Leben* for which redaction criticism is also looking. Matthew reflects the separation of Palestinian primitive Christianity from Judaism (p. 103). Matthew thus counters the fruitless attempt of the mission to Israel with the command for world-wide mission (p. 260). The gospel of Mark, on the contrary, shows no controversy with Judaism, but a concern for the mystery of Jesus' person, for the sublime majesty of the Son of God and the humiliation and disguise of majesty in the Son of Man (p. 260). In Luke's gospel, on the other hand, a didactic trait appears which is aimed at the practical life of a Christian (p. 225). The reason for this trait lies in the fact that the church is moving ever further away from Judaism, is growing stronger within itself and concentrating its attention on the community and its inner life. The internal circumstances of the communities in Paul's mission area are also mirrored here (pp. 226f.). By the manner in which Luke describes Jesus, he intends to bring the influence of Jesus' example so that practical consequences are drawn in the community, too (p. 260). To sum up, the chief idea of each gospel and the manner of its expansion is connected with the internal and external situation of early Christianity at a definite historical period of its development (p. 260).

Most recently, to some degree following Lohmeyer in his method,

G. Schille has attempted to sketch a completely new picture of apostolic Christianity with the help of a traditio-historical investigation. He completely rules out of account the Lucan framework of primitive Christian history as a construction by Luke.[29] In its complexity, this investigation in some respects resembles Hirsch's *Frühgeschichte des Evangeliums*.

B. *The first beginnings in Old Testament Scholarship and in Schlatter*

In the preface of his book *Der Evangelist Markus*, Marxsen points to the fact that, as in form criticism, Old Testament studies prepared the way for redaction criticism. He himself had obtained suggestions for the formulation of his questions from the work of von Rad on the Pentateuch.[30] In fact von Rad demonstrates by means of the Yahwist source that the latter had collected certain material which had become detached from the customs of the cult and had inserted it within the framework of his literary composition.[31]

According to von Rad, Gunkel had almost completely left theological purpose out of account in his studies. This, however, is vigorously pursued and the individual pieces of material are associated by no more than a few fundamental ideas (p. 51). The tradition of the conquest of the country is regarded by von Rad to be the Yahwist's fundamental framework and design. This framework was shaped according to a homogeneous plan; the shaping therefore had been no natural and anonymous growth (pp. 51f.). The Yahwist had brought into the framework of the conquest tradition the Sinai tradition, the patriarchal tradition and the creation narrative (p. 53). But the Yahwist did not only shape his material in accordance with his plan; he also collected it. The story of Joseph provides evidence of this; in it the assembled units retain an individual life of their own, but are governed by a leading fundamental theological conception, which links the history of the patriarchs to the conquest of the country (pp. 59f.).

Von Rad considers that it was the work of the Yahwist alone which made the material of the early history lead up to a goal. The leading

[29] G. Schille, *Anfänge der Kirche. Erwägungen zur apostolischen Frühgeschichte*, Munich 1966.
[30] W. Marxsen, *op. cit.*, p. 5; see also on this A. Descamps, 'Essai d'interprétation de Mt. 5.17–48' in *Studia Evangelica*, Berlin 1959, pp. 156–73.
[31] G. von Rad, 'The Problem of the Hexateuch', in *The Problem of the Hexateuch and Other Essays*, Edinburgh 1966, p. 50.

conception is the growth of the power of sin in the world (p. 64). Thus the general arrangement of the material, i.e. the way in which it is put together, goes back to the Yahwist (p. 67), who is speaking to his contemporaries out of his own concern for the faith (p. 69). He testifies to a story of divine guidance and providence in all spheres of life (p. 71). K. Elliger also agrees on the whole with this opinion of von Rad about the historical composition of the Yahwist, though he assesses the influence of the cultic-sacral tradition more highly.[32]

More important for redaction criticism than von Rad's works are the studies of the gospel of Matthew by Schlatter. Above all in his great commentary, *Der Evangelist Matthäus*, he has noted and used fruitfully for exegesis the fact that in this gospel can be seen the work of a 'church' in handing on the tradition. Yet these remarks of Schlatter have hardly been noticed in the rest of the literature about Matthew. This is certainly due to the fact that Schlatter's works have remained completely dissociated both from the period of literary-critical research and from the method of the form-critical school. To this extent they lacked a methodological foundation, compared with literary and form criticism.[33]

It is not necessary to deal fully here with Schlatter's small book *Die Kirche des Matthäus*. It is written in a very popular style and does not supply any evidence for the assertions made in it. Besides, it is extremely doubtful if so much can really be gathered, as Schlatter attempts to do, from Matthew's gospel about the church represented by Matthew, its relation to Judaism, the internal arrangements of the community and its relation to God. It must be said in opposition to Schlatter that the gospels were written not so much in order to describe a condition, as to strengthen and edify particular regional groups in the whole of the church in which they originated, and as a contemporary answer to questions and problems of these communities, although this opinion is not wholly incompatible with Schlatter's point of view.

In his commentary *Der Evangelist Matthäus* (1929), Schlatter endeavours to deduce from the gospel of Matthew not only the condition of the church represented by Matthew, but also the other problems which in Schlatter's opinion may have agitated this community of the Palestinian church. Schlatter is already using the redaction-critical method in his work to the extent, but only to the

[32] See on this K. Elliger,' Der Jakobskampf am Jabbok', *ZThK* 48, 1951, p. 13.
[33] Cf. W. Trilling, *Das wahre Israel*, p. 2.

extent, that he endeavours to determine a quite definite place in the history of primitive Christianity, a third *Sitz im Leben* for the first gospel. Schlatter tells us in the preface about the method of his approach. He writes that in the gospel of Matthew we are addressed by a man who lives in the Palestinian church and who has written as a member of it and for it.[34] Since Jesus speaks to mankind through his disciples we must ask about the aim and intention of the evangelist's presentation and pursue this problem closely, for scientific research supplies different answers to it (p. *viii*).

Schlatter places definite emphasis on the relative independence of the evangelist, which appears in a specific conception; he adds that the title of the gospel would become open to question if the share of the evangelist in his book had been restricted to putting together two or more records as a mere scribe. Apart from the mutual relationship of Matthew to Mark, the skills and troubles of a scribe who pieces 'sources' together can hardly be evidenced in connection with Matthew (p. *xi*). Schlatter even expresses his intention to keep clear of all conjectures about the early stages preceding our gospels, for 'I call science the observation of what exists, not the attempt to imagine what is not visible' (p. *xi*). Nevertheless, Schlatter, too, has his own quite definite ideas and opinions about the time when the gospel of Matthew came into being and about its literary relationship to Mark: he disputes the dependence of Matthew on Mark (pp. 50 *et passim*), because this makes Matthew's procedure both the dependence of a copyist and at the same time the independence of a constructive thinker (p. 50). He also denies not only Matthew's dependence on a collection of sayings (Q), but even the existence of such a collection at all (p. 51). On the contrary, Matthew, who is identical with the tax-gatherer and apostle Levi, wrote this gospel as a presbyter about twenty years after Jesus' death. It was then used by Mark and Luke for the composition of their gospels (p. 304). Luke's other source over and above Matthew was no book of sayings but a gospel on its own (pp. 357 *et passim*).

On a general view, we are to infer from the form of the gospel of Matthew (the five great complexes of discourses supply evidence for this) not only the personal faith of the evangelist, but also a picture of the first community, of Palestinian Christianity, which shows by the reproduction of the discourses in Matthew that its religious attitude was determined at every step by what it had received from

[34] A. Schlatter, *Der Evangelist Matthäus*, Stuttgart 1929, preface p. *x*.

Jesus. Matthew is handing down to us not his own considerations, but Jesus' utterances, as they had become Matthew's own by his reflection and by his experience (p. 128).

We do not wish to enter here upon a detailed discussion with Schlatter about the time of origin and the question of the sources of Matthew's gospel. We will only state that in order to defend himself against critical research Schlatter has moved the time when the first gospel came into being much too near to the date of Jesus' death. He has done this in order to be able to trace it back to a disciple of Jesus without inserting an intermediate stage as a bearer of the tradition, and at the same time in order to conclude from this its absolute historical trustworthiness. He does indeed admit that in the case of the discourse tradition Matthew abridged the historical picture. For in his opinion the discourses in Matthew's gospel consisted of maxims, i.e. pure, self-contained principles. During their transmission all that Jesus had said to explain these maxims was lost. Besides, it was not certain that the sayings had been spoken in the days of which Matthew was thinking (p. 130). Now what Schlatter believes he can gather from Matthew's gospel about the circumstances of Palestinian Judaism at the time when this gospel came into being is highly problematical. From several passages, for example, from the commissioning discourse (ch. 10), from the saying about the leaven of the Pharisees (ch. 16), from the sayings about the temple-tax (ch. 17) and from the discourse against the Pharisees, he thinks that in so early a period, about the year 50, he can detect a quite bitter enmity, a matter of life or death, between the primitive community and Judaism. Thus it appears in the section Matt. 10.16–23 that the conflict with Israel has been intensified to the utmost limit, so that the complete collapse of the Palestinian church is expected (p. 342). Moreover, the conversation about the leaven of the Pharisees (Matt. 16.5–12) shows that the oppression of the community of disciples makes it difficult for them to obtain their normal food (p. 501).

Certainly some sections from Acts enable us to know that altercations took place with the Jews because Jesus was proclaimed as the Messiah (Acts 4 and 5), that Peter was imprisoned, and that James the son of Zebedee was executed (Acts 12.1ff.). But in other respects we know nothing about an oppression of the primitive Palestinian Christians by the Jews, at least not in the period in which Schlatter places the origin of Matthew's gospel, since they presumably kept themselves very largely within the general framework of Judaism. The situation was different only as regards the Hellenistic Jewish Christians round Stephen and Paul's preaching of the gospel free from the law.

But we are not concerned in our discussion of Schlatter with these historical questions, nor with the origin of the synoptic gospels and their dependence on each other, but only with the method of his approach, namely his estimate of the share of Matthew as an author in his own right in shaping his gospel, and his attempt to fit the first gospel as a whole into the history of primitive Christianity. Although we have considerable objections to Schlatter's separate theses, yet we feel able to value the method of his approach as a contribution towards the consideration of the synoptic gospels in terms of redaction criticism, even though this approach has not been made by way of literary criticism, the two-source theory and form criticism, but in obvious opposition to them.

III

THE GOSPEL OF MATTHEW

A. Günther Bornkamm   *End-Expectation and Church in Matthew*

BORNKAMM'S ARTICLE 'MATTHÄUS als Interpret der Herrenworte' (Matthew as the interpreter of the Lord's sayings) sets out explicitly to be a contribution to the redaction criticism of the gospel of Matthew.[1] He concentrates his attention upon the sayings of Jesus, mainly on the composition of the discourses. In Matthew we find a close association of the idea of the Church with the expectation of the end, a link between ecclesiology and eschatology (col. 341). Thus the Beatitudes in the Sermon on the Mount are the rules of admission to discipleship. The missionary discourse in ch. 10 shows the above-mentioned association, as do the other three sets of discourses in Matthew. Chapter 13, with the seven parables about the kingdom of heaven, expresses the idea that the Church is not only a collection of the elect and the righteous, but a *corpus mixtum* which will not face separation until the final judgment (col. 342). We need hardly stress how true these observations of Bornkamm are for the whole of the discourse to the community in ch. 18; not merely for the section about the power of the keys (vv. 15–18), but also for vv. 6–9, 12–14 and 35, at the end of the parable of the unmerciful servant.

By attaching Jesus' pre-Easter saying firmly to Peter as the rock of the Church (Matt. 16.18) during the time of Jesus' life on earth, the Church, too, is placed under the law of the life and passion of Jesus on earth; her place is indeed after the resurrection, but still before the parousia (col. 346). But these ideas of Matthew can only be learned from the context, in which the ministry of the Church is controlled by the standard of the future decisions of the Son of Man (col. 346). Matthew's christology is controlled by the thought that the Messianic function of the earthly Jesus appears in his interpretation of the law (col. 343). Whereas in Mark an apologetic motive is

[1] G. Bornkamm, 'Matthäus als Interpret der Herrenworte' *op. cit.*, col. 341.

present, the theme that the Messianic confession might not become known until after the resurrection, Matthew expresses the idea that Jesus on earth was at the same time both the Christ and the Son of God who calls his disciples, too, to follow the example of his passion (col. 345). In the gospel of Matthew, which certainly uses many christological titles for Jesus, but correspondingly few eccelesiological designations, the idea of the Church is marked by the strict eschatological separation of those who are called from those who are chosen (col. 344).

This investigation by Bornkamm, which was first presented as a lecture at the *Deutscher Theologentag* in 1954 and published in summary form in the *Theologische Literaturzeitung*, is the preliminary study for the expanded and more carefully documented study, 'End-expectation and Church in Matthew'.[2] Bornkamm subdivides the latter into four sections. In the first, he shows by means of the close association of eschatology and ecclesiology in the chapters containing the discourses, how Matthew sees even the Church to be under the final judgment. In the second section he deals with Matthew's understanding of the law, in the third with Jesus as the one who fulfils the scriptures, especially the law—the christology of Matthew's gospel—and in the fourth and last section with Matthew's ecclesiology.

Apart from the discourse of the Baptist in the gospel of Matthew, Bornkamm examines in the first section only the construction of the discourses as regards the combination of eschatology and ecclesiology in them. In Mark, John the Baptist is given no importance of his own; after a brief mention of him (Mark 1.4–8), the baptism, temptation and public appearance of Jesus begin at once. In Luke his public appearance occurs in a section which is historically fixed and complete in itself (Luke 3.1ff.; 16.16). Matthew, however, connects the Baptist and his message quite clearly with the message of Jesus. Matthew alone connects the preaching of the Baptist with that of Jesus in the same logion (3.2; 4.17). By this means the Baptist, too, becomes a preacher of the Christian community.[3]

Even in the Baptist's preaching (Matt. 3.7–12), the basic concep-

---

[2] First published in German in *The Background of the New Testament and its Eschatology*, Cambridge 1956, now translated from a somewhat more complete and revised version in: Günther Bornkamm, Gerhard Barth and H. J. Held, *Tradition and Interpretation in Matthew*, London and New York 1963. In what follows, quotations are taken from this expanded and revised version.

[3] G. Bornkamm, 'End-expectation and Church in Matthew', p. 15.

tions of Matthew's understanding of the Church appear. This is fashioned by the fundamental conception of the expectation of the coming judgment (p. 16). This conception runs through the whole gospel and also determines the structure of the Sermon on the Mount. From the start, this discourse has an eschatological trend which appears particularly from 7.13 onwards in the saying about the narrow gate—and the following pronouncements (p. 17).

In the missionary discourse in ch. 10, the same trend and connection can be seen. It is suggested by the theme of Jesus' compassion for the harrassed and leaderless people (9.36). Before the actual missionary discourse, the disciples are first exhorted to pray to the Lord of the harvest for labourers (9.37f.). Thus the familiar image of the judgment of the world is applied to mission (p. 18). The last part of the missionary discourse (vv. 17–39) is no longer missionary instruction in the proper sense, but gives directions to the Church as a whole and indicates what the disciples as a whole must expect and endure. Thus here the way and the nature of discipleship are wholly set in an eschatological light. For this purpose, the evangelist has already incorporated here some logia from the apocalyptic sayings of the synoptic discourse about the return of the Son of Man (pp. 18f.).

In the parable chapter, the same contrast between the disciples and Israel, characteristic of the whole gospel, is dominant. Those to whom it has been given to know the mysteries of the Kingdom of Heaven (13.11) are contrasted with the obdurate people condemned by its own guilt (13.14f.). This whole composition is intended to show the importance for the Church of the coming judgment (p. 19). Several things may be gathered about the community represented by Matthew from the discourse to the community. It is still attached to Judaism, as the immediately preceding section (17.24–27) shows, and recognizes voluntarily the taxation of the Jewish communities in the diaspora, though conscious of its own special position. We must also take into account the position of this discourse after Peter's confession and the saying concerning the foundation of the Church (16.18f.), and after the following pericope with the predictions of the passion and the sayings about the suffering of the disciples in following Christ (16.21–28), down to the second announcement of the passion (17.22f.) (pp. 19f.). Matthew has significantly and deliberately set the sayings about the discipline of the community (18.15–18) within the framework of the parables of the lost sheep and of the unmerciful servant (18.12–14, 21–35). For the last parable ends by pointing to the judgment which will fall inexorably on those members of the community who are unwilling to forgive (v. 35) (p. 20). Bornkamm thinks he can find expressions in the parables of the wicked wine-dressers (21.33–44) and the marriage feast (22.2–14) of the thought that the coming judgment applies to the disciples as well; but his arguments are not sufficiently convincing.[4] The introductory verses (vv. 1–3) of the discourse about the Pharisees in particular show that Matthew's community belonged to organized Judaism, and with its sevenfold 'woes' it is quite strongly permeated by the thought of the final judgment (vv. 32–39) (p. 21).

Finally, the apocalyptic discourse in ch. 24, with the eschatological parables in ch. 25, supplies a firm outline of the idea of the Church and its orientation to the last days (p. 21). The thought of judgment in the eschatological parables in ch. 25 is applied throughout to the Church. In these parables, the experience of the delay of the parousia leaves its mark so that the understanding of 'wisdom' changes with the situation. In 24.48 'the delay of the master' is understood as an illusion of the wicked servant, whereas in 25.1–13 the delay in the arrival of the bridegroom is considered to be an actual experience in which the 'wisdom' of the virgins who made provision for a longer period of waiting is confirmed, whereas the illusion of the foolish virgins is the simple fact that they reckoned on his being at hand (p. 23). In the description of the judgment of the world (25.31–46), only one standard is applied, love for the least: it is not important whether a man is a Jew or a Gentile, a believer or an unbeliever. Here it is evident that the discipleship of Jesus is not confined to the company of the chosen, but includes at first the company of those who are called, whose ultimate fate is decided by the doing of God's will (pp. 23f.).

In the section on the understanding of the law in the gospel of Matthew, Bornkamm, after examining the relevant passages,

---

[4] *Ibid.*, pp. 20f. The interpretation of Hasler rejects this decisively. He tries to grasp the redaction theology in this parable by distinguishing three stages in the revision of the traditional material found in the source of the discourses (Q). These are: (1) An eschatological-ecclesiological stage (the Church as a *corpus mixtum* until the judgment). (2) A revision of the tradition as salvation history in the pattern of promise and fulfilment with scriptural proofs (the sending of the Old Testament prophets and Jesus' disciples with the invitation to God's people). (3) A polemical stage of redaction (God's judgment on Israel itself). According to Hasler, the idea of judgment is not directed against the disciples, but (in the third stage of the redaction) against Israel (see V. Hasler, 'Die königliche Hochzeit: Matt. 22.1–14', *ThZ 18*, 1962, pp. 25–35).

arrives at the conclusion that Matthew understands the law in a way which does not differ in principle from Judaism, but he deliberately inserts his understanding of it into the Jewish scribal tradition. It is only the discrepancy between doctrine and deeds on the part of his opponents that brings about the vehemence of his opposition to Judaism and thus to the misuse and failure of an interpretation of the law which does not look for the original meaning of the divine demand and refuses to perceive the essentials of the law (p. 31). In Matthew, the essence of the law is the command of love in its twofold direction, towards God and towards man's neighbour. The cultic law is not disputed; its validity is taken for granted, insofar as it is not misused hypocritically and the weightier matters of the law are not neglected (pp. 31f.).

The third section turns its attention to the relation of law and christology in the gospel. Matthew in particular seeks the authority of scripture vigorously and consistently for all the messianic titles of Jesus, for his teaching, his deeds and his story, for which evidence is provided by the reflective quotations (pp. 32f.). There are hardly any reflections on the relationship between the messianic titles; these occur only in 22.41ff., about the relationship between the title of David and the title *Kyrios*; again in 26.63f., about the relationship between the titles Christ and Son of God, and Jesus as the Son of man who will judge the world. There is a third instance in the story of the entry into Jerusalem (21.1ff.) (pp. 33f.).

The relationship of Jesus to Moses is understood not in the sense of an antithesis, as in John 1.17; 6.32, but in the sense of correspondence. Jesus' teaching, in spite of the authoritative 'But I say to you', is constantly proved from the law and his authority is not simply asserted (p. 35). Bornkamm allows for the fact that the messianic titles of Matthew's gospel are not derived only from Jewish messianology, but already show influences of the Hellenistic community (p. 32).

The last section seeks to determine the ecclesiology of Matthew's gospel. No other gospel is so deeply imbued with the idea of the Church and shaped for use in church as Matthew. That is why it subsequently had a decisive influence in the Church. The whole book contains statements which express the eschatological self-consciousness of primitive Christianity (p. 38). Yet Matthew's gospel shows only the most meagre beginnings of a real ecclesiology, which would enable the Church to be recognized as an independent, empirically circumscribed entity. There is no similar number of ecclesiological concepts and words to correspond with the numerous christological titles and pronouncements. Matthew's gospel confirms throughout that the community which he represented had not yet broken away from Judaism. It still advocates the messiahship of Jesus and the validity of his teaching completely within the framework of Judaism. 'The struggle with Israel is still a struggle within its own walls.'[5]

Matthew's conception is indeed on the one hand dominated by the Jewish tradition (15.24 and 10.5f.), yet on the other hand it is peculiarly open in the direction of the Gentile world (28.19) (p. 38). The saying about the Church in Matt. 16.18, which Bornkamm does not derive from the historical Jesus (p. 45), cannot be grasped from the perspective of the traditional idea of the people of God, but bears an institutional character, marked by the authority in doctrine and in discipline of a particular apostle. The future tense, repeated several times in vv. 18f., points to the fact that Peter as the rock of the Church receives the office of the keys only for the period after the resurrection, but before the parousia. This Church on earth is both different from the $\beta a\sigma\iota\lambda\epsilon\acute{\iota}a$ $\tau\hat{\omega}\nu$ $o\mathring{\upsilon}\rho a\nu\hat{\omega}\nu$ and also quite closely associated with it; for its binding and loosing, its authority in doctrine and discipline and the decisions resulting from it, will be confirmed in the $\beta a\sigma\iota\lambda\epsilon\acute{\iota}a$ to come (pp. 45f.).

Bornkamm sums up the result of his investigation by saying that Matthew is to a high degree an interpreter of the tradition which he collected and arranged; in him tradition and theological conception stand in a mutual relationship to each other, so that theology is placed in the service of the tradition, just as tradition serves theology. Although Matthew is first and foremost a representative of a community, his gospel is by no means simply the outcome of a community's theology; the carefulness and the well-planned nature of his work show him to be a distinct individual in primitive Christian literary history (p. 49).

Bornkamm's study, taken as a whole, must be understood to be a contribution to the theology of Matthew's gospel. He draws attention repeatedly to the evangelist's independent redactional activity in the service of his theological conception. We cannot claim it as a complete redaction-critical sketch of the gospel of Matthew. Therefore the question of its *Sitz im Leben*, in the history of primitive Christianity,

[5] A different opinion in W. Hillmann, *op. cit.*, p. 103.

arises only marginally. The answer to this question is found in Born-kamm's agreement with the studies of J. Weiss and of H. J. Schoeps, who placed the gospel of Matthew close to the epistle of James (p. 50, note 2). It is found in his acceptance of Syria, in the broadest sense, as its place of origin (p. 50, note 3) and also in his assent to Kilpatrick's thesis that the Judaism attacked in the gospel of Matthew must not be identified simply with the Judaism in Jesus' time, but belonged to the period between AD 70 and 135, when the rabbinate accused the Jewish sects of heresy and excommunicated them. This continuing process of controversy with the Judaism led by the Phari-sees, in which the community is tenaciously defending the remaining connections, is clearly mirrored in the first gospel (p. 22, note 2).

In a recent article[6] on the missionary command, Bornkamm has on the one hand sought to give further justification for his earlier position as regards the derivation of the christological titles in Mat-thew, and on the other hand has modified it by partially accepting Michel's ideas. He, too, now calls the missionary command the key text and a kind of summary of the whole of the gospel of Matthew (p. 173). The earlier thesis, that Matthew's church was still linked to Judaism, faded into the background. Instead, the author is under-stood as a Hellenistic Jewish Christian whose work is directed against two different fronts: against Pharisaic Judaism after the destruction of Jerusalem, and against a Hellenistic Christianity in which the law has lost its validity and its significance for salvation under the in-fluence of faith in the *Kyrios*. There is evidence of a passionate struggle on the part of the author against the preaching and mission of the Hellenists who were free from the law (Matt. 5.17–20; 7.15–23; 24.11) (p. 180).

The gospel of Matthew is closely connected, both positively and negatively, with Pharisaic Judaism, and it has preserved important traditions from primitive Palestinian Christianity. Nevertheless, certain elements of primitive Hellenistic Christianity can also be recognized (p. 187). The two have not, however, been fused together eclectically, but woven into unity which is held in tension, so that the elements of one serve to criticize and correct the other. In other words, Matthew wages war on Pharisaic Judaism not only with the tradition of Jesus, but also with the christology of Hellenistic Christianity, and in so doing bursts the bounds of the Palestinian community. But by a

[6] G. Bornkamm, 'Der Auferstandene und der Irdische (Matt. 28.16–20)' in: *Zeit und Geschichte*, Bultmann Festschrift, Tübingen 1964, pp. 171–91.

close connection between law and christology he also seeks to correct a Hellenistic Christianity detached from the law and the prophets, its faith in the Kyrios, and its understanding of apostles, prophets, church and mission (p. 188).

Bornkamm sees the author as a Hellenistic Jewish Christian, who knows Hellenistic Christianity and presupposes it; his attitude towards it is by no means negative, as is clear from his acceptance of the gospel of Mark and his considerably more frequent use of the christological title *Kyrios* (p. 180). Matthew and Paul presuppose a common faith in the Kyrios and the Hellenistic Christian understanding of the Gentiles and the mission to a far greater degree than is usually supposed. Both are also engaged, in different ways, in a struggle against Hellenistic antinomianism and enthusiasm. They are, however, differentiated strongly in their understanding of the law and of 'righteousness' (p. 191).[7]

Of course when Matthew's gospel is understood in this way, several questions remain open. We can certainly understand why Bornkamm regards the 'church of Matthew' as a Jewish-Christian community which belongs to the law and has not yet broken away from Judaism, but is acutely opposed to a teaching and mission set free from the law (pp. 22 and 24). However, he can only describe the missionary charge with its implied universality as 'peculiarly open in the direction of the Gentile world' (p. 39); he is not really able to explain it. For he fails to notice what Michel (following Lohmeyer) has seen, namely that the whole of Matthew's gospel must be understood as having been written on the theological presupposition of Matt. 28.16–20 and must be understood 'by hindsight'. This point of view has been taken over from Michel and substantiated more fully by Trilling.[8] Thus in terms of method we must probably follow Trilling and Strecker in separating the last universalist Gentile-Christian redaction from the narrow Jewish-Christian ideas which are frequently present as well.[9]

[7] A. Vögtle, 'Das christologische und ekklesiologische Anliegen von Mt. 28.18–20' (*Studia Evangelica*, Vol. II, TU 87, Berlin 1964, pp. 266–94), can be seen as a catholic counterpart to Bornkamm's investigation of the missionary command. Vögtle above all draws out the connection in the tradition between Matt. 28.18–20 and Dan 7.13f. Vögtle shares with Trilling (see further below) the view that various earlier parts of the gospel do in fact lead up to the missionary command (p. 293).

[8] O. Michel, 'Der Abschluss des Matthäusevangeliums', *EvTh* 10, 1950/1, p. 21; W. Trilling, *op. cit.*, pp. 6–36.

[9] W. Trilling, *ibid.*, p. 192; G. Strecker, *op. cit.*, pp. 34f.

B. Gerhard Barth *Matthew's Understanding of the Law*

Gerhard Barth is a pupil of Bornkamm. In his dissertation 'Matthew's Understanding of the Law', he approaches the question of the theological peculiarities of Matthew's gospel at a particularly difficult point. In the separate chapters of his investigation he discusses the reason for Matthew's strong emphasis on the expectation of the judgment and exhortation to do the will of God, the interpretation of the Law, the essence of discipleship and the problem how far the Christian life is to be understood in terms of the Law, the connection between Law and christology, and finally the historical context of the antinomians attacked by Matthew.

Barth begins by stating that New Testament scholars have already recognized that the question of the Law plays a special part in the gospel of Matthew; hitherto, however, there has not been sufficient differentiation between the traditional material and the redactional interpretation. He considers it to be the object of his investigation to describe not only how Matthew interpreted individual sayings connected with the Law, but also his whole understanding of the Law.[10]

Next he deals with the 'marked emphasis on the expectation of the judgment' and the 'exhortation to do the will of God'. He proves by means of many individual examples the final thesis of this section, namely, that the strong emphasis must be due to the situation of the author, or else of his community (p. 62). He demonstrates statistically that the concepts which belong to the threat of judgment (e.g. κρίσις, ἡμέρα κρίσεως, μισθός) as well as those which emphasize obedience, doing the will of God (e.g. δικαιοσύνη, κελεύειν, τηρεῖν, ἀνομία) are definitely more numerous in comparison with Mark and Luke (pp. 58f.) Again, of the twelve doublets which occur in the gospel of Matthew, one half belongs to the threats of judgment and to the exhortations (p. 59).

Moreover, only in Matthew does a detailed description of the last judgment occur (7.21ff.; 13.36ff.; 25.31ff.). The meaning of the parable of the tares among the wheat, which Matthew has furnished, is typical of him. Whilst the salient point of the parable is the exhortation to be patient, the interpretation has dropped this idea

[10] G. Barth, 'Matthew's Understanding of the Law', in Bornkamm, Barth, Held, *Tradition and Interpretation in Matthew*, p. 58.

completely. Instead, it gives a description of the last judgment for the entirely hortatory purpose of emphasizing the fact that membership of the Church means no security at the judgment, which will destroy those who disobey the Law. The judge of all the world decides entry into the kingdom in accordance with the one standard which is valid and all inclusive, namely, whether God's will is done. Matthew repeats this thought at every opportunity (p. 59).

The threat of judgment is used throughout as an exhortation to urge the doing of God's will. This doing of God's will is particularly emphasized throughout the Sermon on the Mount, which is already given special importance by its position in the gospel of Matthew. Above all, the last part of the Sermon on the Mount, from 7.13 onwards, unequivocally drives home the fact that at the judgment questions will be asked about deeds alone. The commandments which are to be observed by the disciples are conditions of entry into the kingdom of God. The same trend is present in the whole apocalyptic discourse in chs. 24 and 25, including the parables. Matthew understands the exhortation to be vigilant as an exhortation to do God's will (24.42; 25.13) (p. 61). The great debate with the Pharisees in ch. 23 is also determined by the concern that God's will should be done. For the Pharisees are not reproached because of their teaching, but because of their practice: the contrast is between the external pious appearance and what they actually are (23.5, 28) (p. 61). Whereas in Jesus' proclamation, behaviour in view of the imminent dawn of God's kingdom is the criterion, in Matthew the imminent expectation is already receding and exhortation comes to the fore (p. 61).

Here we must put to Barth the question of method, namely by what criterion he differentiates between Jesus' preaching about the dawn of God's rule and Matthew's account. For after all we have access to Jesus' preaching only through the medium of the evangelist's description. Hence Barth ought to try to prove more fully and to produce evidence for what he regards as the proclamation of the historical Jesus in the gospel of Matthew.

In the section on the abiding validity of the Law, the author of this gospel is disputing, in Barth's opinion, with antinomian teachers of heresy in the community, who teach that the Law was only in force until John the Baptist, and that Jesus had abolished it. Barth has taken over this thesis from Bacon.[11] Barth adduces the following

11 B. W. Bacon, *Studies in St Matthew*, New York 1930, quoted by Barth from G. Strecker, *op. cit.*, p. 137, note 4.

separate proofs for this thesis (p. 63). It is characteristic of Matthew that he designates the godlessness which he is attacking by a compound of νόμος, namely ἀνομία, i.e. lawlessness (pp. 62f.). Compared with the weaker version 'law—prophets' in Luke 16.16, the sequence 'prophets—law' in the saying about the men of violence in 11.13 shows that Matthew does not share the attitude of the Hellenistic community towards the Law, but that he holds firmly to its abiding validity. It appears from the adoption of the conservative sayings regarding the Law, that these correspond to the views of the evangelist, at least to a certain extent (p. 64).

The sayings about the Law in the Sermon on the Mount (5.17ff.) were not simply accepted and handed on by Matthew, but were at the same time interpreted by being fitted into a plan of salvation history (v. 18c) and linked with his christology. According to this, Jesus had not come to annul the Law, but to establish it, and this takes place here through his teaching (p. 70). The controversies with the antinomians, who want to abolish a part of the law, is particularly evident in those passages in which the word πᾶς is used in contexts associated with the Law (p. 71. See Matt. 3.15; 5.18; 7.12; 23.3; 28.20).

In the Sermon on the Mount, Matthew is referring in 7.12 back to 5.17ff., thus regarding all the separate directions between these verses as the contents of the law and the prophets; by this means he intends to confirm their enduring validity (p. 73). Barth does not, like Schlatter, understand the false prophets mentioned in 7.15 (see also vv. 16-20, 22-23) as Zealots, but as antinomians within the community. By enclosing the instructions in the central part of the Sermon on the Mount between verses which were clearly aimed at the antinomians, Matthew understands the whole sermon to be concerned with the problem of the Law (pp. 74f.). Even in his apocalyptic discourse (24.10f.), Matthew is speaking of the same false prophets. By the alteration of the prototype in Mark, he has used the community's experience of false antinomian teachers to describe them as part of the troubles of the last days. This also emerges from the occurrence of the catchwords of the antinomian struggle. The false prophets in 24.11 are not the same as those in 24.24, but antinomian heretics who threaten the life of the community. By this means, antinomianism is once again condemned and its Satanic origin is exposed, for the confusions of the End are a last rearing of Satan's head. This problem is so important to the evangelist that he even shapes the apocalyptic discourse under this viewpoint (p. 75).

In the last section of his work, Barth endeavours to find a place in history for the antinomians attacked by Matthew. He describes them as those who dispute the validity of law and prophets for the Church, since Christ by his coming has brought the validity of these to an end (p. 159). But he rejects an identification of the antinomians both with a Pauline group as well as with the libertines attacked in the epistle of James (pp. 159–164). It is not possible to think that a group of Jewish-Christians had held the view that the Law was not valid for the Church; these must be Hellenistic Christians who, because they lacked works, appealed to their *charismata* (7.21f.).[12]

However, in the case of these antinomian opponents from a Hellenistic group it is no longer a matter of the same problems as in the disputes about the Law during the forties and fifties, when the questions of circumcision and the food regulations were vital. In Matthew there is no mention of circumcision, and in 15.11 it is clear that the laws about food or the law about the sabbath are not involved. It is true that Matthew attaches importance to keeping the sabbath, but he places the law of love above that of the sabbath. Matthew merely emphasizes *generally* the enduring validity of law and prophets for the Church, not in particular disputed cases. The opponents who can be recognized by their bad fruits (7.16–20) and who caused love to grow cold (24.12), may be considered to be libertines (p. 163). But since in Hellenistic Christianity all libertinism shows influences which cannot be ascertained in the opponents attacked by Matthew, Barth describes them as 'ungnostic' (p. 164).

It seems to us open to question whether the passages adduced by Barth are sufficiently convincing to support his thesis about antinomian opponents. On this question the following points must be noted: Matthew 5.17 does not allow us to draw conclusions about a particular group; it rejects only a theoretical possibility (like the redactional introduction in 10.34) and indicates no specific situation; it emphasizes, without being controversial, the rigour of the Law's demands. In Matt. 7.15–20 the context must be heeded: vv. 13f. contain a demand for decision, vv. 21–23

12 *Ibid.*, pp. 163f. Käsemann, too, supports the view that Matthew's gospel is making an attack on two fronts; not, however, against Hellenistic libertines, but against a prophetic, enthusiastic piety on the soil of Palestine, probably represented by the Hellenistic circle round Stephen. In fact Matthew's polemic hits Paul, too; but it is not certain whether the latter is specifically meant (E. Käsemann, 'Die Anfänge christlicher Theologie', pp. 163–6).

are a summons for right action, vv. 24–27 are the concluding parables. The warning against false prophets is only one admonition amongst others in the exhortation to the community, and does not go materially beyond the customary and also similarly indefinite utterances to the length of heresy (e.g. I Tim. 6.3ff.; Titus 1.16). Even Matt. 24.10ff. does not mean a definite heresy in Matthew's community, but a generally applicable warning against false prophets in the Last Days, and this is evident from the apocalyptic context. In fact Matthew's image of the antinomian opponents remains indefinite, a fact which tells against Barth's hypothesis.[13]

Furthermore, we cannot fail to recognize at least a certain abrupt change of logic in Barth's thought. Barth assumed on the one hand that Matthew was merely defending *in general* the enduring validity for the Church of law and prophets (p. 163), not, for example, specifically that of the law dealing with ceremonial with all its separate rules; but he asserted on the other hand that the frequent use of the word πᾶς shows that Matthew was engaged in controversy with people who wished to abolish part of the Law (p. 71). The two theses exclude each other, at least logically, for the little word πᾶς would include the whole ceremonial law with all its separate rules as well. Moreover, in my opinion, the πᾶς in Matt. 28.20 in particular is not conclusive evidence for Barth's thesis (τηρεῖν πάντα ὅσα ἐνετειλάμην ὑμῖν), for Barth fails to notice the fact that the words 'observe all that I have commanded you' are contained in the universalist missionary command; consequently they lose much of the power to carry conviction for the thesis that Matthew wishes to use them to emphasize once again the importance of the Law (understood as Jesus' commands) (pp. 134f.). Besides, the group of Hellenistic ungnostic libertines which he postulates not only remains indistinct and historically intangible, but in addition we know nothing else about such a group. We think it more probable that Matthew's gospel, at least the material worked up in it, is opposed to Paulinism.

We have pointed out the inadequacy of the evidence given by Barth for his thesis about the antinomian heretical teachers of the gospel of Matthew and can now proceed to the third section of his work, which deals with the significance of the commandment of love in Matthew's interpretation of the Law. Opposition to the antinomians is not his only battle-front; there also runs through the whole gospel an opposition to Pharisaism and the rabbinate (p. 76). This opposition is not only a matter of reproaching them with the failure to make theory and practice consistent, for in that case Matthew's Christianity would be a Pharisaism cleansed from failure

[13] So, too, Strecker, *op. cit.*, p. 137, note 4.

in practice. Matthew's view of the Law is also in contrast with that of the rabbinate (p. 76). This contrast must be seen in the light of Matthew's commandment of love (p. 76). This commandment is important as the principle of interpreting the whole of the law and the prophets (7.12), for the commandment of love in the Golden Rule interprets the directions in the Sermon on the Mount in accordance with the commandment of love and is the basis and secret goal of all commandments (p. 80).

The commandment about the sabbath, which is certainly kept in Matthew's community, was qualified by the commandment of love, and a definite rule allowed (12.12) even doing good on the sabbath (p. 79). Matthew does indeed retain the ceremonial law, but it has undergone a reassessment under Christian motives (p. 91). 'With the meaning of the commandment of love as the essence of the Law, the contrast to the rabbinate is given. Matthew regards himself as separated from this not only by practice but also by teaching. He is linked with the rabbinate in holding fast to the whole Law; he parts from it in his interpretation. And not merely in the interpretation of particular questions, but this contrast goes already to fundamental depths and leads to a quite different understanding of the Law' (p. 85).

As regards the range of the valid law for Matthew, it must be said that '. . . the attitude of Matthew to the Old Testament is determined from two sides, corresponding to his double front against the antinomians and the rabbinate. Against the antinomians he defends the abiding validity of the whole Old Testament law. Against the rabbinate, he emphasizes the right interpretation of the law, which can lead him to contradict not only parts of the rabbinic tradition, but also individual commandments of the Old Testament itself. But in his conflict with the rabbinate he also appeals repeatedly to the Old Testament' (pp. 94ff.).

In addition to the application of the commandment of love as a principle for the interpretation of the Law there also arises the question of discipleship, which also involves an interpretation of the Law. The reason for this is the fact that Matthew's understanding of the Christ-event modifies his understanding of Christ derived from Judaism and leads to the interpretation of the Law by the commandment of love *and* by discipleship (p. 104).

In the chapter on the essence of being a disciple, Barth examines the question of the extent to which Matthew understands the Christian life in terms of the Law. As in Mark and Q, the life of discipleship starts with Jesus' call. This call is marked in Matthew by the 'understanding' which is given especially to the disciples. Matthew has omitted all the passages in Mark about the disciples' failure to understand, or has interpreted them differently (p. 106). Matthew does not regard a man's understanding as an achievement, but as a gift and an act of God in him (see Matt. 13.11f., 16f.) (p. 110). It is true that understanding always includes an element of willing (13.15; 15.10; 16.9; 17.12), but this remains completely in the background because understanding is regarded as God's act on a man, as obduracy is God's judgment on a man (p. 110).

Matthew has completely removed the difference in the disciples' understanding before and after Jesus' resurrection as shown by Mark; in so doing he has written the situation of the Church into the life of the disciples during the earthly activity of Jesus (pp. 110f.). This equating of the time is an element of the framework, thus of the construction of the whole gospel (p. 111). The hearer or reader is thus obviously intended to be made a contemporary of Jesus' disciples, to be brought into Jesus' presence. The basis for this construction in Matthew is the presence of the exalted Christ in his community (18.20; 28.20) (p. 111).

There is yet another inference to be drawn from the gospel. On the one hand the evangelist stands particularly close to the rabbinate, but on the other the debate with Judaism has reached a climax of passionate polemic.[14] The church of Matthew does indeed try desperately to cling to fellowship with the Jewish people, yet the situation is very tense and the church is being persecuted (5.10–12; 10.23; 23.24). Therefore God's judgment is pronounced on the Jewish people and they are threatened with being deprived of the kingdom of God. Only Matthew has felt as deeply as Paul the problem that Israel has rejected its Messiah and its salvation. In Matthew the answer to it is the teaching of the culpable hardness of heart until the terrible self-condemnation in 27.25 (pp. 111f.). This theory of obduracy in Matthew reveals the situation of the community after the year 70, when the front against Judaism had become completely hardened (p. 112).

[14] Haenchen has investigated this problem in his study of Matthew 23. The collective verdict of condemnation without nuances and the judgment of history on Pharisaism and the rabbinate does not originate with the historical Jesus, but with the community which was fighting for its existence. For Jesus never attacked them as hypocrites, but as moralists who supposed that they were blameless in the sight of God (see E. Haenchen, *op. cit.*, pp. 59f.).

The constant exhortation by Matthew to do God's will, combined with the threat of the judgment according to works, has neverthless not led to his saying that the Christian can rest on his achievements. On the contrary, the disciples continue to be in God's sight the empty ones, the μικροί, whose life depends on the shepherd's searching love (pp. 121f.). The fact that Matthew as compared with Mark from time to time omits something which disparages the disciples, especially their lack of understanding, is not due to any inclination to excuse the disciples, but is part of the conception of the evangelist who throughout, unlike Mark, reinforces the reproach of lack of faith and obedience (pp. 113), in order to carry on the thought mentioned in the previous sentence.

The fifth section sets out to show the relationship between Law and christology in Matthew. He does not describe the attitude of the historical Jesus with regard to the Law, but already sees in the earthly Jesus the exalted Lord and therefore displays the relation of the Kyrios to the Law. It is possible to find some lines connecting Matthew's christology with his understanding of the Law (p. 125). He certainly shows that his interest in Jesus' lowliness is in the foreground, yet contrasted with this there is a wealth of assertions about his majesty (pp. 125, 129). In this context, the statements about the present rule of Jesus and the presence of the Exalted One in the community are particularly important for the understanding of the Law (p. 131).

Barth follows this up with a detailed study of the last verses of the gospel (28.16–20). He comes to the conclusion that the Easter assurance is not brought to the community by seeing the Risen One, nor is his presence conveyed by physical intercourse with the earthly Jesus. These are brought by the word of the proclamation, which in Matthew, by the same token, is the preaching of the commandments, that is, the Law. From this it follows that preaching the Law brings about the presence of the Exalted One in the community (p. 136). As evidence, Barth adduces the parallel that in Judaism also the presence of the divine Shekinah is bound to the Torah (p. 136).

Here we wish to contradict Barth emphatically. The unequivocal universalistic missionary command alone makes it quite impossible that Matthew should have placed on the lips of the Kyrios, who is sending the disciples as missionaries to all people, words which include teaching about keeping the whole Law. On the contrary, it is necessary here to bring out the fact that Matthew, as the last redactor of the material before him, is thinking not in terms of Jewish-Christian separatism, but of Gentile-Christian universalism.[15]

The saying of Jesus in Matt. 28.20a (teaching them to obey all that I have commanded you) which Barth has interpreted in this manner, does not refer to the 'new commandment' in the sense given to it in the Johannine gospel, nor to the νόμος Μωύσεως as the sum of the individual rules which it had been the achievement of Jesus to interpret afresh and conclusively, but to the whole way of life of God's people as being Christ's command. The interpretation of the πάντα in v. 20 must not be pressed too far. Nor is it followed by the admonition, which occurs in the apocalyptic writings, that nothing must be taken away or added to Jesus' words (cf. Rev. 22.18f.). The purpose of the saying is contained in the positive instructions and comprises Jesus' whole teaching,[16] including the instructions of an ethical nature, which can by no means be understood merely, as Barth supposes, to be restricted to the Jewish Law. The statement that the missionary message (Matt. 28.18–20) is to be preached in order to serve to support the commandments, God's justice (p. 142), is open to question, at least if it is intended to mean that the commandments or God's justice were understood by Matthew in terms of law according to Judaism. Hence an emphatic question-mark must be placed at the end of Barth's theses.

Lohmeyer may have interpreted this passage correctly when he stated that to observe all that Jesus had commanded the disciples denotes more precisely what is meant by being a disciple. The historical and material analogy to this occurs in the Old Testament. As in the Old Testament each member of the people together with the people in its entirety is bound to keep God's commandments, so now all peoples (all disciples) are to be committed to keeping Jesus' commandments.[17] If Barth thinks that Matthew is laying such stress on the support of God's justice in order to express his opposition to the libertine heretical teachers who wish to abolish the law (pp. 152f.), we must recall here once more the critical misgivings which we have urged above against Barth's opinion of this gospel's hostile attitude towards a group of libertines.

In conclusion, we may refer to what Barth writes about Jesus' relationship to Moses, about the Sermon on the Mount and the law of Sinai. Matthew cannot be understood to mean that he wishes to disparage the Mosaic law; he rather seeks, by expounding its real meaning, to lay bare its principles (thus in Matt. 19.1–9, concerning divorce). For Matthew, the law of Moses is the law of God for the

---

[15] Cf. W. Trilling, op. cit., p. 192.

[16] On this cf. W. Trilling, op. cit., pp. 23f.

[17] E. Lohmeyer, 'Mir ist gegeben alle Gewalt', in In memoriam Ernst Lohmeyer, Stuttgart 1951, p. 40.

Church as well. The fact that Jesus' interpretation of the law and his commands did not stand in tension with the Mosaic law is proved by passages in which Jesus' commands are corroborated by the Old Testament (12.1–7; 15.1–20; 19.1–9). The law in force in Matthew's church is identical with 'the law and the prophets'. The Moses typology can only be intended to confirm Jesus' teaching as the real teaching from Sinai (p. 158). Matthew is concerned less to set Jesus' teaching in opposition to the law of Sinai than, on the contrary, with the rabbinic interpretation of it. It is possible to speak of a *nova lex* only in so far as Matthew does not simply share the rabbinate's understanding of the law, but also opposes it. On the other hand, the expression *nova lex* is not justified, because its identity with the law of Sinai is so strongly emphasized (p. 159). The law and saving act of God do not fall apart with the death and resurrection of Jesus, but are closely bound together by Matthew's concern for establishing God's justice. Yet the emphasis on works and on judgment according to works, as well as the manner of attacking the Pharisees in ch. 23, encouraged the development of the early Church in the direction of the *nova lex* (p. 159).

Barth's investigation regarded as a whole can be considered to be a contribution to redaction criticism. For by this method of working he aims at gleaning from the gospel in question what the author had in view by the manner of his presentation. In so doing, Barth has repeatedly pointed out the construction and choice of vocabulary and the characteristic changes which occur in relation to Mark and Q. We are indeed obliged to express critical misgivings about Barth's hypothesis of the gospel's hostile attitude to the antinomian libertines; nevertheless, his description of the hostile attitude against the rabbinate may in essentials prove to be correct. However, this work cannot be claimed as a complete redaction-critical sketch of Matthew's gospel. This follows simply from the limited themes handled. It has to be accepted as a contribution to the theology of the gospel of Matthew based on the method of redaction criticism, especially since no attempt was made, apart from small marginal comments, to determine the third *Sitz im Leben* for the gospel in its present form.

C. Heinz Joachim Held   *Matthew as Interpreter of the Miracle Stories*

With his dissertation 'Matthew as Interpreter of the Miracle Stories', Heinz Joachim Held fills nearly half the collected work

Tradition and Interpretation in Matthew (pp. 165–299). Like Barth, he is a pupil of Bornkamm and associates himself similarly with his teacher's theses which are represented by the two studies printed with his own in the same volume. Held agrees with Paul Wernle's statement that Matthew's gospel is a re-telling of that of Mark,[18] and in this study his aim is to demonstrate that Matthew, when he re-tells the miracle stories taken from Mark's gospel, must be understood as an interpreter with a definite goal in mind (p. 165).

In the first section, Held reviews the individual miracle stories in Matthew, enquires into the evangelist's purpose in re-telling them, and by means of a comparison of the synoptists reaches the conclusion that the miracle stories in particular are affected by the abridgement of the narrative material and the simultaneous expansion of the discourse material (pp. 165f.). Held begins by advancing the hypothesis that the abbreviation of the miracle stories in Matthew compared with Mark is a method of interpretation (p. 166). Here he agrees with an investigation into the healing of the paralytic according to Matthew by Greeven,[19] who formed the opinion that the abbreviation of the expansive Marcan narrative by Matthew was in the interest of concentration on what is essential (p. 69), and that Matthew's curtailment serves to reach the essential point more quickly (p. 74).

Held seeks to confirm this thesis of Greeven's in detail by means of Matthew's miracle stories. In order to do so, he considers that the purpose of Matthew's interpretation must be made evident in each case separately. It is not expressed by the abbreviation alone, but also by the position of the miracle story in question in the framwork of the gospel and by the different wording of the text compared with Mark (p. 167). 'Hence it will be necessary, by a comparison of the versions of the two gospels with regard to abbreviation, setting and wording, to work out the Matthaean interpretation of the miracle stories. A look at the gospel of Luke may help us to recognize the peculiarity of the first evangelist' (p. 167). Held is right in pointing out that in spite of this not all the divergences of Matthew and Luke from Mark could be completely explained, but that allowance must be made for 'the carelessness of popular writing', as Schniewind already pointed out.[20]

[18] P. Wernle, *Die Synoptische Frage*, Freiburg 1899, p. 161.
[19] H. Greeven, 'Die Heilung des Gelähmten nach Matthäus', in *Wort und Dienst, Jahrbuch der Theologischen Schule Bethel NF* 4, 1955, pp. 65–78.
[20] J. Schniewind, 'Zur Synoptiker Exegese', *op. cit.*, p. 139.

Moreover, no doubt many abridgements in Matthew are due to the removal of the elaborations of language and the prolixities of style in Mark, but such explanations are not sufficient, for it has been observed that Matthew shows no interest in descriptive details in the miracle stories (p. 167).

At this point Held must be defended against a criticism which is made in Delling's review.[21] Delling writes that in explaining particular features of the narration, Held had not taken account of the possibility of the *Sitz im Leben Jesu*, the setting in the life of Jesus, and for precisely this reason several difficulties of interpretation arose. But the reply to this is, first, that redaction criticism has on principle only to enquire into the *Sitz im Leben* of the whole gospel, possibly also into the *Sitz* of the individual pericopes in the life of the community. The question of the *Sitz im Leben Jesu* is a matter of history, not of form criticism or redaction criticism.

We cannot contrast the setting of an action or of a saying of Jesus in the life of Jesus with the setting of an individual pericope in the life of a community and play them off against each other. This misconception had already begun in Fascher's thesis for his licentiate,[22] and Bultmann had alluded to it in his review of Fascher's work.[23] We must acknowledge, however, that this was provoked by Bultmann's own use of the term to support his historical scepticism. For this reason, the argument has been repeatedly urged up to the present day in very many works by scholars who recognize the method of form criticism to a certain extent and make use of it, and also by opponents of the form-critical method. Hitherto only Schürmann, and in a certain sense Jüngel too, have attempted to give the term '*Sitz im Leben Jesu*' a meaning which can be accepted from the point of view of the assumptions of the form-critical use of this term. Schürmann speaks, though only in connection with the sayings tradition, of a pre-Easter *Sitz im Leben Jesu*, by which he means a particular setting of sayings of Jesus in the life of the circle of disciples.[24]

Held next reviews the miracle stories in Matthew, which the evangelist has abbreviated in comparison with Mark. He demonstrates by them that the abbreviation of the individual stories is pursuing an essentially theological theme. In this interpretation the

[21] G. Delling, 'Besprechung der Arbeit Helds', *ThLZ* 85, col. 926.
[22] E. Fascher, *op. cit.*, p. 221.
[23] R. Bultmann, 'Besprechung der Untersuchung Faschers', *ThLZ* 50, 1925, col. 316. There Bultmann writes that '*Sitz im Leben*' does not mean the original situation, but the relationship of a historical pericope to a general historical situation out of which the type arose.
[24] H. Schürmann, 'Die vorösterlichen Anfänge der Logien-tradition', *op. cit.*, pp. 342–70, especially p. 351; in addition E. Jüngel, *Paulus und Jesus*, Tübingen 1962, pp. 292–300.

themes concerned are christology, faith and discipleship (p. 169). He substantiates his thesis by the following miracle stories: the healing of Peter's mother-in-law (8.14–15), the summary account of the healing of the sick (8.16–17), the expulsion of the demons of Gadara (8.28–34), the healing of the paralytic (9.2–8), the raising of Jairus' daughter, and the healing of the woman with the haemorrhage (9.18–26), the feeding of the five thousand (14.15–21), the feeding of the four thousand (15.32–38), and the healing of the epileptic boy (17.14–20).

Held has also pointed out that in Matthew not only the abridgement but also the expansion of the miracle stories serves the purpose of interpretation and is concerned with questions of faith and discipleship (p. 193). As examples he takes the following miracle stories: Jesus and the centurion of Capernaum (8.5–13), Jesus and the Canaanite woman (15.21–28), the stilling of the storm at sea (8.18–27), and Jesus' walking on the sea (14.22–33).

Although Held's observations on each of the miracle stories contain some very noteworthy details, we do not want to discuss them more fully; in our opinion his view is fundamentally correct, although in some passages some interpretations are pressed too far.

At the end of the first section, Held seeks the answer to the question why Matthew has not taken over from Mark the two stories about the healing of the deaf mute (Mark 7.31–37) and of the blind man of Bethsaida (Mark 8.22–26). It is very likely that he knew them (p. 209). Their omission could not be adequately explained by pointing out their profane character, nor can the reason be that in Matthew's gospel, where from the outset the disciples are represented as understanding the miracles, the symbolic character of these stories drops out, although it was evident in Mark's composition. In the gospel of Mark they illustrate the opening of the disciples' eyes and ears before Peter's confession which follows, and in which it is taken for granted that their want of understanding has been removed.[25] In the re-telling by Matthew of Mark's other miracle stories it is noticeable that Matthew omits the features suited to the style of miracle stories and the vivid details, but supports his theological revision of the miracle stories with significant points in the story before him. In these two miracle stories, however, no significant points

[25] *Ibid.*, pp. 197f. Similarly W. G. Kümmel, *Introduction to the New Testament*, pp. 209ff.

dealing with the theme of christology, faith or discipleship are available for theological interpretation (p. 209). Evidently they had contained no kerygmatic statement which was of interest to him and which might have been able to justify a re-telling (p. 210).

Held sums up in the following words: 'If one surveys . . . the evangelist Matthew's re-telling of the miracle stories, it is plain that the miracles are not important for their own sakes but by reason of the message they contain. The abbreviations, such as occur, above all, in the healing miracles proper, show that no importance is attached to the details and the pictorial nature of what happened. The expansions of the miracle stories confirm this negative result in so far as, on the one hand, they occur in scenes with conversations about doctrine and have no narrative function (8.5ff.; 15.21ff.). . . . The re-narrating of the miracles of Jesus is undertaken for the instruction of the Church.'[26]

In the second section, Held examines in detail the characteristics of the form of Matthew's miracle stories. He takes for granted the results of the form-critical characterizations of M. Dibelius and R. Bultmann (p. 212). However, he also pays attention to the warnings of Fascher[27] and of Koehler[28] that the different historical situations on which the synoptic stories of miracles rest, frustrate a conversion into pure forms according to their type. Hence the pattern can be perceived more clearly in one story, less so in another. In Matthew, too, the miracle stories are more clearly written up in some cases, less so in others, each time according to the style of the existing tradition (p. 213).

Held, after examining individual miracle stories, comes to the following conclusions, summarized in five points. (1) Matthew's manner of narration is formal, especially at the beginning and conclusion of the miracle stories (pp. 225–41). (2) He omits secondary people and secondary actions as a means of interpretation (p. 233). (3) He has made conversation the centre of the miracle stories and given it decisive significance compared with the narrative portions (pp. 233–7). (4) He frequently uses catchword connections in order to express actual relationships in a self-contained pericope (pp. 237–9). (5) The principle which shapes his miracle stories is

---

[26] *Ibid.*, pp. 210f. A contrary view is taken by W. Marxsen, *Einleitung*, p. 132.

[27] E. Fascher, *op. cit.*, p. 227.

[28] L. Koehler, *Das formgeschichtliche Problem des Neuen Testaments*, Tübingen 1927, pp. 27 and 34.

that faith and miracle belong together; in his miracle stories he brings out more strongly than Mark and Luke the actual circumstances of the faith which saves (pp. 239–41).

In Held's opinion, these five points allow the conclusion that in the first gospel we can speak neither of miracle stories (as Bultmann does) nor of 'tales' (like Dibelius); for the miracles of healing exhibit the form of a conversation and are constructed by means of the request for healing and by Jesus' word of healing so as to present the features of a conversation (p. 242). By stylizing the healing miracles as conversations, Matthew has approximated them to controversies and scholastic dialogues. In its form and subject-matter, a healing story in Matthew reaches its climax in Jesus' saying concerning faith. Regarded as a whole, it is no more than an illustration of this saying. Matthew's healing miracles correspond most closely to the type which Dibelius calls paradigms (p. 242). We cannot class the healings in Matthew with the group designated by Bultmann as miracle stories, but owing to the frequent use of a conversational form, they should rather be classified as apophthegms in Bultmann's sense (p. 243). We can learn from this section in Held's book that he retains in practice, with occasional modifications, the classification of the synoptic material according to types by Dibelius and Bultmann, but deduces the alteration of the miracle stories in Matthew from the conception of the evangelist on the lines of redaction criticism, and not on those of form criticism, i.e. from a *Sitz im Leben* for the individual pericope.

In the third section, Held seeks with the help of the results already obtained to understand Matthew's miracle stories as evidence for his christology. Following Schniewind and Schlatter, he sees the collection of Jesus' miracles in chs. 8 and 9 as having a christological function. The fact that Matthew placed a frame of almost identical verses round the complex of material contained between 4.23 and 9.35 demonstrates that he wishes to portray Jesus within this complex as the Messiah of the word by means of the Sermon on the Mount, and as the Messiah of deed by means of his miracles.[29] Matthew's two chapters of miracles are arranged in a well-ordered cycle (p. 247). He has collected the pericopes in the two chapters under the leading

[29] *Ibid.*, p. 246. Strecker also stresses the close connection between word and miracle. This appears in the fact that in 8.1–9.34 Matthew places ten miracle stories after the Sermon on the Mount. In the missionary discourse (9.35–11.1), words and references to Jesus' deeds stand side by side (11.2–6, 20–24). The same also applies to the summarizing sections, e.g. 4.23f.; 9.35; 10.7f. = θεραπεύειν beside κηρύσσειν and διδάσκειν (G. Strecker, *op. cit.*, p. 175).

thought that the Christ of the miracle stories is at the same time also the Lord of the community (p. 249).

Held identifies four christological themes in Matthew's miracle stories:

(1) Matthew exhibits Jesus' miracles as the fulfilment of Old Testament promises not only by reflective quotations, but also by emphasizing ideas which occur already in the stories, for example, by mentioning the command to the healed leper to show himself to the priest and to offer the gift for his healing (8.4) (pp. 253–9).

(2) He describes Jesus' miracles not as the performance of a wonder-worker, but as that of the servant of God in taking up the cause of the helpless, who thereby proves himself with might to be the one who shows mercy. The idea of the victorious activity of the servant of God is substantiated both by Isa. 53 and also by Matt. 28.18. Lastly, the evangelist sees in Jesus the risen and exalted Lord to whom all power in heaven and on earth is given. The earthly Jesus already acquires the features of the exalted Lord of the community because Matthew displays him in all his triumphant power (p. 259–64).

(3) Matthew portrays Jesus as the helper and Lord of his community. Many individual observations point to the fact that Jesus is intended by his behaviour to be already in truth the risen Lord of the Church; evidence for this also appears in the frequent use of the term of address, Κύριε, and of the verb προσκυνεῖν.[30] The influence of the circumstances of the Church on the miracle stories appears at several points, e.g. in the form, in the omissions and interpolations, in the shaping of the text, in the choice of words and also in the placing of the pericopes within the gospel (p. 267). Just as the discourses in the first gospel are in fact addressed to the Church, so the miracle stories are composed to fit the situation of the Church (p. 268).

(4) Lastly, Matthew exhibits Jesus as the one who gives his disciples a share in his authority. This appears both in the construction of the gospel and in the way the miracle stories themselves are fashioned (pp. 270f.) The idea of entrusting Jesus' authority to his disciples is indeed present in Mark and Luke as well, but it is not worked out so clearly and so impressively as in Matthew, for he has connected the two chapters of miracles closely with Jesus' teaching in the Sermon on the Mount, and he has placed the sending out of the disciples in ch. 10 between the comprehensive description of the

[30] *Ibid.*, p. 265; on this see G. Strecker, *op. cit.*, p. 124.

ministry of Christ in chs. 5–9 and the enquiry by the Baptist in 11.3. Thus the activity of the disciples has a direct christological reference (p. 271).

The fourth section deals with the interpretation of faith in Matthew's miracle stories. He begins by emphasizing once more that in the synoptic tradition as a whole there is a material connection between faith and miracles (pp. 276–84). Matthew understands faith to be both a praying faith (pp. 284–8) and a faith as participation in the miraculous powers of Jesus (pp. 288–91). It is striking in the gospel of Matthew that the disciples are never represented as being in possession of miracle-working power; their authority to perform miracles in faith is mentioned only in those passages in which their failure is told at the same time (17.20; 21.20). The promises of faith are only set before the eyes of those who are not disciples, and it is never the disciples who are examples of faith, only the suppliants. The disciples are repeatedly called men of little faith (8.26; 14.31; 16.8) (pp. 291–4).

Admittedly Matthew never understands the disciples as being completely without understanding, like Mark, but on the other hand they are not able to understand fully, for he has not eliminated the idea of the disciples' lack of understanding everywhere. He has interpreted it differently from Mark (pp. 294f.). The lack of understanding of the disciples in Matthew is in fact a state of affairs within the community of Jesus which rests on the confession of the Risen One. Matthew understands the lack of understanding of the disciples as little faith (pp. 291, 293). Little faith is a form of unbelief, though it does not carry with it falling from faith in Jesus or abandoning discipleship. Little faith means failure to follow Jesus. This conflicting situation is also rendered in Matthew by the concept of doubt (p. 295). 'Both notions are therefore fitted to denote the situation of the disciple who on the one hand directs his faith to the risen Lord, but on the other hand, in view of the facts of this world is again and again in temptation. From this the interest of the evangelist Matthew in these two concepts explains itself. They link the history of Jesus and his disciples in the time before Easter with the history of the Church and her experiences after Easter' (p. 296).

In the last section, Held sums up the results of his investigation against the background of tradition and redaction and understands Matthew as both a transmitter and a redactor. In taking over from Mark the idea of the disciples' lack of understanding he is a

transmitter. In giving it a fresh meaning he is an intepreter. He interprets the idea which he has received in order to bring home its urgent
importance to the disciples of his own day. These three factors in his
transmission belong essentially together in his gospel (p. 296). When
Matthew is handing on the miracle stories, he also both transmits and
interprets. Whilst in Mark's view they serve the dominant thought of
the secret manifestation of the Son of God, Matthew makes at least
some of them serve for instruction about the nature and the promise
of suppliant faith, an instruction just as necessary as the witness of the
wonderful power of its Lord for a church in danger of little faith and
of doubt.[31]

Matthew understands Jesus' miraculous acts as the fulfilment of the
prophets' predictions. The reason for this is that in the sphere of
Jewish thought these acts could only have been considered to be the
acts of the Christ and to have carried conviction as such, if they took
place in the fulfilment of scripture. In Mark, on the contrary, by
being given the style of epiphanies they would have had a missionary
effect in Hellenistic surroundings on their own account.[32] The leading
thought in Matthew's fresh interpretation of the narrative no doubt
already existed in the tradition and is merely worked out by him
more clearly (p. 298). 'If one desires, then, to understand Matthew
as the interpreter of the miracle stories, one must understand him at
the same time as their transmitter. If there is no tradition without
interpretation, the interpretation remains bound neverthless to the
tradition' (pp. 298f.). Matthew is supported in an interpretation of
the miracle stories by the conviction, in the words of his gospel, that
this Jesus has now all authority in heaven and on earth and is present
with his Church until the end of the world (28.18, 20) (p. 299).

We consider the results of Held's study to be basically correct; thus
we need only make a few comments as a general assessment. It may
be that in details minor interpretations have been pressed too far, but
these elements are so firmly embedded in the study that they can
hardly, if at all, be detached from the general conception. If they were,
they would not in any case cause the structure of the study to collapse; they would merely be an insignificant correction of the general
picture; they would not alter it completely. There is as little reason
for regarding this study as a full scale redaction-critical sketch as there

[31] *Ibid.*, p. 297. Similarly also W. Marxsen, *Einleitung*, pp. 134f.
[32] *Ibid.*, p. 297. On the question of the fulfilment of Old Testament prophecies,
cf. also G. Strecker, *op. cit.*, pp. 175f.

is in the case of the investigations of Bornkamm and Barth. This is due from the outset to the theme which has been chosen. Held concerned himself only with the miracle stories, and Bornkamm and Barth also concentrated their attention on a partial review of Matthew's gospel. Emphasis ought to have been placed on the fact that Jesus' acts of authority proved his mission in the sight of Israel (9. 33f.; 11.2–6; 12.28; 15.31). In Matthew they are quite firmly brought into Jesus' life and are intended to substantiate his claim.[33]

Held fails even more than his fellow authors to attempt to determine a *Sitz im Leben* for the whole gospel. Mention is merely made of the fact that Matthew has narrated Jesus' miracles as examples for the community of his day, but this community is not described in any detail. Even an attempt to specify its historical place in the account of primitive Christianity is not undertaken. In Barth this attempt was at least somewhat more noticeable. Instead, Held concentrated his attention more closely on the theology contained in the miracle stories, especially on the christology. To this extent this study is a contribution to the theology of Matthew's gospel. But it is also a contribution to the continuing work on the synoptists beyond the researches of literary and form criticism into a fresh country. By his work Held has shown not only the fact *that* Matthew interpreted the tradition at his disposal so as to serve the preaching of a message relevant to his times, but also *how* he did so.

The article by Greeven, 'Die Heilung des Gelähmten nach Matthäus', is also closely related to Held's study as regards method and theme.[34] It is of about the same length as Bornkamm's article on the stilling of the storm. Greeven agrees in principle with the point of view of redaction criticism and has had a stimulating influence on Held's investigation. As Greeven has set himself a limited aim for his article, he restricts himself essentially to establishing the differences between Matthew and Mark in the miracle stories. In the story of the healing of the paralytic he endeavours to deduce certain theological conclusions. Otherwise he only notes the frequent abbreviations in Matthew compared with Mark (pp. 67, 73f.). He concurs with Held in attributing this refinement in the gospel of Matthew to the aim of getting down more quickly to the essentials (p. 74). Greeven merely points out that this refinement enables us to perceive where Matthew considers the climax of the pericope is to be

---

[33] Cf. G. Strecker, *op. cit.*, p. 177, note 2.
[34] H. Greeven, *op. cit.*, pp. 65–78.

found, and for this purpose the conclusion supplies the best indication (p. 75). Held, on the other hand, tries to grasp this climax in detail and to recognize, as we have seen, what theological themes influenced the fashioning of Matthew's miracle stories.

Greeven seeks to explain the pericope of the healing of the paralytic both according to form criticism by the *Sitz im Leben* of the individual pericope, and according to redaction criticism with the evangelist's conception in mind. For form criticism, this pericope is a paradigm. Jesus' final saying about authority to forgive sins (9.6) is of general significance and serves as a link with the sermon. The paradigm is the illustration of the concluding saying which is the place 'where the pericope joins up with the kerygma' (p. 75). The pericope of the healing of the paralytic in Matthew illustrates how the intention is shifted by the point of view: in this pericope Mark and Luke placed greater value on Jesus' missionary activity, which as a piece of missionary preaching served to win new believers; Matthew, however, is more concerned to instruct community members who already believe (p. 76). In the Matthaean form of this pericope, the community which handed it down has given a sharper outline in several respects to the figure of Jesus, and has traced some of the contours afresh. In other words, it perceives in this pericope the One who gives confidence to his own and who knows men's most secret thoughts (p. 78).

D. Wolfgang Trilling   *The Understanding of the True Israel in Matthew*

Trilling's study *Das wahre Israel* can be called a general redaction-critical sketch of the gospel of Matthew and can be compared with works of a similar kind by Marxsen and Conzelmann on Mark and Luke. It comprises the largest part of his dissertation. A shorter essay on the theme of the Baptist tradition in Matthew was published in another place.[35] It is not evident where this chapter appeared in the dissertation, but its method and purpose indicate that they belong together. This already appears in the first sentences, which refer to the redaction-critical consideration of the gospels and accept it with approval. Trilling writes that in the gospel of Matthew a consistent editorial hand can be observed in the composition of the material

[35] W. Trilling, 'Die Täufertradition bei Matthäus', *BZ*, *NF* 3, 1959, pp. 271–89.

and in the general theological shaping. 'The greatest attention is being paid today to this theological redaction, to its leading ideas and the motives which inspire it, as it carries further the work of literary and form criticism' (p. 271). Trilling's important redaction-critical conclusions in the special article may be summarized here: Matthew interchanges the traditions of the Baptist and of Jesus by putting Jesus' words into the mouth of John and *vice versa*,[36] for John anticipates Jesus' message of the βασιλεία (p. 285). The church of Matthew is not aware of any competition with the community of the Baptist; for no tension can be felt in Matthew between the communities of Jesus and those of the Baptist, whereas the fourth gospel shows evident hostility to the cult of John (p. 286). But in Matthew, Jesus and the Baptist certainly form a common front against the Pharisees (p. 283).

We have already dealt with Trilling's attempt to determine a *Sitz im Leben* for the gospel of Matthew. Admittedly his book *Das wahre Israel* consists of separate studies and because of its selection remains in certain respects fragmentary. But the investigations of Marxsen and Conzelmann also consist of individual studies, and the formulation of the enquiry and the method employed provide an internal cohesion. This applies all the more to Trilling's investigation, since he starts by analysing the missionary command (28.18–20), in which, in his own words, 'the main themes ring out and are focussed like the rays of light through a lens'.[37]

He declares that although there are the three stages in the course of the evangelist's composition it is not his purpose to enquire into the historical situation in the life of Jesus, which is the first stage. He is concerned with the situation of the transmitting church and the redactional activity in the last version, which make up the second and third stages (p. 3). Thus he starts from 'the formulations of the traditional material within the setting of the post-Easter church' and enquires only about the 'span between the traditional matter which had already been shaped and its final incorporation into Matthew's "great gospel"' (p. 4). However, his main concern is to 'throw light upon the fundamental theological ideas of the whole book and to discuss their influence on the present version' (p. 4). At the same time, a distinction must be drawn between the theological views within the transmitted material and the theological views at the stage of the

[36] *Ibid.*, p. 282; G. Bornkamm, 'End-expectation and Church', p. 15.
[37] W. Trilling, *Das wahre Israel*, p. 4.

final redaction, especially in cases in which statements contradict or stand in tension with each other (p. 4).

In the investigation of the missionary command, Trilling takes up some suggestions by Michel. The starting point of the latter was that the whole of Matthew's gospel had been written on the theological presupposition of 28.16–20, and that 28.18–20 is the key for understanding the whole book. Therefore the conclusion teaches us that we must understand the whole book with hindsight.[38] Michel thinks that, when the missionary charge was fixed in its final form, an advance on the road into the Gentile world had already been made and the ἐκκλησία which handed down this saying of Jesus had already gained ground (p. 26). Trilling states that the word of authority was in fact only possible on the strength of the Easter event, but the post-Easter situation is hardly the primary ground for understanding this saying, nor is this saying identical with the statements of early community theology; it is evidence of a higher and more developed stage of christology evolved from the earlier messianic theology and related to the Son of Man saying in Daniel 7.13f. (p. 10).

The command to baptize in Matt. 28.19 is not to be regarded as an interpolation. For although baptism as an institution appears here without warning and some New Testament writings do not mention it at all, the practice is, of course, taken for granted (p. 20). In the central portion of the manifesto, Matt. 28.18–20, vv. 19–20a are concerned with the missionary command and the organization of the community. The character of this passage is not stamped so unequivocally as a missionary command as Luke 24.47f. and Mark 16.15f., nor is its character that of a community rule, as in the instruction about baptism in *Didache* 7. The whole passage is carefully thought out and filled with theological meaning and bears the character of a summary in the most concise form of 'the nature of the Christian' (p. 25). In addition, we must ask whether anything is to be deduced from the statement in the last verse of the gospel of Matthew about the problem of the delay of the parousia. Trilling sees no problem and agrees with Lohmeyer[39] in stating that it is not even faintly hinted how far or how near the day of consummation is. On the contrary, the consciousness of the contemporary experience of the

[38] O. Michel, *op. cit.*, p. 21. G. Schille takes a similar view; the missionary command at the end is the key to the whole gospel, 'Bemerkungen zur Formgeschichte des Evangeliums II', *NTS* 4, 1957/8, p. 113.

[39] E. Lohmeyer/W. Schmauch, *Das Evangelium des Matthäus*, Göttingen 1956, p. 422.

Kyrios is so powerful that it can include all the days to come. The saying indicates the strong faith of the Church, and not apocalyptic speculation.[40]

In order to corroborate his thesis, Trilling also adduces the parables of the wicked servant and the ten virgins (chs. 24 and 25). He comes to the conclusion that these stories had in mind the situation in Matthew's church and bore the character of an exhortation to vigilance. The problem of the delay of the parousia is not standing in the background; there is no sign of this in the rest of the gospel. On the contrary, difficult sayings about the imminent expectation (10.23; 16.28) are retained without significant alteration. In Matthew's church no exaggerated expectation of the parousia prevails, nor is the failure of the parousia to appear felt to present a special difficulty. But for that very reason the exhortation to be prepared, the warning against carefree and wanton living, combined with the menace of the last judgment, is presented with all the greater urgency. As the attention of the evangelist is directed in the first place to the present, however, no hint is given when the last days will take place and the end of the world appears to be neither particularly near nor particularly far off (p. 30).

In the missionary command we can recognize the following themes, which are in the closest connection with the construction and the thematic peculiarities of Matthew's gospel: Matthew's church teaches a completely unqualified universalism of the Christian faith which has no fundamental limits bound to time or to circumstances. In the final saying there is no trace of the difficulties between Jews and Gentiles (p. 34). The parousia as a theological problem is alien to Matthew. The character of the passage is to be understood as fulfilled eschatology, i.e. permeated by the consciousness that salvation has been accomplished. The roots of many views in the passage lie in the Old Testament, especially those of the ideas under-

---

[40] W. Trilling, *op. cit.*, p. 29. Strecker writes similarly: The future of salvation history does not happen as a development which can be deduced. It does not end at a point of time which can be calculated in advance. By emphasis on the suddenness of its arrival, the idea of being able to calculate the time is eliminated (rejection of apocalyptic speculation). But then Strecker makes a qualification: the community has already drawn conclusions from the failure of the parousia to occur and has come to terms with the extension of time. Yet the belief in an unexpected arrival of the parousia still exists, both as an imminent and also as a distant expectation. The stronger idea is that the community is continually aware of the possibility and is never released from the eschatological aspect (G. Strecker, *op. cit.*, p. 242); cf. also W. Schmauch, *op. cit.*, p. 83.

lying it. These are securely established in the structure of the whole gospel, especially in the fundamental declarations of faith. From this it follows that the whole gospel is conceived on the basis of two realities, namely, the reality that the people of God are the Church of Christ and that the reign of God is the reign of Christ. Matthew's gospel must be understood with these two presuppositions in mind (p. 35). In contrast to Trilling, however, Bornkamm sees the delay of the parousia as the background to the conception of the universal mission to the Gentiles. The christological conception of the enthronement of Jesus as *Kyrios* probably contributed to displacing the expectation of the parousia of the Son of Man from the forefront of the thoughts of the early Palestinian community. But faith in the *Kyrios* was not a substitute, with which the later community sought to compensate for its disappointment.[41] The positive force of this faith in the exalted *Kyrios* and his already present lordship which had already arisen early in primitive Hellenistic Christianity prevented the delay of the parousia from becoming a catastrophe for primitive Christianity. In Paul, faith in the *Kyrios* and the expectation of the end are in fact closely associated. The beginnings of this movement seem to have been in the Antioch community, which was a foundation of Hellenistic Christianity (p. 176).

With the results of his investigation into the missionary command in mind, Trilling sets himself the task of demonstrating the theological conception that the people of God of the Old Testament are now the Church of Christ. For this purpose he examines Matthew's gospel under three aspects. (1) In a main section dealing with salvation history he seeks to prove that Israel's crisis was the antithetical background and negative pole for determining the place of the Church in salvation history (pp. 33–7). (2) A doctrinal main section demonstrates that the revelation of the Old Testament was the soil in which was rooted the Church's own understanding of itself as the true Israel (pp. 78–137). (3) An ethical main section aims at proving that the vocation and task of the true Israel is the perfect fulfilment of God's will (pp. 138–88; see p. 36). Each main section is divided into an exegetical and a thematic part. For the questions raised in redaction criticism, only the thematic part is important, but its foundations are laid in the exegetical part.

In the first main section, 'Israel's Crisis', Trilling expounds the parable of the wicked tenants of the vineyard in Matt. 21.33–45 and

[41] Günther Bornkamm, 'Der Auferstandene und der Irdische', p. 176.

the account of the proceedings before Pilate in 27.15–26. Matthew shares with the other synoptists and with almost the whole New Testament the conviction that Israel bears the guilt of Jesus' crucifixion. In his gospel, the people as a whole is the tribunal which pronounces the verdict on Jesus (27.25) (p. 57). It has a role similar to that of the chorus in ancient tragedy; for in both cases it lacks purposeful activity, self-reliance in word and deed. In the gospel of Luke, on the other hand, there is an independent assessment of the people. For him they are the elect, holy Israel, the receptive field for the word of Jesus and of the missionaries. In Mark, again, the people are associated with the evangelist's idea of the messianic secret. They are neither a chorus nor walkers-on, but are emphatically and consciously kept aloof from the act of salvation. They hear the message, but do not understand it; they belong to those who stand outside, to whom everything appears in veiled language; they experience the miracle, but do not believe (p. 58). Matthew, however, assigns to the people in part an independent and supporting function in the saving event. The conception of the people standing outside, taken over from Mark (Mark 4.11), has been combined by Matthew independently with the doctrine of the guilt of the whole of Israel (p. 60). The distance from the whole people has become so great in Matthew that no common ground any longer exists between them; church and synagogue have parted (p. 61).

Trilling deals in detail with this theme of the separation of church and synagogue. He concludes from Matt. 8.11f. that Matthew did not envisage a final conversion of Israel, but that this saying is in essence a judgment and that Matthew regards the chosen people as a people which has been finally condemned (pp. 68ff.). Unlike Mark, Matthew considers the different parties and classes in Judaism as a single and united front.[42] Thus he turns the opponents into types and so constructs another front to which, alongside God and Jesus Christ, the disciples belong much more definitely than in Mark (p. 72). Whereas Mark describes Jesus as a solitary, misunderstood man and keeps him at a distance from the leaders of the nation, from the people, and even from the disciples, Matthew constructs two fronts. On the one he places the leaders of the nation, Herod and the people, all who belong to Israel, and on the other John the Baptist, Jesus and the disciples, all who belong to the 'true' Israel. Compared with this main front, all other fronts in the synoptic tradition lose their

[42] *Ibid.*, p. 71; also G. Strecker, *op. cit.*, p. 140.

importance, e.g. Jesus' relation to his family (Mark 3.20f.) and the attitude towards the rich emphasized by Luke (Luke 6.24f.; 16.14, 19ff.) (p. 73). In this respect Matthew comes nearest to the manner in which the Johannine gospel turns the fronts into types.

The fact that both the synagogue and the church claimed to be the Israel of promise and of election explains the acutely polemical situation in the gospel, which no longer knows any compromise, any willingness to co-operate, any friendly gesture (pp. 75f.). 'From this hostile attitude of the gospel, the alternative between the false and the true Israel follows conclusively. Since only *one* people can be the true Israel, every claim must be denied to the other' (p. 76).

Trilling assumes that the breach between Israel and Matthew's church has already taken place and is mirrored in the first gospel. According to Bornkamm and Barth, on the other hand, the church of Matthew is still living in association with the Jewish society.[43] Without wishing to substantiate Trilling's view in detail here, we are rather inclined to accept it. We think that we can conclude from the probable late date of the origin of the gospel of Matthew after the destruction of Jerusalem (cf. Matt. 22.7) and from the other references adduced by Trilling, that the final rift between Israel and Matthew's church has already been accomplished even though the latter bears a Jewish-Christian character. The passages 17.24–27, 23.1–3, adduced by Bornkamm as the chief arguments for his case, in my opinion provide too narrow grounds to support his view adequately. We consider that all other evidence produced by Bornkamm is best explained by making a distinction between Matthew's material, which undoubtedly contains arguments for Bornkamm's opinion, and the final redaction of the gospel,[44] which is open to a universal Gentile mission without requiring the adoption of the Jewish ceremonial law. This view assumes that this final redaction has not also eliminated the separatist passages and those with traces of legalism. We see here how completely faithful Matthew is to the tradition which he has incorporated.

The second main section, 'The True Israel', is the heart of the whole work. In its expository part it also turns to those passages which contain separatist statements and compares them with the missionary command. Trilling begins by examining the two logia of a strictly separatist nature: Jesus sends the disciples only to the lost sheep of the house of Israel (Matt. 10.5f.); Jesus himself is sent only to Israel (15.24). Trilling regards the saying to the Syro-Phoenician woman (15.24) to be secondary in literary terms compared with the

[43] G. Bornkamm, 'End-expectation and Church', *loc. cit.*, pp. 20, 39.
[44] Thus also G. Strecker, *op. cit.*, pp. 16–18.

saying to the disciples (10.5f.) (p. 82). Trilling compares the pericopes of the healing of the Syro-Phoenician woman's daughter and the healing of the servant of the centurion of Capernaum, which are not mutually exclusive, but have much in common (p. 83). From this comparison he concludes that Matthew held the following opinion: Jesus was certainly sent only to Israel, but he meets with rejection, whereas the Gentiles occupy Israel's place in the kingdom of God because it has repudiated Jesus. Conversely it was necessary for Jesus to be sent only to Israel in order that it might be without defence and that its guilt could be established unequivocally (p. 84).[45] In this matter Matthew takes seriously the Old Testament view, where the Messiah is only the Messiah of Israel; this is not a Jewish-Christian bias, but a theological necessity for Matthew. Therefore 15.24 corresponds to a theological opinion of the evangelist (p. 84).

Trilling next examines the rules for the community in ch. 18. This chapter deals with items of instruction arranged according to their subject-matter in the form of a discourse on brotherliness. It is a code for the community, if not as regards its form, yet as regards its contents, and it refers to the actual circumstances of the church. Trilling also suggests that Matt. 18 might be thought to be instruction for the church leaders, like the missionary discourse in 9.35–11.1, though he considers that the case that Matthew is *only* thinking in these terms is not sufficiently established. Even if Matthew had actual circumstances and a particular instance in mind, the general trend is towards the internal structure of the church, whereas the legal and disciplinary aspect are not in the foreground (p. 100).

In the part of the second main section dealing with particular themes, Trilling sets out to depict an image of Matthew's church and to outline its theological position. The universalism of the missionary command (28.18–20) does not occur without preparation and does not come as a surprise at the end of the book; it is rooted more deeply in the structure of the gospel (p. 101). For instance, in the interpretation of the parable of the tares amongst the wheat the designation of the whole world ($\kappa \acute{o} \sigma \mu o s$) as a field (Matt. 13.38) indicates an un-qualified universalism (p. 103). This also applies to the use of the concept of the $\kappa \acute{o} \sigma \mu o s$ in other passages (Matt. 5.14; 18.7; 26.13). In

[45] *Ibid.*; Strecker takes a similar view. He concludes from this that Matthew for the same reason also distinguishes between two periods in his ecclesiology. With the end of Jesus' life, the restriction to Israel has become out of date and it remains only for the message to be delivered to the whole world (*op. cit.*, p. 196).

the gospel of Matthew, the whole world is the field for the missionaries' labour (p. 103). We must understand the twofold use of ἔθνη in
the reflective quotation from Isa. 42.1–4 in Matt. 12.18–21 to be in
accordance with Matthew's universalism (p. 103). In addition,
Trilling adduces the passages with the phrase 'for a testimony to
them' (εἰς μαρτύριον αὐτοῖς: Matt. 8.4; 10.14, 18; 24.14); however, its
meaning has been vigorously disputed (pp. 104ff.). He comes to the
conclusion that Matthew uses this expression in a positive sense.
'Just a peculiarity of this kind running through the whole gospel can
show that Matthew's universalism is a deeply rooted conception'
(p. 104).

As regards the problem of the region of Jesus' activity according to
the gospel of Matthew, Trilling considers that his ministry of salvation and his fate were accomplished in the area of Israel, as in
Matthew's view Jesus was sent only to the lost sheep of Israel. The
geographical framework of Matthew's gospel was evidently made to
fit this view; for the only journey into Gentile territory and the
miracle occurring there are marked more clearly than in Mark as
exceptions. Besides, Matthew, unlike Luke and John, never mentions
Samaria, apart from the prohibition of the mission there (10.5), so
that the impression is given that Jesus never set foot in Samaria, that
it had actually been a forbidden country (p. 113) for him and the
twelve disciples.

But at least the healing of the two demoniacs of Gadara does not fit
into Trilling's conception (8.28–34). Although unequivocally Gentile
territory is in question there, it is not indicated anywhere that Matthew
considered this healing to be an exception. Trilling's explanation that
Matthew's interest was not attached to this place, and his remark that this
story was provided in the tradition are not good enough (p. 113).

Trilling seeks to delineate Matthew's image of the church
negatively and positively. Negatively, we may say that nowhere does
the mission amongst the Gentiles on the part of the disciples represent
a problem and require to be substantiated by itself; it is treated as a
self-evident fact. There is no mention of specific conditions or presuppositions for the mission to the Gentiles, because the primary
antithesis in Matthew is not between Jews and Gentiles, but between
Israel and the church of the nations (p. 214). His church does not
think of itself as being composed of Jews and Gentiles, but of all
nations. Matthew has developed this view clearly by means of the

breach with the Jews. Behind this there stands the theological view that it was necessary for the Jews to be guilty in order that salvation might come to the Gentiles (p. 215). For Matthew there could no longer be the antithesis between Israel according to the flesh and Israel according to the spirit, because Israel according to the flesh, as a people of the promise and the covenant, no longer existed at all (p. 114).

We can agree with Trilling's last sentence only insofar as he intends it to mean that Israel according to the flesh, i.e. the Judaism of his time, has been in Matthew's view, perhaps under the impression of the catastrophe of the year 70, completely rejected by God. This view is altogether possible, especially since he wrote his gospel with quite different historical presuppositions than those which Paul had when writing Romans 9–11, in which a hope of a final conversion of Israel is still expressed (Rom. 11.25–32). But it is more than doubtful whether we can go as far as Trilling, who follows Munck in writing: Matthew's gospel is the documentation of a new separatism which is directed only to the Gentiles and explicitly excludes Israel, because it refused to accept the message of salvation.[46]

Positively, Trilling seeks to base Matthew's image of the church on the Old Testament. We agree with him that the Old Testament does contain the idea of Israel's vocation to be the light of the world and the bearer of salvation to all peoples (Isa. 42.6; 49.6); but to call this idea the fundamental conviction of the Old Testament (p. 136) is to go beyond the demonstrable facts, even if we bring in passages like Ezek. 5.5; 38.12. In any case, only in Deutero-Isaiah is there in the Old Testament a pronounced idea of mission. Hence Trilling's thesis that Matthew's universalism grows out of the tradition of the Old Testament seems to us too subtle and can at most be explained by the fact of the world-wide diffusion of the church, measured by Matthew's standard (p. 117).

In the section about the theological place of the ἐκκλησία in Matthew, special attention is directed to the eschatological views of the first gospel. The variety of eschatological terminology proves that the eschaton had already become the subject of active consideration. Admittedly the didactic passages about the Last Things stand in tension with the didactic passages about the kingdom of heaven in

---

[46] *Ibid.*, p. 116. Strecker speaks of a dissolution of salvation history. But the missionary message is still addressed to the Jewish people, though only as to one people amongst the others, out of which individuals are called to the new people of God (*op. cit.*, pp. 117f.).

ch. 13; yet present and future do not fall apart. In Matthew, the eschatological exhortation to vigilance occupies the foreground (chs. 24 and 25). To be distinguished from this is the rousing summons provoked by the force of the approaching catastrophe and intended to produce conversion and penitence, whereas the eschatological exhortation is provoked by the pressure of the uncertainty of the date (p. 125). 'The eschatological call to awaken seems to Matthew to be changed largely into an exhortation to be vigilant. The entire passage 24.37–25.13 (with the echo in 25.19) is an exhortation to vigilance of unparalleled urgency, following the saying about the uncertainty of the day and hour (24.36), so that the whole subject-matter is made to apply to the situation of the community' (p. 125).

In the exhortation about the judgment, too, the centre of gravity has been shifted, so that the theme of the urgent proximity of the eschatological event is to a considerable extent replaced by that of the stern judgment. This is intended primarily for the situation of the post-Easter church. It is precisely the situation of the church described by Matthew in dark colours which demands a particularly pungent exhortation concerning judgment; as evil and sin increase, so to the same degree does the need for exhortation become accentuated (p. 126). At this point we should like to raise a main objection against Trilling, that he ought to have brought up the problem of the delay of the parousia under the theme of the eschatological exhortation. In another place he had explicitly denied that Matthew had possibly been aware of this particular difficulty (pp. 131–6).

A careful examination of the two ἐκκλησία passages in Matthew (16.18; 18.17) enables Trilling to reach the conclusion that Matthew's bias leads him to demonstrate that this *ecclesia Christi* is the true people of God and to identify the one with the other.[47] Matthew also emphasizes firmly the contemporaneity of the church (p. 136), but the tone of the gospel taken as a whole is attuned less to the idea of a constitutional ecclesiology expressed in the *ecclesia* passages than to the conception of the people of God and to the laws of its inner nature (p. 137).

Lastly we must give an account of the third main section of

---

[47] *Ibid.*, p. 136. According to Strecker, Trilling has not made a sufficient distinction between the evangelist's own understanding and his object. Matthew certainly understood the church to have occupied Israel's place, yet Matthew did not wish to prove this (contrary to Trilling), but to portray the life of Jesus in his significance for salvation history. At the centre of his book is the christological presupposition of the *ecclesia*, but not the *ecclesia* itself (*op. cit.*, p. 189, note 1).

Trilling's study. He makes a very detailed exegetical examination of the collection of sayings dealing with the question of the Law in the Sermon on the Mount (5.17–20), in order to penetrate into the meaning of what the evangelist intended to convey in these verses (p. 138). From the point of view of literary criticism this passage is an artificial composition of four logia which are held together by the conjunctions οὖν in vv. 18 and 20 and γάρ in v. 19. Regarded form-critically, the logia are four different types of sayings, each with a different centre of gravity (p. 158). In v. 17 it is the mission of Jesus to bring to fulfilment by his teaching God's will in the scriptures, in v. 18 the enduring validity of the scriptures containing the prophetic pronouncements which are fulfilled by the events of history, in v. 19 the instruction to observe faithfully all the commandments and in v. 20 the summons to the disciples to greater righteousness (p. 158).

The sayings also offer different pointers towards their individual *Sitz im Leben* in the church. Thus v. 17 refers to the theology of Matthew's church concerning the Messiah, v. 18 to its theology of the Law, v. 19 to the discussions amongst the Jewish Christians about the Torah and v. 20 to the ethics of Matthew's church in its controversy with Phariseeism and the rabbinate (p. 158). In the subject-matter, three different modes of understanding the Law appear: according to v. 17, the Torah is intended to be brought to fulfilment, according to v. 18 it has an inviolable, permanent character because all that is prophesied in it must come to pass, and according to v. 19 it is the summary of all the individual commandments on the careful observance of which a position in the kingdom of heaven depends (p. 159). The primary problem for Matthew seems to be the fresh assessment of the revelation in the Old Testament, and compared with this the question of the validity of the individual commandments becomes unimportant. The scriptures are regarded by Matthew as a whole, and no part of it, not even a particular aspect of it, can be detached (p. 159).

The part of the third main section dealing with the subject-matter treats of the practical demands and of the fulfilment of the Torah, which is their theological foundation. Matthew places the greatest weight on doing God's will and thereby emphasizes God's presence vigorously; for actual observance is now already the criterion for true membership of God's kingdom. In accordance with this a strong emphasis is always laid on practical obedience; his ethics are those of obedience (p. 162). For Matthew, the fundamentally compelling power which really shapes action is the will of God. From the point of view of its content the briefest expression of this will of God is the demand to be perfect. The form of this expression comprises the whole abundance, the full measure of active achievement; its content includes especially the demand for perfect love, which knows no bounds and takes God's love as its standard (p. 169). Compared with the other synoptists, in Matthew the law of love has been enriched by several elements and stands even more firmly at the centre of ethical instruction (p. 169). The exhortation to love pervades Matthew's gospel from beginning to end. He has in mind only the love of one's neighbour carried into effect by word and deed; it is as impossible for Matthew to think of love without works as to think of loving God without loving one's neighbour (22.38f.). This love does not consist in thoughts and sentiments, but urges action, especially in the sermon on the judgment of the nations in 25.31–46 (pp. 169f.).

Finally, Trilling discusses the antitheses of the Sermon on the Mount. He had already emphasized earlier that the gospel of Matthew modified the understanding of the Torah by referring back to the overriding principle of God's will and the intensification of the law of love. Over and above this, the Torah is brought to fulfilment in the antitheses of the Sermon on the Mount by heightening its demands (p. 180).

The common principle of all the antitheses is not to replace the Torah of the Old Testament by a fresh one, nor is it merely to interpret anew the Torah in order to bring to light a purer or deeper conception of its contents (p. 186), but it is to proclaim new ethical standards which continuously confront the precepts of the Old Testament Torah. What was in question in the case of the Old Testament Torah was not its validity in general, but in particular the standards of ethical behaviour as they were understood by the tradition, for which in fact fresh ones were substituted. In this sense Jesus could be called the new lawgiver and the Sermon on the Mount the new Torah, though the problem of the validity of the Messianic Torah must not be confused with this (p. 187).

Here we are brought to the end of the description of Trilling's work. We were able to concur in essentials with his exposition. We would like to express our agreement with Trilling's thesis that there are tensions in the gospel of Matthew, some of which are considerable and of theological importance, which raise the problem as to whether the gospel is Jewish Christian or Gentile Christian in character. We agree with him also that these tensions are best explained by the differences between the varied traditional material and the final redaction of the gospel.[48] We can hardly allow ourselves to think in terms of alternatives, Jewish Christian or Gentile Christian. For if we assume the gospel of Matthew to be a church's witness to itself and the result of a lengthy transmission, then at the stage of the last redaction we must also reckon with this church being made up differently, so that the distinctions between Gentile and Jewish Christians played merely a small part or no longer any part at all.[49] Trilling regards his distinction between the material and its final redaction as a version of the earlier conception, developed further by the questions posed by redaction criticism, that the canonical gospel of Matthew is a Gentile Christian revision of a Jewish Christian prototype, a conception which occurs in Baur, Hilgenfeld and Zahn amongst others and, in a modified form, as a Judaistic Jewish Christian source in Hirsch (p. 192).

Schreiber seeks to explain the different features of the gospel of Matthew by the statement that Matthew has combined Hellenistic and Jewish-Christian traditions into a unity in tension. He combined Mark and the sayings source in such a way that the legalistic ethic deriving from Judaism could have a combined effect with the idea of reward which stemmed from Hellenistic Christianity. Matthew's basic tendency is in fact derived from Hellenistic Jewish Christianity, which undertook the final redaction of the sayings source and through Matthew also used the gospel of Mark to follow his intentions. Matthew could thus have been either a Jewish or a Gentile Christian.[50]

If we compare Trilling's work with the studies of Bornkamm and his pupils which have been discussed, it must be said that Trilling's study, unlike the other three works, is to be seen as a redaction-critical sketch of the whole of Matthew's gospel. This description

---

[48] *Ibid.*, p. 192. According to Hasler, the redactional revision of the tradition available to Matthew was not a single operation by a school or a theological personality, but a process and at the same time a witness of a church which, by degrees and then finally, parted company with the synagogue (V. Hasler, *op. cit.*, pp. 23–35).

[49] Cf. W. Trilling, *op. cit.*, p. 200; similarly A. Jülicher/E. Fascher, *op. cit.*, pp. 287ff.

[50] J. Schreiber, *Theologie des Vertrauens*, p. 50, note 1.

arises particularly out of the last paragraph headed 'Conclusions and Prospects', in which Trilling summarizes the result of his investigation under four aspects.

Bornkamm and his pupils deal merely with the *aspects of certain sections* of the theology of Matthew's gospel and discuss only marginally the redaction-critical questions treated in greater detail by Trilling. Moreover, they do not give so central a place to the partial aspects of this theology which they discussed as Trilling did to the problem, raised by him, of the church's understanding of itself as the new people of God and true Israel. It is true that Trilling made an exhaustive examination only of particular passages in this gospel; yet it was just these which served to corroborate his conception— especially he was able to bring in additional references over and above the passages examined individually. His approach 'with hindsight', that is to say, with the missionary command in mind, proved particularly fruitful in opening up the problems of the gospel. This confirmed the fact that in 28.18–20 'the main themes ring out and are focussed like the rays of light through a lens' (p. 4).

In this connection, we wish to direct attention to Lohmeyer's study, an exegesis of the conclusion of Matthew's gospel.[51] He does not in fact consider, like Michel, that the whole gospel was written with the theological presupposition of 28.18–20; yet it is interesting to see what conclusions, some of them of a redaction-critical nature, Lohmeyer draws from the variant forms of the text of verse 19b with the command to baptize. We know that the familiar text contains the threefold formula 'baptizing them in the name of the Father, and of the Son and of the Holy Spirit'; in his pre-Nicaean writings, however, Eusebius renders this passage: 'Make disciples of all Gentiles in my name'. Out of this variation Lohmeyer constructs a whole historical and theological edifice and links it with the idea, already developed in his study *Galiläa und Jerusalem* and in his commentary on Mark, that primitive Christianity had a twofold origin in Galilee and Jerusalem.

This thesis recurs here again in an altered form. He thinks that two different movements in primitive Christianity are embodied in these variant texts just quoted. The one, using the Eusebian form of the text, did not regard the sacrament of baptism, originating from John, but the imitation of Jesus, discipleship, as the decisive criterion of the eschatological fellowship. The other movement with the current

[51] E. Lohmeyer, 'Mir ist gegeben alle Gewalt', *op. cit.*, pp. 22–49.

threefold form of the text regarded baptism as a necessary condition of salvation and had traced back to Jesus' example the form of baptism in the name of the Father, the Son and the Holy Spirit (p. 32). The practice of baptism in the name of Jesus alone, combined with the bestowal of the Spirit, as attested in the Acts, does not run counter to this, because the essential and historical conditions in the command to baptize in the gospel of Matthew are different from those in Acts. For the picture of baptism in the Acts is derived from the Jerusalem tradition, but the formula in Matthew's gospel from primitive Galilean Christianity (p. 32).

Now Lohmeyer's thesis stands or falls with the strength of the evidence of the form of the Eusebian text. F. C. Conybeare, in ZNW 2, 1901, pp. 275ff., proved that Eusebius quotes the missionary charge without the threefold formula only in his pre-Nicaean writings.[52] The use of the threefold formula in the post-Nicaean writings of Eusebius could also be derived from the influence of the dogmatic decisions of the Council of Nicaea. Nevertheless, the evidence for Lohmeyer's view is still not substantiated by the fact that Eusebius quoted merely the abbreviated form (p. 29). Trilling mentions an investigation by B. H. Cuneo, who discusses Conybeare's work and demonstrates that the shortened form in Eusebius by no means proves that he did not know the threefold formula, because in all the passages in which he employs the short form the detailed form is not required by the context.[53]

If this is correct, then it puts an end to Lohmeyer's idea of tracing back the text variants to two different movements in primitive Christianity. Similarly his theory that Matthew's missionary command entrusts the mission to the Gentiles until the end of the world only to the primitive Christianity of Galilee is also untenable (p. 44). However, he is right in stating that this missionary charge is not on the same lines as those actually pursued by Paul in his missionary work (p. 43), and that it does not belong to the latest material peculiar to Matthew. Some scholars urge a later date for the missionary command because they think that this is the only explanation for the attitude of the Jerusalem community towards Paul's mission to the Gentiles; but they have overlooked the fact that the point at issue was not the right to convert the Gentiles, which was established from the beginning, but the lines on which to pursue the work (p. 43).

[52] *Ibid.*, p. 29; see further W. Trilling, *op. cit.*, p. 20, note 96.
[53] B. H. Cuneo, *The Lord's command to baptize. An historical investigation with special reference to the works of Eusebius of Caesarea* (Diss. Washington 1923), quoted by Trilling, *op. cit.*, p. 21, note 96.

Even if Matthew's missionary command does not agree completely with Paul's method (according to Acts, Paul baptized only in the name of Jesus and did not approach the Gentiles until after his attempts to convert the Jews had proved fruitless), it is an extremely doubtful proceeding for Lohmeyer to attribute the missionary command in Matthew to the primitive Galilean Christianity which worked in Decapolis and Syria (p. 43). This attribution stands or falls with the very existence of a special Galilean Christianity in general which is in itself open to question.

E. Martin Johannes Fiedler   *Matthew's Understanding of Righteousness*

Amongst the studies which are at least closely connected with the redaction-critical approach to Matthew's gospel, we can reckon the unpublished dissertation (Halle 1957) of M. J. Fiedler, *Der Begriff DIKAIOSYNH im Matthäus-Evangelium, auf seine Grundlagen untersucht* (*An investigation of the basis of the concept DIKAIOSYNH in Matthew's gospel*). It can certainly be called only a small section from the theology of the gospel of Matthew since it is confined to an examination of the seven passages in Matthew in which the concept δικαιοσύνη occurs (3.15; 5.6, 10, 20; 6.1, 33; 21.32). This is preceded by a full history of the concept in which its significance is examined in Greek literature, in the Septuagint and in Hellenistic Judaism. Fiedler's approach must be judged redaction-critical insofar as he declares it to be his intention to interpret the relevant statements in Matthew as they appear in his gospel without subjecting them to source-critical analysis (p. 104). He justifies this course of action explicitly by reference to Conzelmann's examination of Luke's writings (p. 104, note 45).

Fiedler sees in this concept in Matthew an important element in the debate with Pharisaic Judaism which is carried on vigorously by the first gospel; especially in the Sermon on the Mount it is a battle-cry in the controversy with Israel (p. 164). He emphasizes in particular the controversial factor in the concept δικαιοσύνη in Matthew. The concept belongs to the debate with a Judaism which rejects the Messiah, and not to the Jewish-Christian sphere of Matthew (*pace* Feine/Behm, *Einleitung in das Neue Testament*, 9th edition, p. 52). Its context is the pronouncements in which Matthew attacks Judaism. The δικαιοσύνη of the community is contrasted with that of Israel, which has rejected the Messiah (p. 165). Knowledge of the content of this concept became a criterion by which to distinguish between the Christian community and disobedient Israel (p. 167).

An article by A. Descamps on the antitheses in the Sermon on the Mount and the introduction to them ought also to be mentioned here.[54] He proceeds explicitly in accordance with the point of view of redaction criticism and distinguishes between three stages in the tradition: Jesus' sayings, the stage of the transmission of the tradition, and the stage of the redaction of the traditional material (pp. 171–3). He is concerned to establish the fact that the question as regards method cannot be: 'Form-critical *or* redaction-critical', but must be: 'Both together'. In order to bring out the three different stages of the tradition he works in precisely the reverse direction to that mentioned above, namely from the existing tradition back to Jesus' original words. In this process he distinguishes a threefold *Sitz im Leben*: that of the redactor, that in the community and that in the life of Jesus himself (p. 159).

He begins by attempting to pick out from the whole complex the interpolated editorial comments (pp. 160–6), then to identify the circumstances of the tradition in the community (pp. 167–9), and finally to arrive at the sayings of Jesus as the source of the tradition (pp. 169f.). Behind this article there lies the apologetic purpose of identifying a definite stock of 'authentic' sayings of the historical Jesus by means of posing questions according to the 'most modern' method of the time. But it is not the real aim of redaction-critical research to pursue the investigation from the existing tradition back to the sayings of the historical Jesus, but only to establish through comparing the synoptists with each other by what changes the traditions handed down in Matthew and Luke differed from those in Mark. The intention is to draw from this comparison conclusions about the theological conceptions of the evangelists and the *Sitz im Leben* of the gospel concerned. However, the material peculiar to the evangelist is particularly unsuitable for such an investigation; and the collection of passages examined by Descamps (5.17–48) consists mainly of such material. We must not, however, fail to recognize that his attempt to determine a threefold *Sitz im Leben* borders closely on the task of redaction-critical research as formulated by Grundmann.[55]

[54] A. Descamps, 'Essai d'interpretation de Mt 5.17–48', *Studia Evangelica*, Berlin 1959, pp. 156–73.
[55] W. Grundmann, *Das Evangelium nach Markus*, p. 23.

F. Georg Strecker   *Christology and Ecclesiology in Matthew*

The inaugural dissertation of Georg Strecker, *Der Weg der Gerechtigkeit, Untersuchungen zur Theologie des Matthäus*, represents a more advanced stage in redaction-critical research, insofar as it enters into a dialogue with all the redaction-critical investigations into the synoptic gospels which have appeared up till now, rather than limiting itself to the gospel of Matthew.

In terms of method, Strecker takes for granted form criticism and the two-source theory (pp. 9–14). Even though he does not appear to admit that redaction criticism in theory ranks as an independent method of research, *in fact* his place is in the ranks of redaction-critical scholars. For he seeks to investigate Matthew's theological ideas, and for this purpose to isolate the stage of redaction and to put the author into his sociological place (p. 10). Thus Strecker deviates from redaction criticism only in theory; in practice he follows its principles. His conclusions bear this out. In contrast with Marxsen and Conzelmann, who make a sharp distinction between redaction, i.e. the editorial activity of the evangelists, and the tradition, Strecker emphasizes the *basic unity of tradition and redaction*. Thus he does not define the situation as being that of an individual, but lays stress on his unity with the community which he represents (pp. 14 and 34).

Strecker's investigation can also be considered as a general redaction-critical sketch. It differs from Trilling in some individual conclusions, but not in its conception as a whole; for both make a distinction in terms of method between material handed down to them and the editing of this material by the evangelist. The chief difference between the two studies is that they approach Matthew's gospel with different questions. The reason for this is that the first versions of both studies were produced at the same time, thus independently of each other. It was only when Strecker prepared his study for publication that he was able to discuss Trilling's work which had been published in the meantime.

Trilling discusses chiefly the salvation-historical encounter between church and synagogue, together with the problem of the fulfilment of the Law. Strecker, on the other hand, lays the main emphasis on the christology and ecclesiology of Matthew's gospel, and discusses the questions of eschatology, of God's saving acts in history and of ethics in this connection. In doing so he already finds in Matthew's gospel the division of salvation history into periods resulting from the delay of the parousia (shown by Conzelmann to exist in Luke's historical work). In Matthew the eschatological element is not eliminated as a result: the problem is solved dialectically, for according to Matthew's ideas both the imminent and the distant expectation have their place (p. 242). This thesis represents what is new in Strecker's work. The historical element is not subordinated to the eschatological element; they are not alternatives, but they complement each other mutually (p. 185), and together contribute to shaping the work by the influence they exert on each other. Both themes express the same understanding of history, namely, that the life of Jesus should be brought into the categories of salvation history, in which the division into linear periods is combined to form a unity with the eschatological significance of time for salvation (p. 185).

In the introductory section, Strecker also raises the question about the contemporary background of the work, hence about the problems of the author and the so-called third *Sitz im Leben*. The place of the author (redactor) is not to be found in a genuinely Jewish sphere; the use of the Septuagint suggests that he lived in a Hellenistic environment and was a Hellenistic Jewish-Christian (p. 29). The use of the Septuagint provides evidence for the fact that his theological standpoint was amongst the Gentiles (p. 34). He often assimilated his quotations to the Septuagint insofar as he took them over from Mark or Q. It cannot be concluded from the scriptural quotations that the evangelist knew Hebrew.[56] Matthew's reflective quotations, which are introduced by a standard formula, are peculiar to Matthew (1.23; 2.6, 15, 18, 23; 4.15f.; 8.17; 12.18–21; 13.(14f.,)35; 21.5; 27.9f.); they exhibit a form differing from the Septuagint and related to the Massoretic text. But they are not derived from the evangelist's own translation; they are already pre-Matthaean and were taken over by him from a collection of Old Testament citations. Only the introductory formula is the work of the evangelist.[57]

Strecker explains the separatist Jewish Christian and universalist

[56] *Ibid.*, pp. 28f. Jeremias concludes from the quotation of the sh^ema that Matthew's mother-tongue was Aramaic, but that his prayer-language was Hebrew (Jeremias, 'Die Muttersprache des Evangelisten Matthäus', *ZNW* 50, 1959, pp. 270–4).

[57] G. Strecker, *op. cit.*, pp. 50 and 82ff. Kümmel calls in question Strecker's statement that the reflective quotations in Matthew came out of a separate written source (W. G. Kümmel, *Introduction to the New Testament*, p. 79). For a criticism of the thesis of a book of Testimonia, see too: M. Rese, *Alttestamentliche Motive in der Christologie des Lukas*, Bonn 1965, pp. 326–36.

Gentile Christian features, which cannot be made consistent with each other and contradict each other, in the same way as Trilling. Trilling traced the Jewish Christian features back to a stage with Jewish Christian characteristics during the transmission of the traditional material, but the Gentile Christian features to the final redaction.[58] Strecker thinks that the Jewish Christians represented an earlier stage in the life of the community, but that the evangelist should be assigned to Gentile Christianity, after a fresh Gentile Christian generation had replaced Jewish Christianity (p. 35).

According to Strecker's main thesis, since the synoptic gospels concur in coordinating the historical with the eschatological, it follows that their outline (vita Jesu) is no accident, but expresses the fundamental unity of these gospels. But in the execution and combination of the historical and eschatological themes, room was still left for the individuality of each evangelist (p. 49). The problems of the eschatological elements in Matthew are not a simple matter of 'either-or', but of 'not only—but also' (p. 49). Strecker places Matthew in the same line as the historically-minded Luke, and in this he follows Bultmann, who has argued that Matthew and Luke did not develop further the type of gospel developed by Mark, but reinforced its historical nature by including whatever historical tradition was still accessible to them.[59]

In his main section dealing with the christology of Matthew's gospel, Strecker examines first the historical themes, and second the eschatological ones. Matthew's thinking is determined by a historical bias, so he expounds the christology, too, in historical terms. This appears in his view of time and in his geographical ideas (p. 86). Thus the concept of καιρός in Matthew has no eschatological significance, for the End, the eschatological καιρός, is still awaited, because the time is not yet fulfilled. In Mark, on the other hand, the concept stands in tension between the 'already now' and the 'not yet' (pp. 88f.). Matthew, like Luke, links Jesus' life to history by mentioning his birth in the days of Herod (p. 90). Matthew describes the time of Jesus as a section out of the past which happened once for all and could not be repeated. Only at that time had the Jewish people had the possibility of making a decision for its destiny in salvation history;

[58] W. Trilling, op. cit., p. 192; cf. also p. 200.
[59] R. Bultmann, History of the Synoptic Tradition, p. 371. But in another place Bultmann has contrasted Matthew and Mark with Luke's historical-theological presentation: Theology of the New Testament II, p. 119.

but it let slip its opportunity by rejecting Jesus' call to repentance. The moment of collapse in the history of salvation occurred at the end of Jesus' life. The destruction of Jerusalem (Matt. 22.7) expresses the fact that the condemnation had been accomplished (p. 117). Regarded as a whole, Matthew's tendency to turn his gospel into history writing is not incidental, nor is it manifested merely by a few details; it determines fundamentally the redactional view of the gospel. Matthew represents Jesus' life from his birth to his resurrection as a particular epoch. Before it lay the 'preparatory' period (the genealogy in 1.1–16). From his present, the evangelist looks back to the particular past of Jesus' lifetime. The epoch of Jesus certainly has a special place in the passage of time, but it is clearly marked off from the end of history still to be expected (p. 122).

In his section about the eschatological theme in Matthew's christology, Strecker tries to show how the eschatological aspect of the christological conception acquired its shape. Even though Matthew presents Jesus' life in historical terms, his christology cannot be grasped exclusively from this point of view. For the historical Jesus already anticipates the *eschaton* by his acts of authority (8.29) and makes the claim to be the eschatological Κύριος (22.41–46). In this way, Jesus' epoch is taken out of the sphere of merely historical categories and has a supra-temporal relevance (p. 123). The concept Κύριος, which occurs forty-four times in Matthew (six times in Mark), is found particularly in the eschatological parables, and thus it has an eschatological stamp (p. 123). In Matthew, the disciples address Jesus *only* as Κύριε, even in those places where another term appears in Mark; his opponents, however, call him διδάσκαλος or ῥαββί. This indicates that Matthew has deliberately projected into the life of Jesus the community's confession of the exalted Lord. He understands Κύριος as a designation of sovereignty for the future Lord. This term shaped the image of the historical Jesus. It invests the man on earth with the colours of the eschatological Lord and represents the Κύριος to come as the one who has come (p. 124).

Strecker concludes from his examination of the christology of Matthew's gospel that the evangelist did not take Mark's scheme as the pattern for his book by chance. He drew a continuous line from the birth to the death and to the resurrection in order to present a life of Jesus. He contrasted this section of history with the time preceding it and with that following it. In that the Old Testament (reflective quotations) points forward to it and after the resurrection a

new epoch, the time of the Church and its mission, begins, the life of
Jesus has in Matthew the historical character of a period of time
complete in itself (pp. 184f.). The elements of history in Matthew's
redaction confirm the thesis that the synoptic composition of the
gospels is to be understood as a description of Jesus' life, and that this
is to be explained by the disappearance of the imminent expectation
(p. 185). The time of Jesus was for Matthew the time of the revelation
of the way of righteousness; the time of the prophets was marked
primarily by their indication of the central point of salvation history;
this is now continued in the Church after Israel's rejection of its
privileged position.[60]

    Thus Strecker has already demonstrated for Matthew's gospel
what Conzelmann has established as the characteristic trait of Luke's
twofold book, namely the pattern of three epochs, the time of Israel,
the time of Jesus and the time of the Church. Strecker names as the
motive for Matthew's gospel the *fact* of the delay of the parousia; on
the other hand, Conzelmann speaks of the *problem*, produced by this
fact, which led to a crisis and necessitated the composition of Luke's
history in order to surmount this crisis. Strecker has contrasted
Matthew and Luke with Mark's gospel; but he has found traces of a
historical point of view in Mark, too, and he has thus rejected the
excessive emphasis on the eschatological factor in Mark by Marxsen.[61]
Strecker considers that in all the three synoptists the history of salvation has been divided into periods and that the difference between
them consists in Mark placing the Messianic secret and Luke the mere
fact of the continuity of salvation history in the foreground, whereas
Matthew has interpreted the eschatological factor in salvation history
in an ethical sense (in the discourses): i.e. the eschatological demand is
proclaimed at the centre of salvation history and is put into practice
as an example by Jesus and the Baptist (p. 186).

    The short part of Strecker's study examines the ecclesiological
views in Matthew's gospel. It is concerned primarily with christology
instead of ecclesiology (p. 189). Even when an ecclesiological problem
is raised, an allusion is made to the different periods in salvation
history (9.14f.). Matthew 21.43 points forward to the Gentile church
and distinguishes it clearly from the time of Jesus. In his ecclesiology,

    [60] *Ibid.*, p. 188. On Matthew's conception of history cf. E. Dinkler, 'Geschichte
und Geschichtsauffassung', *RGG* II, 1958³, col. 1479.
    [61] G. Strecker, *op. cit.*, p. 48, note 2; also p. 186, notes 1 and 2: 'motive of
fulfilment in Mark 1.15; 14.49'. Mark, too, is aware of a further epoch in salvation
history after the resurrection, cf. Mark 4.21–23; 9.9.

too, we must reckon with the evangelist's historically-minded bias. This appears in the description of the circle of the disciples which is contrasted with the Κύριος, as a compact group, and portrays by anticipation the later community (pp. 190f.).

Matthew distinguishes two epochs in ecclesiology as well; he associates the situation of the Twelve with the life of Jesus (p. 196), who are described as witnessing by what they see and hear (13.16f.) (p. 198). He has reserved the term μαθητής exclusively for the Twelve (p. 192). He has drawn a consistent parallel in the missionary discourse between Jesus and the disciples, for *their* acts of authority represent the *eschaton* in these passages (cf. 10.1b with 8.29), although their preaching is connected with healing (10.5–8) (p. 185).

The person of Peter displays a juxtaposition of positive and negative features both in the tradition and in the redaction. Matthew has brought out Peter's negative traits more strongly than Mark (p. 204). His person forces its way out of the tight framework of the historical uniqueness of the situation of Jesus' life, and is significant primarily not as history, but as typology. For example, it happens that Matthew speaks of Peter where Mark mentions the disciples (cf. Matt. 15.15 with Mark 7.17, see also Matt. 16.23); the disciples can also take Peter's place (cf. Matt. 21.20 with Mark 11.21; Matt. 24.3 with Mark 13.3; Matt. 28.7 with Mark 16.7). This suggests an anticipatory description by the subsequent community. In the juxtaposition of positive and negative traits in the person of Peter we see what the Christian in the community is like, for Peter is his prototype (p. 205). 'The person of Peter becomes transparent in view of the contradictory existence of the Christian. By nature it belongs as a whole to the larger circle of problems of Matthew's understanding of the community and of mankind' (p. 206).

Strecker shows through many passages that the themes in the gospel of Matthew often burst the framework of the life of Jesus and enable the situation of the community to be recognized, e.g. in the ἐκκλησία passages in Matthew 16.18 and 18.17 (p. 207). Matthew describes the community both as an eschatological entity and as a *corpus mixtum*. The correspondence of the community with the former people of God (21.43) and the frequent concrete directions on questions of church order show that Matthew's ecclesiological pronouncements refer not to an invisible, but to a visible sociological entity (p. 214). The parables of the tares amongst the wheat (13.24–30) and of the fish net (13.47–49) cannot fail to be understood as pointing to the future. But by means of the idea of the sowing of the seed by the Son of Man (in the interpretation, v. 37) a previous epoch of time is inserted (p. 215).

The community as a *corpus mixtum* in the world is a presupposition for the exhortation which extends throughout the discourses of Matthew's gospel and determines them continuously; thus actual abuses are concerned, with which the fellowship of the church has to reckon. The community also takes for granted the existence of wicked men and stands permanently under the eschatological demand on its way through time, until the judgment brings the final separation (Matt. 22.9–14) (p. 218, also note 3).

In Matthew, the character of the community is understood essentially from the point of view of salvation history. It takes the sacred past (Jesus' ethical demands) as its standard and at the same time it lives with the future in view. The relationship of each member to the eschatological imperative is also determined within time. The attitude of the individual to the eschatological demand must be understood dialectically: on the one hand, the Christian when following Jesus gives concrete form to the eschatological δικαιοσύνη; on the other hand, he does not attain to Christian perfection once and for all, but is exposed to the temptation to sin as a perpetual menace. Thus the existence of a Christian is understood by Matthew as a permanent movement between assent and refusal, fulfilment and non-fulfilment of the eschatological imperative (pp. 235f.).

Matthew refuses to interpret the eschatological expectation in a speculative way. Instead of this he is concerned with exhortation; this appears in connection with the parables of the Second Coming (24.27–39) in which exhortation is implicit, and in the formalized statements about the fate of the righteous and the unrighteous which raise the question of works (25.31–46). His interpretation directs our gaze away from the future back to the present and expresses the fact that the ethical intention is the central and invariable element throughout salvation history (p. 242).

The content of Strecker's book is reproduced as it were in a shorter version in his article 'Das Geschichtsverständnis des Matthäus', *EvTh* 26, 1966, pp. 57–74. There he develops further the point that the gospel of Matthew presupposes the change of theological situation between the first and second generations of Christians. Whereas in the first generation the arrival of the parousia was still expected, in the second generation there is already the problem of adaptation to an extended existence in time (p. 60). The redactors of the synoptic gospels have a share in the beginnings of 'Early Catholicism' in the New Testament insofar as they presuppose the consciousness of the delay of the parousia and have drawn the consequences from the altered theological situation. The course of history comes into view in that both the past and the future are to be accounted for (p. 61). Against Trilling's new edition of *Das wahre Israel* (1964[2]), he points out that the gospel of Matthew is to be interpreted in christological rather than ecclesiological terms (p. 71). Trilling's work is an instructive example of the way in which the new discovery of historical criticism in modern Roman Catholic exegesis does not automatically lead to an adoption of results worked out on the Protestant side (pp. 71f., note 43).

G. Reinhart Hummel   *The Controversy with Judaism in Matthew*

Hummel's investigation also arose out of a dissertation (1960) dealing with the problem of 'The Controversy between the Church and Judaism in the Gospel of Matthew'. Like the studies of Trilling and Strecker, it attempts to determine the historical place of the first gospel in the history of primitive Christianity by means of the redactional work of the evangelist. To this extent it also belongs to the redaction-critical sketches of the first gospel as a whole. Since it was composed later than the studies already discussed, it also enters into a dialogue with redaction-critical work which had appeared earlier.

Hummel inclines more to the standpoint of Bornkamm and Barth than to that of Trilling and Strecker on the question of the relations of the communities represented by Matthew. As the title of his study indicates, he places his chief emphasis on the passages in Matthew in which a controversy with Judaism appears. The evangelist carries on the controversy as a man of the Church. In this debate with Judaism he demonstrates at the same time the nature of the Church over against Judaism and the attitude it adopts or ought to adopt in the matters in dispute. 'He allows us to have an insight into the controversy with Judaism.'[62] We need to know the peculiar structure of Matthew's church and its actual relationship to Judaism. The theological statement of the first evangelist could be understood best as

[62] R. Hummel, *Die Auseinandersetzung zwischen Kirche und Judentum im Matthäusevangelium*, München 1963, p. 9.

an answer to the problem presented to him by this historical situation (p. 10).

Hummel shares the view of Bornkamm and Barth that Matthew's church had not yet parted from the Jewish community, but nevertheless feels itself to be in process of consolidating a decided life of its own.[63] The synagogues are for Matthew's church those of Pharisaic Judaism; however, the Christians did not attend their services (p. 29). The instruction to pay the temple tax (17.27), as well as the beginning of the discourse about the Pharisees (23.2f.), tell against a separation from Judaism.[64] The pericope about the temple tax still belongs in fact to the period before 70, but by including it the evangelist wished to say that the community should not refuse to pay the tax and thus separate itself from the Jewish society and slam the door against the mission among the Jews. Here Matthew enunciates his principle for intercourse with Judaism: 'not to give offence to them' (pp. 103, 105). The hardships mentioned in the logia about persecution presuppose the juridical competence of Judaism, i.e. that Christians at whom Matthew is aiming belong to the congregations of the synagogues. He certainly mentions experiences in the Jewish war, insults, calumny, flogging, hate and persecutions, but nothing is said about exclusion from the synagogue in 5.11, unlike Luke 6.22 and John 9.22; 12.42; 16.2 (pp. 30f.).

Hummel therefore understands Matthew's church to be a Jewish Christian community, but he thinks that here 'Jewish Christian' does not mean early Judaism, nor Ebionism either, for circumcision and the mission to the Gentiles are no longer urgent problems of the day. Matthew's gospel is rather evidence for the fact that, after 70, 'Jewish Christian' and 'universal Church' are no longer mutually exclusive antitheses (p. 26, note 54). Gentile Christians, too, belonged to Matthew's church and the evangelist is endeavouring to impress a new Christian pattern on the Jewish forms which had been retained (p. 32). Since his church was not yet completely excluded from the society of Judaism it cannot have come into being later than 85 (p. 32). In Pharisaic Judaism after 70, the place of the temple had been taken by the Law, which increasingly occupied the centre of the stage and gave Judaism its closed nature. Then, in the course of this consolidation round the Law, the Christians were driven out (pp. 34f.).

[63] *Ibid.*, p. 33. Cf. p. 64. For a criticism see N. Walter, 'Tempelzerstörung und synoptische Apokalypse', *ZNW* 57, 1966, p. 46, note 37.
[64] *Ibid.*, pp. 31f. The same passages are also the main evidence for Bornkamm.

Thus, in general terms Hummel supports the opinion that Matthew's church had an inherent independence and was completely detached from Pharisaic Judaism, and that it was Jewish Christian in character. So long as it was not excluded from the synagogue society it maintained its connection with it. Hummel shares with Dobschütz the view that the evangelist was a converted Jewish scribe of the Pharisaic movement (p. 159).

Hummel proceeds from the hypothesis that the first gospel does not reflect especially Jesus' debate with his Jewish opponents. On the contrary, the evangelist has introduced into this debate the picture of the Judaism of his time. For it is evident that the manner in which the Jewish groups and movements are described reflects not only his theological views, but also the circumstances of his day (p. 12). Hummel indicates the manner of the debate with Judaism in Matthew's delineation of the Pharisees, in his attitude to the Law, to the temple, to the cult with its sacrifices, to the problem of the Messiah, and to the new people of God.

He is able to prove by means of a comparison with Mark and Luke that Matthew by his redactional work gives greater prominence than the other synoptists to the Pharisees. They appear as often as possible as Jesus' opponents; in the controversies (Matt. 12.24, 38; 21.45; 22.34f.) and even in conflict with the Baptist (3.7). In addition to the discourse in ch. 23 significant programmatic sayings are directed against them (5.20; 15.13f.). In the account of the Passion, the other synoptists differ from Matthew in mentioning them only in the question about the Pharisees; but Matthew also inserts them in 22.15 and 27.62 (p. 13). He is concerned that they should share the guilt for Jesus' passion. As the real opponents of Jesus they reflect the situation in Matthew's time, when they had obtained the ascendancy amongst the Jews after the destruction of the Temple. He names them together with the scribes more frequently than Mark and Luke; hence he is not able any longer to distinguish them clearly (p. 14). Matthew directed the woes in ch. 23 against the Pharisees as well as against the scribes, although originally some had been directed only to the Pharisees, others only against the scribes. Thus he is acquainted only with Pharisaic scribes (p. 15). Compared with Mark and Luke he speaks more frequently about Sadducees (3.7; 16.1, 6,11,12; 22.34). These passages originated unequivocally with the evangelist and showed that the differences in doctrine between the two movements were meaningless for him since he only notices what is common to both (p. 19). Matthew's description of the chief priests and elders gives proof of care and accuracy. He never mentions the elders alone, but always with the chief priests, or else together with these and the scribes. They play a part only in connection with the Passion (pp. 21f.).

Hummel examines the controversy between Matthew's church and Pharisaic Judaism over the correct understanding of the Law, above all as it is reflected in the conflict stories. His comparison with the parallel stories in Mark shows that Matthew has nearly everywhere incorporated the circumstances of his church in Mark's prototype (pp. 34–52). In Mark, too, the conflict stories to some extent throw light on the situation of the community which he represents, for whom Christ is the end of the Law. Nearly all the conflict stories in Mark show that his church prides itself on its freedom from the Law (p. 52). In Matthew the aim of these stories is on the contrary not to express a christology, but to justify the authority of the community over its life in terms of the *halakah*. He has brought Mark's christological conflict stories back into the sphere of halakic discussion (p. 54). Matthew's christology sees in Jesus above all a messianic interpreter of the Torah. Compared with Mark, the conflict stories in the gospel of Matthew display a marked apologetic trait. The reason for this is that his church is defending itself against Judaism. The subject-matter of the polemic is the Pharisaic misuse of the Law. This polemic no longer has an undertone of propaganda, but announces the judgment (15.12–14) (p. 55). Matthew thus no longer expects his Pharisaic opponents to be converted and struggles with them in order to maintain his own theological position. He never makes a christological declaration against commands of the Torah, nor against customs of the Pharisees without producing evidence from scripture for it (9.13; 12.5–7) (p. 56).

Hummel, like Barth, also takes account of the fact that Matthew is debating with an antinomian movement within his own church (p. 56). He sees Hellenistic libertines in this church (p. 65). This argument, conducted in two directions, connects Matthew with Paul, though their solutions differ; for Paul in Romans develops his concept of faith as an antithesis to legalistic Pharisaic piety on the one hand and to guard against possible libertine effects on the other (p. 66).

According to Hummel, the antitheses in the Sermon on the Mount are not directed against Jewish opponents, but against the disciples. Thus they draw attention to matters within the church and do not, like the controversial discourses, reflect the debate with Judaism *directly* (p. 74). In 5.17–20, the antinomians were forced to submit to the authority of the letter of the valid Torah, and over and above this were led to obedience to the Torah as expounded by Jesus. The community endangered by antinomianism is bound by the Torah and is not led away from it (p. 71). However, the antitheses had the same purpose as the rules about piety in ch. 6, namely a separation *in spirit* from Phariseeism by the community (p. 74). For Matthew, the Sermon on the Mount regarded as a whole is the foundation of the church which resulted from the new messianic interpretation of the Law of the new Moses in opposition to Pharisaic Judaism (p. 74). The Jewish scribal tradition is not neglected altogether, but is subjected to a critical judgment, for which the law of love and the main commands of the Decalogue are the most important criteria (p. 75).

Next, Hummel examines Matthew's relationship to Judaism as shown by his statements about the temple and the sacrificial cult. No dramatic breach can be felt (p. 77). On the one hand, in some passages earlier material has been revised and still presupposes the existence of the temple (23.16–22; 5.23–24; 8.4; 17.24–27) (pp. 79ff.). On the other hand, Matthew looks back on the destruction of the temple which has taken place and regards Pharisaic Judaism as already judged; in this case the threats of judgment in ch. 23 are the echo of the Jewish war (p. 89). The woes against the Pharisees were in Q directed originally against the Pharisees and partly against the scribes; in Matthew, however, they are against Judaism under the leadership of the Pharisees (p. 87). In the parable of the king's marriage feast, an allegory of salvation history (22.1ff.), the reason for the destruction of the temple is the rejection of the post-Easter message (p. 85). Further references to the condemnation which had already taken place occur in Matthew 21.39ff.; 27.25; 27.51 (pp. 83ff.).

Matthew does not inveigh against the cult and its sacrifices. This is because when the gospel was composed after the destruction of the temple, this question was no longer of urgent importance (p. 96). According to the view of the evangelist, his community had been set free from service to the temple. This liberation had taken place in their hearts through the words of Jesus which had been authenticated by the Old Testament (Hosea 6.6, in Matt. 12.7; cf. 9.13) and in the outside world by the judgment of the year 70 (p. 103). The *Sitz im Leben* of the quotation from Hosea 6.6 is the controversy of his church with Judaism over the problem of coming to terms theologically with the ending of the sacrificial cult by force (p. 99). Matthew does not know the difference between a temple made by hands and one not made by hands, and this latter temple, even if it had been built anew eschatologically, could not have acquired for him the significance which it had in Judaism. Matthew's theological conception does not demand as a spiritual necessity a new building of the temple in the last days (pp. 106f.).

The most profound contrast between Matthew's church and Judaism is the church's faith that Jesus is the Messiah (p. 109). Scriptural proof is the most important form of this controversy (p. 111). Hence the redactor inserts the title 'Son of David' conspicuously in the foreground when compared with Mark and Luke (p. 116). Matthew attaches great significance in the debate especially to this title as a messianic name of honour (p. 120). This is evident particularly in the Beelzebub discourse (12.22–45), out of which Matthew has created a debate about Jesus' messiahship by associating it with the theme of the Sonship of David and expanding it materially. The days in Jerusalem and the controversy between Jesus and the Jewish authorities were also linked by him with the theme of Jesus' Davidic sonship (p. 119, cf. p. 122). The Judaism with which the evangelist has to do resembles in his view the man who had been set free from one demon and is now possessed by seven (p. 127).

It is only in the question of the Law that Matthew argues with Judaism on the basis of Old Testament passages, i.e. on the same common basis. He does not do so when discussing Jesus' messiahship, because for him the confession of the messiah is not a question of the right understanding of scripture (p. 127). Hence for Matthew scriptural proof does not belong to esoteric instruction but to the public debate with Judaism; and the formula introducing the quotation describes Jesus' career and influence as the eschatological fulfilment of the prophets' predictions to Israel (p. 131). Therefore Matthew does not produce indiscriminate evidence from scripture, but prefers the prophets as the source of messianic prophecies of Jesus (Mark 14.49: 'But let the scriptures be fulfilled', Matt. 26.56: 'That the scriptures of the prophets be fulfilled').[65] For him Jesus' arrest and

[65] In some scriptural proofs Matthew even gives the name of the prophet (2.17f.; 3.3; 4.14; 8.17; 12.17; 27.9).

passion are not the fulfilment of a particular passage from the prophets, but of the prophetic writing as a whole, i.e. Jesus' passion is for him the conclusion of the history foretold by the prophets and the end of Israel's history as far as they had prophesied it (p. 134).

Hummel proceeds to show that in Matthew's view the earthly Jesus had existed only for Israel. His miracles for Gentiles did not yet authorize the mission to the Gentiles, but by presenting mercy as the decisive mark of Jesus' messiahship they provided the spiritual presupposition for the mission to the Gentiles (p. 140). Matthew demonstrates the result of rejecting Jesus by the phrase ἀπ' ἄρτι (23.39; 26.29, 64) in polemical passages against Judaism; 'from now on', until the parousia, Jesus is no longer Israel's Messiah. This phrase is not pointing forward to the parousia, but back to the past, to an epoch which is finally finished. The time of Jesus' visible presence is over for Israel (p. 141). Thus the kerygma of Jesus' exaltation is at the same time a message of judgment on Israel; for the exaltation brings Jesus' activity among the Jews to an end and clears the way for the Gentile mission (p. 142). Faith opens the door into the βασιλεία (8.10) for the Gentiles, whereas the sons of the βασιλεία are cast into the darkness (p. 146).

According to Hummel, Matthew regards the relation between Israel and the Church from the point of view of a replacement of the Jews in salvation history by a new people of God. Israel's lack of faith breaks up the relationship between itself and the βασιλεία (p. 148), and separates the faithless Israel from its past (p. 150). Israel itself has destroyed the privilege of being destined for the βασιλεία at the end of time (21.43); therefore this prospect is promised to the Church, but only with the eschatological proviso that it bring forth fruits (p. 149). Its existence is the consequence of Jesus' rejection by Israel, and the sayings which repudiate Israel (8.11f.; 21.43) are at the same time the grounds for the Church's call (p. 153). The replacement of Israel in salvation history by a new people of God does not, however, ensue automatically, and membership of it does not imply a guarantee, for the Church, too, is a *corpus mixtum* (p. 156). It is not simply analogous to the Israelite community, but is focussed on Jesus as the Lord of the Church (p. 155). For Matthew, the relationship of Church and Israel is not determined by the notion of salvation history (as it is in Luke; cf. Conzelmann), but by that of the law and the judgment (cf. also Bornkamm) (p. 156). What is common to both is the Torah, on which also their continuity is based. Additional characteristics of Matthew's inner attachment to Judaism are the Christian scribe, authoritative teaching and discipline, and the complete contrast to paganism. For Paul, on the other hand, law came in only incidentally (Rom. 5.20) and the continuity is based on faith grounded in the promises (Abraham) (pp. 156f.). Hence Paul does not start at Sinai, but even earlier (p. 158).

Matthew's church, in spite of its external membership of the association of the synagogue, is nevertheless something fundamentally new when compared with the Israelite national community. Matthew indicates what this newness involves by the phrase 'it was said to the men of old'. For him, the antitheses of the Sermon on the Mount are the foundation of the Church laid by Jesus' messianic interpretation of the Law in opposition to Pharisaic Judaism. This opposition is constitutive for his understanding of the Church and of lasting theological significance, for his community believes that it possesses the right understanding of the Torah and of Old Testament prophecy (p. 161).

A critical comment to be made on this work of Hummel, as on that of Barth, would be to raise the question whether Matthew's gospel is in fact directed towards two fronts. Allegedly antinomian polemic seems rather dubious, as does membership of the synagogue group. The relevant passages might go back rather to a stage in the traditional material before the final redaction, just as in some passages the material employed still presupposes the existence of the temple, whereas Matthew's thesis of Israel's rejection looks back unequivocally to the destruction of Jerusalem. The same must be said about the problem of universalism and of the mission to the Gentiles in Matthew. The real key to the understanding of the gospel of Matthew is in fact the missionary comment. From here alone, real light is first shed on the controversy with Judaism. It was the connection between a universalistic missionary command and the proclamation of the replacement of the former people of the covenant in salvation history which had to be clearly worked out. From this point of view it naturally becomes open to question again whether Matthew's church is still tied to the law as understood by the Pharisees, indeed, whether it wishes to go even beyond it. Instead of this the Pharisaic understanding of it is actually turned upside down. We must also ask whether in Matthew the idea of salvation history is to be excluded. Such a theory is already made impossible by the fact that Matthew, especially by means of the scriptural proofs, is in continuity with the Old Testament and is by his orientation open to the period of the Church.

H. Manfred Punge *Eschatology and Salvation History in Matthew*

Our sentence mentioned above, which presupposed that Matthew's thinking is in terms of salvation history, makes the problem of the 'relation of the final events and salvation history in Matthew's gospel' a burning one. This is in fact the subject of an unprinted dissertation from Greifswald, which therefore concentrates particularly on an examination of chs. 24 and 25, comparing them with the existing synoptic parallels, especially with Mark 13. In these chapters there is an interest on the one hand in the way the eschatological events take their course, and on the other in the actual present of Matthew and its position in the sequence of the final events. Hence it follows that for the evangelist, eschatology in the strict sense is a completion of God's history of salvation which is already approaching in the past and in the present.[66]

In terms of method this investigation is not a redaction-critical work in the strict sense, at least theoretically; for in the opinion of the author reliable criteria could not be obtained for uncovering the stages of redaction which undoubtedly exist and their *Sitz im Leben*. Thus he felt that a direct literary dependence of Matthew on Mark was open to question. The comparisons with the other synoptists are not considered in terms of literary history, but merely as determining objective relationships. Accordingly he does not look at Matthew's peculiarities in terms of redaction criticism in the real sense, but only in the perspective of the exegesis of the gospel as a whole (pp. 2f.).

In the course of his study, Punge raises questions about Matthew's present, about the expectation of the end and the understanding of the kingdom of God in Matthew. Whereas Hummel in his study examines the role of the temple and of the cult with its sacrifices in Matthew's controversy with Judaism, Punge is mainly concerned with the connection between the destruction of Jerusalem and the eschatological events. Matthew has detached the destruction of the temple from the context of the events at the end. Its date is of no consequence as a sign of the end.[67] In Matthew there is no connection between the Jewish war and the beginning of the fulfilment, for in

---

[66] M. Punge, *Endgeschehen und Heilsgeschichte im Matthäus-Evangelium*, Theological Dissertation (in typescript), Greifswald 1962, p. 5.

[67] *Ibid.*, p. 16; cf. also N. Walter, *op. cit.*, pp. 38–49.

his book the historical references of Mark 13.14 are lacking. He understands the 'desolating sacrilege' to be the apocalyptic sign foretold by the prophet Daniel, yet without any reference to the present time (p. 18).

The future tense in his eschatological discourse shows his inclination to regard the events of that time as historical. Matthew sets the time of Jesus and his own time within the pattern of prophecy and fulfilment, and in this way he intends to ensure that Jesus' sayings are valid for later times as well. Admittedly he, too, has a line of junction between present and future time (p. 35). But this line does not run along the points which are parallel to Mark 13.20 or Luke 21.24, i.e. in Matt. 24.22, but is seen already in Matt. 24.14b (par. to Mark 13.10), namely at the period of mission in which the evangelist is standing. The τέλος here is still something to be expected, but it is not possible to gather from Matt. 24.3–31 how long the eschatological existence of the community with its lively expectation of the end had already lasted. Nor can we learn how near or how far he reckoned the end to be, towards which he is pointing in 24.13 and of which he is describing the separate stages from v. 15 onwards (p. 36).

The section on the expectation of the end contains Punge's efforts to work out the fact of the delay of the parousia, especially in a discussion with Michaelis and his rejection of it, but also with Trilling and Klostermann; here he follows Grässer and Conzelmann. The 'nevertheless' of the waiting period as a result of the length of the time is an indication of actual delay (p. 41). But Matthew's intention is not to broach the actual problems of the delay, but to reduce their impact. Jesus has already announced the long period, hence there is no cause for anxiety; but the background is the experience of the delay (p. 44, note 1). This experience of the delay must not, however, result in the surrender of the imminent expectation; it might also lead to the conclusion that the time of arrival was now at last at hand (Matt. 24.48–51) (p. 48, note 2). The uncertainty of the time of the arrival of the parousia merely excludes *being bound up* with its nearness (p. 51). Whereas Conzelmann and Grässer see in Luke's two books a first example of the solution of the eschatological problem which does not require repeated revision as the delay continues, for Punge Matthew's gospel already shows the signs of such a permanent solution. It is therefore not a transitional form with the nature of a compromise (p. 52).

In Matthew, then, the date of the parousia is uncertain and an intense temporal expectation is lacking; nor is there a *direct* reference to the *eschaton*.[68] Whereas in Mark watching is an eagerness to be on the look out for the signs of the times, because the καιρός had become uncertain, in Matthew it is a life lived in constant watchfulness in expectation of the goal, which includes salvation.[69] The example of Noah, too (24.37–41), is a summons to be ready, as the appropriate behaviour in view of the end; in Matthew those who wait do not observe the signs of the times as in Mark, but the command of the Lord who will call them to account at his parousia (24.45–51; 25.14–30) (p. 56).

Punge follows Bornkamm in working out in Matthew the connection between the expectation of judgment and the parousia (24.40, 41, 51; 25.12, 21, 23, 30). Those phrases, which strain the framework of the parables, already point forward to the description of judgment and a sifting in 25.31–46. In this pericope, which is the climax and conclusion of the eschatological instructions, the eschatological expectation is indeed directed to the appearance of the Son of Man, but mainly to the last judgment and the separation (similarly already in 24.3). The peculiar quality of Matthew's idea of the judgment within the frame of the eschatological discourse is achieved by interpreting the expectation of the end in moral terms, with the help of redactional interpolations from the special material and additions (p. 59). In spite of its being directed to the present time and its tasks, and in view of the open date of the end, Matthew's gospel announces the eschatological determination of men's task and their accounting for it (p. 65).

Punge lays particular emphasis on those passages in Matthew which are in evident antithesis to the particularist restrictions and qualifications of the eschatological statements and conceptions of Mark, thus for example Matt. 24.14; 26.13; 28.19, cf. with Mark 13.10; 14.9. Matthew has expanded the pericope in 24.23–25 = Mark 13.21–23 by means of vv. 26–28. In this way Matthew shows his concern, not for the suddenness of the parousia, but for its universality (8.11) (p. 67). It takes place everywhere and is not tied

[68] *Ibid.*, p. 53. Matt. 24.42–44 is a combination taken from Mark 13.35a and Luke 12.39f.
[69] *Ibid.*, pp. 54f. Matthew demands γρηγορεῖτε and γίνεσθε ἕτοιμοι (24.42, 44), whilst Mark demands ἀγρυπνεῖτε and βλέπετε (13.33). Thus Matthew gives a fresh interpretation with γρηγορεῖτε, also in 25.1–13; for the antithesis of 'watching—sleeping', he substitutes 'being ready—not being ready'.

to a fixed place (against Lohmeyer's Galilee hypothesis). Moreover, 24.30 in particular, unlike Mark 13.26, shows a trend towards expansion: 'The universalism of Matthew's gospel has created appropriate eschatological conceptions for itself here; just as the εὐαγγέλιον τῆς βασιλείας is no longer a hole and corner affair, so the parousia, too, is no longer tied to a particular place, but takes place everywhere.'[70] According to Matt. 24 and 25, the ultimate event will apply not to a band of elect persons in *one* place, but to *all* within the jurisdiction of the Son of Man, i.e. to all peoples (p. 70).

Punge's investigation of the idea of the kingdom of God in Matthew deals in particular with the parables of the kingdom in Matt. 13 and works out in them the perspective of salvation history. By means of his composition he has made the trend towards salvation history the central theme of ch. 13. Interest in salvation history is to the fore, especially in the parables of the tares among the wheat (vv. 24–30) and the net (vv. 47–50) (p. 104). Matt. 13.41–43, too, is not primarily a hortatory warning, but imparts insights into salvation history (like vv. 31–33); a sketch of the course and of the background of salvation history, of which the underlying theme is the βασιλεία (p. 103). Thus in ch. 13 the kingdom of God is the subject of instruction, not about eschatology but about the history of salvation, and the concept βασιλεία τῶν οὐρανῶν does not, after all, belong in Matthew to the terminology of eschatology but to salvation history, of which eschatology is only a part (cf. Matt. 21.43; 23.13; 6.10b; 6.33) (p. 105). Punge's opinion about the differences between Matthew and Luke in dividing up the periods of salvation history and in fitting the Baptist into them agrees largely with that of Conzelmann, Trilling, and Bornkamm (the saying about men of violence in Matt. 11.12f. = Luke 16.16, pp. 112f.; cf. p. 130). In Matthew's view, the Baptist no longer stands on the side of the old era, but already on that of the new (p. 115). The words βιάζεσθαι and βιαστής in the saying about violence are addressed with a polemical intent to the former elect people who rob the new people of their title and dispute it (p. 129).

Punge is able to show how Matthew already presents the history of the community in his gospel by means of the pattern of promise and fulfilment; hence he has no need of an Acts of the Apostles like

[70] *Ibid.*, p. 68. Punge also cites Matt. 25.32 to confirm the abolition of the barriers (*ibid.*, p. 69).

Luke. The problem of the possibility of taking the gospel to the
Gentiles and of the right to engage in this does not arise for Luke
until the early history of the Church. In Matthew, however, it is
already solved by the fate of the Son of Man in accordance with the
paradigmatic significance of the *vita Jesu* (especially in the ἦλθον-
sayings (pp. 162f., note 1). Matthew brackets Israel with the *vita
Jesu* and the *vita Jesu* with the era of the community, in the pattern
of prophecy and fulfilment (p. 171, note 4). Thus there are points of
contact between Matt. 24.10 and 26.31 on the one hand and Zech.
13.7 (image of the shepherd) on the other, and also between Matt.
24.14 and 28.19, between 24.7b and 27.51, 54 and 28.2. Thus Jesus'
predictions in the apocalyptic discourse already come true for the
first time in chs. 26 to 28 in the pattern of prophecy and fulfilment
(pp. 167f.). These passages determine the era of fulfilment which
starts at the life and death of Jesus and lasts till the completion of the
aeon, when the chain of events announced in Matt. 24 comes true.
This chain belongs directly to the beginning of the woes, which is
also meant to be contemporary with Matthew.[71] It is Matthew's
view that the last stage of God's history with his people since Jesus'
coming is not, as in Mark, merely a transitional stage, which is
significant in view of the time of its fulfilment, but an independent
era of salvation history with a definite value and meaning of its own
(p. 172). In Matthew's view, the period of Jesus and the missionary
period did not form two different eras in the history of salvation
(against Marxsen, *Evangelist Markus*, p. 64), but two different stages
within one era of the fulfilment of the law and the prophets (p. 198,
note 2).

The result of our description of the redaction-critical works on
Matthew's gospel has been that there are two problems for which
different solutions are offered, namely the problem of Jewish
Christianity in Matthew's gospel and the problem of the separation
of Matthew's church from Judaism. On both problems Trilling and
Strecker on the one hand, and Bornkamm, Barth, and Hummel on
the other represent different points of view. Trilling and Strecker

[71] *Ibid.*, p. 171. Against Marxsen (*Evangelist Markus*, p. 64). Punge calls in
question the fact that for Matthew Jesus' death forms a particular caesura in the
course of salvation history. Since Matthew is especially concerned with his own
time (28.16ff.), he enquires more about the quality of what is new than about the
time of its arrival. For him the new era already begins with the Baptist and appears
after that in a different way (*ibid.* p. 171, note 3).

have, however, perhaps made it probable by means of convincing arguments that the separation of Matthew's church from Judaism had already taken place, and that it is no longer possible to speak of Matthew's Jewish Christianity, at least in the last redaction of the material, but only in the stage before the final redaction.

IV

THE GOSPEL OF MARK

A. Willi Marxsen   *Mark's Topical Eschatology*

MARXSEN'S INVESTIGATION CONSISTS of four separate studies: of John the Baptist, the geographical outline of the gospel of Mark, the concept εὐαγγέλιον in Mark and the apocalyptic discourse in Mark 13. It is true that they are independent in themselves, but they are held together by the use of the same methodology. Marxsen notes that the four studies were intended at first as independent articles, but it appeared during his work on them that they were much more interconnected than had been assumed at first.[1] In each study Marxsen starts with Mark's statement and then compares this with 'its development in the great gospels' of Matthew and Luke; in so doing he traces the differences between these two great gospels and their contrast with Mark back to the different conception of the evangelists when composing their gospels.

Riesenfeld, too, had already pointed out that in the gospel of Mark we have the deliberately executed work of one man[2] and that the arrangement of the gospel is the result of the evangelist's theological meditation or of his procedure (p. 160). Both studies appeared at about the same time, but were not influenced by each other, and they were certainly not dependent on each other. However, Marxsen later included Riesenfeld's suggestions in his dissertation when he prepared it for publication.

In his analysis of the Baptist tradition, Marxsen starts with the challenging thesis of M. Kähler that the gospels are 'Passion narratives with an extended introduction'[3] (p. 17). He follows K. L. Schmidt[4]

[1] W. Marxsen, *Der Evangelist Markus*, Göttingen 1956, p. 16.
[2] H. Riesenfeld, 'Tradition und Redaktion im Markusevangelium', *op. cit.*, pp. 158f.
[3] M. Kähler, *The so-called historical Jesus and the historic, biblical Christ*, ET Philadelphia 1964, p. 80, note 11.
[4] K. L. Schmidt, *Der Rahmen der Geschichte Jesu*, Berlin 1919, pp. 18f.

and differs from Lohmeyer[5] in maintaining that Mark is composing the pericope about the Baptist with hindsight (p. 18). Just as the tradition before the Passion story must be read with the cross in mind, so the story of the Baptist must be read with Jesus in mind. The pronouncements of the Baptist are thus christological pronouncements and interpreted the Jesus-event in a certain manner. But the Baptist has no independent significance (p. 19). The reflective quotation placed at the beginning of the Baptist tradition in Mark 1.2f., a 'composite' quotation made up of three Old Testament passages, is in Mark 'a prophecy looking to the past' (p. 21). The desert, the site of the Baptist's activity, is no geographical place; instead it gives to the Baptist the qualities of one who fulfils the prediction of the Old Testament prophets (p. 22). Thus Mark is using a statement which is in itself geographical with a theological purpose (p. 22).

The same is true of Mark's temporal statements. Even the fact that Jesus succeeded the Baptist is not a succession in time, but an essential succession in a formal pattern in salvation history (p. 23). The word $\dot{a}\rho\chi\dot{\iota}$ in Mark 1.1 is not the starting point of a development which is coming to an end, but a starting point from which something already in existence can be traced.[6] The preceding event receives a quite new quality when seen with Jesus in mind; it becomes the real prophecy and John becomes the real fore-runner of Jesus. The evangelist sees both the prophecy and the fore-runner, i.e. John, as a real part of the gospel.[7]

Marxsen next examines the modifications of the Baptist tradition in Matthew and Luke. Mark gives the 'desert' a theological significance, but in Matthew (3.1) and Luke (4.1), the concept is altered to denote a place and thus receives a local meaning (p. 18). The Old Testament composite quotation from Mark 1.2f. is given a different

[5] E. Lohmeyer, *Evangelium des Markus*, p. 10.

[6] *Ibid.*, p. 24; according to M. Karnetzki, 'Die letzte Redaktion des Markus-evangeliums', *op. cit.*, p. 173. $\dot{a}\rho\chi\eta$ does not just designate a point, but the whole of the event to be described in what follows. The title $\dot{a}\rho\chi\eta$ means that an event is being described which does not end with the resurrection of Jesus. It is continued in the preaching of the Apostles. It has its beginning in the activity and proclamation of Jesus and is legitimated by it.

[7] *Ibid.*, p. 25. According to Schweizer, for Mark the time of salvation foretold by the Old Testament is the time of the kerygma. This begins with the Baptist, is taken up by Jesus and continued in the preaching of the Twelve, and it flows finally into the world-wide church of the Gentiles ('Anmerkungen zur Theologie des Markus', *loc. cit.*, p. 36).

character in Matthew 3.3 and is no longer a prophecy directed towards the past, but one which supplies a foundation; nor is it, as in Mark, a part of the gospel, but precedes it. Matthew gives more thought than Mark to the use of the Old Testament quotations: because the announcement of the prophet has taken place, the event which happens is proved to be the fulfilment of the promise (p. 29).

Whereas in Mark the event as it were proclaims itself, for Matthew it is the proclamation in the Old Testament, in prophecy, which gives the New Testament event its quality. Matthew is concerned with the question whether what is reported actually happened (p. 29). Mark's theological sequence of the Baptist and Jesus becomes in Matthew a temporal sequence. Mark connects the preliminary history in its essence with Jesus, but Matthew supplies a preliminary history of the Baptist to be understood as having happened in time. This appears particularly in the family tree with its establishment of a connection with the patriarchal era; for it is only a genealogy beginning with Abraham, and no longer an *arche* in Mark's sense.

In Luke the historicizing element in the presentation plays a still larger role than in Matthew. It is true that he, too, is not better informed about what actually happened, but he uses his historicizing presentation in order to carry out his theological conception of salvation history. He makes a clear distinction between the Baptist and Jesus and corrects the sequence in Mark. By Jesus' baptism the story of the Baptist is already at an end, for Luke mentions the arrest of the Baptist paradoxically before Jesus' baptism (3.19f.), and then gets himself out of the difficulty by not mentioning the Baptist's name again at Jesus' baptism. In this way Luke has eliminated the significance of the Baptist for Jesus' baptism. The Baptist has for him no longer the eschatological significance which he had in Mark, and is no more than a prophet who is not, as in Mark, part of the gospel. Except in the preliminary story, Luke is not aware of any correspondence between John and Jesus as types.[8] The Baptist has significance only at a particular point in salvation history, immediately before the story of Jesus. He does not belong to the βασιλεία, but stands before it (p. 31). Thus it appears from the comparison of the synoptists how it was possible to break up Mark's conception with some slight alterations, and to reconstruct the material. By this means Luke was able to take over the material almost unchanged, and needed merely

[8] This is emphatically disputed by H.-W. Bartsch. See his book, *Wachet aber zu jeder Zeit*, Hamburg 1963, pp. 44f.

to rearrange it and to connect it up in his redaction. The evangelists were men whose conception differed more from each other than a superficial comparison would lead us to surmise (p. 42).

The real material core of Marxsen's book (apart from the study of the concept εὐαγγέλιον) is the second study dealing with the geographical scheme of Mark's gospel. Lohmeyer had already tried to draw conclusions about the situation of the primitive community from the geographical statements in the framework and in the separate traditional pericopes. He could even write that hardly any biographical detail is mentioned in Mark's gospel without having a theological significance.[9] Mark's composition represents the point of view of a believer and not a biographical narrative (p. 160).

Marxsen takes up this idea of Lohmeyer's but emphasizes that an even stronger distinction than that in Lohmeyer must be made between the traditional material and the work of the evangelist. The statements about places in the traditional material ought to be examined by form criticism, those in the framework by redaction criticism; the framework must be taken completely seriously as the work of Mark, whilst the traditional material goes back to an earlier period (p. 34). Moreover, it would certainly have been possible for Mark to create out of the material before him a different plan, perhaps one like that of the fourth gospel. For behind the passages in Mark 10.46f.; 11.2f.; 14.3, 13ff., 49; 15.43 there is a view according to which Jesus had already been in the neighbourhood of Jerusalem before the Passion (p. 34, note 25.).

Marxsen takes up Lohmeyer's interpretation of the concept 'Galilee' as being a theological factor. He attempts to demonstrate that the name 'Galilee' has been inserted throughout by the hand of the evangelist. Galilee as a place name has a theological importance and is intended to show that Galilee is the 'place' of Jesus' activity in the same way as the desert is the 'place' of that of the Baptist (p. 39). This appears, too, from the fact that in Mark the crucial proclamation of Jesus is always made in Galilee (p. 39). Now Mark is writing because he is interested not in biography, but in *kerygma* (p. 41). The fact that Mark concentrates Jesus' ministry so largely in Galilee is doubtless connected with the significance of Galilee and the Galilean community for the primitive church at the time of Mark. Hence the reason why Mark brought Galilee into prominence is the situation of the community in his day (p. 40). The local Galilean

[9] E. Lohmeyer, *op. cit.*, p. 162.

tradition in Mark might be an indication of the gospel's place of origin and might lead to the further inference that the early church tradition that Mark's gospel originated in Rome is wrong (p. 41).

After examining geographical statements in Mark's gospel, which tell of Jesus' sojourns and his activity outside Galilee, Marxsen raises the question as to the role played by Galilee in the complex of Mark's Passion story. He attributes special importance to the two passages Mark 14.28 and 16.7, in which mention is made of the fact that the Risen One will go ahead to Galilee and of the announcement of his appearance there. He deals in detail with the problem of the real ending of Mark's gospel. Many scholars, including Bultmann,[10] assume that the original ending of the gospel after Mark 16.8, which is said to have reported appearances of the Risen One in Galilee, has been lost (p. 285). Marxsen, however, attempts to understand the end of Mark's gospel on the presupposition that it actually ended with Mark 16.8. He disputes the fact that the passages usually adduced for the purpose, 14.50; 14.27f.; 16.7; John 16.32; 18.8, support the thesis that the disciples fled to Galilee (p. 52, note 1). Marxsen does not take the two passages Mark 14.28 and 16.7 (p. 53, note 2) either as allusions to Jesus' appearances in Galilee, or, like Lohmeyer, as a promise of the parousia,[11] but as being connected with the importance which the Christian community had at the time when Mark's gospel was written.[12]

The evangelist inserted verse 16.7 into the context of 16.1–6, 8, which, as the latest stratum of the tradition, reflects the situation of the evangelist. In the context of Mark this redactional note is to be related to the parousia expected by the evangelist (p. 54). 'The breaking off after verse 8 becomes intelligible. If Mark in verse 7 intends to prepare for the parousia, then after verse 8 its arrival cannot be mentioned. This "see him" is still in the future for Mark. The parousia is still awaited. At the same time we then understand the orientation of the gospel to Galilee. That is where Mark is expecting the parousia. We understand why there is a central point here, why (in Mark's time!) the communities "gather" by the lake.

---

[10] R. Bultmann, *History of the Synoptic Tradition*, p. 285, note 2.

[11] E. Lohmeyer, *Galiläa und Jerusalem*, pp. 10–12; *id., Evangelium des Markus*, pp. 354–8.

[12] W. Marxsen, *op. cit.*, p. 54. Schweizer writes that the use of the word εὐαγγέλιον in Mark shows that, beginning with the Baptist, including Jesus and reaching as far as the world-wide Church, the summons was to repentance (E. Schweizer, *op. cit.*, p. 37).

In this way we can accept the existing text. We need no longer postulate a lost ending, the contents of which would in any case present a serious problem' (p. 54).

We might infer that Marxsen has points of contact with Lohmeyer. But behind Lohmeyer's interpretation is his thesis of a twofold origin of primitive Christianity, whereas Marxsen argues that the gospel of Mark came into being at the beginning of the Jewish war in the year 66, when the original community fled from Jerusalem to Pella, which in fact lies in the land east of the Jordan (Peraea), but belonged politically to Galilee.[13]

Marxsen's interpretation has been challenged by J. Schreiber. He sees Mark 14.28 and 16.7, which are interpolations by the evangelist into the revised tradition, as a polemical message of the Exalted One addressed to the Palestinian Jewish Christians in Jerusalem who rejected the kerygma of the Hellenistic community which dominates the approach of Mark's gospel. The disciples, with Peter at their head, are to come from Jerusalem to Galilee in the land of the Gentiles, in which Mark also includes Tyre, Sidon and the Decapolis, where they will see Jesus as the exalted Son of God, just as he appeared to them previously at the transfiguration, and the Gentile centurion (15.39) already saw him under the cross.[14]

Further, Marxsen holds the opinion that we are not justified in doubting the fact that contrary to Mark's hope the parousia after all failed to appear. He had expected it to be immediately at hand. Matthew and Luke had already discovered this error and altered their parallel text, in Matt. 28.7f. and Luke 24.6–9, accordingly.[15] The spurious ending of Mark appended later is possibly connected with the delay of the parousia. In its place Matthew and Luke have given reports of appearances (p. 58). Marxsen explains the differences between Matthew and Mark in the Easter story by the fact that Mark was still living in imminent expectation of the parousia, whereas for Matthew the time had already begun to lengthen. Matthew created,

[13] This is the view of A. Schlatter, *Evangelist Matthaeus* (on Matt. 19.1); cf. W. Marxsen, *op. cit.*, p. 47, note 6. The possibility of this combination is disputed by Strecker (in his review of Marxsen's book, *ZKG* 72, 1961, p. 146). Josephus also tells against this (*B.J.*III, 35–40), cf. M. Karnetzki, 'Die galiläische Redaktion im Markusevangelium', *ZNW* 52, 1961, p. 245, note 22. Cf. also H. J. Schoeps, 'Ebionitische Apokalyptik im Neuen Testament', *ZNW* 51, 1960, 101–11, especially pp. 105–7, 110.

[14] J. Schreiber, 'Die Christologie des Markusevangeliums', pp. 176f.

[15] Marxsen, *op. cit.*, 58. Punge disputes an imminent expectation in Mark. He tones down the previous signs and assertions of signs so that they mean a relative imminent expectation (M. Punge, *op. cit.*, p. 25); cf. also E. Haenchen, *Der Weg Jesu*, p. 24, note 26.

as it were, an interim solution by inserting a period of missionary work (p. 63).

This has been disputed, in our opinion rightly, by Conzelmann and Strecker. Conzelmann points to the fact that even in Mark 13 delay of the parousia is already playing a part, and therefore this does not happen for the first time in the two 'great gospels'; according to Strecker, the very existence of the synoptic gospels and the similarity of their plan is a consequence of the delay of the parousia.[16] Punge also stresses strongly that the problem of the delay occurs as early as Mark. He had already experienced the delay of the parousia after the exodus to the land east of the Jordan, and is now attempting to fill up the time until then. Past events extended up to Mark 13.20 and the last event begins at v. 24. The intervening verses, 21-23, the period of the pseudo-Christs and pseudo-prophets, are the time in which Mark is living.[17] The evangelist conceived the delay in such a way that he can still hold firmly to its nearness. This 'nevertheless' is a fresh element and an indication of an actual delay (p. 26). The expectations which arose in view of the events of the years 66-70 were again toned down by Mark. He is not intending to issue a first summons to depart from Jerusalem, but to justify the exodus which had become open to question because of the delay. He is bringing the tradition of Jesus into line with the parousia in Galilee, which is nevertheless imminent (p. 28). Dinkler speaks of a reply in apocalyptic terms to the problems arising from the delay of the parousia.[18]

Marxsen describes the conclusion of Matthew's gospel as being, as it were, timeless, for after the conclusion of the time of Jesus, Matthew makes a new era begin which lasts until the end of the world. Before the beginning of the time of Jesus there was, for Matthew, the time of the Old Testament which the evangelist has linked together with the time of Jesus by means of the proofs from scripture peculiar to him. As for Matthew, the time of Jesus becomes an epoch between two others; the presentation of it is effected in his gospel on the lines of a *vita*, by turning Mark's design into a history and making it a continuous progression, a succession of happenings in the actuality of which he is interested. The groups of discourses which are fitted into this framework mirror his own times (p. 64). Strecker has demonstrated this historicizing work of Matthew in detail. Conzelmann has done the same for Luke's historical books.

[16] H. Conzelmann, 'Geschichte und Eschaton nach Markus 13', *ZNW* 50, 1959, p. 211; G. Strecker, *Weg der Gerechtigkeit*, p. 43 *et passim*.
[17] M. Punge, *op. cit.*, p. 24.
[18] E. Dinkler, *op. cit.*, col. 1478.

According to Marxsen, Luke has completely eliminated the eschatological significance of Galilee (p. 64). In his works, Mark's conception of Galilee has been modified and Galilee has become an era in Jesus' life alongside two others, in which Jesus gathered together those who went up to Jerusalem with him. In Luke, Galilee has no theological significance, nor any local one either; for the third gospel is planned particularly with Judaea and Jerusalem as the place of the temple in view. Nor does Luke wish to know anything of a departure of the Risen One to Galilee; he has omitted Mark 14.28, and in Luke 24.6 by a small juggling trick he has turned Mark 16.7, which was a prediction of a departure *to* Galilee, into a prophecy made about Jerusalem *in* Galilee. In this way the eschatological expectation of Mark becomes a piece of past history in Luke.[19] Luke also brings the time of Jesus to an end in order to compensate for the failure of the parousia to appear, by letting the time of the Church begin with the Ascension and Whitsuntide. In Luke's gospel the author becomes aware of the extension of the time by the delay of the parousia, and he endeavours to come to terms theologically with this by means of salvation history, 'the continuous course of which has been arranged and condensed in Luke's two books' (p. 66).

With these last statements Marxsen is in close agreement with Conzelmann's investigation of Luke's work; this is also the case in the following statements, in which he makes a comparison of the theological conceptions of the gospels of Mark and Luke. The leading theme in Mark is the place, in Luke, the time. In Mark, the self-contained unity is provided by the orientation towards a place. Mark does not yet envisage the problem of time in the sense of its continuity; Luke is the first to do this. In his work there is a succession of eras of time, with the time of Jesus as the centre. Thus in Luke, time is the relevant factor of this historicizing presentation; the statements about places are only a means of carrying out his conception. The cause for the differing conception of each of the evangelists is to be sought in the fact that the distinctive difficulties which each of them had to overcome were expressed in the different work of redaction as being the method by which each of them presented his conception (p. 69).

[19] *Ibid.*, p. 65. According to Schreiber (*op. cit.*, p. 182), Luke was no longer able in 24.6, like Mark in 16.7, to attack Jewish Christianity in Jerusalem, because when his gospel was written it was no longer in existence.

Marxsen certainly acknowledges Bultmann's criticism of Lohmeyer's thesis of a twofold Christianity in Galilee and Jerusalem,[20]
but at the same time he modifies it in the light of the redaction-
critical method. For we ought to ask at what time Mark assumed this
community to exist. Since redaction criticism raises the question of
the time of the evangelist and his community, it follows that Mark
presupposes this Galilean community only in the late 60s, and therefore Paul could never have known it (p. 70, note 3).

On the other hand, we may certainly enquire how it happens that Acts,
which also came into being later than Mark's gospel, knows nothing of a
community in Galilee, if we leave aside the passage in Acts 9.31, which we
described as a mere summing up. In that case, Marxsen would have to
attempt to explain it by the hypothesis that the Christian community
which had existed in Galilee in 66 had meanwhile perished during the
Jewish war.

Marxsen considers that a direct inference about the setting of the
gospel of Luke is not possible. The community in Jerusalem is an
invention by Luke, insofar as it could not have been in existence at the
time after the year 70 when he wrote his work. But in fact Luke did
not want to vindicate any place, but to assimilate the problem of what
had been experienced meanwhile in the lengthening period of time.
For behind Luke there stands a community which has to settle the
delay of the parousia, and tackle the fresh problems of the second
and third generations. Jerusalem is excluded as the place where
Luke's gospel was written. This gospel is only orientated towards
Jerusalem insofar as within Luke's two books the city has the
significance of a central point, which is at the same time a point of
transition. It is towards Jerusalem as the place of the temple that
salvation history in the time of Jesus as the centre of time is orientated
(p. 71). But at the same time it is in Jerusalem that the third era
begins, the road of the gospel into the world. Until then, in Luke, the
whole of what is happening, the activity of Jesus, has been consistently
restricted to Palestine. Not until then does Luke break out of the
boundaries of that land. 'To turn back to Galilee would, in the opinion of the evangelist, mean a retrograde step as regards not only the
place, but also its importance. Thus Good Friday, Easter and
Ascension are followed by Whitsuntide, and the missionary period'
(p. 72). Luke is living in this missionary era. It is not important for

[20] See R. Bultmann, *Theology of the New Testament I*, p. 37.

him whether at the time of writing his gospel a Christian community still existed in Jerusalem. But as a believing historian it was important to him that at one time the gospel went out from Jerusalem to Gentile lands. Possibly there is in Luke even an underlying polemic against Galilee as the early home of the gospel, and a defence and assertion of the equal rights of the missionary communities (p. 72).

Marxsen deals exhaustively with Mark 16.7, the interpretation of which is much discussed, especially with regard to the relationship in time of the resurrection and the parousia. The advocates of the thoroughgoing eschatology in particular use this verse as evidence for their ideas that Jesus has supposed no interval of time between resurrection and parousia. Marxsen, however, is not enquiring about Jesus' opinion, but about the ideas of the evangelists (p. 73). Mark could not have understood resurrection and parousia as events following each other directly, or even coinciding, for the very reason that he was, after all, writing his gospel between these two events. But he relates them to each other by eliminating the interval between them. He has the resurrection behind him; the era of the resurrection in which Christ rules as the Risen One has thus in fact begun and will be concluded by the approaching parousia. This era is, however, no continuous progression of time in Mark; instead, by his editorial work, it has become reduced essentially to a transition between resurrection and parousia (p. 74).

We can allow Marxsen's thesis to stand only if we also accept as the third *Sitz im Leben* for Mark's gospel the 'historical place' determined by him. For if we do not share his hypothesis that Mark's gospel was written at a time of intensified expectation of the parousia in the primitive community, which had fled from Jerusalem at the beginning of the Jewish revolt in Galilee, then we cannot accept his conclusions either. For Marxsen's theses fall to the ground if we assume that the tradition of the early Church concerning the place where the gospel of Mark was written and the time when it came into being could be correct.[21]

We can only describe as equally open to question and as a hypothesis Marxsen's conjecture that there is an identity, or at least a close relationship, between Mark 14.28 and 16.7 and a statement in Eusebius' *Church History* (III.5) in connection with the departure of the community from Jerusalem, that the leaders had been granted

---

[21] Schreiber calls Marxsen's opinion to this effect an indefensible thesis (*op. cit.*, p. 171).

an oracle (χρησμός) by means of a revelation (δι' ἀποκαλύψεως).[22] Since the gospel is the message of the evangelist announced to his own time, the community are assumed to have set out on the strength of this oracle from Jerusalem to Galilee. However, since the parousia had not yet appeared when the evangelist wrote his gospel, he could not record the fulfilment of Mark 16.7, and therefore Mark's conception requires the conclusion of the gospel to be after 16.7 (p. 77).

Critics indeed generally emphasize the questionable nature of Marxsen's hypothesis. But it is no use attempting to explain, like Karnetzki, the orientation of Mark's gospel to Galilee by asserting that these Galilean features are only to be found in a stratum before the final redaction. Karnetski relies for this on the source theories of Bussmann, who maintains the existence of a Galilean redaction (B) for the historical source (G), which had been used by Matthew and Mark in an edited form, and by Luke in the original wording. According to Karnetzki, Marxsen's results do not apply to the last redactor, but to the penultimate revision of the material. The final redactor was a member of the Roman community. Karnetski locates the Galilean redactor and his community in the Syrian region adjacent to Galilee, but he rejects the idea of a mood of strong eschatological tension, and instead he asserts a falling off in waiting and watchfulness.[23] But the question is whether the problem is solved simply by shifting the Galilean features of Mark's gospel from the evangelist to a fictitious redactor.

In the third study, the examination of the concept εὐαγγέλιον, Marxsen poses the question whether it is really correct to denote the works of the three synoptists by the term 'gospel' or whether important differences between them are not smoothed out by this common name (p. 77). The result of his analysis of the synoptic material is that Mark's gospel is the sole source of this concept, for Matthew did not introduce the concept εὐαγγέλιον into his book of his own accord, nor from his own sources; in Luke, on the other hand, only the verb εὐαγγελίζεσθαι occurs (p. 81, cf. p. 78). Matthew deals altogether independently with his material and uses the concept in

---

[22] W. Marxsen, op. cit., pp. 75f. Thus also H. J. Schoeps, op. cit., p. 105. Strecker calls the tradition handed down by Eusebius a legend with historical value (ZKG 72, 1961, p. 146).
[23] On this see M. Karnetzki, 'Die galiläische Redaktion im Markusevangelium', op. cit., pp. 238–72; cf. also id., 'Die letzte Redaktion im Markusevangelium', op. cit., pp. 161–74.

those places where in his opinion it is appropriate, whereas in comparison with Mark he omits it (4.17; 16.25) or replaces it with something else (19.29) where he considers that it *does not belong* (p. 82). In any case, this concept in Matthew is associated with his groups of discourses and shows that for him the 'gospel' is a group of discourses of this kind, and that is the reason why he does not take it over from the Marcan original in 4.17; 16.25 and 19.29. Since the whole of the synoptic material only contains the concept εὐαγγέλιον in those passages where it is found in Mark, or in the passages in Matthew which depend on Mark, the most probable explanation is that it was Mark who introduced it into the tradition (p. 82).

Moreover, Mark placed this concept in 1.1 at the head of his whole book and thereby created at the same time the designation for the works of Matthew and Luke (p. 83). Here it is almost a title and is intended to describe and to denote the whole work as εὐαγγέλιον. Thus the whole of Mark's gospel is to be read as an announcement and a summons, not as an account of Jesus (p. 87). Hence εὐαγγέλιον in Mark 1.1 is to be understood with Mark's present in mind; the whole gospel is constructed against the background of this verse.[24]

Even in Mark 1.14f., where the concept εὐαγγέλιον occurs, it cannot only be explained by its context in a summary report, the formulation of which goes back to the evangelist himself, but both verses must again be understood in the light of the situation of Mark, who is here making use of the missionary terminology of primitive Christianity. Hence it is primarily the Risen One who is speaking here and who sums up his preaching in these verses. The material which is then worked up further in the gospel is in Mark's view an interpretation and development of this preaching assisted by the tradition of the earthly Jesus (p. 88). The words in Mark 1.14, 15 are in fact the beginning of the preaching of the Risen One in the evangelist's view and not a beginning of the preaching of the historical Jesus. So this preaching is not directed to Jesus' contemporaries, but to the communities in Galilee, amongst whom Mark is living and is telling them the gospel of the Risen One: 'I am coming soon'.[25]

The understanding of the concept εὐαγγέλιον in Mark, regarded as a whole, shows that this evangelist uses it to express the way and

[24] *Ibid.*, p. 87. For the concept εὐαγγέλιον in Mark cf. also Marxsen, *Einleitung*, pp. 123f.
[25] *Ibid.*, p. 89; for a criticism cf. also M. Karnetzki, 'Die letzte Redaktion des Markusevangeliums', *loc. cit.*, esp. pp. 171f.

means in which the Lord is present in his community. For Mark, Jesus is both bringer and content of the gospel and not only one of the two (p. 90). What matters to Mark in the first place is the preaching which represents the one who is preached. This confirms that Mark is writing a sermon which is a gospel (p. 92).

In Matthew, a certain change in the use of this concept can be established in comparison with Mark. The concept not only shows connections with groups of discourses, but also is never used in Matthew without qualification (p. 92). The reason for this change in comparison with Mark is that Matthew no longer, like Mark, identifies εὐαγγέλιον with Christ; he no longer understands Jesus as the content, but as the bringer and preacher of the gospel (p. 92). In consequence Matthew places the emphasis on Jesus' preaching, whereas Mark has displayed Jesus in action. Thus in Matthew the main interest lies in the groups of discourses which were created by him and placed in his framework to give the appearance of a history, by which he intended to say that Jesus had already spoken these discourses. But all his discourses enable us to recognize clearly Matthew's own situation, which he has historicized by making Jesus give this instruction and teaching. So, for Matthew the discourses are 'gospel'.[26]

The evangelist records especially the instructions to the disciples which had gained paradigmatic significance for the community in Matthew's time (p. 94). In his gospel, the preaching received a framework orientated to history. The result of placing the preaching in the story of Jesus was to give a twofold character to Matthew's work; on the one hand it contains preaching to the community for his time, but on the other it traces this preaching back to Jesus' story and thereby substantiates it (p. 94). Matthew introduces into Mark's framework his idea that the gospel is the preaching because Jesus practised it, and he replaces the concept in those places which do not agree with his understanding of it (Matt. 4.17; 16.25), or he qualifies it in accordance with his own meaning (4.23; 9.35; 24.14; 26.13) (p. 95).

Luke consistently avoids the noun εὐαγγέλιον, because in fact he distinguishes the preaching of Jesus and the preaching of the apostles. Consequently his book is no 'gospel' in Mark's sense, nor a βίβλος with gospels in Matthew's sense, but 'a life of Jesus'. For him the time of Jesus as 'the centre of time' has paradigmatic significance and

[26] *Ibid.*, p. 93; for a criticism of Marxsen's interpretation of the complexes of speeches cf. also W. Schmauch, *op. cit.*, pp. 84, 86.

plays a role apart. It is true that the preaching given by Jesus has
something to say to Luke's community also, but it must be kept
separate from the preaching of the contemporary community.
Luke distinguishes the time of the Church from the time of Jesus,
even though he relates and applies the two to each other. Hence it
happens that Luke can use the concept εὐαγγέλιον only in the
second part of his work (p. 95). The verb εὐαγγελίζεσθαι does not
express the same meaning (p. 96), but only indicates oral preaching
which is sometimes paraphrased more precisely by denoting its
content as βασιλεία τοῦ θεοῦ (p. 97).

Summing up, Marxsen writes about the different use of this
concept in the synoptists, and at the same time he describes the
characteristics of these writings as follows: 'Stated concisely, the
difference is that Mark is really writing a gospel; Matthew in his
book offers a collection of gospels linked aetiologically with the life of
Jesus; Luke writes a *vita Jesu*'.[27] The particular characteristic of
Mark's gospel, that it is a preaching in a concrete situation, has been
lost in Matthew and Luke, and use of the same concept for quite
different books has led to the differences being ironed out. Thus it
was merely a small step to give the same name to the work of John;
in fact the logical development pointed the way directly to a harmony
of the gospels. Mark forms an important key point in the development
of the significance to this concept started by Paul, and it can be said
truly of him that he is an evangelist in the fullest sense of the word
(pp. 100f.).

We should like to make the following comments on this study of
Marxsen: Marxsen was right to examine the varied uses of the concept
εὐαγγέλιον in the three synoptists, and to work it out clearly. We can
agree with his result in the case of Luke's gospel, but not in the case of
Mark, because we do not share his thesis of the *Sitz im Leben* of Mark's gospel
in the history of primitive Christianity. To the same extent, we are also
unable to accept the historical deductions drawn from the differing use of
this term in Mark in comparison with Matthew and Luke.

As regards the groups of discourses of the gospel of Matthew, here, too,
it cannot be made altogether probable that the evangelist understood them
as 'gospel'. In the case of Matt. 24.14, we must ask Marxsen whether the
preacher may be separated from his doctrine; for, in that the community
propagates Jesus' message, the preacher becomes necessarily the one who is
preached. This applies particularly to Matt. 26.13. Since the genitive
τῆς βασιλείας is missing here, the τοῦτο acquires a stronger emphasis.

[27] *Ibid.*, p. 101, note 1; cf. also *id., Einleitung*, pp. 142f.

Thus the expression τὸ εὐαγγέλιον τοῦτο refers to the story of the Passion, not to a doctrinal section.[28] But the fact that the Passion story is a narrative section contradicts Marxsen's thesis that 'gospel' in Matthew signifies groups of discourses which the evangelist is presenting in his book.[29]

Moreover, it seems to us very risky to refuse the three other New Testament gospels apart from Mark the name of 'gospel' as their legitimate type. It is not admissible to wish to deny altogether that the name 'gospel' is justified on account of the undoubtedly different theological conceptions of the writers of the New Testament gospels. The fourth gospel may not use either the noun or the verb in question, but it belongs nevertheless to the same type. For in spite of all the difference in the details of their fundamental construction, all *four* gospels are in the last resort alike; this is also true of their aim. We do not think that this aim in the synoptic gospels is different from what is formulated by the fourth evangelist as the purpose of his gospel (20.30f.), and especially of the σημεῖα contained in it, to awaken faith in Jesus as the Messiah by bearing witness to his own faith.

Marxsen developed the same idea in a lecture held at the *Theologentag* in 1956 on the 'form' of the synoptic gospels. This lecture is to a large extent identical with the substance of his inaugural dissertation. At any rate, much of what had been worked out in the third study of his inaugural dissertation appears again in this lecture. In it he has given a correct view of the difference in the endings of the synoptic gospels: Matthew's gospel is concluded, Luke's gospel is planned to be continued, Mark's gospel has an end which remains in tension.[30] But to conclude from the beginning of these gospels that Mark alone is a εὐαγγέλιον, Matthew on the other hand is a βίβλος γενέσεως and Luke a διήγησις[31] seems in my opinion to be carrying interpretation too far. We also consider it open to question that only Mark is thought to be preaching to fit *one* concrete situation, whereas the church of Matthew, on the other hand, is living in a permanent situation which begins with 28.18–20 and will continue to the end, and for this purpose needs a record.

On the other hand, however, it must be stressed that Marxsen has laid too strong an emphasis on the 'quality of the moment'; that is, on the

[28] Cf. G. Strecker, *Weg der Gerechtigkeit*, p. 129.
[29] *Ibid.*, p. 129, note 2. In his *Einleitung*, p. 134, too, Marxsen has maintained the thesis that only the discourses of Matthew's gospel are to be understood as 'gospel', not the whole book.
[30] W. Marxsen, 'Bemerkungen zur "Form" der sogenannten synoptischen Evangelien', *ThLZ* 81, 1956, col. 347.
[31] *Ibid.*, col. 347; cf. on this also *id.*, *Einleitung*, p. 143.

particular occasion for producing the gospels. In this respect they differ fundamentally from the Pauline letters. Redaction criticism can undoubtedly make a contribution to an approximate determination of the occasion.

But this cannot be established with complete certainty even in all the Pauline letters; how much greater is the difficulty in the case of the synoptic gospels! The occasion is to some extent evident only in the letters to the Romans, in the two letters to the Corinthians, and the two to the Thessalonians, whilst in the letter to the Galatians and in the captivity letters, the opinions disagree as to the time and place of composition. It can only be said that in the synoptic gospels a continuous development of the primitive Christian church is reflected from Mark through Matthew to Luke and his two books; but the relation of Matthew to Luke must not be taken as a series in time, but as a juxtaposition in terms of locality and theology. It is also open to question whether the works of Matthew and Luke may be called a critical exegesis of Mark's gospel (col. 348). It is probably better, as Wernle does, to call them new versions of the gospel of Mark, written from the point of view of a later time and for a later time. The break in attitude towards the imminent arrival of the parousia occurs between Mark on the one side and Matthew and Luke on the other, but the problem of the delay of the parousia is also there in Mark 13, as Conzelmann has pointed out.[32] In the gospel of Matthew, however, it appears still more clearly.

Strecker would explain the fact that the synoptists wrote their gospels wholly as an account of the life of Jesus, from the process of historicizing which arose out of the gradual disappearance of the imminent expectation. In all the three synoptists, the underlying motive of the *vita Jesu* is salvation history. They are also alike in dividing salvation history into periods; the theme of fulfilment already occurs in Mark (1.15; 14.49), which presupposes a continuing time and makes a break between the time of Jesus and the situation after the resurrection, which is followed by a new, further era of salvation history (Mark 4, 21ff.; 9.9).[33]

In an article, S. Schulz also investigates the concept εὐαγγέλιον in Mark and assigns Mark a key position in the history of the theology of primitive Christianity. His real significance does not lie in the Messianic secret, in the parable theory or in the fact that his work is a passion narrative with extended introduction, but in the fact that he is the first and *only* person to have written a gospel. The works of Matthew, Luke and John

[32] H. Conzelmann, *op. cit.*, p. 211.
[33] Thus G. Strecker, following W. Wrede, *Das Messiasgeheimnis in den Evangelien*, Göttingen, 1913[2], pp. 65ff., *op. cit.*, p. 186, note 2.

are not gospels.[34] In Mark, the gospel is no longer as in Paul a message of good news delivered verbally or by letter, but a story (p. 136).

As Paul did not have the mass of Jesus traditions from the primitive community and Hellenistic Christianity, he could not write a gospel. At this point, Dibelius' theory of the preaching must be corrected, as the Jesus traditions were not part of the missionary kerygmatic material and were not handed on to the missionary Paul by the Antiochene community (p. 141).

It was not Luke, but Mark, who wrote the first *historia Jesu*. Luke merely took up the impulses which led to the creation of the gospel of Mark and carried them through to perfection; Luke is the creator of a *vita Jesu* in the full-scale form of Romano-Hellenistic historiography (p. 143). The decisive feature for Mark is the Hellenistic epiphany christological pattern of humiliation and exaltation, with the mystery of the son of God, the theory of the parables and the cross as the sign of the eschatological epiphany of the son of God. Mark thus reinterpreted the Jesus traditions which he took over in a radical new way by means of the Hellenistic epiphany christology (p. 144).

We can now discuss Marxsen's fourth study, which analyses Mark 13. Here an attempt is made to understand this chapter as arising out of the situation at the beginning of the Jewish war, in which the evangelist is writing with the imminent parousia in view (p. 102). By means of this last study all four formally independent studies are combined in a unity. Marxsen attaches great importance to emphasizing the unity of Mark 13, understood as a unity within the evangelist's work (p. 106), without paying attention to the various elements of the tradition which may have been incorporated and which Kümmel is the latest to have endeavoured to disentangle.[35]

Marxsen, on the other hand, is not concerned with these problems of literary criticism and source analysis, but with the discovery of the 'message of Mark 13', and for this purpose he analyses this chapter so as to be able to recognize Mark's own work and hence his point of view (p. 108). He is right in not confining himself to an examination of the origin of the individual traditional passages and to the determination of the original meaning of these passages; he tries to find the meaning of the whole chapter in the context of Mark's conception (p. 112).

The interpretation of this chapter is also made to serve his thesis

[34] S. Schulz, 'Die Bedeutung des Markus für die Theologiegeschichte des Urchristentums', *Studia Evangelica*, Vol. II, TU 87, Berlin 1964, p. 135.
[35] W. G. Kümmel, *Promise and Fulfilment*, London 1957, p. 98.

regarding the time and place in which Mark's gospel came into being. From the literary seam which can be detected between Mark 13.1 and 13.2, he deduces that Mark perceives a connection between the two verses and is looking ahead to the early destruction of the temple. This is certainly an indication both of the time as well as of the place of its composition, and for these there can certainly be no question of Rome, because from there the course of the destruction of the temple could not be watched (p. 113; also note 7).

This argumentation is by no means convincing. We consider it to be quite possible that the gospel of Mark could have been composed in Rome between 66 and 70, and that the author, in the capital city of the world, could be prepared for the possibility of the temple being destroyed. Moreover, at that time an apocalyptic mood can also be conceived in the city of Rome, for here, after the insurrection of Vindex in Gaul and ferments in Spain and North Africa, Nero was murdered. Then came the year of three emperors, Galba, Otho, and Vitellius (68–69), to be followed on July 1, 69 by the proclamation of Vespasian as emperor and his forcible seizure of authority throughout the empire. Punge accepts Marxsen's Galilee hypothesis, but he places the time when Mark's gospel was written in the period after 70. He thinks that Mark understands the destruction of the temple to be a part of the Last Events, since in Mark 13.2, 4 he fits it into the landscape of the apocalyptic discourse. But he is speaking with the destruction of the temple already behind him, for in 13.14 the evangelist is not concerned with the profanation, but with the destruction of the sanctuary.[36]

Marxsen sees in Mark 13.14 the evidence for his thesis that the gospel is geographically orientated away from Jerusalem, and he conjectures that behind it stands the exodus of the primitive community from Jerusalem to Galilee, which was of course connected with the threat to the temple (pp. 115f.). In particular the phrase ὁ ἀναγινώσκων νοείτω, in v. 14, which Marxsen calls 'the most direct form of address in the whole gospel' (p. 124), is seen by him as a proof that the gospel of Mark came into being at the beginning of the Jewish insurrection; he calls it a cleavage in the life of the reader, who is thereby led as it were from the present into the future.[37]

[36] Cf. M. Punge, op. cit., pp. 6–13; similarly, N. Walter, op. cit., pp. 43, 48.

[37] Ibid., p. 125. For Conzelmann, the gulf between present and future does not appear until v. 24. He turns Marxsen's interpretation upside down. What Marxsen stresses as the real message of Mark 13, Conzelmann sees as the false teaching which must be rejected. He looks for a solution to the problems of eschatology in principle and more or less postpones the parousia indefinitely: 'Geschichte und Eschaton nach Mark 13', op. cit., p. 215.

In comparing Mark 13 with Luke 21, Marxsen comes to the conclusion that Luke wants to interpret Mark's apocalyptic outlook from the standpoint of his own later period (p. 131). For him the prophetic apocalyptic predictions of Mark 13 are pronouncements of the historical Jesus, but Luke is contemplating these pronouncements at a time when they had already been partly fulfilled in the community (p. 133). Luke has read Mark 13 on the presupposition that Jesus was speaking there about what would come to pass. What had happened since then had proved to Luke that Jesus was right. Thus Luke is standing between predictions which had been fulfilled and a fulfilment which was still awaited; for the events which had already occurred were a confirmation for him of the reliability of pronouncements about events which were still awaited. Luke had also made some corrections to the predictions in Mark by assimilating the predictions to what had in fact happened. Here the most serious alteration was the elimination of the expectation of the parousia in the context of the destruction of Jerusalem in Luke 21.7, compared with Mark 13.4 and Matt. 24.3 (p. 134).

In comparison with Luke 21, Matt. 24 shows not only similar features, but also some of a quite different kind (p. 135). Matt. 24.3 introduces a discourse dealing exclusively with the parousia which is still awaited, the time of which is, however, completely uncertain and is no longer linked with any contemporary pronouncements. Matthew alone uses the expression *parousia* here, the only place in his gospel in which he employs it at all; he does so in order to indicate the theme of his discourse. Thus there is a seam here which separates present and future; though basically Matthew is marking out epochs not of time, but of importance (p. 136). What Mark in 13.5–13 indicates in his description as the situation immediately before the parousia has become in Matthew a permanent situation; for he has removed the idea of the End which is to be found in these verses in Mark and has placed the rest in his missionary discourse in 10.17–21. There Matthew is speaking about the permanent situation, long before the parousia discourse. Matthew is making a distinction between the era of mission with its persecutions, described in ch. 10 as his own present time, and the era of the parousia in Matt. 24f. as in the future.[38]

[38] *Ibid.*, p. 138. It seems to me questionable whether in ch. 10 Matthew really means to describe his present as a permanent situation. In fact he is there describing the first epoch of church history, the controversy with Israel (10.5), in which

The fact that the description of the permanent situation does in fact belong to Matthew's own conception is evident in 28.20 as well as in ch. 25, where the theme of watchfulness from Mark 13.33–37 is transformed into the theme of buying up the time, of good housekeeping (Matt. 25.13, 14–30) (p. 138, note 3). In this way, by rearranging the traditional material and dividing it up into several groupings, Matthew gives us in ch. 24 a pure parousia discourse which takes us step by step to verses 26–31 containing the description of the parousia of the Son of Man, and before them he indicates the signs which are to precede this parousia (p. 139).

Thus Matthew has driven into the background the imminent expectation of the parousia, although it can still be recognized in the parts of the tradition which he has accepted (Matt. 24.34). He has done this by detaching the portions relating to his own time from their connection with the end of time, and by making them a group of sayings by themselves (ch. 10). The remainder acquires the exclusive character of a parousia discourse (p. 139). Since Matthew's gospel reflects the period of the Church engaged in missionary work, the missionary discourses would also have this period in view. They might be concerned with Matthew's own time and be speaking about the fate of the missionary disciples; but they might also be dealing with future matters such as the parousia, and be deducing from them conclusions for the present, as in ch. 25. Whereas Mark in ch. 13 is compressing and concentrating present and future, Matthew has sorted out this compression into a juxtaposition of groupings. Sometimes this sorting out is nearer to the original traditional material than is the case with Mark's compressed composition, because Mark had directed towards *one* point material which diverged with a different σκόπος towards different σκόποι, whereas Matthew has again placed the different σκόποι *side by side* (p. 139).

In his summing up, Marxsen writes about Mark and his synoptic parallels: 'Mark's gospel is *one* sermon; ch. 13 is a part of it which fits into the whole. The material accepted from the tradition is revised and made to apply to the actual contemporary situation. The

---

there was still in fact contact with Israel (10.17–23), even if it is characterized by the persecution of the community. The first evangelist thus deliberately incorporated material from Mark 13 into his commissioning discourse. The first epoch of church history, i.e. the missionary activity to Israel, ends for Matthew with the destruction of the temple, and the gospel is now turned to the Gentiles (28.19) (cf. also N. Walter, *op. cit.*, p. 46, esp. note 37).

imminent expectation of the parousia determines the general
purport throughout. The Risen One is speaking. Matthew's gospel is
a *collection* of sermons. The contemporary situation which gave rise
to it is therefore much more difficult to perceive. . . . However, as
regards this situation it may be said that it is the time in which, after
relinquishing the imminent expectation, the missionary church is
taking shape. To the direct speech of the proclamation there is
added the motive of teaching. The speaker is the one who is always
with his own until the end of the world. . . . Luke is a historian.
He is constructing from the angle from which he sees his own times
and from his own experience of it the first "Church History", which
begins with Jesus.'[39]

Finally, a few comments on the concluding chapter of Marxsen's
investigation, before we give a critical appreciation of his conceptions
and his method. In his final remarks, Marxsen attempts to approach
the conception of the evangelists and the type of their works from a
more distant point; for this purpose he starts from a suggestion of
Emanuel Hirsch and examines the concluding remarks of the
evangelists in which the intrinsic object of the whole can be seen.[40]

With regard to Luke's gospel, Marxsen emphasizes that since it is
the first part of a work which is to be continued (Luke 24.49), it is
orientated unequivocally towards the second part, and therefore the
third gospel must be understood (in terms of redaction criticism)
with the Acts of the Apostles in mind. However, the orientation of
the gospel towards Jerusalem is not due to the situation of the author;
the central point of the gospel is significant as being the central point
of salvation history. The lines of the gospel are drawn towards
Jerusalem; from there the message goes out into the world, and Luke
is situated at the end of one such missionary line (p. 141). In
Matthew's gospel, which in comparison with Luke has been brought
to a conclusion, the situation may be deduced from the missionary
command in Matt. 28.18f., which states the intrinsic aim of the whole
book (p. 142). This description of the first gospel brings Marxsen
into close material accord with the statements of Michel and Trilling.

According to Marxsen, Mark's ending differs in a peculiar manner
from those of the other two synoptists. Mark's gospel does indeed

[39] *Ibid.*, pp. 139f. Marxsen also calls the second gospel *one* sermon in his *Einleitung*, p. 129.
[40] E. Hirsch, *Frühgeschichte des Evangeliums I*, Tübingen 1941, p. 182, cited by
Marxsen, *op. cit.*, p. 141.

come to an end at 16.8, yet it points beyond this ending, and the intrinsic aim of the whole gospel lies just in the fact that this ending is an open one (p. 142). It is true that Matthew and Luke have adopted his scheme, but they have also at the same time 'extended' Mark's gospel into their own time. By means of their orientation and intention something really new has come into being (p. 142). In that case the addition of a secondary ending to Mark's gospel means that this has been assimilated to the existing form of a gospel found in Matthew and Luke, and this had been a necessity in a later situation when the parousia, expected by the evangelist to be very near, had not taken place (p. 143).

Yet the passages, Mark 14.28 and 16.7, can hardly be applied to the parousia, but rather to the resurrection appearances. For in the New Testament ὁρᾶν and ὀφθῆναι are used indiscriminately, e.g. ὁρᾶν for the Risen One in Matt. 28.7, 10; John 20.18, 20. Moreover, both examples in Mark are connected with the person of Peter. That might be pointing in anticipation to an appearance to Peter, which is also mentioned in Luke 24.34; I Cor. 15.5; and John 21.[41]

Marxsen rejects the answer frequently given to the question how several gospels came to be written, namely that a later one was intended to attack an earlier gospel. Mark's successors had merely endeavoured to tell the old matter in a new way and to bring it 'up to date'; for they were exegetes of the earliest gospel and had intended to proclaim the message by means of their interpretation of Mark's gospel, which was directed quite definitely to the present time of the exegetes. It is from this exegesis of the later gospel that redaction criticism attempts to determine the *Sitz im Leben* for the gospels (p. 144).

Another essay of Marxsen, which arose out of his study of Mark's gospel, and is to a large extent identical with his inaugural lecture, must be mentioned here. It deals with Mark's so-called parable-theory, and sets out to explain it on redaction-critical principles.[42] So it is only consistent that Marxsen raises an objection against Jeremias, who believes he can claim the logion in Mark 4.11f. as a very early saying which has its *Sitz im Leben* in the life of Jesus after Peter's

---

[41] Thus also W. G. Kümmel, *op. cit.*, pp. 77f.; see especially G. Strecker, *ZKG* 72, 1961, p. 145.

[42] *Id.*, 'Redaktionsgeschichtliche Erklärung der sogenannten Parabeltheorie des Markus', *ZThK* 52, 1955, pp. 255–71.

confession, during the time of Jesus' esoteric preaching.[43] Marxsen asserts on the contrary that the course of Jesus' life cannot now be reconstructed, and that the evangelist's redactional principle of arrangement ought not to be turned into a biographical one; for not only Mark 4.1–34, but the whole gospel has been composed by Mark, and the position of a passage in the whole book must always be ascribed to him (p. 257, note 1).

After analysing the chapter of parables in Mark 4 and separating the sources conjectured in it from the interpolations of the evangelist (pp. 258–63), he comes to the conclusion that this work of revision by the evangelist was determined by his conception (p. 271). The chapter of parables makes it clear how Mark by adding a verse, part of a verse, or only an idea, sets out to interpret the source before him and to make intelligible to his contemporaries how he understood his sources, or at any rate wanted them to be understood (p. 164).

It had already been recognized by form criticism that the parables had originally been spoken to meet a particular situation; yet in the course of their transmission the framework describing the scene had dropped out and merely the discourse itself was preserved; thus they gave support to several interpretations. They were soon interpreted allegorically, and were also made useful for exhortation by means of a fresh interpretation (p. 265). For this purpose the parables received a new framework, or a verse was interpolated which was intended to tell how the parable ought to be understood at the time of the primitive community or of the evangelist (p. 266). Mark represented the bearers of this new interpretation as the circle of enquirers (Mark 4.10; 7.17), particularly by enlarging this circle; by this means he had his own contemporaries in view (p. 266). In Mark 4.10 he doubled the number of listeners by adding to the Twelve a further circle of listeners. In this way, Mark expresses the fact that not only the disciples of former days, but the whole community, is now interrogating the Lord. Moreover, by altering the singular of 'parable' to the plural in Mark 4.10, the message of this one parable becomes a paradigm for preaching generally, the preaching in the community at the time of the evangelist. This is effected in literary terms by the evangelist's identification of this community with the circle round Jesus (p. 267).

William Wrede had explained the failure of those who listened to the parables to understand them and the interpretations given to

[43] J. Jeremias, *The Parables of Jesus*, London and New York 1963, pp. 13f.

them as being due to the theme of the messianic secret, which he regarded as the adjustment between the unmessianic life of Jesus and the messianic worship of Jesus after Easter.[44] Marxsen, on the other hand, attributes this theme as well as the commands to be silent to Mark's redaction. The messianic secret occurred in the preaching at the time of the evangelist and was concerned with the μυστήριον, which is revealed to the community, but remains an enigma to those outside.[45] Mark cannot be said to have a special theory about parables, unless perhaps this is understood as a statement about the evangelist's message (p. 271).

It must have become evident that this essay is connected closely in method to the book already discussed. It could also be understood as the fifth study in Marxsen's inaugural dissertation.[46] It is now appropriate to attempt a general criticism of Marxsen's studies in Mark's gospel. In doing so we shall repeat some points already mentioned in the detailed description.

(1) We should like to emphasize strongly the fruitful possibilities of redaction criticism as a method, and to welcome it in principle. It is to the undisputed credit of Marxsen that he has gathered together

---

[44] W. Wrede, *Das Messiasgeheimnis in den Evangelien*, Göttingen 1913[2], pp. 64ff., 227ff. Wrede, however, saw the theory of the secret revelation of the Messiah as pre-Marcan because it appears in the gospel of Mark in an undifferentiated way and with numerous variations (*op. cit.*, p. 145). Strecker, however, sees its specific nucleus (referring to Bultmann, *History of the Synoptic Tradition*, p. 346) as a redactional peculiarity of Mark ('Zur Messiasgeheimnistheorie im Markusevangelium', in *Studia Evangelica*, Vol. III, Berlin 1964, p. 93). As further recent literature on the Messianic secret in Mark see also G. H. Boobyer, 'The Secrecy Motive in Mark's Gospel', *NTS* 6, 1960, pp. 225–35; U. Luz, 'Das Geheimnismotiv und die markinische Christologie', *ZNW* 56, 1965, pp. 9–30; R. P. Meye, 'Messianic Secret and Messianic Didache in Mark's Gospel', in *Oikonomia*, Cullmann Festschrift, Hamburg-Bergstedt 1967, pp. 57–68; E. Schweizer, 'Zur Messiasgeheimnistheorie bei Markus', *ZNW* 56, 1965, pp. 1–8.

[45] W. Marxsen, *op. cit.*, p. 220. Cf. also H. Baltensweiler, 'Das Gleichnis von der selbstwachsenden Saat (Markus 4.26–29) und die theologische Konzeption des Markusevangelisten', in *Oikonomia*, pp. 69–75.

[46] In view of what has just been said, there is no justification for Strecker's reproach to Marxsen that he has left out of account in his book a problem which is as central for understanding the editorial work of Mark as Wrede's theory of the messianic secret (the review of Marxsen's book: *Der Evangelist Markus, loc. cit.*, p. 147). In the four other studies there was simply no place for it, because of their themes, but there certainly was a place in the problem of Mark's parable theory. However, Strecker's criticism that Marxsen has only treated sections taken out of Mark's gospel, and therefore has not exhausted all the possibilities for a strict confirmation of his hypothesis, is justified (*op. cit.*, p. 147). A redaction-critical investigation of the prophecies of passion and resurrection in Mark is, in fact, offered by Strecker himself (*ZThK* 64, 1967, pp. 16–39).

the principles of research already existing in redaction criticism, and has illustrated the nature of this new method of treating the subject matter.

(2) In spite of this welcome in principle to Marxsen's methodological procedure *in terms of method*, we should like nevertheless to utter a warning against possibly employing too great subtlety, a danger which in our opinion Marxsen has not avoided. For it is surely open to question whether the authors of the gospels when writing their works really thought matters out in the detail that Marxsen believes he can perceive.[47]

(3) Our warning applies in the first place to the term 'gospel' for the works of the synoptists, the term on which Marxsen throws some doubt as the designation of a type. We cannot be convinced that this term is justified only for Mark's gospel, in spite of the individual observations which Marxsen has made on the differing use of the term in the three synoptic gospels. It also seems to be doubtful whether a modification in the term can be deduced in the passages in Matthew in which the first evangelist has omitted it in comparison with Mark, whereas these omissions by Matthew can also be substantiated by the subject matter. Thus he has probably omitted the term in Matt. 4.17 in comparison with Mark 1.14 because he wished to describe the message of Jesus and of the Baptist on parallel lines (cf. Matt. 3.2) and in 16.25, compared with Mark 8.35, and in Matt. 19.29, compared with Mark 10.29, the material reason for omitting the term εὐαγγέλιον is probably the fact that Matthew wished to lay stress on the person of Jesus.[48]

But in spite of this differing usage in the synoptists, it still does not follow that Mark intended to use it as a classification for his whole book, and that Matthew and Luke did not do so. In our opinion, no difference in the type can as yet be deduced from the differing theological conceptions. The term 'gospel' as it is generally understood in fact signifies for all the four first books of the New Testament only what the Church regarded and understood them to be, namely the four different variations of the one message of Christ, Christ's good news and good news about Christ. Even if this term was first used by Mark and became thereafter the designation of the books of Matthew, Luke, and John as well, its use in Mark 1.1 does not

---

[47] For the problem of the evaluation of traditions taken over from the community cf. also E. Haenchen, *Der Weg Jesu*, p. 23.
[48] Thus G. Strecker, *ibid.*, p. 146.

signify that it was intended to be understood as a classification. In our opinion, the character of Mark's work would not have been altered if βίβλος had appeared in his first verse, as in Matt. 1.1, or διήγησις as in Luke 1.1, or βιβλίον, as in John 20.30.[49]

(4) We have already pointed out that we cannot agree with Marxsen's conclusion about the historical situation when Mark's gospel came into being, in spite of the fact that he has worked out a convincing picture of Mark. At any rate, we do not think it at all impossible that this gospel could have received the shape which in fact it possesses, even if it had been written in Rome according to the evidence of the tradition of the early Church in the time between 66 and 70; for Mark, who was most probably a Palestinian Jewish Christian, possibly a native of Galilee, could follow the events in Palestine even from Rome, without it being necessary to assume his presence in Galilee. There are too many arguments against the hypothesis of its composition in Galilee for the primitive community which had left Jerusalem. These arguments are:

The explanation of Jewish customs (Mark 7.3f.; 14.12; 15.42), the translation of Aramaic words (Mark 3.17, 22; 5.41; 7.11; 9.43; 10.46; 14.36; 15.22, 34), the reference to Roman marriage law (Mark 10.12), the use of many Latin expressions (Mark 4.21; 5.9,15; 6.27, 37; 7.4; 12.14, 42; 15.39, 44, 45 et passim),[50] not least the fact that Jesus' message and actions are addressed to Gentiles as well (Mark 11.17; 13.10; 14.9); for these reasons the composition for Gentile Christian communities seems to us to be assured. No trace can be observed of a Jewish Christian theology and bias, which would certainly have to be present if the gospel of Mark had come into being in the primitive community which had fled from Jerusalem. We consider it to be a task for redaction-critical research in particular to use its methodological presuppositions for an examination of Mark's gospel in order to find a Sitz im Leben. This might perhaps be defined as being in the period of 66 to 70 in the community in Rome, which consisted mainly of Gentile Christians. This examination should scrutinize the tradition of the primitive Church by means of the method of redaction criticism. For this purpose, help might probably be given by a hint of Harder, who understands Mark 13 as a Christian revision of apocalyptic

---

[49] A different opinion in W. Grundmann, Evangelium nach Markus, p. 1.

[50] Above all, we consider Marxsen's objection that the Latinisms in Mark's gospel belong to the tradition, not to the redaction (Evangelist Markus, p. 41, note 1) ill founded; in that case, we would have to ask why the redaction did not eliminate them. We consider them on the contrary to be editorial additions in order to make the gospel more intelligible to readers in Rome, whom we have assumed to be Gentile Christians.

material which treated of the extension of the Christian Church and its controversy with the synagogue and the state government.[51]

(5) We put the further question to Marxsen, how Mark could be supposed to have eliminated the interval between resurrection and parousia, when after all more than thirty years had elapsed from the resurrection until the writing of the gospel without the Lord having appeared? Is the evangelist supposed still not to have been conscious of an experience of time, in the sense of a delay of the parousia? The historical element must not be removed from Mark's gospel, for Marxsen asserts that its revised tradition had an eschatological bias. An argument against this appears in the term ἀρχή (Mark 1.1) which does not remove the element of time, since the ἀρχή is based on the Old Testament prophecy and introduces the appearance of the Baptist. The temporal line is then continued in Mark 1.14 by μετὰ Τὸ παραδοθῆναι. Moreover, Mark establishes a series of chronological and topographical links.[52]

(6) We certainly consider it possible that in the situation presupposed by Marxsen the expectation of the parousia could have become intensified; that is, of course, assuming that this situation is defined correctly. But in that case we would have to raise the question why Mark is supposed still to have composed a gospel in writing when he expected the parousia to be so imminent. Can a work like the gospel of Mark be composed at all in a period of such confusion?[53]

(7) Finally, we consider that we are also still entitled to ask whether too strong an emphasis on the fact that the individual evangelists were bound to time and situation, might not result in their message being made a relative one. A warning must be uttered against the desire to understand the gospels as works written for a

[51] G. Harder, 'Das eschatologische Geschichtsbild der sogenannten Kleinen Apokalypse Markus 13' in: *Theologia Viatorum* 4, 1952/3, p. 98. For a criticism of Marxsen's Galilee hypothesis, see also E. Haenchen, *Der Weg Jesu*, pp. 459f., note 23.

[52] Examples in R. Bultmann, *History of the Synoptic Tradition*, pp. 339ff. See also Strecker's discussion, *op cit.*, p. 145, and *id.*, *Weg der Gerechtigkeit*, p. 48, note 2.

[53] Punge also brings out the fact that a concise, clearly worded leaflet would have sufficed to call for flight. For this purpose there would have been no need of a well-thought-out gospel. Mark had wished instead to give to his community a new basis for its existence in a new situation. In our opinion, however, this situation cannot be placed in Galilee, but, owing to the reasons given in (4), in Rome, though certainly in connection with the end of a Christian community in Jerusalem in consequence of the Jewish war. Marxsen's pupil A. Suhl follows his teacher in defining the place and time of origin of the gospel. For the problem of a leaflet as the basis of Mark 13 see N. Walter, *op. cit.*, pp. 39f.

particular occasion and restricted to their time. This applies indeed to most of the Pauline letters, although this view could be supported there with greater justification. It would, of course, also affect the question of the binding force of the New Testament writings in general as well as the question of the canon. But the discussion of this systematic problem is not our task; we merely wished to indicate its existence.

This brings to an end the discussion of Marxsen's works on Mark's gospel. W. Grundmann's *Commentary on Mark* (1959) considers the redaction-critical works of Marxsen quite fully. The new edition of this commentary was said to be necessary in consequence of the questions raised by redaction criticism in its research into the synoptists, just as the first edition of Hauck was influenced by the first result of form criticism.[54] The effect of redaction criticism is particularly clear in the passages of the commentary on Mark which are of particular importance, the four studies of Marxsen's inaugural dissertation.[55]

Ernst Haenchen's great commentary *Der Weg Jesu* also makes use of the redaction-critical approach in detailed exegesis, but does not combine the individual observations to provide an overall view of the theology of Mark.

B. Alfred Suhl   *The Old Testament in Mark*

In Suhl's redaction-critical investigation of the Old Testament citations and allusions in Mark the main thesis is that Mark, unlike Matthew and Luke, did not make use of the Old Testament in the pattern of prophecy and fulfilment. Matthew is concerned with the fulfilment of individual passages of scripture understood as prophecy. He thus seeks to provide proof by means of the ascertainable fulfilment of individual scriptural prophecies. Luke, on the other hand, is concerned rather to demonstrate the realization of the plan of God in the juxtaposition of different epochs of salvation history and also in the juxtaposition of salvation-historical events within the individual epochs (p. 42).

Suhl does not therefore speak of a scriptural proof along the lines

---

[54] W. Grundmann, *op. cit.*, p. 23.
[55] This applies to the pericopes about the Baptist: Mark 1.1–8 (pp. 25f.); Mark 1.14–15 (pp. 36f.); Mark 3.7–12 (p. 75); Mark 4.10–12 (p. 91); in addition, Mark 13.1–37 (pp. 259–72); Mark 14.28 (p. 289); Mark 16.7 (pp. 321–3).

of prophecy and fulfilment in Luke's total conception, but only in connection with the missionary speeches in Acts, in direct preaching in a missionary situation (p. 166). Even where Luke only stresses the fulfilment, he clearly thinks in terms of salvation history as a sequence of prophecy and fulfilment, as can be seen immediately in a contrast between Luke 22.22 and Mark 14.21. The picture in Mark is much less clear. Apart from the first announcement of the Passion ($\delta\epsilon\hat{\iota}$ in Mark 8.31), he has only three general remarks about the need to be in accordance with the scriptures (Mark 9.11–13; 14.31; 14.49) (pp. 43f.).

The echoes of the wording of Old Testament passages in the Marcan passion narrative are therefore not to be interpreted along the lines of the pattern of prophecy and fulfilment; they are accounts of New Testament events in Old Testament colouring, i.e. the Jesus event took place $\kappa\alpha\tau\dot{\alpha}\ \tau\dot{\alpha}s\ \gamma\rho\alpha\phi\dot{\alpha}s$ on the basis of the Easter faith. In Mark, the fulfilment is not yet constructed according to the existing Old Testament prophecy, but on the contrary Old Testament phrases are used in the description on the basis of the New Testament circumstances. This sort of use of the scriptures was to be found in part even before Mark.

Against Suhl's interpretation it must, however, be pointed out that while explicit scriptural proof plays no obvious role in the Marcan passion story, Mark 14.27 contains a scriptural proof along the lines of the prophecy-fulfilment pattern. The general assertion that events are according to the scriptures, such as can be found in Mark 14.21, 49, fits this pattern very well. We must also remember the echoes of Old Testament passages (e.g. Mark 14.18, 34, 62; 15.24, 34) which Christian Maurer—in my view, rightly—describes as 'de facto scriptural proof'.[56] This 'de facto scriptural proof' can also be detected elsewhere in the gospel of Mark, where Suhl merely concedes that we have a general assertion that events are according to the scriptures (pp. 137, 157, 160). To a large extent Suhl makes this thesis serve his view that the gospel of Mark has a heightened expectation of the end, so that it is to be understood as a topical address to the present (cf. pp. 160–8). In this connection it is necessary only to refer back to the critical remarks which have already been made about Marxsen's general view.

[56] See his article 'Knecht Gottes und Sohn Gottes im Passionsbericht des Markusevangeliums', *ZThK* 50, 1953, esp. p. 7.

C. James M. Robinson   *The Problem of History in Mark*

In his consideration of Mark's gospel, Marxsen laid strong emphasis on the fact that it was directly affected by events in his own time, and thus thought that he could establish a direct imminent expectation of the parousia based on the impact of contemporary events; Robinson's book, on the other hand, is characterized by exactly the opposite one-sidedness. In it Mark's conception is to be understood as determined by Jesus' struggle with Satan, so that the story of the temptation is given—in my opinion wrongly—a central significance.[57]

The fact that this work comes from an Anglo-Saxon exegetical tradition involves a different methodological foundation. In consequence, the work cannot be claimed as a redaction-critical study in the real sense, even though its title, *The Problem of History in Mark*, displays its concern and brings out strongly the historical tendency of the evangelist. The fact that Mark's gospel is approached from the point of view of its understanding of history surely implies that Robinson wishes to determine the place of this gospel in theological terms, even if he does not endeavour beyond this to raise the question of the temporal and geographical *Sitz* of this gospel. Therefore we shall only discuss particular parts of this book which are of importance for redaction criticism.

Marxsen in his studies had emphasized again and again that the evangelist Mark had wanted to preach and to proclaim the gospel in his book. Robinson, on the other hand, emphasizes the fact that Mark wished to be a *narrator* of history.[58] His gospel is not only intended to reflect what the Christian faith understood itself to be, its understanding of history also sees itself as having been formed and determined by the reality contained in the history of Jesus.[59] Mark's conception of fulfilment in history is not that of a rationalist who clings narrowly to the wording of the Old Testament prophesies and wants to see everything fulfilled literally. But in his view history is nevertheless

---

[57] Cf. G. Strecker, *op. cit.*, p. 48, note 2.

[58] J. M. Robinson, *The Problem of History in Mark*, London 1957, p. 21. There is an earlier German version, *Das Geschichtsverständnis des Markusevangeliums*, Zürich 1956, which differs at points from the later English one; page references are to the English version unless otherwise stated.

[59] German edition, p. 10.

determined according to a divine plan and has a meaning the truth of which can be recognized and declared.[60]

Robinson bases these assertions on his examination of the passages about the Baptist in Mark, which he compares with those of the other synoptists. Marxsen, too, has taken an interest in these passages. We can see at once when comparing Robinson with Marxsen that he poses different questions, though he examines the same passages, and he arrives at different conclusions. Marxsen had thought that the pericope about the Baptist in Mark 1.1ff. was the point to which the gospel could be traced back, i.e. to the time of the Baptist and of the Old Testament prophecy.[61] Robinson claims that in comparison with the gospels of Matthew and Luke, Mark's gospel starts deliberately from so late a time in Jesus' story, because this abrupt point of departure contains at the same time a relative assessment of the history before and after John; the point of departure in Mark's gospel is not due to such external reasons as lack of information about the earlier stages in John's life, but according to Mark's conception a new form of history at a higher level starts with the beginning of Jesus' public ministry (p. 56).

Mark distinguishes history before and after John (p. 57) and makes both a positive as well as a negative evalution of Jewish history. He evaluates it negatively insofar as he considers it merely as a preliminary to real history, but positively insofar as the preparatory history receives its vindication in the fulfilment of the prophecies of the Old Testament (pp. 47f.). Yet the gospel of Mark is not restricted in its use of the Old Testament to the prophetic material alone; it also recognizes the validity of the Old Testament law (Mark 7.10; 10.7f.; 10.19; 12.29–33), it occasionally rejects the tradition of the Pharisees by an appeal to Moses (7.1ff.), and Moses as well by an appeal to the creation narrative (10.2ff.) (p. 58).

In Robinson's exegesis the struggle with Satan (exorcism of demons) moves firmly into the centre of the theology of the second gospel (pp. 33–46). But the struggle with Satan and the demons is surely not the key to understanding Mark. A much greater weight is attached in his theology to the teaching of Jesus. The exorcisms of demons are above all intended to teach that the nature of Jesus' teaching is that of a divine act of soveriegn power, for ἐκβάλλειν is connected with κηρύσσειν (1.39; 3.15; 6.12f.) or θεραπεύειν (1.34). But the passages in which Jesus is said to be teaching

[60] German edition, p. 16.
[61] W. Marxsen, *Evangelist Markus*, p. 88.

(διδάσκειν) are more numerous. This is very frequently the case in the redactional sections (1.21f.; 2.13; 4.1; 6.2, 7; 10.1). The success of this teaching is often shown by the nouns qualified by πᾶς or ὅλος (1.28, 39; 4.1; 6.33, 55; 9.15; 11.18). The universal effect of Jesus' message, especially of his healing and teaching, is therefore particularly important to Mark.[62]

It is noteworthy how in ch. 5 of his study Robinson distinguishes between Mark's own history at the time when he wrote the gospel and the history of Jesus which Mark is describing (pp. 54, 63). It is just this idea which shows a point of contact with the questions posed by redaction criticism, for Robinson states in his book that in Mark the history of Jesus is also quite different from the subsequent history, just as Mark makes a distinction between the pre-Christian history and the history of Jesus (p. 63). But this contact in method is present in Robinson's book only in this particular chapter, which significantly has the title 'History since AD 30 in Mark'. In the preceding chapters, on the other hand, the influence of form criticism as represented by Dibelius and Bultmann is much more strongly felt.

Robinson devotes a special section to ch. 13, which is so important for grasping Mark's understanding of history. He names two facts as being especially significant for the correct interpretation of this chapter: first that the language of the Marcan apocalypse at times clings to the form of prophecy, so that its pronouncements can be fitted better into an apocalyptic history than into the narration of actual historical events; secondly, that Mark's apocalypse agrees in part so completely with the events in the history of the first century and with what is reported in the Acts of the Apostles, that it appears to present history in the form of a *vaticinium ex eventu* (p. 61). This tension in the Marcan apocalypse must be clearly recognized; in any case, in it the experiences of the community were understood as having been predicted by Jesus and modelled after his history (p. 62).

Robinson rejects Harder's thesis which makes a sharp distinction in Mark 13 between Mark's and Luke's 'view of history' and states that Mark's presentation goes beyond the dimensions of the historical. He emphasizes that both evangelists have in common an eschatological view of history. He rejects as too subtle Harder's antithesis that Luke gives an 'interpretation of Mark 13.14–20 from contemporary history', whilst 'Mark sees the destruction of the temple precisely not as a political event, but as an occurrence which goes beyond the

---

[62] Cf. E. Schweizer, 'Anmerkungen zur Theologie des Markus', *op. cit.*, pp. 38f.

dimensions of the historical, and therefore as eschatological' (p. 62, note 3).

Here we must put to Robinson the question whether by maintaining a common eschatological view he does not ignore the existing differences and bring them down to a common level; there is also the further question whether in Luke we can speak at all of an eschatological view of history in its full meaning, which would in that case have to be defined as a view of history which is marked by the imminent expectation of the parousia and does not reckon with a long continuance of the present conditions in the world, as is obviously the case in the Lucan historical work.

The section which examines the role played by the Gentile mission in the understanding of history in Mark's gospel is also important. According to this, the eucharist and other cultic elements are not the only parts of the life of the community which are rooted in the life of Jesus; Mark also suggests that the missionary activity of the community also goes back to the lifetime of Jesus and his example (3.13ff.; 6.7ff., 30), for the missionary activity of the disciples likewise exhibits itinerant wanderings, privation, healing the sick, exorcism of demons and the witnessing, the same ingredients as those of which Jesus' ministry was composed (p. 64). Mark has also rooted firmly the event of great historical importance for the primitive community, the Gentile mission (p. 64), in the history of Jesus. But this event is in itself a matter of the years between Jesus' life and the time when Mark wrote his gospel. The impact upon Mark of this process in universal history appears particularly in the important role played by Gentiles and Gentile territory, especially in Mark 6–8 (pp. 64f.).

Here Robinson, unlike Marxsen, may have a correct view. The latter did indeed examine the geographical statements of Mark's gospel about Jesus' journey to the Gentile region,[63] but he drew no conclusions from them which could have been the outcome of an inquiry in terms of redaction history, namely, that behind them there is reflected the success, or rather the fact, of the Gentile mission when Mark's gospel was written. But this does not necessarily imply that missionary work in these areas only at the time of the composition of Mark's gospel is concerned, for Acts 9.2; 11.19 suggests a much earlier time for this work. Marxsen attempts to cut out this sojourn of Jesus in the Gentile area outside Galilee, instead of interpreting it from the point of view of redaction criticism.

[63] W. Marxsen, op. cit., pp. 41–47.

This shows once again (p. 41) how Marxsen subordinates all details in Mark's gospel to his main thesis concerning the time and place when this gospel came into being. Our criticism of Marxsen is supported by a comment of Schille, who is of the opinion that Marxsen in his examination of the notes about places comes to no real conclusion because he takes no account of the aspect of missionary history.[64]

Robinson goes on to write that Mark understood the presence of the Gentiles in the Church theologically, and even in the passages in which he speaks of Gentiles, they are nevertheless already Christians for him. This theological appraisal is based on the historical fact that the Gentiles had entered the community in such proportions as to put them on the same footing as the Jews with regard to the saving significance and prophetic meaning of Jesus' history (p. 65). Robinson thinks that this idea could be suggested by the two stories of the feeding, and especially by the occurrence in them of the numbers seven and twelve, which might be brought into connection with the community of Jews and Gentiles in Acts 6.1ff. (p. 65). We cannot accept this hypothesis of Robinson, but we may note his hint that Mark placed both feedings in the Decapolis, and that perhaps the disciples' failure to feel responsible for the crowds (Mark 6.36) and Jesus' firm attitude that there was after all enough for everyone,[65] is an allusion by Mark to the solution of the problem of the Gentile mission.

Robinson is right in pointing out that in Mark, Jesus' death has a particular significance for the inclusion of Gentiles in the community, and in this connection he mentions the cleansing of the temple (11.17), the anointing in Bethany (14.8f.), Jesus' death 'for many' (10.45; 14.24), the tearing of the curtain of the temple (15.38), and the confession of the centurion at the foot of the cross (15.39).[66] Similarly, Robinson can rightly describe the parable of the wicked husbandmen (12.1–11) as a unified presentation in which the various traces of the entry of the Gentiles into the community and the establishment of a new people of God are brought together (p. 66). The parable once more confirms on a small scale the view of the course of history which occurs again and again in Mark: first the time of the prophets, then the time of Jesus, and lastly the time of the Church (p. 66).

[64] G. Schille, 'Die Topographie des Markusevangeliums, ihre Hintergründe und ihre Einordnung', *ZDPV* 73, 1957, p. 133, note 2.

[65] German edition, p. 98.

[66] German edition, p. 99.

Opinions certainly differ very much as to whether the division of the history of salvation into periods occurs as early as Mark. Marxsen disputes this on the basis of his presuppositions. Strecker has proved this convincingly for Matthew's gospel, and Conzelmann for Luke's two books. Robinson's standpoint coincides largely with the thesis of Cullmann, who challenges the assertion that the delay of the parousia is already reflected in the synoptists and ventures the opposite thesis that Mark is already thinking in terms of salvation history. He particularly rejects Conzelmann's thesis that Luke's book is the outcome of the crisis of the delayed parousia.[67] Yet Cullmann, on the other hand, accepts the elaboration by Conzelmann of a pattern of salvation history in Luke, though unlike Conzelmann he does not regard this pattern as a special case within New Testament theology, but as one that is present throughout (col. 9).

Strecker likewise supports the existence of a pattern of salvation history as early as Mark's gospel. This formalism is common to them all. In Mark its special character consists in the Messianic secret, whilst in Luke the fact of the continuity of salvation history stands firmly in the foreground.[68]

All in all, it can be said that Marxsen and Robinson have diametrically opposed understandings of Mark, seeing that for Robinson, Mark represents past history, which has significance for salvation as a decisive victory over the powers of evil, whereas Marxsen stresses very strongly the character of the gospel of Mark as proclamation.[69]

D. Philipp Vielhauer *Christology in Mark*

In his article 'Erwägungen zur Christologie des Markusevangeliums',[70] Vielhauer presents a critical discussion of Wrede's theory of the messianic secret. He is concerned with the question of the significance of the story of Jesus for Mark's christology. He describes Bultmann's thesis, that in the gospel of Mark the Hellenistic kerygma – of Christ (the Christ-myth) has been combined with the tradition of the story of Jesus,[71] as problematic. Mark may have collected, composed and interpreted his material for Hellenistic readers, but it – is questionable whether Rom. 3.24 and Phil. 2.6–11 were the normative kerygma for him, for the tradition of Christ's atoning death has its

[67] O. Cullmann, 'Parusieverzögerung und Urchristentum', *ThLZ* 83, 1958, col. 9.
[68] G. Strecker, *op. cit.*, p. 186. For a critical discussion of Conzelmann's division into periods of salvation history cf. also H. Flender, *St Luke: Theologian of Redemptive History*, London and Philadelphia 1967.
[69] Cf. also A. Suhl, *op. cit.*, pp. 13f.
[70] In: *Zeit und Geschichte*, Bultmann Festschrift, Tübingen 1964, pp. 155–69.
[71] R. Bultmann, *History of the Synoptic Tradition*, pp. 347f.

roots in the primitive Palestinian community and is not constitutive of Mark's christology. It occurs only in Mark 10.45 and 14.24, and is completely missing from the predictions of the passion and in the passion story proper. The dominant theme there is rather the divine δεῖ with the proof from scripture and the idea of fulfilled prophecy.

Wrede's theory of the messianic secret must also be modified, as it is not simply to be interpreted as an apologetic theory (p. 156). According to the results of form-critical investigations, the material in the tradition used by Mark was not unmessianic, but had already been shaped by particular christological ideas, especially in the miracle stories and the passion narrative (p. 157). After investigating the different christological titles in Mark (pp. 157–66) and comparing the passages on the baptism, transfiguration and crucifixion, Vielhauer (with reference to Eduard Norden) advances the hypothesis of of an enthronement pattern with the elements of apotheosis or adonptio (baptism), presentation or proclamation (transfiguration) and enthronement (crucifixion), which are rounded off by the acclamation (the confession of the centurion in Mark 15.39) (p. 167).

A theological interest can be seen developing in the composition of th ebook, and can be seen in the threefold designation of Jesus as son of God at the baptism, transfiguration and crucifixion, whereas the corresponding remarks by the demons are regarded as illegitimate because they are premature and come from the wrong side (p. 166). For Mark, Jesus becomes son of God in the full sense of the word at the crucifixion, not at the baptism. The evangelist keeps the disparate material together by means of an enthronement ritual. He interprets the story of Jesus from the baptism to the crucifixion as an enthronement. Here lies the relevance of the earthly story of Jesus for the christology of Mark and this story as a saving event, though the presentation of its happenings in the baptism, transfiguration and crucifixion is determined by the theory of the messianic secret (p. 168).

Vielhauer considers his enthronement hypothesis as an expansion of the theses of Martin Kähler (the gospel of Mark as a passion narrative with an extended introduction) and Wrede (the theory of the Messianic secret) in asserting that in Mark the *theologia crucis* determines the theory of the secret. For Mark, the earthly story of Jesus is not a subject of apologetic, but of the saving event. 'The book of secret epiphanies' is a proclamation of salvation, i.e. εὐαγγέλιον (p. 169).

E. Johannes Schreiber   *Theology of Trust*

Johannes Schreiber's investigation *Theology of Trust* begins from three statements in Wrede's study of the messianic secret: (1) that the gospel of Mark is not an account of historical facts but a testimony of faith; (2) that above all, the purpose of the author in writing the gospel needs to be investigated; and (3) that psychology should not be misused in the quest of the historical Jesus (p. 11).

Taking account of redaction-critical works published earlier, and in view of the difficulties of a redaction-critical investigation of the gospel of Mark because of our scant knowledge of the sources employed by Mark, Schreiber prefaces his study with some methodological considerations about a comparison of the synoptic gospels.

The starting point is that Matthew and Luke reject a theological idea of Mark's when they repeatedly alter particular notions of Mark in their parallel passages or delete certain phrases (p. 15). As well as using a comparison of the synoptic gospels to establish the theology of Mark, it is also necessary to compare passages within the gospel of Mark itself, i.e. to investigate a passage of the text in the context of the gospel (p. 15). If Matthew and Luke are then brought in as well, it becomes clear that the many small and great alterations were determined above all by the different theological conceptions of the evangelists (p. 16). With reference to Wrede, Schreiber forms a rule of exegesis that the less an account in Mark can be understood as a historical report, the more theologically important it is for him (p. 18, cf. pp. 160, 205).

The redaction critic is primarily interested in the tradition, because the tradition apart from the redaction gives a further point of comparison with Mark's outline, and helps us to understand this better. Schreiber designates the redactional verses, in connection with the selection and ordering of the tradition, as the *ipsissima vox* of the evangelist, by which he brings the tradition into accord with his own view (p. 19).

With reference to Wrede, Schreiber points out that Mark principally expresses his theology in narrative form. 'The Marcan theology is to be found in events, in the course of action, in details of place and time, and not only in the spoken word.' What people say in Mark is commented on by the course of action in which they are involved, i.e. word and event stand in correspondence, so that the usually very brief redactional remarks of the evangelist, often spread out formally over the whole gospel, indicate the significance of this correspondence to the reader (p. 20).

As Schreiber begins from Martin Kähler's thesis that the gospels are passion narratives with extended introductions, he sees the starting point for an investigation of Mark's theology in the account of the crucifixion in 15.21b–41, which he derives from two different traditions. These have been collected by the evangelist and supplied with additional comments (pp. 32–49). Schreiber derives both traditions of the crucifixion from Hellenistic Jewish Christianity; the first goes back to Simon of Cyrene, whereas the second tradition possibly goes back to the Hellenistic group (around Stephen) in the primitive community (pp. 62, 66, 69f., 82).

All in all, Schreiber sees the gospel of Mark as needing to be interpreted very much in the light of the fourth gospel; here he seems to be influenced by Bultmann's commentary on John. Thus he is of the view that Mark does not know an imminent expectation of the end, which only promises salvation at the apocalyptic end, as hopes like those in Matt. 19.28 are alien to him. For Mark, salvation and judgment are already included in the cross; the eschaton is already present. He thus rejects Marxsen's thesis of an acute expectation of the end in Mark and alters this to the conception that, in view of the delay and to refute false ideas of the parousia, Mark *nevertheless* held to an imminent end (against Conzelmann and Vielhauer) (p. 85).

Schreiber engages in lengthy exegetical investigations to demonstrate that Mark 13 is not concerned with the imminent expectation of the parousia. Here he is much more concerned with the missionary interest of Gentile Christianity, the total Christianization of Jewish apocalyptic material along the lines of Hellenistic Christianity (pp. 126–45). Whereas K. L. Schmidt wanted to eliminate the topographical details in Mark as being historically worthless, Schreiber seeks to use them as a means of interpreting the account of the messianic secret in redaction-critical terms, e.g. house, mountain, wilderness, boat (pp. 126–69).

For Marxsen, the orientation of the gospel of Mark towards Galilee was grounded in the fact that the evangelist wrote for and in the Christian community in Galilee. Schreiber sees the impossibility of the travel routes of Jesus in Mark 6–8 as proof that the evangelist understands the district of Galilee as 'Galilee of the Gentiles' by including the adjoining Gentile area of Galilee. This is to show that Jesus' earthly work was directed above all to the Gentiles (see. pp 170–84; 210).

In terms of the history of religion, for Schreiber a Gentile Christian Hellenistic theology stands behind the gospel of Mark, which is decisively stamped with certain gnostic ideas (p. 218). Here he considers Vielhauer's assumption of a three stage enthronement pattern in Mark as moulding the story of Jesus from the baptism to the crucifixion, not as a counter-thesis, but as a meaningful enlargement (p. 223). He regards the redeemer-man dualism, the hiddenness and exaltation of the redeemer as an eschatological event and the victory over the powers which essentially determined Mark's conception as all being gnostic elements (p. 227).

In the basic ideas of Mark's redaction it should be noted that the evangelist dealt with great freedom with his traditional material. He has altered it, often reinterpreted it in a radically new way and formulated whole verses and sections quite independently, using such freedom to present one and the same message in all its variety and breadth. He did not want to present an unmessianic life of Jesus in messianic terms (against Wrede). His is not the work of an unskilled redactor or a modern historian, who preserved the elements of tradition like an archivist with the greatest care; he consistently proclaimed the description of the God-man Jesus as a message of the crucified and the risen one (p. 230).

In summary, Schreiber works out the following basic theological ideas:

(1) Mark is writing his gospel as a passion narrative with an extended introduction, to show that the way of Jesus and the proclamation of the Gospel and thus the life of Christians is determined by the will of God: discipleship of Jesus may mean loving God and sacrificing one's life for it.

(2) He has presented the life of Jesus and the disciples in the messianic secret. This shows that the will of God takes redeemer and redeemed to life through suffering and concealment.

(3) He interprets Jesus' death as exaltation and enthronement. In this way, the divine will of love embodied in Jesus is the last authority for decision over life and death, for rejection or confession of the crucified one means judgment or deliverance.

(4) By his account of Jesus as miracle worker and exorcist, Mark seeks to show that the one who is veiled in the messianic secret in the

sign of the cross and unconditional love is the one who is now exalted and acts with authority.

(5) As teacher and proclaimer of secret mysteries and the gospel, Jesus works in such a way that his proclamation and teaching are in the end simply testimony to the love of God that summons men to life with Jesus and thus to true life in love.

(6) To follow Jesus' call unconditionally means to be a disciple of Jesus and to experience his presence, which now gives a share in the divine spirit even in suffering (Mark 13.11) and gives life in love (Mark 10.29f.) (pp. 233f.).

V

LUKE'S TWO BOOKS

INTRODUCTION

WHEN WE DISCUSSED the redaction-critical works on the gospels of Matthew and Mark, we were able on the whole to consider these gospels in isolation from each other. But the situation regarding Luke's gospel is different, insofar as here we must at once also refer to the Acts of the Apostles and consider the two parts of Luke's historical work as a unity, because of their intimate and indissoluble connection with each other.

The method of form-critical study could not be confined to the synoptic gospels,[1] but was already extended by Dibelius himself to other New Testament writings.[2] In the same way, in redaction-critical studies Acts, too, was from the beginning included in the approach to the problem. Here Dibelius has played a considerable part with his form-critical articles on Acts. Thus he was led to perceive that an investigation of this kind answers questions about the literary intention of the author, and that in consequence the further question about the meaning of the whole work must be added to the question about the small units.[3]

The article 'The Speeches in Acts and Ancient Historiography' is of importance here. In it, Dibelius writes: 'The historian's art begins where he no longer contents himself with collecting and framing traditional events, but endeavours to illuminate, and somehow to interpret the meaning of the events.'[4] This quotation might give the impression that Dibelius wishes to regard the author of Acts as being on the same level as the historians of antiquity. But in the face of this

---

[1] Cf. on this E. Fascher, *op. cit.*, p. 2.
[2] M. Dibelius, 'Zur Formgeschichte des neuen Testaments', *ThR NF* 3, 1931, pp. 207–42.
[3] On this see also H. Greeven, 'Heilung des Gelähmten nach Matthäus', *loc. cit.*, p. 66.
[4] M. Dibelius, *Studies in the Acts of the Apostles*, London 1956, p. 138.

possible misunderstanding he emphasizes the fact that in his speeches in Acts Luke is in the last resort after all not a historian, but an evangelist.[5] In Acts he was able to work up the material which he uses with greater freedom than in the gospel, and in spite of adopting different methods when writing Acts from those he used in his gospel, in the second work, though in a higher sense, he remained an evangelist (p. 185).

The article 'The First Christian Historian' must be mentioned as well (pp. 123–37). In it, Dibelius emphasizes the fact that in Acts Luke was endeavouring to illuminate and somehow to present the meaning of the events which he recorded, and that he was not satisfied with collecting them and giving them a framework (p. 125). Luke's work consisted especially in bringing out the meaning of the trend of an event, for instance the influence of the Spirit when the gospel crossed over from Asia to Europe or when Paul appeared upon the Areopagus in Athens (pp. 129f.). Here he stresses the momentous meaning of the fact that the gospel stands face to face with Greek wisdom (p. 130).

Dibelius has understood Luke not as a modern historian, but certainly as a genuinely classical historian who does not reproduce everything with photographic fidelity, but displays only what is typical and significant. By this means Dibelius has paved the way from his form-critical investigations of the Acts to a redaction-critical investigation of this second part of Luke's historical work. M. Rese points to this fact in writing that with his works on Acts, Dibelius created the methodological presuppositions for a theology of Luke, which were, however, only really used by Vielhauer.[6] 'In Dibelius' works on Acts, the step between form criticism and redaction criticism has been taken' (p. 13).

A. Hans Conzelmann   *Luke's Idea of Salvation History*

The results of Conzelmann's investigation of Luke's theology are contained mainly in two works. The first is an article, 'Zur Lukas-analyse',[7] which contains in embryo everything that is later amplified and substantiated in the book *Die Mitte der Zeit*.[8] We can restrict

[5] *Ibid.*, p. 185. W. Marxsen calls Luke a believing historian (*Einleitung*, p. 138).
[6] M. Rese, *Alttestamentliche Motive in der Christologie des Lukas*, Bonn 1965, p. 15.
[7] Printed in *ZThK* 49, 1952, pp. 16–33.
[8] First edition, Tübingen 1954; third edition, Tübingen 1960. ET of the second edition: *The Theology of St Luke*, London and New York 1960.

ourselves in the main to this book because it repeats the ideas of the article which is more in the nature of a programme.

The book, *The Theology of St Luke*, is a combination of Conzelmann's dissertation and inaugural thesis. The dissertation, which was entitled *Geographical Ideas in Luke's Gospel*, appears again in the first part of the book under the heading 'Geographical Elements in the Composition of Luke's Gospel'. In addition, its results are included elsewhere.

Conzelmann is concerned to bring out what is typical and characteristic of Luke in his book. It is only natural that in doing so he takes more account of the gospel than of Acts. The chief reason for this is the fact that for the investigation of Luke's gospel there are at his disposal two other works very similar in construction, subject matter, and contents, namely the gospels of Matthew and Mark. These serve the purpose of comparison and thus throw into relief the ideas which are characteristic of and peculiar to Luke. There is no similar work to which reference can be made for the study of Acts; the apocryphal Acts cannot be taken into consideration owing to their completely different nature.

Conzelmann sets aside to a large extent the question of the sources which Luke may have used. He has on the whole no particular theory about sources, but accepts the classical two-document theory. The search for a specifically Lucan theology starts from the hypothesis that Luke's two books had a quite definite and clearly recognizable conception throughout, and that this conception both gave the material used a uniform stamp[9] and also led to the literary idea of a double work. Conzelmann must of course assume that the author wished to bring his work to an end with Acts in the form before us, and did not intend to write a continuation of it, as has been conjectured for example by Zahn, because of the abrupt conclusion of Acts.

We, too, see no sufficient reason for the hypothesis that the author might have had in his mind a plan for a third part, especially since the scheme formulated in Acts 1.8 was in fact carried through. Hence we consider it to be justified that Conzelmann uses criteria drawn from Acts in his consideration of Luke's gospel, and that his assessment of the gospel is determined directly by Acts.

[9] The manner in which Luke made even non-Christian material serve his conception by his redaction is proved convincingly by Vielhauer, who consciously accepts Conzelmann's method in his study of the 'Benedictus of Zechariah' in

In the introduction Conzelmann formulates the principles of his method. Although he sets out to address some new questions to the gospels and thus to go beyond form criticism, he does not speak of a new method. Nevertheless, the working out of the characteristics of Lucan theology presupposes a completely different estimate of the role of the author from that of form criticism. In Marxsen's introduction, by contrast, a new programme for the redaction-critical investigation of the gospels is already formulated, and this is done with complete realization of his independence of the form-critical method, in spite of the full debt owed to it. Conzelmann has to some extent accomplished a pioneering task by being the first to open up a new problem regarding a gospel as a whole, and by not restricting himself merely to partial aspects.

Conzelmann sees the distinction between his methodological procedure and that of form criticism to lie in the fact that he means to attempt a positive exegesis of the framework of Jesus' story, whereas form criticism in the main examined the individual pericopes, and studied the framework only with the intention of destroying it by demonstrating its secondary nature.[10] Conzelmann, on the other hand, endeavours to examine it in its present condition apart from particular literary theories. If Luke's historical work is a self-contained scheme, a literary-critical analysis is only of secondary importance because a variety of sources does not necessarily imply a similar variety in the thought and composition of the author.[11]

Conzelmann naturally assumes a definite source theory, namely the two-document theory that one source of Luke's gospel is the gospel of Mark. For in working out Luke's peculiarities, Conzelmann reaches his conclusions mainly by comparing Luke with Mark. He is of the opinion that Luke deals with his sources in a radically critical manner and only retains that part of the wording which fits smoothly into his conception.[12] 'He takes over word for word a large part of Mark's material and destroys Mark's redaction, the arrangement of the gospel, so thoroughly that hardly one stone remains upon the other. This alteration is small in quantity, but decisive in quality. In

---

Luke 1.68–79. (See his article of the same name in *ZThK* 49, 1952, pp. 255–72.) For Luke's conception see also G. Klein, 'Lukas 1.1–4 als theologisches Programm', *Zeit und Geschichte*, Bultmann Festschrift, pp. 193–216.

[10] H. Conzelmann, 'Zur Lukasanalyse', *op. cit.*, p. 18.
[11] *Id.*, *The Theology of St Luke*, p. 9.
[12] *Id.*, 'Zur Lukasanalyse', p. 19.

place of Mark's arrangement he has devised a completely original one, developed out of his own typical opinions.'[13]

In his study, *Die lukanische Geschichtsschreibung als Zeugnis*, Morgenthaler saw the design of Luke's historical work as based on the principle of two parts; Conzelmann sees it as influenced by the idea of a division into three parts, which he derives from objective and theological criteria. Thus Luke divides the time between creation and the world's end into three epochs; (1) the time of Israel, the Law and the prophets, which is concluded with John the Baptist; (2) the time of Jesus' earthly ministry as the anticipation of the future salvation, characterized by the absence of Satan, the peace of God, and the realization of salvation which extends up till Jesus' passion; (3) finally, the present time, the historical epoch between the exaltation and the return of Christ, the time of the Church with temptation and persecution which it can indeed surmount, the time in which the Church is Israel as being the bearer of salvation and Jesus' ministry is continued by the spirit.[14]

Conzelmann's choice of the title for his book *Die Mitte der Zeit* (The Middle of Time) corresponds to this proposed division, for the object of Luke's gospel is to describe the central section, the history of Jesus' ministry. In this central period of time, namely Jesus' life, we can recognize, according to Conzelmann, a tripartite construction to which three stages in Jesus' life and ministry correspond: (1) the time in Galilee, from Jesus' call at his baptism to be the Son of God, and the collection of witnesses to his call (Luke 3.21–9.50) (pp. 27–60); (2) Luke's travel account, with the disclosure of the decision to suffer and the preparation of the disciples for the necessity of suffering (Luke 9.51–19.27) (pp. 60–73).

It is noteworthy in Conzelmann's discussion of the travel account, that in spite of the several notes about places (Luke 9.52; 17.11), which might be hints, the narrative does not consider it a journey through Samaria, though Lohmeyer did so and thought that by not mentioning Decapolis, Phoenicia, and Peraea as spheres of Jesus'

---

[13] *Ibid.*, p. 19. Marxsen is of the opinion that Luke wished to replace both the other gospels, for according to the Lucan prologue the criterion by which he wished to improve them is historical reliability (cf. W. Marxsen, *Einleitung*, p. 138).

[14] *Ibid.*, p. 32; in addition, *The Theology of St Luke*, pp. 16, 148, 170. Dinkler, who to a large extent follows Conzelmann, also speaks of Luke's well-thought-out view of history, in which the succession of the epochs is regarded as a necessity for the fulfilment of scripture (*loc. cit.*, col. 1479). The same division into three parts in Luke's book is also supported by W. Marxsen, *Einleitung*, p. 139.

ministry, Luke had won Samaria as a fresh area.[15] Conzelmann, on the other hand, offers the opinion that Jesus' awareness that he must suffer expresses itself as a journey (p. 65). Conzelmann substantiates his assertion, that according to Luke's view Jesus did not set foot in Samaria, with the pertinent comment that Samaria is first described as a mission area in Acts (p. 41, note 1), whereas the omission to mention Galilee as a mission field in Acts must be traced back to the fact that these communities are derived from the activity of Jesus himself (p. 41).

It is also striking that Conzelmann does not let the account of the journey end at Luke 18.14, from which point onwards Luke again agrees with the plan of Mark's gospel, but continues it up to 19.27. In the next verse, the account of the entry into Jerusalem then begins. Conzelmann emphasizes particularly that the extent of the account of the journey is not to be determined by the source-material employed, but by the work of arrangement carried out by the author (pp. 72f.). It is true that Luke receives from his sources suggestions for drawing up a journey, but in the elaboration and use of the motif for the arrangement of Jesus' life he is quite independent. The journey is therefore to be considered merely as an invention and its essential meaning has yet to be brought out (p. 73). Finally, the third period deals with the end of Jesus' life from the entry into Jerusalem until his death (Luke 19.28–23.49).[16]

Hence Conzelmann is concerned first to consider the framework of Jesus' story without paying attention to the problem of the historical facts of Jesus' life (pp. 9f.). The chronological framework had already been broken up by K. L. Schmidt, the geographical one by Lohmeyer, who replaced it by identifying local traditions (p. 10, note 4). According to Conzelmann, the framework of Jesus' story is now neither chronological nor geographical in its nature; it is kerygmatic and is amplified by means of narrative material about Jesus and sayings of his. 'The process by which the gospels were formed proves to be that of the filling out of a given kerygmatic framework with the narrative material about Jesus and the traditional sayings of the Lord. This has been realized for a long time, but it needs to be stated more precisely by bringing out more sharply than hitherto *each* evangelist's understanding of the kerygma' (p. 12).

[15] E. Lohmeyer, *Galiläa und Jerusalem*, p. 42.
[16] *Ibid.*, pp. 73–94. For the significance of these three pericopes in the life of Jesus see also pp. 14f.

In a first stage of the transmission during the collection of the material up to Mark's redaction and the collection of the logia, the kerygma was simply handed on; in a second stage, namely that of Luke, the kerygma itself becomes the subject of reflection. This is seen in Luke's critical attitude to his tradition and the positive formation of a new picture of history out of the components available to him, which he uses as stones for a fresh mosaic (p. 12). This may clarify the question how far such formulations contain a fresh assessment of the evangelist, compared with that of form criticism, as a theologian of a distinctive character. We must by no means consider Luke's method of operation as that of a historian, in the sense of asking about the reliability of his reporting (p. 12).

It was not Conzelmann's aim to investigate prototypes and sources and to reconstruct historical events, but to answer the question of Luke's attitude to his predecessors and to see how he conceived of his task in the context of the contemporary Church's understanding of doctrine and history. 'First of all the meaning of the text before us must be investigated regardless of our idea of the probable course of historical events, regardless, that is, of the *picture* which Luke gives of the latter' (p. 13). For this purpose it is also necessary to define Luke's own historical position in the context of the Church's development; in Marxsen's terminology, the *Sitz im Leben* of the evangelist and of his community. The way in which Luke looks back on the ἀρχή of the Church as something unique and unrepeatable presupposes a certain distance in time. What distinguishes him is not that he thinks in categories of promise and fulfilment, for he shares this with the other evangelists, but the way in which he produces out of the material handed down to him a picture of the course of salvation history (p. 13).

Luke presents the time of Jesus and the time of the Church as two epochs of a comprehensive course of salvation history, which are each distinguished by their special characteristics. Thus there are instructions given by Jesus which were meant to remain valid permanently (those of the Sermon on the Plain), and some which were intended only for the situation at that time and are annulled in the following period (instructions for preparations in the missionary discourse in 9.3; 10.4, which would be explicitly cancelled for the following period by 22.35–37) (p. 13). Luke can no longer simply project questions of his day into the time of Jesus; his aim is rather to bring out the peculiar character of each period (p. 13).

Taken as a whole Luke's theology of history is determined by two
factors: (1) 'Luke is confronted by the situation in which the Church
finds herself by the delay of the parousia and her existence in secular
history, and he tries to come to terms with the situation by his account
of historical events' (p. 14). (2) In Luke's description of the period of
the Church, the last period of salvation history, he differentiates
again between his own time, that in which the author is living,
and the time of the apostles as eye-witnesses when the Church was
founded. He did not wish to bring his picture of the primitive church
into harmony with his own time, but to show the difference between
them, nor did he wish to reform the church of his day in accordance
with the example of the early one, for its necessary corollary, the
theory that decadence had meanwhile set in, is lacking. However,
in spite of his deliberate separation from the earlier community,
Luke nevertheless preserves the continuity with the present one (p.
15). Thus the fact that the two books of Luke belong together and
yet are separate, results on the one hand from the continuity of
salvation history, and on the other from its divisions (p. 17).

Conzelmann devotes his examination of Luke's historical work,
and especially of the gospel, to the exegetical demonstration of this
hypothetical outline of three periods in salvation history and three
periods in Jesus' life; in doing so he reckons, of course, with the fact
that not every passage fits into this design. He calls such passages
remains from the utilized sources which have not been completely
assimilated; however, these examples of inadvertence do not exceed
the measure of what is customary, even in the case of good historians
in antiquity (p. 19, note 1).

In the first main section Conzelmann deals with the 'Geographical
Elements in the Composition of Luke's Gospel' and works out the
three periods in Jesus' ministry in accordance with Luke's theory.
He also investigates the role of the Baptist in Luke's gospel. Luke
gives a remarkably vague picture of the area of the Baptist's activity.
He associates it neither with Galilee nor with Judaea, because
according to Luke's conception both of these are Jesus' sphere of
work alone. In Luke the Baptist's sphere is Jordan, the sphere of the
old period, whilst Jesus' activity takes place elsewhere. Unlike Mark
and Matthew, Luke explicitly suppresses in 3.3 the fact that people
came to the Baptist not only from the area of the Jordan, but also
from Jerusalem and Judaea (p. 20).

In Mark and Matthew, the Baptist is regarded from the point of view of the approach of the new eschatological era. He is its fore-runner, like Elijah: a sign of its approach (p. 22). Luke has indeed admitted existing material, but has recast it in characteristic fashion. In Luke, the Baptist no longer has a direct relation to the ultimate happenings, but has a definite position in a continuous history of salvation which in the meantime lasts for an immeasurable period. In Luke, John no longer marks the dawn of the new aeon, but only the division between two epochs of a continuous history (Luke 16.16). After John, the break-through into the ultimate happenings is no longer to be expected; merely a fresh stage in the process of salvation is reached, the Baptist himself belonging to the earlier of the two periods. Since Luke no longer considers the Baptist to be the preacher of the approaching kingdom, his preaching of repentance has become his real task (p. 23). Apart from the prologue, Luke does not re-cognize any typological correspondence between the Baptist and Jesus; he has even eliminated hints of this kind on the one hand by omitting the narrative of the Baptist's death in order to exclude the possible wrong interpretation of a typological correspondence, and on the other hand by emphasizing that John is dead and cannot return (cf. Luke 9.9 with Mark 6.16 and Matt. 14.2) (p. 24, also note 1).

The Baptist is described by Luke by means of the categories of the former epoch as a prophet and preacher of repentance, and not by those of a new epoch as a forerunner, Elijah, and a sign of its arrival. Where Luke describes his baptism as a baptism of repentance, stress is laid on what it lacks compared with Christian baptism of the spirit (Acts 1.5; 11.16; 18.24–19.7). Hence the Baptist in Luke has a clearly defined function at the centre of salvation history and his activity is a preparation for Jesus, but not his person; he remains subordinated to the task of Jesus in the same way as the whole epoch of the Law (p. 24). Thus the Baptist does not belong in Luke to the premonitory signs of the parousia, for Luke recognizes only Jesus' resurrection as a prelude to the parousia, though it is still separated from it by a long period of time (p. 24, note 2).

In Luke, too, topographical statements have a certain symbolic theological significance. Thus the mountain is even more than in his fellow evangelists a place of prayer, the scene of esoteric manifesta-tions and of communication with the higher world; on it there can be for him neither temptation nor public preaching.[17] It is true that

[17] *Ibid.*, p. 29. For topographical details in Mark see J. Schreiber, *Theologie des Vertrauens*, pp. 210–13.

in Mark the mountain is already a place and a revelation, but Luke has increased its symbolic significance still more (6.12); we ought not to ask about its particular position, but it is the place to which the 'crowds' do not come. The people always remain behind when Jesus, alone or with his disciples, ascends a mountain (cf. Luke 9.37 with Mark 9.9 and Matt. 17.9) (p. 44). The mount of the transfiguration cannot be regarded as a geographical site either, but only as a site of an epiphany (p. 57). It is noteworthy, too, that the eschatological discourse in ch. 21 is not sited by Luke, as in Mark (13.3) and Matthew (24.3), on the Mount of Olives, but in the temple, because for Luke the mountain cannot be the place for teaching, but only for prayer (p. 79). By the 'lake', too, Jesus is always alone with his disciples. Like the mountain, the lake is also the place of manifestations (p. 44). In Luke's conception, the lake at the stilling of the storm is just the fitting milieu for the manifestation of power (p. 49). In Luke Jesus is never publicly beside the lake, and its shore is no permanent abode for Jesus (p. 42). The place where Jesus meets the people is the plain. This is brought out, for example, by the fact that in 6.17 Luke replaces the shore in Mark (3.7) (πρὸς τὴν θάλασσαν) by 'plain' (ἐπὶ τόπου πεδινοῦ) and thereby prepares the setting for the discourse (p. 44). When he descends from the Mount of the Transfiguration the people first meet him on the plain (9.37) (p. 59).

But here we must ask whether Conzelmann is not sometimes too subtle. At least the exegetical foundation in the text for the assertion that the plain alone was the place where Jesus met the people seems to us very restricted. Moreover, in view of the fact that the gnostics used such statements to denote spiritual conditions,[18] it is natural to ask whether this can be assumed for Luke as well.

Conzelmann considers the so-called travel account (Luke 9.51–19.27) to be particularly important for the theology of Luke's gospel. For him the division actually occurs with the story of the transfiguration (9.28–36), which introduces a fresh stage, namely that of Jesus' consciousness that he must suffer, just as the story of the baptism was the opening of the period of Jesus' messianic awareness.[19] Even before Conzelmann, the travel account had often led scholars (e.g. Wellhausen, Schlatter, K. L. Schmidt, and Bultmann)

---

[18] This question is put by Winter in his review of Conzelmann's book, *ThLZ* 81, 1956, col. 37.
[19] H. Conzelmann, *op. cit.*, pp. 58f.; also p. 63, note 1 against Schlatter.

to observe a tension between the material and its insertion into a pattern of a journey. But whereas for them the impossibility of establishing a route for the journey out of the geographical statements ('Jesus' route cannot be reconstructed on our map of the country—Luke did not possess a modern map') (p. 63, note 6) served to call this journey into question altogether by proving the secondary character of its framework, Conzelmann, by working out the theme of the journey, endeavours to grasp a specifically Lucan christology (p. 62).

The preceding complex of topics in Luke 9.18–50: Peter's confession, the first announcement of the Passion, transfiguration and second announcement of the Passion, is influenced by the way in which the journey beginning in Luke 9.51 is to be presented as a progress to his passion, which differs from the earlier travels in just this respect (p. 63). In Luke, the journey begins after the fact of Jesus' suffering has been disclosed but not understood in the announcement of the Passion. The goal of the journey is the place where the suffering must take place for theological reasons (13.31–35) (p. 65). 'Jesus' awareness that he must suffer is expressed in terms of the journey' (p. 65). Luke has broken up the compact complex of predictions of the Passion in Mark (8.31; 9.31f.; 10.32ff.) by inserting the journey between them; and he has in his turn enclosed the journey within the predictions (9.22, 44; 18.31–33; also 17.25).[20]

It has always been a special problem to establish the course of the journey. It has nearly always been laid in Samaria. Conzelmann considers that the reason for placing this journey in Samaria is to be found not in the text but in our maps, for Luke 17.11 suggests the conjecture that Luke had no accurate picture of the country (p. 66). He seems to imagine that Galilee is inland, but adjacent to Judaea, that Samaria is north of Judaea (Acts 8.1,25; 15.3) possibly because in his two books the whole of Palestine seems to be seen from abroad.[21] In the ancient geographical statements of the Greek and Roman authors, too, this vagueness about Palestine prevails, and the mental picture which Luke is conjectured to have had can be verified straight out of Pliny (p. 69, note 1). Now, if according to Luke's idea Galilee has a common boundary with Judaea, there is no need to make Jesus' route go through Samaria or Peraea, and the strange route

[20] *Ibid.*, p. 64, note 1; for the travel theme in Mark cf. J. Schreiber, *op. cit.*, pp. 190–203.
[21] *Ibid.*, p. 70; similarly W. Marxsen, *Einleitung*, pp. 141f.

from Galilee to Jericho is explained by Luke's geographical ideas.[22] In the only passage in Luke (9.51–56) which actually takes place in Samaria, we have a rejection, so this argument, too, falls to the ground.[23] Moreover, Luke 10.29–37 and 17.11–19 (merciful and grateful Samaritans) are not local Samaritan traditions, but only happen to mention Samaritans; the standpoint of the traditional matter is that of Jerusalem (p. 72).

According to Lohse, Luke does after all set out to describe a journey through Samaria, but he had far too little material. Most of the pericopes of the narrative must be placed in Galilee or Judaea.[24] The merciful and the grateful Samaritans bear witness to the fact that Jesus' missionary activities had borne fruit in Samaria as well. The real mission to the Samaritans was indeed first begun by Philip in Acts 8.4ff., but Luke had already sketched out in anticipation in Jesus' earthly life (the travel account) the road which his disciples would take after Easter in the power of the Holy Spirit (Acts 1.8). Acts shows the progress of the gospel from the Jews to the Gentiles; but the ministry of the earthly Jesus is the theological reason for the missionary task of the Church (pp. 10f.).

Conzelmann reaches the conclusion that the author of the gospel has only arranged the material as a 'journey', and that his editorial work extended to all groups of material before him. 'The journey is therefore a construction, the essential meaning of which is yet to be brought out. It will not do to dismiss it by pointing out the geographical discrepancies' (p. 73). This essential meaning has been explained more fully by Conzelmann in the following words: 'the journey motif and the description of Jesus' ministry are not only not integrated with one another, they are positively incompatible. Yet this very combination is a basic characteristic of Luke's account. Jesus does not make directly for Jerusalem. The journey is simply one of the forms that Jesus' ministry takes. It is not the outcome of the fact that Galilee has rejected him, but of the fact that it is God's will that he should suffer. . . The purpose of the journey is not merely to bring about the inevitable change of place, in order to reach the

---

[22] *Ibid.*, p. 71. Lohse questions Conzelmann's opinion of Luke's geographical ideas. We must not overestimate Luke's lack of knowledge of Palestinian topography (E. Lohse, 'Missionarisches Handeln Jesu nach dem Evangelium des Lukas', *ThZ* 10, 1954, p. 6, note 8a).

[23] H. Conzelmann, *op. cit.*, p. 72. Lohse finds the theological idea which is the keynote of the travel account in 9.51. Here Luke expresses the fact that at this time a part of the promise of salvation history is being fulfilled (*op. cit.*, p. 6).

[24] E. Lohse, *op. cit.*, p. 9.

place of suffering; it is also in itself something of divine appointment, which may not be brought to an end too soon, because it has a function of its own' (pp. 67f.).

Conzelmann next examines the material theological significance of the geographical entity, Jerusalem, in the context of the third period of Jesus' mission, the passion. He establishes the fact that Luke develops his eschatology in explicit relation to it. This already appears in Luke 19.11, where the disciples understood their approach to the city as an approach to the parousia instead of to the passion. Thus they have a wrong conception of both christology and eschatology. In Luke Jerusalem has nothing to do with the parousia, for which the καιρός is still a long way off, but only with the resurrection. Luke 19.11 gives the parable of the pounds, which follows in vv. 12–27, a fresh interpretation and makes it refer directly to the delay of the parousia (p. 74).

Luke's main purpose is to stress the distinction between the entry into Jerusalem and the parousia. For Matthew, the entry was a direct type of the parousia (23.29). In Luke it is not directed to the city, but to the temple. The fact that Jesus takes possession of the temple is not eschatological typology but ecclesiological typology; on this he bases the claim of the Church to be the true Israel. Political apologetic is also present here. Luke deals with the contradiction between the non-political christology and the fact of the entry by altering the people's cry of rejoicing in 19.38 from that in Mark 11.9, 10 and by omitting the kingdom of David (p. 75). The continuous description in Mark of the entry into the city and the temple (Mark 11.11) is divided by the insertion of the destruction of Jerusalem (Luke 19.39–44) between the scene of acclamation on the Mount of Olives and the entry in the form of the occupation of the temple. Conzelmann emphasizes the fact that this is a consistent redactional shaping by Luke, which is not to be explained by the use of various sources (p. 76).

Luke also breaks up the pattern of days in Mark. In this way he creates the impression of a fairly long period of activity in Jerusalem, a period of equal importance to the two preceding ones, a period marked by the absence of miracles and a special kind of teaching.[25]

Conzelmann attaches particular importance to working out Luke's political-apologetic bias in his description of Jesus' trial; Luke 23.2

[25] *Ibid.*, p. 77; for the scheme of days in the Lucan and Marcan accounts of the activity of Jesus in Jerusalem cf. also J. Schreiber, *op. cit.*, p. 149.

brings out clearly that Luke describes the Jews' accusations against Jesus as a deliberate lie. By this means Luke wished to explain clearly to the Roman persecutors of the Christians of his own day that even the proceedings against Jesus, as well as those against the Christians, were based on Jewish slander. Luke supplements this apologetic by his christology, for in exhibiting Jesus' messiahship he wants to create the opinion that the Jewish accusation has been brought forward illegally (p. 85). The political-apologetic trend becomes quite clear when the verdict is given: Luke mentions explicitly that Pilate declared Jesus to be innocent and that he made several efforts in favour of the accused. Pilate does not in fact condemn Jesus to death, but hands him over to the will of the Jews (Luke 23.25). The mocking by the Roman soldiers is omitted by Luke and is replaced by that of Herod and his men (23.11) (p. 87). Luke does not even mention explicitly that the execution was by Roman soldiers, but suppresses their nationality; in the same way he replaces the mockery by the Romans with repeated mockery by the Jews (p. 88). After comparing the statements in Acts about Jesus' death, Conzelmann reaches the conclusion that Luke regards the Gentiles as acting in ignorance, and the Jews as bearing the burden of guilt in respect of salvation history.[26]

The second main part of Conzelmann's book deals with Luke's eschatology. Together with the third main part about Luke's conception of salvation history, it forms the real core of the book. It is here that Conzelmann has worked out the basic idea which underlines both of Luke's books, that Luke replaced the imminent eschatological expectation by the conception of a salvation developing step by step. Conzelmann constantly compares Luke's statements with the corresponding parallel passages in Mark and infers Luke's different attitude to the problem of eschatology from the changes he has made.

S. Schulz interprets Luke's conception of a salvation history, not as a history of election understood in Old Testament, late Jewish, Jewish-Christian terms, but as a history of providence interpreted in Romano-Hellenistic terms with a direct demonstration of the continuity of the working of the divine providential will ('Gottes Vorsehung bei Lukas', ZNW 54, 1963, p. 111). He sees in the composite words with προ- which often occur in Luke an expression of the

---

[26] *Ibid.*, p. 92. But it must be said against Conzelmann that in Acts 3.17 and 13.27f., both the people and their leaders are called ignorant. In Luke 23.34, too, the ignorance of the Jews, not of the Romans, is meant.

central idea of a divine plan. This happens in a different kerygmatic situation, because the proof from scripture is no longer effective among Gentile-Christian readers, who no longer had any relationship with the Old Testament. Thus the idea of a *prognosis* (Providence) is new in Luke. Luke no longer identifies revelation exclusively with scripture, but with the nature of God (pp. 105f.). The context of Luke in the history of religion is the Roman ideology of Fate, accompanied by related motives from the Graeco-Hellenistic worship of ἀνάγκη. To these is added in Luke a christological orientation, i.e. he has kerygmatized this religious heritage (p. 112, cf. p. 113.) In Acts, Luke has placed sermons and apologias from the apostles at the decisive turning points, in which the testimony of the apostle is an instrument of the divine plan (p. 116). In the same way, the spirit plays a great part at decisive moments as the director of the divine providential will: the baptism of the Ethiopian treasurer, the baptism of Cornelius, the missionary journeys of Paul (p. 115).

Conzelmann must presuppose, even though tacitly, that the eschatology of Jesus or (and?) of the primitive Christian community was determined by an imminent expectation of the parousia. On the one hand he actually expresses this presupposition: 'Luke employs for his reconstruction of history the traditional material, which is stamped with the view that the last days have already arrived' (p. 96), but on the other hand he declares that he is not concerned with the eschatology of Jesus or that of the primitive Christian community, but with the eschatological conceptions which Luke displays and takes for granted in his two books (p. 95).

Now it can indeed be seen from comparing Luke with Mark that in the corresponding passages Luke has altered Mark's gospel which lay before him and which is stamped even more firmly with the imminent expectation; but this does not assure us that the eschatological views given by Mark were in fact those of Jesus. It is just these questions which are to a very high degree controversial in New Testament study. This appears, for example, from the fact that Kümmel (on the basis of Mark 9.1 and Matthew 16.28; Luke 9.27) expresses the opinion[27] that Jesus reckoned with the beginning of the complete rule of God by the end of the generation then living, whilst Albert Schweitzer thinks on the basis of Matt. 10.35 that Jesus expected the parousia to be immediately imminent in his own lifetime.

Conzelmann presupposes that eschatology, as an imminent expectation felt at that time (by this he means Jesus' expectation)

[27] W. G. Kümmel, *Promise and Fulfilment*, pp. 27f.

cannot by its very nature be transmitted by tradition; only the idea of the expectation can be handed on. The delay of the parousia which Luke was already aware of having experienced, has for him become a basic element in the construction of the fresh expectation.[28] Thus Luke has stretched out the 'last days' (Acts 2.17) to a longer period, the period of the Church, and has thereby shifted the understanding of the 'last days'. In his thought the spirit is no longer an eschatological gift in itself, but a provisional substitute for the possession of ultimate salvation, and this makes it possible for the faithful to exist in the continuing life of the world and bestows the strength for missionary work and endurance in the persecutions.[29]

•Conzelmann shows the shifting of the eschatological aspect in Luke in a number of examples. In Luke the Baptist is not the apocalyptic forerunner, but is seen in line with all the other prophets and stands as the last of the prophets before Jesus (Luke 16.16) (p. 101). The Baptist brings to a close this period of the Law and the prophets in salvation history, but he does not yet pass out of it, for in Luke he does not yet proclaim the kingdom of God (unlike Matt. 3.1) (p. 102). The preaching of the Baptist (Luke 3.10–14) contains a timeless ethical instruction in the place of an eschatological call to repentance. After baptism, he does not call for repentance, but raises demands about the manner of life required. Thus exhortation is included in the Baptist's preaching (p. 102). 'Matthew's aim is to draw out the parallel between John and Jesus, whereas Luke's is to emphasize the difference between them' (p. 114, note 2).

Conzelmann deals in detail with the eschatology in Luke 21. He compares this chapter with Mark 13, but rejects the hypothesis of a non-Marcan prototype in order to explain the differences from Mark 13 as they are stressed, especially in English and American research, under the influence of the widespread theories of a proto-Luke. He traces back all the variations from Mark to the editorial work of Luke, carried through in accordance with a definite plan (p. 125). Careful comparison of the two discourses shows that the strongest

---

[28] H. Conzelmann, *op. cit.*, p. 97; cf. also J. Schreiber, *op. cit.*, pp. 57–59.

[29] *Ibid.*, pp. 95f. Strecker disputes that in Luke the spirit is the substitute for the parousia which has failed to appear; for in the tradition it is precisely the spirit which is regarded as the eschatological gift of salvation. He expressly supports the reading ἐν ταῖς ἐσχάταις ἡμέραις against Joel 3.1 LXX and Codex Vaticanus. The period of the Church, too, is understood in eschatological terms with the gift of the spirit. That the eschaton determines the present appears from the eschatological motivation of the exhortations and hence of Christian life, e.g. Luke 17.20ff. (*op. cit.*, p. 47, note 4).

motive for Luke's reshaping is the failure of the parousia to appear. Luke explains the failure as God's plan, but on the other hand he emphasizes the suddenness of its irruption. Since this ending is still far off, ethical rules demanding a Christian life take the place of the arrangement for a short interval. The summons to this Christian life is no longer dictated by a definite limited period, but by the fact of the future judgment (pp. 131f.).

Conzelmann rightly emphasizes that the exhortation in Luke 21 derives its special tone from the prevailing persecution (Luke 21.12–19). But here Conzelmann ought to go on to ask which persecution Luke could have in mind; for this is the question of redaction criticism about the *Sitz im Leben* of the evangelist and his task in the history of primitive Christianity. The persecution of Nero can be ruled out. The possibility of an allusion to the persecution under Domitian is possible. It might refer to circumstances similar to those reflected later in the correspondence between the Emperor Trajan and Pliny, the governor of Bithynia about 112. Not only are persecutions by the Gentiles mentioned (21.12c), but also by the Jews (21.12b). Besides, we should also ask what is the relationship of the statements about persecution in Luke 21 to the accounts about the conflicts with the Jews in Acts. If a note of political apologetics with regard to the Roman state is unmistakable in the corresponding accounts in Acts, we ought to ask now if this is also the case in Luke 21. E. Haenchen points out that with 21.19, Luke has reached his own present. All the events narrated before this have already happened (*Der Weg Jesu*, p. 455).

An important role is played by Jerusalem in Luke's eschatology. The evangelist indicates the fate of the city in the Jewish war; but at the same time he keeps it quite distinct from the Christian expectation of the end. Whereas Mark interprets the historical part of the events around Jerusalem as already eschatological signs, Luke proves them to be an uneschatological process (p. 133). We must ask Conzelmann here whether this difference between Mark and Luke is not connected with the fact that Mark wrote his gospel *before* the destruction of Jerusalem and interpreted this destruction already awaited at that time, as an eschatological sign. On the other hand, Luke, who did not write until after it had happened, could no longer understand this destruction as an eschatological event, since the parousia had still failed to arrive: consequently he had to alter his Marcan prototype accordingly.

In the third main part, 'God and Salvation History', Conzelmann demonstrates that Luke also undertakes to work out in his two books a theological discussion of the problems of the Church's relation to its environment due to the extension of the time, which had at the beginning been overshadowed by the imminent expectation. Luke discusses these matters in a wide-ranging reflection on the position of the Church in the world; he determines its position there in terms of salvation history and draws out the rules necessary for its attitude towards the world.[30]

To begin with, he examines the indications in Luke's work of political apologetic, which he finds especially in the story of the passion, and in some parts of the missionary journey (p. 138). However, he rejects the theory that Acts might be a written vindication for use in Paul's trial (p. 137, note 1). This follows simply from the fact that he dates Luke's book several decades after Paul's death. In any case, the political apologetic is not adapted to the single case of Paul's trial, but is fundamental in character; besides, it can be read between the lines throughout Luke's gospel. It allows for the state to last for a long time; thus it stands on the far side of the imminent expectation. An attempt is now made to enter into a conversation with the state and to reach a permanent settlement, whereas formerly it had only been endured eschatologically (p. 138). As evidence, Conzelmann adduces the following passages: The sermon of the Baptist with its ethical instructions addressed to officials of the state, the military and the administration, conveys to them the correct moral teaching. This implies loyalty to the state (Luke 3.10–14). The messianic programme in Jesus' first speech in Nazareth (4.18) is non-political in character (p. 138). Jesus' political inoffensiveness is confirmed even by Herod (9.7–9; 23.8–11) (pp. 138f.). However, we do not think that the reason given in 3.19 for the Baptist's arrest is of a non-political nature, as Conzelmann supposes (p. 138); to criticize the moral behaviour of an oriental potentate is not only not non-political, but highly dangerous!

The description of Jerusalem in terms of salvation history (13.34, 35) refutes any idea that the journey had a political meaning; it is traced back to a divine plan ($\delta\epsilon\hat{\iota}$) (13.33). In the acclamation of the people at the entry the concept of the lordship of David is replaced by the title of king, which for Luke is non-political; this completely deprives the entry of a political-messianic character (19.38) (p. 139). Luke leaves no doubt about the limits of loyalty when a confession to

[30] *Ibid.*, p. 137. Cf. also E. Käsemann, 'Begründet der neutestamentliche Kanon die Einheit der Kirche?' *EvTh* 11, 1951/2, p. 14.

kings and governors is required (12.11); yet he also allows for a wisdom which they cannot resist. Luke takes Pilate, Gallio, Felix, and Festus as examples to show what must be said to the state and of what the state must take note, if it does not wish to abandon its own legal position; for to confess oneself to be a Christian implies no crime against Roman law (pp. 139f.).

The reverse side of this loyalty is the evidence that the Jews are lying in their accusations. In Acts there is only one case of Roman intervention in a Jewish agitation which had already occurred.[31] The Gallio-scene is a picture of ideal behaviour on the part of the state officials (p. 142). In Luke's opinion there is no genuine conflict between God and the Emperor, nor does one arise out of the cult of the Emperor (p. 148, note 4).

Luke's political attitude is marked by two points of view; towards the Jews he maintains that God must be obeyed rather than men (Acts 5.29), towards the Empire that what is Caesar's should be rendered to Caesar, what is God's to God (Luke 20.25) (p. 148). Conzelmann also lays stress on the fact that Luke's apologetic writing is not only a part of his practical attitude to the world, but that it rests on fundamental reflection along the lines of salvation history. The cardinal themes along these lines in Luke's plan are connected with the discontinuance of the expectation and the resulting attempt to reach a long-term settlement over the world conditions (p. 149).

In the discourses in the first part of Acts, we can see how Luke has now transferred to the Church the concepts which were originally applied to the position of Israel in salvation history, especially the traditional terminology of 'people' (λαός) (pp. 162f.). This is merely mentioned in advance, because Wilckens will be dealing with the missionary speeches in the Acts particularly from the point of view of redaction criticism.[32]

The fourth main section, 'The Centre of History', examines Luke's christology as it is presented by the development of the position of Christ at the centre of salvation history. The centre of time, the period of Jesus' ministry, separates the first era, the time of Israel, from the time of the Church, the last era. This centre is also marked as the

---

[31] *Ibid.*, p. 140. Marxsen is of the opinion that nevertheless Luke shows no anti-semitism, but that it is his purpose to engage in conversation with the state (*Einleitung*, p. 141).

[32] U. Wilckens, *Die Missionsreden der Apostelgeschichte*, Neukirchen 1961 (ET in preparation).

period which is free from the activity of Satan (Luke 4.13; 22.3).[33] In the context of Luke's christology, Conzelmann, after analysing the statements about the relation of the Father to the Son, reaches the conclusion that Luke has given no thought explicitly to this essential relation, but that he has accepted the concept of subordination which he found in the tradition before him. According to this concept, Jesus appears as the instrument of God, who alone determines the plan of salvation. But from the standpoint of the community Jesus' activity appears to be in complete unity with that of the Father. Moreover, the relation between the Father and the Son is regarded mainly from the point of view of the division of the history of salvation.[34]

Luke no longer counts on a parousia which is actually imminent, but only on the reality of a future act of judgment, though he does not reflect on its distance in time; hence the figure of Jesus is now seen by him in a historical past. It is true that the parousia, as well as Jesus' life, is significant for the present day; but an important change has taken place. The significance of the parousia for Luke's present time no longer consists in its being near at hand, but in the fact that at some time in the future it will be of decisive importance. For Luke's present, Jesus' significance appears in a twofold aspect: by the outpouring of the spirit he shows himself to be the living one in heaven, and by the communication of his words and deeds he is also present in the picture given of him in the tradition (pp. 186f.). We must not deduce from Luke's eschatology that one should be resigned to the failure of the parousia to appear. On the contrary, in view of the fact that the fulfilment of scripture has already taken place in Jesus' appearance, his historical scheme is intended to urge that men should not feel resigned, but that in the interval they should disregard the moment of the parousia and take comfort in the fact that this appearance of Jesus has been a unique event in time (p. 195).

[33] H. Conzelmann, op. cit., p. 170. A different view in G. Baumbach, Das Verständnis des Bösen in den synoptischen Evangelien, Berlin 1963, pp. 162f.

[34] H. Conzelmann, op. cit., p. 184. Glombitza adds a supplement to Luke's christology by his examination of the titles διδάσκαλος and ἐπιστάτης in Luke. He states that διδάσκαλος applied to Jesus in Luke occurs only in the mouth of strangers. The title is avoided often in comparison with the other synoptists. Instead he uses the title ἐπιστάτης (found only in Luke in the New Testament), and he does so because in his view Jesus is a man with full authority. The title appears particularly in passages in which Jesus is challenged to reveal his full authority (5.5; 8.24; 8.45; 9.35, 49; 17.13). The considered use of these titles is the

In the last main section Conzelmann investigates Luke's view about the Church and the appropriation of salvation. In Luke the individual believer stands in the Church, which by its mediation makes it possible to render insignificant the temporal distance of the individual from the period of Jesus. For the nearness of this event is replaced by the Church's continuous activity (pp. 207f.). Luke intends to show by his picture of the Church how the message takes place in the midst of the world as it pursues its way. This life of the Church is presented by describing the primitive community as an example, and also by reflecting on the unique quality of that situation. For Luke does not wish to depict a timeless ideal of a church nor to demand from his contemporaries that they should restore or preserve the conditions of those days. Luke presents the Church as the successor of Israel, but beyond this he offers no speculation about its nature (p. 209).

In Luke the position of the Church in the world is conditioned by persecution, and it is the task of the Church as conceived by Luke to make possible the endurance of the Church in the third era of salvation history.[35]

Here the question must certainly be raised whether Conzelmann is correct in his view that in Acts Luke has drawn the picture of an *ecclesia pressa*. He certainly mentions persecution, but also a connection between persecution and propagation of the Gospel (Acts 5.41-42; 9.15-16). In my opinion the general tone of Acts is determined by the growth of the Church, whilst the persecutions are only short episodes and contribute directly to the extension of Christianity, as for example the persecution in

---

expression of Luke's theological conception; he wishes to show that the Church in this world is not a school of philosophers and that Jesus is not the head of such a school; for the title ἐπιστάτης is not used anywhere else for the head of a school of philosophers (see O. Glombitza, 'Die Titel διδάσκαλος und ἐπιστάτης für Jesus bei Lukas', *ZNW* 49, 1958, pp. 275-8.

[35] *Ibid.*, pp. 209f.; G. Braumann's thesis ('Das Mittel der Zeit', *ZNW* 54, 1963, p. 121), that the starting point for understanding Luke's intention is to be sought in his account of the persecution of the church seems to me to be questionable. In his view, it expresses the problems of Christian faith at the time of Luke more comprehensively and more topically than the delay of the parousia. In fact, however, the viewpoint of political apologetic must be kept in mind in the account of the persecutions of the church, and this is only one—and by no means the central— aspect of the Gospel of Luke. Moreover, for Luke a persecution never reaches its goal, but always has a contrary result, as Acts shows. But Braumann bases his thesis merely on the eschatological texts in Luke.

connection with the stoning of Stephen (Acts 8.1–2, 4–5; 11.19–21) and the ambushes laid by the Jews for Paul which always resulted in the Gospel being handed on to the Gentiles (Acts 13.45–51; 14.4–7, 19–21; 16.19–34; 17.5–10; 18.6–11; 19.8–10). Finally Paul, as a prisoner, brings the Gospel into the capital of the world. Thus the picture given in the Acts is dominated by the picture of a victorious advance by the Gospel. In this way the purpose announced in Acts 1.8 as the subject-matter of this book has been accomplished and the path of the Gospel has been traced from Jerusalem through Judaea and Samaria to the ends of the earth. These words may be intended to mean Rome, perhaps even the whole area within the *Imperium Romanum*.

Conzelmann rejects the idea of describing Luke's concept of the Church in terms of early Catholicism, for the later concept of offices in the Church is only slightly developed by him. He is indeed aware that some men perform official duties in the communities (Acts 11.30; 14.23; 20.28), but there is no question of establishing definite concepts. We cannot speak of early Catholicism until there is in existence a firmly regulated idea of a tradition and order of succession with a firm chain for the transmission of offices. Instead of this, everything is made to depend on the special role of the apostles and evangelists in transmitting the spirit; there is nothing about offices. The office-bearers in Luke's day are therefore still qualified by the spirit and not yet by a particular succession (pp. 217f.). His church and its history are not yet considered as a factor in salvation in the sense of being an object of faith. True, it is also a necessary medium for handing on the message, but it is not yet an entity playing a part in its own right in the saving events. Thus the third article of the creed is not yet actually developed. But Luke has certainly created the presuppositions for it, since he describes the existence of the Church in the categories of salvation history (p. 225).[36]

Lastly, Conzelmann examines Luke's soteriology. Luke describes the Christian life not in spiritual, but in ethical categories. In spite of the reference to God's activity when a man is converted and becomes a believer, the man's share is also brought out (p. 226). Now that the long period of the Church has been substituted for the imminent expectation, the road to salvation becomes a matter of concern and the theme of the message is no longer the coming of the kingdom, out

---

[36] *Ibid.*, p. 225; for the problem of early Catholicism see also E. Käsemann, *Exegetische Versuche und Besinnungen* I, pp. 130–4, 158–68, 198f.; II, pp. 29f., 240f. and 241 n.1., 249, 264.

of which the summons to repentance had previously arisen of its own accord (p. 227).

Moreover, eternal life as an object of hope for the individual believer has been moved into the distance, since the eschaton as understood by Luke no longer denotes a present, but a future eventuality. In Luke, the believer no longer possesses eternal life himself, but only the hope of it. But this is stronger than the distance in time until the dawn of God's kingdom, and it is already guaranteed by the existence of the Church and the presence of the Spirit. Thus future life is no longer dependent on the nearness of God's rule, and as a hope it can await the fulfilment of the promise (p. 230). Because the period of time after conversion is extended, the themes which influence the shaping of daily life became more prominent, and independent ethical considerations begin to be defined. The *vita Christiana* replaces the eschatological community with its imminent expectations. Practical problems are treated by preference, and arise out of the situation of the Church in the continuing world. Luke is the first to have thought out the connection between the delay of the parousia and exhortation (12.35–38), even though this connection had been already recognized earlier.[37]

Luke developed his ethics out of traditional material, not out of ideals, but he selected for emphasis particular matters in the circumstances of his time. Neither in the gospel nor in Acts is poverty an *ideal*. Even the possession of property in common is not an ideal which holds good for the present time, but is a feature belonging to the early days of the Church. Luke no longer demands it for his own times (p. 233). 'Luke's ethical thinking is determined not by "imitatio" but by discipleship, in a form appropriate to the particular time. Therefore there is no ideal of the "imitatio" of the apostles either' (p. 233).

We will now endeavour to produce a final verdict on Conzelmann's work:

(1) By a careful comparison of Luke's gospel with that of Mark he has set out the modifications made by Luke in the parallel text

---

[37] *Ibid.*, p. 232. Strecker advances against Conzelmann the view that in Luke it is not a question of de-eschatologizing in consequence of the extension of the time, but of modifying the understanding of eschatology itself. For salvation history as understood by the synoptists is simply a matter of connecting the historical with the eschatological aspect. This follows from the fact that Luke presents the history of salvation in contrast to that of the world: Luke 3.1; Acts 14.15–17; 17.24–27 (G. Strecker, *op. cit.*, pp. 47f., note 2).

of Mark, and has thus detected the difference in the theology of the two evangelists.

(2) His inclusion of Acts in the investigation must be seen against the background of the studies in Acts by Dibelius and Vielhauer. Conzelmann goes further than Dibelius in so far as he places not only the author of Acts, but the author of the gospel as well, in the ranks of the 'historians'.

(3) Following Lohmeyer, he has attempted to look closely at the framework of Jesus' story as an entity of a special kind and to interpret it, although he does not share Lohmeyer's theory of two primitive communities in Galilee and Jerusalem. Conzelmann brings forward fresh points of view, especially when analysing the travel account.

(4) Conzelmann has not advanced any particular theories as to the sources of Luke's gospel; on the contrary, he has called them irrelevant and has instead taken for granted the classical two-document theory.

(5) What is new in Conzelmann's work is above all the elaboration of the central basic idea of Luke's two books, namely that Luke, in consequence of the failure of the parousia to appear, has given up the imminent expectation of it and put in its place the theory of a history of salvation which proceeds in stages. The idea of regarding Luke's historical work as the result of the crisis of the delayed parousia has been accepted particularly by those scholars who belong directly or indirectly to the school of Bultmann. In the discussion with Cullmann, who in his study *Christ and Time* sees the whole New Testament dominated by the thought of salvation history, Conzelmann himself certainly stands on Bultmann's side; he regards the idea of salvation history first as a product of the disappointed imminent expectation and as a theory conceived by Luke. The problem of the influence of the delayed parousia on the division of salvation history into periods in the synoptists has been solved in a different way by Strecker. He has elaborated in Matthew's gospel, too, the indications worked out by Conzelmann of a tripartite character in salvation history, and has identified them to a lesser degree in Mark as well.[38]

(6) We must, however, put to Conzelmann the question whether he does not lay too strong an emphasis on this idea and thus approaches fatally close to 'consistent' eschatology, which in fact regards the failure of the parousia to appear and the crisis resulting from this as the prime mover in the development of primitive

[38] G. Strecker, *op. cit.*, pp. 122, 185; see especially the appendix on Matthew.

Christianity. We ought at least to expect from Conzelmann a definite statement as to whether he regards the non-appearance of the parousia as the element in Luke's historical work which basically determines it, or as merely one amongst others. On this point it seems to me that Conzelmann's conception needs to be put right. On the other hand, he may have seen correctly that Luke explained away the possible shock felt by faith when the imminent expectation remained unfulfilled, by shifting the emphasis in his historical writing rather on to the past and the present, and by replacing the expectation of the speedy coming of the kingdom by the notion of the activity of the Holy Spirit.[39] Luke does indeed reckon with the imminent expectation of the end, even when he describes the history of Israel, the time of Jesus and that of the Church as the elapsing of a divine plan. Nevertheless, the end is possible at any time (cf. Luke 12.38 with Mark 13.35). Perhaps we must also make a distinction, as Strecker does, between eliminating what is eschatological and modifying the structure of the eschatological self-understanding. He has demonstrated that the historical method, not only in Luke but particularly in Matthew as well, does not mean elimination, but that in spite of the structure being modified, the orientation towards eschatology, the dialectic between history and eschatology, remains the determining element.

(7) As regards his methodology, we must ask Conzelmann how he obtained the criteria for discovering the original eschatological expectation of Jesus and of the early Christian community. This question is just as acute in Grässer's study of the problem of the delay of the parousia.

(8) Unlike Marxsen's redaction-critical studies Conzelmann has not attempted to determine a *Sitz im Leben* in the primitive Church for Luke's historical work as a whole. Instead, he has restricted himself to working out the theological characteristics of this work. We can, however, learn indirectly from many individual comments that he places it at the extreme end of the apostolic era, in any case some time after the destruction of Jerusalem.

(9) We cannot occasionally resist the impression that Conzelmann draws too far-reaching conclusions from some few isolated observations in order to be able to carry through his conception, or that he bases his theses on too few references in the text, or indeed on none. Thus Baumbach has shown that contrary to Conzelmann's view (*Theology*

[39] Against this see G. Strecker, *ibid.*, pp. 47f., note 2.

of St Luke, p. 170) the time of Jesus between Luke 4.13 and 22.3 was by no means the 'centre of time' exempt from sin, but that it contains statistically the majority of statements about Satan (8.12; 10.18; 11.14ff.; 13.10ff.) and that Luke in 10.1–20 actually represents the mission as a victorious struggle against Satan and as a 'prefigurement' of the time of the Church which began on Whit Sunday. Even the statements about Satan in Acts serve to demonstrate the victory over Satan of the Spirit at work in the missionaries and the community.[40] Nevertheless, on the whole Conzelmann's book has given a quite decisive stimulus to the latest research on Luke.

B. Walter Grundmann *The Gospel of Luke*

In his commentary on Mark (1959), Grundmann had pointed out explicitly that his exposition is a necessary new edition of the first edition of the commentary by F. Hauck, written under the influence of form-critical work, and that it was now prompted by the questions posed by redaction criticism.[41] An explicit reference to redaction-critical research does not in fact occur in his *Commentary on Luke* (1961), but in fact the redaction-critical method has also decisively influenced him here; for he goes further back still and discusses the whole study of the synoptists since the turn of the century, beginning with the source criticism of Wellhausen, Bernhard, and Johannes Weiss, continued through Bussmann to Emanuel Hirsch, and then the commentaries of Schlatter and Klostermann and form-critical work since the fundamental studies of Bultmann and Dibelius.

The extent to which redaction-critical findings have a share in Grundmann's exegesis is shown, for example, in the fact that he denotes Luke's historical work, following Marxsen,[42] as διήγησις (Luke 1.1); here he announces the fact that from the very first Luke did not plan his work as the history of Jesus Christ, but included in it at the same time the progress of the preaching from Jerusalem to Rome (p. 1). Naturally Conzelmann's commentary exerted an even greater influence than Marxsen's on that of Grundmann. Grundmann also refers again and again to the shorter articles written in connection with Conzelmann's studies by Lohse (p. 2, note 5; p. 6, note 17 *et passim*), Wilckens (p. 2, note 7; note 6; p. 6, note 16 *et passim*), and Luck (p. 4, note 9 *et passim*).

[40] G. Baumbach, *op. cit.*, pp. 182f.
[41] W. Grundmann, *Evangelium nach Markus*, p. 23.
[42] W. Marxsen, *Evangelist Markus*, p. 13 *et passim*.

We may use some examples to show the extent of the influence of Conzelmann and Marxsen on Grundmann's commentary. He emphasizes with Conzelmann that in Luke's conception the story of Jesus is the middle of time (p. 452), but this does not thereby bring eschatological expectation to an end (pp. 4f.). Luke's conception must be understood bearing in mind the situation at the time when the gospel was written, the chief features of which were that it was the end of the apostolic age and that the parousia had not appeared. Thus it became necessary both to ward off the Gnostics' mythicizing of the historical and eschatological actions of God, and to detach the expected parousia from definite points of time (p. 5). Marxsen evaluates this procedure positively against the background of Gnosticism, but qualifies Conzelmann's assertion that Luke had removed eschatology from Jesus' preaching: 'When time was experienced as a problem with which one had to come to terms, the complicated eschatology was lost. Its futuristic elements were retained, and the spirit and the name provided compensation for the contemporary elements which were now excluded. In this way, in spite of the experience of the lapse of time the danger of falling into Gnosticism was averted.'[43]

Grundmann accepts the difference between the gospels of Mark and Luke worked out by Marxsen's redaction criticism, and he expresses the opinion that Luke's gospel, unlike that of Mark, had become an account intended to safeguard the testimony of eyewitnesses at the end of the apostolic age for the era of the Church; his standpoint is the Church which believes in Jesus Christ (pp. 5f.).

The appraisal of the apocalyptic discourse in its Lucan form (Luke 21) is influenced strongly by Marxsen's study. It is made to fit the historical situation which had changed in comparison with that of Mark, and it has detached the time of the parousia from that of the Jewish War; on the other hand, it is influenced authoritatively by the image of the apostolic age in Acts (p. 14). Thus we can already see to how large an extent Grundmann has made use of the opinion expressed by Conzelmann on Luke's eschatology.[44] He also accepts Conzelmann's thesis of Luke's political apologetics towards Rome which occur in his historical work.[45] In general he observes the

[43] W. Marxsen, *Exegese und Verkündigung*, p. 27; quoted from W. Grundmann, *op. cit.*, p. 5, note 12.

[44] *Ibid.*, p. 29; cf. also p. 378 (on Luke 21).

[45] *Ibid.*, p. 31; also on Luke 20.20ff. (p. 373); on the scene of the arrest (Luke 22.47–53) (p. 413).

principle laid down by redaction criticism that the task of research today is not to establish fresh source-theories,[46] but to investigate Luke's work as a whole, how it was fitted together by the evangelist out of his prototypes and bears unmistakably his own stamp (p. 17).

Conzelmann's influence makes itself felt particularly in the analysis which is made of the Lucan travel account. Conzelmann had argued that Luke presented Jesus' going to Jerusalem as his going to suffering, his awareness of his suffering as a journey.[47] Schneider, on the other hand, in his analysis of the travel account had pointed out the trend here towards teaching and exhortation as well,[48] and he perceived in it that Luke was shaping ecclesiology and ethics in order to mould the church and the life of individuals, in view of the delay of the parousia (p. 218). Grundmann now sums up the insights of both these scholars and concludes that Luke's travel account portrays Jesus as a teacher facing death, who knows about his death and is resolutely on his way towards it (p. 200).

By means of repeatedly interspersed travel notes, the whole section is divided into three parts; each of these mentions the travel situation at the beginning, and in between inserts sections from Jesus' teaching in longer excursuses. (1) Luke 9.51–13.21 with the excursus in 11.1–13.21; (2) 13.22–17.10 with the excursus in 14.1–17.10; (3) 17.11–19.27 with the excursus in 17.20–19.27.[49] Schneider had also emphasized that the so-called community theology had grown out of Jesus' sayings, not the other way round, and that Luke by the manner in which he reports and groups the material is serving a purpose which extends beyond the original historical situation into the situation of the community;[50] Grundmann, on the other hand, asserts against Schneider's point of view a 'not only . . . but also'; for 'Luke's work as an author which contains aspects of christology and salvation history is itself community theology; but it is filled out with Jesus' sayings which give it weight. However, its wording is not only a literary question, but is at the same time stamped by theology.'[51]

[46] Thus also H. Conzelmann, *The Theology of Luke*, p. 9.

[47] H. Conzelmann, *op. cit.*, p. 65.

[48] J. Schneider, 'Zur Analyse des lukanischen Reiseberichtes' in: *Synoptische Studien, Alfred Wikenhauser dargebracht*, Munich 1953, p. 219, also pp. 220f., 223.

[49] *Ibid.*, p. 200; *id.*, 'Fragen der Komposition des lukanischen Reiseberichtes', *ZNW*, 50, 1959, p. 259.

[50] J. Schneider, *op. cit.*, p. 221.

[51] W. Grundmann, 'Fragen der Komposition des lukanischen Reiseberichtes', *loc. cit.*, p. 258, note 25.

C. Eduard Lohse   *Luke the Theologian of Salvation History*

In two articles, Lohse has taken up the suggestions of Conzelmann, especially as regards his method, though without having been dependent on him in writing. First, he understands the author of Acts and the third gospel to be a theologian working according to a plan with a definite conception, and secondly, he understands both parts of Luke's historical work as a material and theological unity. This already appears in the titles of the two essays: 'The Significance of the Account of the Pentecost in the Framework of Luke's Historical Work'[52] and 'Luke as a Theologian of Salvation History'.[53]

The first article aims at illustrating Luke's concept, seen in similar terms to those presented by Conzelmann, by a particular example; the second attempts to substantiate more fully the salvation-historical view of Jesus' life and the history of the Church worked out in Luke's historical books. The fact that Lohse takes roughly the same standpoint as Conzelmann shows that shortly after 1950 the question of the theology of the gospels was as it were in the air, like that of form criticism about 1920. It is unmistakable that Lohse has described Luke's particular theology with *sympathy*, whereas Conzelmann restricted himself to a purely objective rendering of this Lucan theology without appraising it, and Vielhauer criticizes it severely in comparison with Paul's theology.

Lohse refuses to solve the problem of the story of Pentecost either by analysing the sources (pp. 426f.) or by discovering analogies with the help of the history of religion (Jewish feast of weeks and harvest festival) (p. 430). A solution can be found only by enquiring what Luke wanted to express by means of this story (p. 430). By bringing the story of Pentecost into connection with the promise of the prophet Joel, he places the events which he reports in a context of salvation history (p. 432). Luke has constructed the story of Pentecost out of the theme of the promise which is being fulfilled. For him, this is the beginning of a new period of salvation history, the last stage before the parousia of Christ and the end of the world, so that Pentecost is at the same time the conclusion of the events which began with Jesus' Passover meal in Jerusalem (p. 433). Thus the story of

[52] E. Lohse, 'Die Bedeutung des Pfingstberichtes im Rahmen des lukanischen Geschichtswerkes', *EvTh* 13, 1953, pp. 422–36.
[53] E. Lohse, 'Lukas als Theologe der Heilsgeschichte', published in *EvTh* 14, 1954, pp. 256–75.

Pentecost, fitted firmly into the framework of Luke's historical work, points back into the past to the promise of the Risen One (Luke 24.49) and forwards into the future to the Christian Church. Thus it is the gateway at the beginning of Church history. Consequently the story of Pentecost bears the stamp of Luke's theology of salvation history, whilst the statements of the external framework are for Luke uninteresting and superfluous, so that the accurate statements of a historian are not to be expected (p. 434).

Lohse has attempted in the other article to explain in more detail how far Luke can be claimed as a theologian of salvation history. What he writes about the external literary method of Luke in his use of the traditional material handed down to him does not in fact go beyond what has long been common knowledge amongst scholars; yet his appraisal of it is fresh, although he remains of course, as we have already said, completely within the framework of the findings which Conzelmann has already presented. Luke places his historical work completely at the service of his theological task (p. 261).

Lohse had already stated in the article previously discussed that Luke used the theme of realized fulfilment at particularly important turning points (p. 261), and he had given as an example of this the fact that the travel account (Luke 9.51) and the story of Pentecost (Acts 2.1) were introduced by almost the same words (p. 432). He deduces from this that Luke had taken as his subject and his task the description of the course of the events which were being fulfilled, and the demonstration by his outline of how the events of salvation continued, beyond the life of the earthly Jesus, in the Church (p. 264). Luke, therefore, does not intend simply to present the early Christian kerygma of the death and resurrection of Christ, but he sketches a Christian view of history in which the salvation events continue to happen in salvation history within the Church until the end of time (p. 265). From his position in the Church which believes in Jesus Christ, Luke now divides up the course of salvation history into separate sections (p. 266). It is in accord, too, with this advance and course of salvation history that Jesus in Luke's gospel, and Paul in Acts, go first into the synagogue of the Jews (p. 267). For Luke, salvation history reaches its goal in the parousia, but until then a prescribed series of ultimate events must be unrolled. Luke has arranged the synoptic apocalypse taken over from Mark into separate sections, and has therefore postponed the end still further (p. 275, also note 81).

It may have become evident by these few remarks how much Lohse depends on the preceding work of Conzelmann, to whose programmatic ideas he has attempted to give a concrete form.

D. Ulrich Luck   *The Retreat to Form Criticism*

Luck makes an attempt in his article 'Kerygma, Tradition and History of Jesus in Luke'[54] to advance beyond redaction criticism. In fact, however, he does not do so, but turns back to the form-critical studies of Dibelius; for he follows Dibelius' thesis that Luke's gospel is not itself the content of the preaching of his day, but the guarantee for this content.[55] As a counter to redaction criticism he stresses that even when an outline of salvation history in Luke has been worked out, his real theological concern has not yet been grasped, and the problem of his theology has not yet been solved (p. 53). It does not become quite clear what Luck wants to set against redaction criticism, or with what he wants to replace it; for in spite of his critical objections to it he remains to a large extent within the framework of its questions and answers. He does so, for instance, when he states that Luke in his gospel attempts to solve the problem of understanding past history as divine history with the present activity of the spirit in mind (p. 65), or when he remarks that Luke in the design of his historical work brings about the continuity between the Church and the life of Jesus, and seeks to grasp the unique character of Jesus' story for his contemporaries (p. 66).

E. Hans-Werner Bartsch   *The Admonition to Constant Watchfulness*

Hans-Werner Bartsch's book *Wachet aber zu jeder Zeit!* (Be vigilant at all times) is the printed version of a lecture series given by Bartsch on Luke's gospel. The very title of the book is a programme, a radical contrast to the interpretations of Luke's work by Conzelmann and Grässer and other representatives of the redaction-critical method which eliminate its eschatology. Bartsch certainly concedes that Luke wants to correct the existing views, but he disputes vigorously that the imminent expectation is the problem with which Luke is dealing, and that it is rooted in the point of departure of Christian faith (p. 7 *et passim*).

[54] U. Luck, 'Kerygma, Tradition und Geschichte Jesu bei Lukas', *ZThK* 57, 1960, pp. 51–66.
[55] *Ibid.*, p. 56; cf. M. Dibelius, *From Tradition to Gospel*, p. 15.

In terms of method Bartsch does not in fact start from redaction criticism, but from the form-critical approach of Dibelius, which was to enquire consistently about the motives of the tradition and of the redaction (p. 9, cf. p. 11). But as he presupposes that in his version of the gospel Luke has made corrections to the two other synoptists, he is in fact working on the lines of redaction criticism as well. The starting point of his criticism of Conzelmann and Grässer is Lohmeyer's thesis (*Galiläa und Jerusalem*) that the primitive community had originally expected Jesus' resurrection and parousia to be one and the same event. Luke's theological purpose is to deal with the breakdown of the gnostic-Christian view of the identity of resurrection and parousia. What he is resisting is on the one hand the false doctrine mentioned in II Tim. 2.18, which asserts that the resurrection has already taken place (cf. I Cor. 15.12), on the other hand the complete falling off of interest in eschatology as a result of the breakdown of the views held hitherto. Luke had indeed on the one hand given up the idea of a definite time for the parousia, but on the other hand he emphatically urged constant readiness for an imminent end (pp. 8f.).

It follows from the prologue to his gospel that Luke does not wish to disparage his predecessors (like Josephus), but that he lays stress on his connection with them. Bartsch describes the work of the author as the first piece of Christian literature which is nevertheless rooted in the tradition of the community and its purposes. He shares with Dibelius the view that Luke wishes by means of his two books to introduce the Christian message into literature (p. 13, cf. p. 14). According to the prologue to the Acts of the Apostles, Luke wished to write in his gospel an account of all that Jesus began to do and to teach, but in Acts he wished to report the deeds of Jesus as the exalted one who carries on his activity in the spirit through his own (p. 13). Bartsch differs from Haenchen, Vielhauer, and Wilckens in seeing Luke as the physician and Paul's companion of that name (Col. 4.14) who is also identical with the Lucius in Rom. 16.21. The information given in II Tim. 4.11 also deserves to be trusted, since the Pastoral Epistles reproduce the tradition about the year 100 (p. 14).

As a result of his basic thesis about Luke's gospel, Bartsch begins his exegesis with the Easter stories. Since he starts from Dibelius' preaching theory and regards as primary the interest in preaching which had begun with the Easter preaching, he can state that 'the gospel offers the material for the preaching of the first community and must be understood with this in mind' (p. 15). Nevertheless, the Easter stories in the synoptic gospels are only a late step in the development; perhaps the empty grave is only an attempted proof of the factuality of the resurrection and a substitute for the original view that the appearances were the beginning of the return. With Dibelius, and contrary to Wilckens, he traces the pattern of the missionary sermons in the speeches of Acts back to an early formula (p. 15). Luke had expunged the references to Galilean appearances because he had discovered in the interval that the parousia had not begun with the events in Galilee. He had expunged these appearances like other predictions which had not been fulfilled. The reference to the appearances in Galilee, understood as the start of the parousia, signified the first postponement of the parousia, but still preserved the connection with the resurrection (pp. 21f.).

The rest of the exegesis of Luke's gospel presented in this study made by Bartsch takes the pericopes in turn and begins with the early stories. Bartsch considers that these were also based on the Easter event, and on the particular understanding of it handed down by the community. Their truth content does not consist in the history reported, but in this very point of departure: the Easter event which had caused them to be reported. All the early stories must be understood as a declaration by the community which confesses that, on the strength of the Easter event which brought the community into being, the Kyrios Jesus had been Kyrios from the beginning. The early stories are authoritative because they are founded on the community's confession of the Easter event, not on the accuracy of Luke's historical research. Especially the association of the Baptist and Jesus in the birth story of John supports this understanding. Bartsch can even express it thus: 'The praises of the angels' song were first heard by the community at Easter', and, 'the worshipping shepherds are identical with the centurion under the cross' (p. 34). Bartsch differs fundamentally from Conzelmann in his exegesis of Luke's description of the relationship between Jesus and the Baptist. Whereas Conzelmann disputes that they correspond typologically except in the early stories, Bartsch maintains that they do so even outside these stories. For instance: the Pharisees and lawyers rejected the Baptist as they rejected Jesus (Luke 7.30); Luke employs the same expression εὐαγγελίσασθαι for Jesus' preaching in 4.18; 4.43; 9.6 as in 3.18 for the preaching of the Baptist; Luke also deletes the passage about the Baptist's ascetic way of life to be found in Mark 1.6. Whereas the absence of an account of the Baptist's death in Luke is taken by Conzelmann as a proof that Luke wished to avoid establishing a parallelism with Jesus, Bartsch explains this omission by the desperate expedient that the corresponding legend was missing in the version of the second gospel before Luke; for Mark 6.17–29 is an interpolation (pp. 44f.). Bartsch disputes Conzelmann's view that Luke had separated the areas of activity of the Baptist (Jordan) from those of Jesus, for Jesus was active in Jericho which is also on the Jordan; but he forgets that in Luke's Jericho stories (ch. 18 and 19) this geographical term does not occur (p. 45). Bartsch disagrees with Conzelmann that Luke has eliminated the Baptist's role of forerunner. According to Luke 16.16, Luke does understand the Baptist as the end of the old covenant and not as a forerunner; that is why he also omitted the conversation during the descent from the Mount of the Transfiguration and Mark 15.35f. But Luke does not do this (p. 88), because in his view a new era begins with Jesus to which the Baptist does not belong. For in fact by means of his three eschatological discourses in chs. 12, 17 and 21 Luke emphasizes more strongly than Matthew and Mark Jesus' eschatological message and explicitly rejects the decline of eschatology (Luke 12.45f.). Looking back dispassionately, he states that the parousia did not take place when Jesus rose again, but that we must still wait for it. He shaped the passion story as a martyr's story and not as an eschatological occurrence. He draws a parallel between the Baptist and Jesus, and he does not identify the Baptist with Elijah, because he did not mark the beginning of the eschatological happenings (p. 46f.).

For Luke, the Baptist is the forerunner only in the sense that both were seen to be parallel, but not in the sense that with Jesus the end had already come and that the Baptist was a forerunner of this end. So in his revision of the material concerning the Baptist, Luke is actuated only by a historical, and not by any theological point of view.[56] In Luke, the account of Jesus' baptism becomes merely the description of how the word of God came to Jesus, but contrary to Mark's account the baptism is not understood eschatologically in the nature of a sign. In Luke 3.2, the word of God came to John as well; this again produces a parallelism. Thus for Luke, Jesus and John are

[56] *Ibid.*, p. 47. Cf. also the exegesis of the discourse about the Baptist in Luke 7.18–35, *ibid.*, pp. 82ff.

both historical figures who have not ushered in the final events; but the Baptist is not a caesura between two eras of the one continuous history (p. 53).

Bartsch considers Luke's Sermon on the Plain to have a more eschatological stamp than Matthew's Sermon on the Mount, which has a somewhat hortatory tone. The direct form of address in the Sermon on the Plain has its *Sitz im Leben* in preaching. With the Sermon on the Plain and its character in mind we might conclude from Luke's gospel that the eschatological message was its central theme (p. 75f.).

Bartsch makes the account of the journey finish in 18.14, unlike Conzelmann who does not end it until the entry into Jerusalem (Luke 19.29ff.). He also disagrees with the latter's statement that Jesus' awareness of his suffering is expressed as a journey; in his view Jesus' life is directed towards suffering. He thus rejects Conzelmann's theological consistency, while recognizing the connection between travel and suffering (pp. 94f.).

It is the fundamental thesis of Bartsch that Luke is not rectifying the imminent expectation nor is he engaged in removing eschatology from the tradition, but is only eliminating with complete consistency the identification of resurrection and parousia. Hence Bartsch pays special attention to the eschatological sections in Luke (12.13–13.9; 17.20–18.8; 19.11–27; 21.8–31) in order to use them to expound his basic thesis again and again. To assume an imminent expectation in the primitive Church is merely a working hypothesis which requires constant scrutiny. Therefore the question must be raised whether Luke's conception is consistently to relinquish the imminent expectation and at the same time consistently to sustain the primitive Christian conception and thus consistently to criticize the imminent expectation of Jesus. We might ask, on the contrary, whether Luke does not intend to criticize the expectation of primitive Christendom which had already been modified.[57]

Bartsch starts from the working hypothesis that primitive Christendom did not take over Jesus' imminent expectation but testified that it had been fulfilled. From the correction of Mark 14.62 in Luke 22.69 he draws the conclusion that the original conception had been to identify resurrection and parousia. The work of Luke is to be

---

[57] *Ibid.*, p. 107; cf. also the redaction-critical context analysis of an eschatological section in Luke by G. Klein, 'Die Prüfung der Zeit (Lukas 12.54–56)', *ZThK* 61, 1964, pp. 373–90.

understood as a correction of this original conception of primitive
Christendom. The same purpose is served by the correction and modification of the eschatological pronouncements in the transmission of
Jesus' sayings (p. 10). In the parable of the pounds (Luke 19.11–27) he
corrects the view that there is a connection between the suffering and
death of Jesus and the Kingdom of God (παραχρῆμα in v. 11); this had
originally been expected when Jerusalem was approached (p. 110).
The words in the parable about watchfulness (Luke 12.35–46),
inculcating the duty to be constantly prepared for the expected
parousia, also show awareness of the fact that Jesus' resurrection had
not brought in the Kingdom (p. 112).

Bartsch attaches great importance to the evidence that Luke
refuses to answer the question when the parousia will take place. He
corrects the original view unequivocally but develops no alternative
to it, except possibly that of a distant expectation (p. 111). Undoubtedly the expectation of the immediate proximity of the final crisis is
also the decisive factor in the parable of the fig tree in Luke 13.6–9.
But the group of eschatological pronouncements in Luke 12f. does
not contain an answer to the question about the time of the parousia
(p. 113).

Bartsch regards the group of sayings in Luke 17.20–18.6 as being
explicitly concerned with the question of the time of the parousia and
the day of the Son of Man. Similarly the logion in Luke 17.20f.
(ἐντὸς ὑμῶν), about which there has been so much debate, is used by
Bartsch to serve his main thesis; originally it meant that the Kingdom
of God had come with the resurrection, as Jesus had promised.

In Luke, however, it means in its context the rejection of attempts
to fix its fulfilment. The promise as such is upheld and transmitted
without alteration; only the date is rejected: it may well appear
suddenly. Luke 17.22–24 also rejects the same view and denies that
men are already living in the days of the Son of Man. Instead, Luke
clings to the apocalyptic conception that the end will break in with
incalculable and overwhelming power (pp. 115f.). Against Conzelmann, Bartsch maintains that in the parable of the importunate
widow (Luke 18.1–8) there is no commendation of prayer as a custom
during the long period until the parousia, but the petition is expressed
for the ardently expected day of the parousia. The framework with
which Luke has surrounded this parable shows a very tense imminent
expectation to which he is issuing a summons (pp. 119f.).

In his exegesis of Luke's synoptic apocalypse Bartsch largely follows

Conzelmann so far as the pronouncements about the destruction of Jerusalem are concerned. Luke understands the destruction of Jerusalem, as he does the persecutions of the community, not in the context of the arrival of the eschaton, but as events in history (pp. 119f.). In Luke's version of the synoptic apocalypse, in comparison with that of Matthew and Mark, the Gentile mission is eliminated; Bartsch explains this fact by saying that Luke adheres consistently to the imminent expectation and therefore he rejects the condition that *first* the gospel must be preached to all nations. He is aware of no conditions for the end, and in v. 32 he also retains the saying from Mark 13.20 because he adheres to the imminent expectation which had replaced the view that the end had a connection with Jesus' death and resurrection. For this reason he has altered the ἀλλ' οὔπω τὸ τέλος from Mark 13.7 to πρῶτον ἀλλ' οὐκ εὐθέως τὸ τέλος in Luke 21.9. But this indicates no postponement of the time (contrary to Conzelmann), but only the construction of a succession of preceding events and of a succeeding end. Luke keeps the saying that the end is near, but cuts out the words ἐπὶ θύραις (cf. Mark 13.29 with Luke 21.31) (pp. 201f.). In Luke 21.32 the evangelist emphasizes the imminent expectation in a manner which is already almost a paradox. He has directed the succeeding warnings towards an *imminent* end, so that it does not cause an unexpected surprise (p. 123).

We shall recapitulate Bartsch's basic conception so as to reach a verdict about it. He assumes that Christian eschatological views started with the imminent expectation of Jesus. As a second step primitive Christianity assumed by reason of the appearance of the Risen One that the resurrection of Jesus and his parousia were one and the same. But in historical retrospect, Luke corrects this view on the basis of experiences up till then, and turns to intensify the imminence of the expectation, detaching it from any particular point of time whilst enjoining constant readiness.[58]

We consider that this conception, which in the last resort is based on Lohmeyer's construction of the history of early Christianity, is mistaken in its approach, in spite of its apparently imposing consistency. No attention is paid to Paul, who never suggests that resurrection and parousia are expected to be identical; at the most he thinks of present and future eschatology side by side,[59] a juxtaposition and

[58] See also his essay, 'Zum Problem der Parousieverzögerung bei den Synoptikern', *EvTh* 19, 1959, pp. 116–31.
[59] Cf. W. G. Kümmel, 'Futurische und präsentische Eschatologie im ältesten Christentum', *NTS* 5, 1958/9, pp. 113–26, especially pp. 123–5.

an intermingling of the experience of the present as the eschatological time of salvation and at the same time an eager anticipation of the impending eschatological consummation (cf. I Thess. 1.9f.; 4.13ff. with Gal. 1.4; Rom. 1.4 with I Cor. 11.26 and I Cor. 16.22) (p. 126); nor does Bartsch at all take into consideration the fact of the Acts of the Apostles. He ignores completely the basic principle of redaction criticism that Luke must be interpreted with the Acts in mind. It is indeed correct that Luke, unlike Matthew and Mark, has in his synoptic apocalypse eliminated the proclamation to the Gentiles from the context of the eschatological events, but in Luke 21.12–16 the fate of the missionaries of Acts is already described in anticipation.

It is admittedly correct, too, that Luke does not say, like Mark in 13.10, that the gospel must first be preached to all nations, and in comparison with Mark 13.27, omits the fact that the believers will be spread over the whole world; but in Acts he does in fact describe both these happenings. It is certainly not correct to say that Luke in ch. 21 eliminates the mission to the Gentiles because he clings consistently to the imminent expectation and rejects the condition that the Gospel must first be preached to all nations. For Acts contains no trace of all this; in fact, according to Acts 1.8 it is the scheme of the whole book to portray the advance of the Gospel to all nations, and Acts 1.7, 11 directly excludes an imminent expectation on Luke's part.

It is true that Luke preserves passages containing an imminent expectation in his gospel, but Acts shows that this has become only of minor significance and a doctrine of the last things. In fact it plays no greater role in Acts than it still does today in textbooks of dogmatic theology. The solution of the difficulties in Luke arising out of the delay of the parousia has remained the solution of the Church until the present day.

F. Philipp Vielhauer: *The Lucan Falsification of Paul*

Vielhauer stimulated an examination of Luke's work in terms of redaction criticism by raising the problem of a possible theology of Luke. In his article 'On the "Paulinism" of Acts'[60] he posed the question whether a specifically Lucan image of Paul can be found in Acts. Whereas Haenchen questions by means of external evidence whether Luke, the physician and companion of the apostle, is the

[60] 'Zum "Paulinismus" der Apostelgeschichte', *EvTh* 10, 1950/1, pp. 1–15.

author of the two Lucan books, Vielhauer on the other hand emphasizes the internal evidence, the different theology of Paul portrayed in Acts compared with the Paul of the epistles, and for this reason he declares himself against the authorship of Acts by the companion of Paul. Vielhauer is concerned more with Luke the theologian and his place within the history of primitive Christianity than with determining the relationship of tradition and composition in Luke.[61]

However, Vielhauer's enquiry into the characteristics of specific-ally Lucan theology is concerned merely with Paul's speeches in Acts, whereas Conzelmann dealt with the Lucan writings as a whole. Vielhauer writes: 'the enquiry into the Paulinism of Acts is at the same time an enquiry into a possible theology of Luke' (p. 1). Dibelius had already accomplished profitable work on the problem of a 'possible theology of Luke', so that Vielhauer could reply to it with the thesis that the specific achievement of Luke was a theology of history. He does indeed agree that Luke has an independent theology; but at the same time he vigorously criticizes its theological authority by pointing above all to the explicit contradiction between the theology of Luke's Paul and that of the Paul of the New Testa-ment epistles.

Vielhauer examines Paul's speeches in Acts with regard to four themes: natural theology, the law, christology and eschatology. He compares the statements in Paul's speeches with those in the Pauline epistles:

(1) The Areopagus speech (Acts 17) shows that the natural theology advocated in it has a function quite different from that in Rom. 1, for the λόγος τοῦ σταυροῦ has no place in it, because Luke has eliminated christology from this sermon of Paul's to the Gentiles. Moreover a fundamental contrast to Paul's actual conception of pre-Christian and Christian being appears in Acts 17. By claiming that pagan history, culture and religion was a preparatory history for Christianity, Luke in Acts 17 comes close to the apologists (Justin) but is remote from Paul (p. 5).

(2) Acts describes Paul, the missionary to the Gentiles, as a Jewish Christian, loyal to the Law, in other words as a true Jew, because, unlike the obdurate Jewish people, he believes in Jesus as the Messiah.

[61] On this, see also M. Rese, op. cit., p. 16. See, too, the brief account by Rese, 'Zur Lukas-Diskussion seit 1950', Wort und Dienst, Jahrbuch der Theologischen Schule Bethel, NF 9, 1967, pp. 62–67.

According to the testimony of the epistles, Paul does indeed adapt himself to a considerable extent, but he is inflexible where the essence of the gospel is threatened (p. 6). In his epistles Paul certainly taught on the lines for which the Jews reproached him of apostasy from Moses, denying that salvation came through the Law, that circumcision was a condition of salvation and that Jewish customs were significant for salvation. On the other hand, Acts shows that the reproaches of the Jews were unwarranted and gives as the reason for the Jews' enmity against Paul the jealousy of rivals or lack of faith in Jesus' messiahship, but never the doctrine of freedom from the Law (p. 7). Luke as a Hellenist has never experienced the Law in its significance as the way of salvation (p. 11) and no longer realizes the fundamental nature of the dispute concerning the Law. Luke speaks only of its incapacity, but Paul speaks of the end of the Law, which is Christ. In the doctrine of the Law in Acts the λόγος τοῦ σταυροῦ has no place, because here it has no meaning (p. 10).

(3) The difference between Luke and Paul lies in their christology (p. 10). Paul's christological statements in Acts are not specifically Pauline, nor are they Lucan, but they belong to the primitive community and bear an adoptionist character (Wilckens differs); they indicate no christology of pre-existence. The Lucan Paul's conception of the work of Christ differs from that of the Paul of the epistles, for in the latter the cross is both the judgment of all mankind and reconciliation (p. 11). But Acts says nothing about the significance of the cross for salvation; it understands the death of Jesus as a judicial error and a sin of the Jews in spite of their knowledge of the scriptures in which the Messiahship and death of Jesus was foretold. The Jews had unconsciously contributed to the fulfilment of this prediction (p. 12).

(4) Eschatology is almost entirely lacking in Paul's speeches in Acts. It appears only discreetly on the margin as a hope for the resurrection of the dead and faith in Christ's return as judge of the world (Acts 17.30f.) and for this reason it is a motive when exhorting to penitence. In this way it has been moved from the centre of Pauline faith to the end, as a *locus de novissimis*. Here Luke differs from Paul as well as from the primitive community; for both these had lived in the imminent expectation which had determined not only the motive of Paul's mission, but also his relation to the world in the words ὡς μή (I Cor. 7.29ff.).[62]

[62] *Ibid.*, p. 12. Kümmel calls in question Vielhauer's statement that eschatology

According to Paul's view nothing essential could still happen between Easter and the parousia, particularly no further history of salvation; but for Luke the time between Pentecost and the parousia is that of the Spirit and of the spread of the Gospel throughout the world, and thus a heightened history of salvation. For him the imminent expectation has disappeared and the delay of the parousia is no longer a problem. Luke has replaced the apocalyptic expectation of the primitive community and the christological eschatology of Paul with the pattern of salvation history, promise and fulfilment. It is evident not only from the subject matter but from the very fact of the existence of Acts how uneschatological is Luke's way of thinking. The handing on of information is the concern not of the man who is expecting the end of the world, but of the man who is reckoning with its continuance (p. 13). Accordingly Luke's historical writing is to be regarded as a symptom of a Christendom which has lost interest in eschatology and has been shaped by the world (p. 14).

Vielhauer sums up with the conclusion that the christology of Acts is pre-Pauline, and that its natural theology, conception of the law and eschatology are post-Pauline. There is no specifically Pauline thought in Acts, and the 'Paulinism' of the Acts consists merely in its zeal for the universal mission to the Gentiles and its veneration for the greatest missionary to the Gentiles. This material distance between the description of the Paul of Acts and the Paul of the epistles is certainly also a matter of time, and therefore the writer of Acts cannot be claimed to be the companion of Paul. Moreover the author, owing to the presuppositions of his historical writing, no longer belongs in terms of the history of theology to primitive Christendom, but to the early Catholic Church in process of formation.[63]

This article has not failed to have a stimulating effect on today's discussion of Luke, and has produced a whole series of articles in

---

in Luke is merely a *locus de novissimis* (W. G. Kümmel, *Introduction to the New Testament*, p. 121). He writes that Luke has not given up the imminent expectation, but that this has lost its quality of urgency. He lays greater stress on the present as the time of salvation (*ibid.*, p. 102; cf. also p. 122).

[63] *Ibid.*, p. 15. Marxsen, too, does not regard Paul's companion as the author of the two books, but he denies explicitly that his conception is an early Catholic one (*Einleitung*, pp. 149, 151). Kümmel also calls in question against Käsemann, Vielhauer and Klein the early Catholic character of the Lucan work (W. G. Kümmel, *op. cit.*, p. 122) and rejects its authorship by Paul's companion (*ibid.*, pp. 105, 123–30).

periodicals.[64] In addition, it has certainly been definitely fruitful and
of influence for Conzelmann's studies and Haenchen's commentary
on Acts. In controversy with Vielhauer, however, the question which
he poses only in terms of the history of theology, of a theology of Luke,
becomes a dogmatic question about the evaluation of Luke. This
dogmatic aspect is also dominant in the works and statements of
Käsemann.[65]

G. Ernst Haenchen   *Working out Luke's Method of Composition
in Acts*

By his study of the Acts of the Apostles, Haenchen has likewise
advanced quite decisively the investigation into this New Testament
book in recent research. His contribution is to be found not only in
his essay 'Tradition and Composition in Acts'[66] but especially in his
great commentary[67] which, in the words of Conzelmann, has far
surpassed all existing commentaries in the understanding of Luke.[68]
The soundness of this exposition is shown not least by the fact that the
commentary passed through four editions in five years; the third one
has been thoroughly revised, especially in the very detailed introduction, compared with the first edition, and the fourth contains an
appendix on the latest history of research. Haenchen's commentary
is in every aspect in dialogue with research into Acts since about 1950
and gives a resumé of what has been produced under the influence
of Vielhauer's article (see above) which appeared in that year.

The first-mentioned article by Haenchen might be considered the
result of his preliminary studies for the commentary. He lays
particular emphasis on the necessity of going beyond the method
employed in the era of source criticism, which wanted to restrict the

[64] Recorded in E. Haenchen, *Die Apostelgeschichte*, Göttingen 1959[12], p. 45,
note 4; cf. also E. Grässer, 'Die Apostelgeschichte in der Forschung der Gegenwart', *ThR, NF* 26, 1960, pp. 93–167.

[65] See E. Käsemann, *Essays on New Testament Themes*, London 1964, esp. pp.
27f., 91f.; cf. also M. Rese, *op. cit.*, pp. 16, 19.

[66] 'Tradition und Komposition in der Apostelgeschichte', *ZThK* 52, 1955,
pp. 205–25.

[67] *Die Apostelgeschichte* (Kritisch-exegetischer Kommentar über das Neue Testament, begründet von Heinrich August Wilhelm Meyer, third part, 10th edition
1956, 12th edition 1959, 13th edition 1961). Conzelmann is for the most part
agreed with Haenchen in his commentary on Acts (1963). Conclusions from his
The Theology of St Luke appear in the relevant passages in detailed exegesis.

[68] H. Conzelmann, 'Geschichte, Geschichtsbild und Geschichtsdarstellung bei
Lukas', *ThLZ* 85, 1960, p. 206.

original work of the author merely to assembling the various available source-writings and combining them into a whole (p. 206). Haenchen attempts to define afresh this relationship between tradition and composition, which has hitherto been wrongly conceived, by ascribing to the author many passages as the product of his own work as a writer, which had previously been regarded as components of the tradition or sources. Haenchen concedes to earlier research that Luke never worked without making *any* use of traditions. But he doubts whether these had been an early and coherent account of the apostolic age. On the contrary, they were composed of all kinds of material of different origins and different dates, and Luke was the first to create the different scenes by means of his own writing and by combining the traditions of extremely different kinds to make up the unity of a lively and vivid scene (pp. 208f.). At the same time, Haenchen does not wish to give the impression that Luke simply invented some of the scenes which he has composed. On the contrary, it was his intention for example to depict the Lord's brother James at the Apostolic Council (Acts 15) by means of the speech placed in his mouth, in accordance with the image of him which survived in the community (p. 210). In doing this Luke was proceeding like all historians of antiquity. The planning of scenes in his writings was based on the picture of the Church as a whole in the past (p. 210).

Haenchen adduces the example of the three accounts of Paul's conversion (Acts 9, 12 and 26) as evidence for the fact that Luke shaped the history of the apostolic age, not according to the criteria of our way of thinking, which is imbued with our historical practice, but according to his own independent ideas. The differences in the three accounts cannot be traced back to the use of different sources (p. 210), but Luke adapted the account in each case to suit the context in which he was telling it (p. 211). He was acquainted with only one single tradition of Paul's conversion, yet in the three passages, by means of his work as a writer, by cutting, supplementing and altering, he made them component parts of a larger whole and thereby achieved the object of his description (p. 217).

Luke was by no means just a man who collected and handed on, but he showed himself to be a deliberately creative writer (p. 217). Not only did he create and fashion out of separate traditional pieces great and vivid individual scenes, but in addition, by means of the succession of scenes which he produced, he was the first to make the history of the apostles into a historical composition (p. 217). We must not make demands on the book of the Acts which, because of its purpose and the conditions of its composition, it neither could nor wished to fulfil. We must not look in it for a formal report, nor for a self-portrait of the apostolic era, but for the image by means of which a later period of the Church has interpreted its past (p. 225).

It is, of course, obvious how large a share in the composition of the Acts Haenchen ascribes to its author; it is also just as obvious that he follows Dibelius in emphasizing (in my opinion, too strongly) the historian in Luke as the author of Acts. We can only welcome the fact that Haenchen does not spend too much time in analysing sources, especially as he is already sceptical for methodological reasons about the possibility of being able to reconstruct them; instead he attaches much greater importance to examining Luke's work as a writer.[69]

All the aspects mentioned so far crop up again in the commentary on the Acts. In the introduction, Haenchen makes clear by his account of the recent history of research what position he himself occupies; by this means he brings out, according to Conzelmann's words, 'both the continuity of research and the newness of the questions raised.'[70] Thus he carries on the line which leads from Paul Wendland's study of the literary forms of primitive Christianity, which represent the transition from the criticism of trends and sources to that of form and style;[71] this line is continued by Dibelius, who applied the principles of form-critic research to Acts,[72] and it finally reaches Haenchen himself. He concurs with Conzelmann's thesis that owing to the failure of the parousia to appear, Luke replaces the imminent expectation by a theology of salvation history ✓ with successive periods and has provided eschatology, too, with a history.[73] Haenchen himself, however, lays the chief stress on

[69] In the 12th edition Haenchen has indeed devoted a special paragraph to the problem of sources, but he is extremely sceptical about the possibility of reconstructing them (*op. cit.*, pp. 73, 80). In the article 'Das "Wir" in der Apostelgeschichte und das Itinerar' (*ZThK* 58, 1961, pp. 329–66), he also calls in question the existence of the itinerary of the journey conjectured by Dibelius as a source and pattern of Paul's journey, and he leaves open the possibility of such a work at most in the case of the third journey (*ibid.*, p. 357). Marxsen, too, is sceptical regarding the possibility of being able to recognize the sources utilized in the Acts (*Einleitung*, p. 148).

[70] H. Conzelmann, *op. cit.*, col. 242.

[71] E. Haenchen, *Die Apostelgeschichte* 1956[10], p. 29.

[72] *Ibid.*, pp. 30-34. In the 12th edition, recent research is described in more detail in pp. 32-47.

[73] E. Haenchen, *ibid.* (1959), p. 46.

demonstrating that the book of Acts is not a straightforward series of stories (strung together) but a skilful piece of writing with recognizable laws.[74]

This view of Haenchen is also substantiated by the following summary: 'In consequence, our image of Acts has been altered for us. Hitherto we read and studied it particularly in order to learn from it something about the apostolic era and we only enquired how far it was historically accurate. Today we are beginning to see that it is a skilful composition, not a straightforward narrative, and that we must grasp the principles of the composition in order to do justice to it. But at the same time it becomes evident that in it we are faced with an independent theology which must be taken seriously' (p. 41).

We may indeed question whether this commentary of Haenchen is to be reckoned as a form-critical or a redaction-critical study. The fact that it depends so much on Dibelius' articles might naturally suggest the former, but we have already endeavoured at the beginning of this chapter to demonstrate what a stimulating significance Dibelius' essays on Acts have had on redaction-critical research as well. We must add to this Haenchen's relationship to Conzelmann over method, which seems to justify a description of his work at this point. The fact that Haenchen's commentary can be placed amongst redaction-critical investigations appears in my opinion most clearly in that section of the introduction in which Luke is described as a theologian, a historian and an author.[75] It is just in this passage that Haenchen also speaks of the manner in which Luke fits the speeches which he himself composed into the context of Acts.

Dibelius had explained the variety of styles of the speeches by the fact that they were adapted for particular occasions.[76] Haenchen takes as an example of this thesis Paul's speech in Acts 22, and uses it to illustrate Luke's method of working. He says that this speech occurs without much connection with its context and that it does not enter at all into the actual accusation against Paul of defiling the temple, but deals with the right to convert the Gentiles.[77] In this speech of Paul, Luke does not let him enter at all precisely into the accusation against himself, because he was not in the least concerned to delineate Paul's controversy with his opponents of those days, but rather the controversy between Christianity and Judaism at the time

[74] *Ibid.* (1956), p. 41.
[75] This applies only to the 12th edition. In the 10th edition the corresponding paragraph deals with the author and his times.
[76] *Ibid.* (1956), p. 81; cf. Dibelius, *Studies in the Acts of the Apostles*, p. 164.
[77] E. Haenchen, *op. cit.*, p. 82; cf. M. Dibelius, *op. cit.*, pp. 158f.

when Acts was written (p. 563). 'There was in fact no particular dispute between Judaism and Christianity such as the alleged defiling of the Temple, but the general one of the conversion of the Gentiles to Christianity, the admission of Gentiles by Christian baptism into the people of God' (p. 563). Thus in Paul's speech in ch. 22 the author of the Acts skilfully fused the former times of Paul with the present day of Luke (p. 565).

Whilst in the first edition of his commentary (1956), Haenchen had given as the heading of paragraph 6: 'The book, its author and its times', when he deals with the same questions in the third edition (1959), he significantly entitles paragraph 7: 'Luke as Theologian, Historian and Author', and paragraph 8: 'Luke and Paul'. This is not a direct expression of a modification in his point of view, but it is certainly a shift of accent. This means that in the latest revision, attention is drawn much more strongly than hitherto to Luke's share in Acts and to the relation of the picture of Paul derived from his letters to Luke's picture of the apostle. In this revision, use is made of the results of the research into the Acts which has been set moving again since Vielhauer's essay. Haenchen examines especially the theological problems of the day discussed in Acts, which he names as the imminent expectation of the end and the mission to the Gentiles without the law (pp. 84f.).

Luke denied the imminent expectation and rejected the question whether this world would soon come to an end as irrelevant for Christian life. On the contrary, Christians should reckon with the fact that the world will endure. Whilst the author of the fourth gospel looks upon the chronological extension of the time after the saving events as being without significance, Luke grapples seriously with this extension and enquires about the place and the manner of God's saving activity (p. 86). Haenchen agrees fully with Conzelmann (p. 86) about Luke's division of salvation history into three periods. The period of Jesus is connected with the period since Jesus by means of the word of God which, in the mission amongst the Gentiles, represents the link between the two eras (pp. 87f.). The real end of his story ought indeed to be the return of Christ; but as this is concealed in an unknown future, Luke as a historian was able only to report what had actually happened and was obliged to stop somewhere before this end. This suggested the description of the course from Jerusalem as far as Rome as a well-rounded historical unit (p. 88).

Acts constantly takes into consideration the political and theological aspect of the fact that Christianity, although it does not
observe the Jewish law, has not interrupted the continuity of salvation history and that by detaching itself from Judaism it might lose
the toleration guaranteed to that religion (p. 90). As Haenchen shows
by many examples, Luke has portrayed the initiators and leaders of
the Christian mission not as having apostatized from their Jewish
faith, but as having been loyal to it; and he shows that God led them
unambiguously and irresistibly to the Gentile mission (p. 90). Yet
the various attempts to build a bridge between Jews and Christians
in Acts are no longer missionary propaganda by Luke to win Israel,
for he no longer hopes like Paul for the conversion of the Jews. The
pointers to the bond with Israel are merely intended to guarantee
that the present continuity of the history of salvation is in accord
with the divine will (p. 91). In actual fact, the spread of Christianity
was not so simple and homogeneous a process as appears at first from
Acts, especially as a number of communities at Paul's mission
stations were founded by unknown Christians. Luke has not drawn
the often interrupted line of the actual development, but its ideal
curve (pp. 92f.).

What Haenchen writes about the relationship between Luke and
Paul is particularly important. Several considerations lead him to
the conclusion that the author of the two Lucan books cannot be the
same as the doctor and travelling companion of Paul named in Col.
4.14. He reaches this deduction on the strength of various separate
facts.

(1) Luke, like Paul, considers the crucial problem to be the mission
to the Gentiles without the law; yet Luke does not know of Paul's
solution, according to which the law leads not to God, but into sin.
Luke, however, substantiates the Gentile mission without the Law
by the revelation of the will of God through miraculous signs (Acts
9.1–19a; 10.1–11.18; 13.1–4) (pp. 99f.).

(2) Luke's picture of Paul differs in several respects from that in
the Pauline epistles. Thus Luke depicts him, like Peter, as the great
miracle-worker (Acts 13.6–12; 14.8–10; 14.19–20; 19.12; 20.7–12;
28.3–6), whereas the real Paul claims at most the sign of apostleship
(II Cor. 12.12). Whereas the Lucan Paul is a consummate orator
with the impressive eloquence of a Demosthenes (Acts 13.16–41;
14.15–17; 17.22–31; 21.40; 22.1–21; 23.1, 3, 5, 6; 24.20–21; 26.2–23,
27; 28.17–20, 26, 28), the real Paul was by no means a master of

extempore speech, but appeared to be a poor speaker and was unimpressive (II Cor. 10.10). The real Paul claimed apostleship on an equal footing with the Twelve, whereas Acts is only aware of the Twelve as apostles (in spite of 14.4, 14) (pp. 100–2).

(3) The account of the relationship between Jews and Christians in Acts is incompatible with the Pauline epistles; in Acts the tension between them arises out of the Christian preaching of the resurrection, but in fact it arose out of Paul's teaching about the Law and the missionary practice which went with it (pp. 102f.).

Hence according to Haenchen the picture of Paul and the missionary situation in Acts shows that no fellow-worker with Paul is speaking here, but a man of the subsequent generation who is explaining in his own fashion things which he had not himself experienced. The real Paul is replaced by a Paul as a later era imagined him (p. 103). Thus, as we have already mentioned, for Haenchen it is especially external evidence which is decisive for calling in question the authorship of Acts by Luke the physician and companion of Paul. With Vielhauer, on the other hand, the decisive factor was the different theological position of the Lucan Paul compared with the historical Paul.

We must not fail to recognize that in Haenchen we can observe a modification in the assessment of the place of Acts in the history of Christian theology. In his first study of Acts, he still followed Vielhauer in many respects,[78] but in his third revision (12th edition) he declares that he cannot claim Acts as evidence for the development of early Catholicism.[79] He adduces the following reasons for this:

Luke does not yet advance a theology of the episcopal office, like Ignatius of Antioch, nor does he yet know of any doctrine of an overriding ecclesiastical organization; for apart from Acts 9.31, the word ἐκκλησία in this book always denotes merely the individual community. Nor does Luke develop any sacramentalism of a φάρμακον ἀθανασίας. Instead, the real subject of Acts is the growth of God's word, which is preached by men, but substantiated by God through signs and wonders (p. 46). Hence Luke's theology is no fall from Pauline heights, for he had never stood on them; it is one of the many varieties of Gentile-Christian theology which developed more or less independently of Paul beside and after his theology. The germs which later grew into early Catholicism had already come into

[78] *Ibid.* (1956), pp. 6, 8 and 9.
[79] *Ibid.* (1959), p. 46.

being before Luke's time in this Gentile-Christian theology (pp. 46f.).

We cannot fail to observe that in this matter Haenchen is defending Luke against the material criticism which Vielhauer had made. But it is doubtful whether he has refuted Vielhauer. In any case, Haenchen has not been able by his discussion to dispose of the theological differences between the Lucan Paul and the Paul of the epistles demonstrated by Vielhauer; indeed he did not really even enter into them.

We must, however, warn Vielhauer, too, against excessive subtlety. Haenchen is undoubtedly correct in saying that Luke had never stood on the heights of Pauline theology. Yet even if Luke might have known the Pauline epistles and might nevertheless have made no use of them, we must not explain this by his lack of theological training and his inability to appreciate the historical hints sparsely contained in them. On the contrary, we may attribute his procedure to the fact that in view of his particular theological conception he did not consider it to be his task to deal with this theological material. Unfortunately, we do not know whether Luke was acquainted with Paul's epistles. If we did, we could save ourselves the trouble of enquiring whether it is at all possible to examine Luke with regard to the Pauline theology, because in that case Luke himself would have given a decisive negative reply.[80] Doubtless there was no *collection* of the Pauline epistles in existence at that time.

Considerable weight must be attached to Eltester's objections to Vielhauer's criticism of Luke's description of Paul. He does indeed accept the four differences brought out by Vielhauer between the real Paul and the Lucan one; but he thinks that Luke was *unable* to understand Paul's dialectic. In his view, Luke's description of Paul provides evidence for the way in which a *Greek* (unlike the oriental Ignatius) had accepted Christianity; it shows how he was obliged to accept it in the altered circumstances of the post-apostolic era; for fresh problems had made him become an independent thinker. John resolutely lets the glowing image of the heavenly Christ shine through the image of the Jesus of the synoptic tradition who lives in lowliness, and he combines the two in a dialetic full of tension; Luke, on the other hand, puts one after the other. This is his tribute to history.[81]

The difference between Luke and Paul does not depend on the interval

<hr>

[80] See on this O. Bauernfeind, 'Zur Frage nach der Entscheidung zwischen Paulus und Lukas', *ZSTh* 23, 1954, p. 88, note 51.
[81] W. Eltester, 'Lukas und Paulus', in *Eranion* (*Festschrift für H. Hommel*), Tübingen, 1961, p. 9.

of time, but principally on the fact that Luke was a Greek. In spite of the same acknowledgment of the Risen One, the Greek Luke had a different horizon from the former Jew, Paul. Luke read the Old Testament only as a prophecy directed to Christ, and had not recognized, as did Paul, the Jew, the intrinsic difficulties arising between a religion of grace and one of works (p. 16). Luke never *could* have described as a problem the Pauline antithesis of Law and gospel, because it was no longer a problem of his own day (p. 15). Paul understood the Law to have been abolished by Christ, but Gentile Christianity struggled through to this only by degrees. 'It is not appropriate to require of Luke, who stood at the beginning of this road, the theology of Paul, although he was his pupil' (p. 17).

H. Ulrich Wilckens: *The Lucan Conception of Christian Missionary Preaching*

Ulrich Wilckens' dissertation for his degree, *Die Missionsreden der Apostelgeschichte* (The Missionary Speeches in Acts) is intended to fill a gap in previous research into the Acts of the Apostles, and for this purpose it examines some missionary speeches form-critically and traditio-historically. Wilckens presupposes the conclusions of Dibelius' studies of Acts (pp. 12–16, 19f.); he also places himself in the tradition of research begun by Vielhauer and continued by Conzelmann and Haenchen (pp. 28f.). He carries on their investigations into the specifically Lucan theology. For he accepts the fact which they have established, that Luke's two books are based on a clearly recognizable general scheme which is stamped uniformly on the material taken over from the prototypes and which led also to these two books being conceived. Within the self-contained scheme of Luke's two books, the sermons of the apostles have a central significance (p. 28).

Dibelius had not yet carried out a proper traditio-historical analysis of the missionary speeches in Acts, because he took into consideration only those passages in the Acts which in his opinion were most useful for his purpose. He assumed that the first missionary speeches were of a traditional nature and were not specifically Lucan (p. 30). Wilckens concerns himself with the problem whether the first missionary speeches in the Acts may be claimed as decisively important material on which to build a traditio-historical study of the development of primitive Christian theology (p. 30). He takes as deserving attention Peter's sermon on Whitsunday (Acts 2.14–39), Peter's speech to the people after the healing of the lame man (Acts

3.12–26), Peter's speech before the Sanhedrin (Acts 4.9–12), the defence of Peter and the apostles before the Sanhedrin (Acts 5.30–32), Peter's sermon before Cornelius (Acts 10.34–43), and Paul's sermon in the synagogue in Pisidian Antioch (Acts 13.16–41). In addition, Wilckens has devoted yet another article to Peter's sermon before Cornelius,[82] but its conclusions appear again in his dissertation. The study attaches most importance to the sermon on Whit Sunday, the sermon before Cornelius and the sermon at Antioch in Pisidia. Stephen's speech is omitted because of its special character and a certain significance for the problem under discussion is attributed merely to its conclusion (Acts 7.51f.) (p. 31, note 1).

Wilckens sets out to show by means of a detailed analysis of the first missionary speeches which is based on the history of the tradition, that this kind of examination necessarily leads to a redaction-critical result and how it does so (p. 190 note 1). Thus Wilckens starts off from the form-critical presuppositions contained in Dibelius' work, but unlike Dibelius, he wants to underpin by a separate proof the thesis that in these speeches we are not concerned with the evidence of the earliest tradition, but merely with the specific trend of the theologian Luke (p. 29). He substantiates his special concentration on the first missionary speeches with the sentence: 'In terms of composition, these speeches are to be considered the decisive centre of his narrative' (pp. 28f.).

In all the six speeches under examination, Wilckens works out a pattern of construction in which the structure and purpose is somewhat the same. It usually consists of six parts. In Peter's Whit Sunday sermon the pattern exhibits the following six sections: a link with the circumstances by means of a scriptural quotation leading up to the kerygma, the miracles and death of Jesus, his being raised up (with a proof from scripture), a summary assertion (v. 36) and finally a call to repentance and salvation (p. 37). Peter's speech before Cornelius occupies an exceptional position because its construction and individual features are different from the others. It, too, starts by alluding to the circumstances, but then it makes no further reference to them (p. 49). It lacks the call for repentance and very little is said about the evidence of the prophets. The same pattern also occurs here, but it is modified in a particular way, so that the portion containing the kerygma has been expanded and has become the predominant main portion and presents almost a short *historia*

[82] *Id.*, 'Kerygma und Evangelium bei Lukas', *ZNW* 49, 1958, pp. 223–37.

Jesu (p. 50). Paul's speech in Pisidian Antioch again shows this pattern of six sections (p. 54). The demonstration of this structural pattern leads Wilckens to the conclusion that in spite of the almost identical pattern, each sermon is given its particular shade of meaning. The same structure with varying shades of meaning is meant to show that the sermons are typical examples of the apostles' defence in an actual situation at any given time (p. 55).

Wilckens next examines the framework of the individual speeches. He rejects the hypothesis that the sermons were inserted by Luke secondarily into the context of the respective narrative. On the contrary, it must be affirmed that the sermons in question are without exception perfectly consistent with their context, that they apply to it and are also stamped by it in detail; indeed the whole sequence, namely, narrative and speeches, are the work of Luke; they belong to his scheme and have a decisive function in it (p. 71).

We shall not illustrate this conclusion of Wilckens by all the speeches treated by him, but merely by Peter's sermon before Cornelius, especially as this speech is of particular importance and Wilckens has devoted another article to its examination. We have already seen that the pattern worked out by Dibelius with its main features of kerygma, scriptural proof and exhortation to repent,[83] does not really fit the speech to Cornelius in the strict sense, but that the kerygmatic part is much expanded in comparison with the other speeches, that the scriptural proof is reduced by the same extent and that the exhortation to repent and be saved is lacking. The different character of this speech compared with the other ones is due to the fact that the conversion of Cornelius as the first Gentile[84] is an event of epoch-making significance in church history for Luke.[85] The speech before Cornelius is also different from the others, because it is not a missionary speech in Luke's sense and did not need to effect a

---

[83] M. Dibelius, 'The Conversion of Cornelius', in *Studies in the Acts of the Apostles*, pp. 111f.

[84] In fact the first conversion of a Gentile was that of the treasurer from Ethiopia (Acts 8.26–40), although it must also be admitted that Luke has not attributed crucial significance to it in his scheme, but has done this instead to the conversion of Cornelius; this appears from the fact that Luke alludes to it again in his account of the Apostolic Council (Acts 15.7–8, 14). Luke has even avoided presenting the treasurer as a Gentile. 'Otherwise Philip would have anticipated Peter, the recognized initiator of the mission to the Gentiles' (thus E. Haenchen, *Die Apostelgeschichte*, 1959[12], *ad. loc.*=p. 264).

[85] U. Wilckens, *op. cit.*, p. 65; *id.*, 'Kerygma und Evangelium bei Lukas', *loc. cit.*, p. 236.

conversion. This had been brought about by God long before. Hence at the conclusion the call to repentance and to receive salvation is lacking, and the sermon ends with a theory of scriptural proof, which contains a mention of the forgiveness of sins (10.43) (p. 67). The differences between the sermon in Acts 10 and the other sermons are to be ascribed to the fact that Luke wishes this one to be understood as a synopsis of his gospel (p. 70). Therefore here the section about Jesus occupies nearly the whole space, whereas scriptural proof and exhortation to repentance recede very markedly into the background.[86]

The character given to Luke's gospel in the prologue agrees with the structure of Peter's speech before Cornelius. For in conformity with the prologue of Luke 1.1–4, it is the purpose of the gospel to be a definite and accurate arrangement of the traditional material in a definite order; its substance has been guaranteed by the original apostles as witnesses and is already known (p. 229).

In this passage Luke has altered the pattern of the missionary sermon into the pattern of the shape of the gospel. He shows here the genre of the gospel as a secondary modification of the *kerygma*, a process in which the material of the gospel is an expansion and arrangement of originally kerygmatic material.[87] Luke himself shaped the construction and subject-matter of this sermon, and in doing so followed closely the arrangement and construction of the third gospel (p. 235). 'This sermon of Peter has been intentionally shaped by Luke as a synopsis of his gospel. Accordingly its form is characteristically different from the other sermons of the apostles: these are missionary sermons; the sermon in Cornelius' house is catechesis—not kerygma, but gospel' (p. 236). The differences worked out by Wilckens in this missionary sermon compared with the other speeches are at any rate a warning against treating all the speeches in the book of the Acts alike, and serve as an inducement to make an attempt to interpret each of them in view of the actual situation in which they have been placed by the author. The redaction-critical method, consistently applied in this way, thus may lead beyond the conclusions of Dibelius and allow Luke's achievement as an author and a theologian to become even more evident.[88]

---

[86] *Id.*, 'Kerygma und Evangelium', *op. cit.*, p. 229.

[87] *Id.*, *Missionsreden*, p. 69; 'Kerygma und Evangelium', *op. cit.*, p. 229.

[88] See on this E. Grässer, 'Die Apostelgeschichte in der Forschung der Gegenwart', *loc. cit.*, pp. 135f.

In his *Studies in the Acts of the Apostles,* Dibelius had propounded the thesis that Luke had indeed formulated the details of the speeches, but had derived their pattern from an early tradition of sermons and also found detailed kerygmatic formulations already in existence.[89] In Wilckens' opinion, the question ought also to be raised whether the pattern of the sermon pointed out by Dibelius might not be detected in non-Lucan texts as well. This Dibelius has not attempted, but has always only taken it for granted (p. 73). He merely adduced I Cor. 15.1, 3–8 in order to substantiate his assertion that there was an existing traditional pattern for the first speeches in the Acts.[90] But now Wilckens has demonstrated in a very careful analysis that the sermon pattern in the first missionary speeches is not to be found in I Cor. 15, but that there are fundamental differences between the two. These are:

(1) The speeches in Acts merely report the fact of Jesus' death; in I Cor. 15.3b, on the other hand, there is a mention of the soteriological significance of Jesus' death ($\dot{\upsilon}\pi\grave{\epsilon}\rho$ $\tau\hat{\omega}\nu$ $\dot{\alpha}\mu\alpha\rho\tau\iota\hat{\omega}\nu$ $\dot{\eta}\mu\hat{\omega}\nu$).

(2) I Cor. 15 speaks only of the death of *Christ;* however the missionary speeches speak of Jesus being killed.

(3) I Cor. 15 lacks any statement about the story of Jesus' passion and in contrast to Acts, no mention is made either of the action of the Jews or of the manner of Jesus' death. It is not the death as such, but its soteriological significance, that is the purpose of the statement.

(4) In contrast to the missionary speeches, I Cor. 15 lacks any reference to Jesus' life before his death (p. 77).

(5) Admittedly, use is made of scriptural proof in both passages; but in the missionary speeches it is merely intended to be evidence from the Old Testament for the fact of the death and resurrection; in I Cor. 15.3f., however, it bears witness to the soteriological significance of the death and the resurrection 'on the third day'.

(6) In both passages, the word 'raised' is used, but the 'third day' is mentioned only in Acts 10.40 (p. 78).

(7) There is merely one traditio-historical connection between I Cor. 15.5 and Luke 24.34, the mention of the first appearance of the Risen One to Peter (p. 79). Wilckens, having established these facts, reaches the conclusion, in opposition to Dibelius, that 'I Cor. 15 does not provide evidence for the sermon tradition conjectured by

[89] M. Dibelius, 'The Speeches in Acts and Ancient Historiography', *op. cit.,* p. 165; *id., From Tradition to Gospel,* pp. 16f.
[90] M. Dibelius, *From Tradition to Gospel,* pp. 17–22.

Dibelius on the basis of the speeches in the Acts'.[91] This applies to all the other passages in the epistles in which tradition with an earlier stamp has been detected in the present arrangement of the text (p. 80). But Wilckens now works out from two passages in the epistles another pattern of missionary kerygma which is found in I Thess. 1.9–10 and in Heb. 5.11–6.2. In I Thess. 1.9–10, there are the following individual components: turning from idols to God, the expectation of the parousia, the resurrection and the deliverance in the judgment to come (p. 81). The patterns in both passages, as certain distinctive features show, had nothing to do with pattern of the missionary speeches, so far as the history of the tradition is concerned (p. 84). In the Acts of the Apostles on the one hand, however, and in I Thessalonians and Hebrews on the other, there are completely different kinds of tradition. Their one common statement is that about Jesus being raised (p. 85).

Wilckens has found firm points of contact between the pattern occurring in the two passages in the epistles and two other missionary speeches of Paul in Acts, both addressed to Gentiles: the speech in Lystra (Acts 14.15–17) and the speech on the Areopagus in Athens (Acts 17.22–31) (pp. 86f.). In the Areopagus speech in particular, all three components of the pattern of I Thess. 1.9f. are present:

(1) Repentance as a turning from idols to serve God.

(2) The end of the period of men's ignorance and of God's condoning their service of idols, with an allusion to the world judgment to come.

(3) The resurrection of Jesus is adduced as evidence that the announcement of judgment is correct (pp. 87f.).

It follows from this that Paul, too, was acquainted with this pattern which Luke placed in his mouth in a sermon before Gentiles (p. 88).[92] The existence of Jewish-Christian missionary preaching has been more or less firmly established historically; the subject-matter of such a sermon to Jews by Jewish Christians was probably like a continuation of Jesus' preaching (Matt. 10.7) in material, structure

---

[91] *Ibid.*, p. 80. On the relationship between a revised tradition and Luke's version see also B. M. F. Van Iersel, '*Der Sohn*' *in den synoptischen Jesusworten*, Leiden 1961, pp. 33–51. Schneider supports Dibelius against Wilckens and maintains with Mussner that the pattern employed is a traditional one (J. Schneider, 'Der Beitrag der Urgemeinde zur Jesusüberlieferung im Lichte der neuesten Forschung', *ThLZ* 87, 1962, col. 409).

[92] *Ibid.*, p. 88. Lerle does not derive the sermon in Lystra from Luke's theology. He thinks that it has been inserted by the author into his two books, but that in

and object (p. 90), and nothing else can be determined about the manner of the Jewish-Christian mission. Nevertheless the historical value of the first missionary speeches of Acts must be called in question or at least strictly qualified in view of the whole literary and theological nature of Acts. The traditional nature of the pattern of the sermon in the first missionary speeches cannot be demonstrated whereas in the case of the others in Acts (Lystra and Athens), evidence for their pattern can be found in the tradition (p. 91). This suggests the hypothesis that Luke himself created the pattern of the missionary speeches as far as Acts 13. In doing so he used the Hellenistic-Christian missionary pattern which was handed down and was known to him, (and on which he had based the sermons to the Gentiles in Acts 14 and 17) for the construction of a corresponding pattern of a Jewish-Christian missionary sermon (p. 91).

In order to substantiate this thesis, Wilckens examines the meaning and the function of the speech pattern in Luke's theological conception of Acts. According to this, the speeches of the apostles were intended to throw light on their witness to Jesus as the prime mover of salvation history and to bring this fact out (p. 95). For this purpose the apostles' speeches stand in each case at the significant turning points of what happened in the church history described by Luke (p. 99). At the decisive points they are shown as the moving force which determines the course of events. Thus the history of the Church opens with the Whit Sunday sermon; the turning point to the Gentile mission appears in the sermon before Cornelius, and in ch. 13 the last call to the Jews for repentance is sounded (p. 96). The speeches before the Gentiles already differ in their design from those before the Jews. This difference in the kind of sermon is determined for Luke by his theology. In his view the Jews are drawn from the beginning of the first era of salvation history into God's election and promise (p. 96). But with the approach to the Gentiles the structure of the sermon must be modified, because the Jews have now dropped out of salvation history and the Gentiles have been drawn into it (p. 98). Hence in Luke's scheme two phases of church history appeared, namely the mission to the Jews and that to the Gentiles;

---

language and themes it is earlier than they are and its theology and the nature of its concepts are stamped by the Septuagint. It is a record of the preaching to the Gentiles in its beginnings and originated in the time before Paul's conflicts with the Judaizers. Thus he considers it to be largely reliable (E. Lerle, 'Die Predigt in Lystra, Acta 14.15–18', *NTS* 7, 1960/61, pp. 46–55, especially pp. 54f.).

the differences between them are seen in the different form of the sermon; the sermon before the Jews referred to their position in salvation history, the sermon before the Gentiles referred to the situation of the Gentiles (p. 99). Hence it follows that 'in the present context in Acts, the form of the speeches, in particular their fundamental pattern, must be understood throughout with Luke's whole scheme in mind' (p. 99). Only in the construction of the speeches in chs. 14 and 17 can a traditional pattern of a Gentile-Christian missionary sermon be established; this cannot, however, be demonstrated in the case of the Jewish-Christian sermons in chs. 2 to 13. It is the subject-matter and design of precisely *these* speeches which cannot be detached from the special situation of the Jews in salvation history; for this reason the hypothesis is probable that Luke himself shaped this pattern of the Jewish-Christian missionary sermon (p. 99).

Wilckens is not content to examine the meaning and function of the speeches in the plan of the Acts; he also interrogates the separate parts of the sermons with a view to discovering whether they contain early kerygmatic material from the tradition and what position the first missionary speeches of the Acts occupy within the history of the tradition of the primitive Christians (p. 100). For this purpose, he examines the first missionary speeches for statements about John the Baptist, Jesus' ministry before his death, the condemnation and death of Jesus, his being raised and exalted, the christological titles and finally the calls for repentance contained in the sermons and the preaching of salvation.

The references to the Baptist (10.37: 13.24f.) contained in the speeches were not only formulated by Luke in conformity with his own theory about the Baptist (cf. Conzelmann on this); they also follow quite closely the wording of the Baptist's statements in the gospel, which was modified only slightly so as to render Luke's own meaning clear. Thus Luke was the first to bring the Baptist into the kerygma of the missionary speeches in order to emphasize that the Baptist did not form part of the Jesus event itself, but that as the last prophet he has his place in the pre-Christian era of the history of salvation before Jesus' first appearance (p. 105). The description, too, in Acts 10.37–39 (see also Acts 2.22) of Jesus' ministry before his death was composed by Luke himself; for its source he used only his own gospel (Luke 23.5, also Acts 1.21f.) (p. 108). On the other hand, the statements about Jesus' condemnation and death appear in all the sermons and form the central part of their outlines (Acts

2.22–23.36; 3.13–15; 4.10, 27f.; 5.30; 7.52; 10.40; 13.27f.) (pp. 108f.).

Next Wilckens examines the history of the tradition of these statements and compares them with the formulations of Luke's passion story. His conclusion is that it can be demonstrated that Luke formulated the statement in the missionary speeches about Jesus' condemnation and death by following his own gospel closely (p. 136). Thus, for example, the synopsis of Jesus' passion story in Acts 3.13–15 is a summary, even down to its details, of Luke's own story of the passion (Luke 23.3–6; 23.13–15) (p. 131). In Acts 3.15 Jesus' death is described as the act of the Jews and their immediate fault, which corresponds exactly to the description of the passion in the third gospel, but differs characteristically from Mark's description (pp. 128f.).

Luke certainly accepted the statements about Jesus' resurrection, which were handed down to him by Mark in the predictions of the passion, but he understood them in the sense of a conception of 'being raised'. This corresponds to the subordinationist quality in his christology, according to which it was God who acted in the raising of Jesus (pp. 149, 139). By contrast the statements about Jesus' exaltation do not play so central a role, but occur only in Acts 2.33; 3.20; 5.31 (p. 150); of these 3.20 is a traditional piece from Baptist circles and is made to appear Christian in a makeshift way (p. 154); yet in these three passages there is no basis for the influence of a tradition which regards the raising up and the exaltation as a single event. In other respects the conception of the outpouring of the spirit in connection with the statement of the exaltation is due to Luke (p. 155).

Wilckens then scrutinizes the christological titles in the missionary speeches. We need call attention only to the title Χριστὸς τοῦ θεοῦ (see Acts 3.18; 4.26 especially, and also Luke 2.26; 23.35). In Luke this denotes Jesus' pivotal function in the history of salvation. It also contains the fundamental reason for the subordinationist quality noticeable in Luke's christology, according to which it is God who plans and directs the history of salvation; in Luke's book *God* uses Jesus as his pivotal instrument for salvation history. The setting of Jesus over against God throughout Luke's book is therefore based by Luke on his general scheme of salvation history (p. 163).

In general, Luke has drawn all the christological titles in the context of the missionary sermons from the tradition, but he has consistently impressed on them the different meaning of his own christological scheme, the structure of which is determined by his main idea of salvation history. From this, all the different titles derive their particular significance in salvation history and they all denote the pivotal function given to Jesus by God at the centre of time, in fulfilment of all the promises given in advance (p. 178).

Finally, Wilckens deals with the statements in the missionary speeches relating to the call for repentance and the preaching of salvation. Whilst in the other speeches only one or two themes occur, in Acts 2.28–40 we find all the themes of a synopsis of a Christian sermon used for proclaiming salvation in a definite order, in an 'ordo salutis' (p. 178). These are repentance, baptism in the name of Jesus, reception of the spirit, membership of the Church as being the number of the saved (2.47) and reception of salvation (pp. 178f.).

Another pattern of conversion underlies Paul's speeches in Acts 14 and 17. Luke has undoubtedly taken this from the Hellenistic-Christian missionary practice in general use in his time, and which is found also in I Thess. 1.9f.; Gal. 4.8 and in Heb. 5.11ff.[93] However, the ordo salutis in the speeches before the Jews bears a special character. In his description of the Jewish-Christian phase of church history, Luke himself changed the Hellenistic-Christian pattern of conversion with which he was acquainted into an ordo salutis for the Jews who had incurred guilt (p. 181). Wilckens proves also by Luke's descriptions of the reception of salvation how he fitted them into the framework of his general scheme of salvation history by using different traditions (p. 186). In this way he brings out emphatically God's unique soteriological initiative with regard to men's reception of salvation (p. 183). He sees the same significance for the convert of Jesus' fate and person in Jesus' pivotal function in salvation history, and he understands salvation to be membership within the sphere of the

[93] Ibid., 179. Dibelius considers the speech on the Areopagus to be a Hellenistic speech which with the exception of the last verses is stamped by Stoic philosophy and piety (see his two essays 'Paul in the Areopagus' and 'Paul in Athens', in Studies in the Acts of the Apostles, pp. 26–77 and 78–84); on the other hand, Eltester lays stronger emphasis on the influence of the Old Testament belief in creation in shaping this speech. The speech is the earliest evidence for a blending within Christianity of the biblical belief in creation with worldly piety, and it has been introduced by the Greek Judaism of the Diaspora (see W. Eltester, Gott und die Natur in der Areopagrede, BZNW 21, Berlin 1954, pp. 202–27, especially p. 226f.). Hommel even traces the material of the Areopagus speech completely back to Posidonius. It was next revised by a Hellenistic Jew. Then Luke took it over and gave it its last revision. (H. Hommel, 'Neue Forschungen zur Areopagrede', ZNW 46, 1955, especially pp. 169f., 172.)

fulfilment of salvation history, i.e. of the Church, which, after Jesus had completed his course, entered into the succession of Israel (p. 185).

It follows from the description so far that Wilckens in his detailed examination of the first missionary speeches in Acts has endeavoured to demonstrate that the theology represented in them cannot be considered in traditio-historical terms as evidence for the beginnings of primitive Christian theology. It must be regarded as programmatic evidence for Luke's theology; in fact a large part of the individual material contains specifically Lucan theology. Wilckens has ascertained this by comparing the relevant individual traditions in the speeches in Acts with the Gospel of Luke and particularly with his passion narrative. Hence he attaches special value to proving that the theology of the speeches is a specific theology of Luke. Thus he can write concerning the author of the two books by Luke: 'The speeches of the apostles in Acts are to be assessed above all as summaries of his theological scheme; they are not evidence of an early, still less of an earliest, primitive Christian theology, but of Lucan theology in the closing years of the first century.'[94]

In his work, Wilckens has set himself in clear and direct opposition to the scholars who consider this theology of the speeches to be of the earliest possible date. Dibelius in one passage denotes Peter's speeches in the first part of the Acts as 'variations on a kind of original community theology';[95] thus he takes it for granted that this theology is very old. However, in his articles on Acts he never pursued this problem of the history of the tradition any further and he did not reach this conclusion as to its age by detailed analysis, even in his *From Tradition to Gospel*, in which he merely takes it for granted that the kerygma contained in these speeches represents a very early type (p. 17). He attempts to substantiate this allegedly old type by maintaining that the christological statements exhibit an adoptionist character and give the impression that in Luke's opinion the man Jesus became the Messiah only by his exaltation (p. 16). But now Wilckens has clearly called in question the adoptionist character of the christology in the missionary speeches. In his opinion, the passages appearing to have an adoptionist sound are to be interpreted as evidence in their context for a

[94] *Ibid.*, p. 186. Glombitza in his analysis of Paul's speech in Pisidian Antioch has attempted to separate the tradition employed and Luke's revision of it (O. Glombitza, 'Acta 13.15-41, Analyse einer lukanischen Predigt vor Juden', *NTS* 5, 1958/9, pp. 306-17). He has followed here the procedure of W. Nauck who has attempted the same thing in his essay 'Die Tradition und Komposition der Areopagrede', *ZThK* 53, 1956, pp. 11-52.

[95] M. Dibelius, 'The Acts of the Apostles as a Historical Source', in *Studies in the Acts of the Apostles*, p. 105.

subordinationist quality in christology and are to be assigned to a relatively late date. Luke's christology is rooted in his particular scheme of salvation history, according to which God alone plans and directs salvation history and for this purpose uses Jesus as his pivotal instrument for salvation history (pp. 191, 163).[96]

Thus we can repeat that Wilckens has emphasized strongly Luke's share in the theological shaping of his material. He can even write that owing to modern scholarship Luke is rising in the exegetical sky as a new constellation, welcomed by some, giving offence to others, and that his scheme had a strong formative influence on the theological history of what is called early Catholicism (p. 189). At first he attracted to himself the attention of the scholars studying the history of the tradition, as one who merely handed it on. 'Luke was wanted as a hack writer—and he showed himself to be a theologian!' (p. 189). Luke, as a son of the post-apostolic era, not only took over the characteristics of early Catholic theology, but also stamped and shaped them extremely effectively as a theology for the time to come. In this way he became the distinctive theologian of early Catholicism at its beginnings. It is in this that his theological significance consists, not in the fact that he hunted up allegedly very early traditional material and preserved it for subsequent generations (p. 192).

Wilckens seeks to use the first missionary speeches as evidence of Luke's theology, and in so doing his study joins forces with the redaction-critical studies of Luke, although he started from Dibelius' form-critical investigations. This demonstrates clearly what a close relationship in the history of research exists between form criticism and redaction criticism. The results of redaction criticism have grown directly out of form-critical analysis.

Thus Wilckens understands Luke's theology to be the result of the situation in which he was assumed to be, when early Catholicism was developing at the end of the first century. He assesses Luke's theology quite positively as appropriate to its time,[97] and he does not let himself be drawn, like Vielhauer, into a violent criticism of Luke as

[96] U. Wilckens, op. cit., pp. 191, 163; M. Rese also emphatically challenges the adoptionist character of the Lucan christology in the speeches in Acts (Alttestamentliche Motive in der Christologie des Lukas, Diss. Bonn, 1965, p. 206).

[97] Wilckens writes (ibid., p. 218) that, in spite of aggravating shortcomings compared with Paul, the construction of Luke's work as a piece of theological history must be regarded as a great achievement with an approach which we cannot do without; in spite of these shortcomings, it exhibits Luke as the most significant theologian of the post-apostolic period.

compared with Paul. He understands both of them with the situation of each in mind, recognizing fully their theological differences. Wilckens works out four differences, based on the different historical situations of Paul and Luke:

(1) Paul received his tradition from Antioch, the centre of his missionary work, from the initial period of Syrian Gentile Christianity which still had quite a unilinear historical tradition. On the other hand, the traditional stock in the shape of ideas and formulae available to Luke at a later time was very diverse in kind, in consequence of the rapid expansion of Christianity into the area of the Western Mediterranean. So Luke had been obliged to reduce it to a coherent sequence of ideas because in his day there was certainly no longer a homogeneous theology in the possession of the communities (pp. 196f.).

(2) The stock of traditions in the case of Paul was restricted to kerygmatic, liturgical and hortatory material, whilst he lacked the bulk of the synoptic tradition about Jesus; despite Dibelius' sermon-theory, the synoptic tradition about Jesus probably did not belong to the stock of missionary kerygmatic material. On the other hand, the greatest part of the tradition available to Luke consisted of what was handed down about Jesus, and it was then Luke's task to permeate this with the various kerygmatic and liturgical traditions of his day (pp. 197f.).

(3) Moreover, Luke and Paul stood in different positions in the history of religion. Paul had on the one hand to enter into thorough discussion with Jewish theology, and on the other to interpret his theological position to gnostic communities, who lacked from the start any understanding of Jewish theology; thus he was continuously facing two quite different fronts. Luke, as a Hellenist, stood at some distance from Judaism, and for him its theological tradition was merely a heritage of the church, and not directly his own; the Old Testament, however, had in his view long been a Christian book (pp. 198f.).

(4) In addition, the position of the Christians in their surroundings had changed. In Paul's time the persecutions took the shape of limited local conflicts at the most; in Luke's time persecution was already a general phenomenon, and the problem of the attitude of the Christians to the power of the Roman state was also present. Consequently there is in Luke a trend to demonstrate that Christians, and Paul in particular, were loyal citizens, and that the Roman authorities

were fair and friendly witnesses of the Christians' loyalty and in-
nocence, but that the Jews, on the other hand, were permanent
troublemakers (pp. 199f.).

We must mention here that Grundmann, differing from Vielhauer,
Conzelmann, Haenchen and Wilckens, puts forward Luke, the doctor and
travelling companion of Paul, as the author of the two Lucan books. The
theological differences between Luke and Paul and the external disparities
between the Paul of history and Luke's Paul (worked out by Vielhauer and
Haenchen) are explained by Grundmann in terms of the later period with
the fresh problems of its day. Luke, with his intellectual tendency to
synthesis, faces these new problems and endeavours, by modifying the
tradition about Jesus and the period of time which he shared with Paul,
to draw an image for the post-apostolic generation as it appeared to him
when he undertook to write his work. His readers are Hellenistic Christians
from communities in Greece, as the tradition also attests. The author had
not in fact been an eye-witness of Jesus' story, but he is looking back to the
apostles' time and he reaches out from the apostolic era into the era of the
developing Early Church, the course of which his influence helped to
determine.[98]

In general terms, it may be said of Wilckens' study that, so far as
we can see, he is still standing alone up till now in maintaining the
thesis that in the first missionary speeches of Acts Luke was not
revising early traditional material, but that he fashioned and created
the content, form and construction of all these speeches. Even
Haenchen holds a different opinion on this point. Wilckens' reasoning
seems at first extremely alluring, consistent and convincing; but on a
closer scrutiny of this thesis doubts about it do crop up. Is the
traditio-historical relationship between the pattern worked out in the
missionary speeches in Acts 2 to 13 and that in 14 and 17 really what
Wilckens makes it out to be? Does it in fact prove what it is intended
to prove? We think we can use three passages in the Acts to call in
question the strength of the evidence for the patterns which he had
demonstrated:

(1) In the speech to the elders of Ephesus at Miletus, Luke places
on the lips of Paul the words (Acts 20.21) that he has testified both
to Jews and to Greeks μετάνοια towards God and faith in our Lord
Jesus Christ. According to this sentence, Paul presented to *both*
audiences, not only to the Gentiles, but also to the Jews, two items
in the missionary pattern, which according to Wilckens belong only

[98] W. Grundmann, *Evangelium nach Lukas*, p. 39.

to the pattern of missionary speeches to the Gentiles, and in fact have points of contact both in terminology and subject-matter with Acts 17.30f., I Thess. 1.9 and Hebrews 6.1b.

(2) In Paul's defence before Agrippa, too, Luke has put into Paul's mouth words declaring that he had preached to Gentiles *and* to Jews that they should repent, turn to God and perform deeds worthy of repentance (Acts 26.20). But these are items which according to Wilckens belong only to the missionary sermons to *Gentiles*.

(3) As regards Paul's sermon to the elders of the Jews of Rome, it is said, though in an indirect, condensed and summary style, that Paul has testified to them of the Kingdom of God, and has preached about Jesus from the law of Moses and from the prophets. If we compare this wording with that in the first missionary speeches examined by Wilckens, only two items, kerygma and scriptural proof, are mentioned as the subject matter of this sermon to the Jews, and not the summons to repent which would be altogether relevant here and, in view of the situation which is presupposed, ought not to be lacking as in the speech before Cornelius.

It follows from the observations on the three foregoing passages that Luke has by no means carried out the pattern of the sermon to the Jews and the Gentiles respectively with such complete consistency as Wilckens has assumed. Thus the strength of the argument for his thesis has lost some of its power to carry conviction. We do not intend to reject the whole of Wilckens' scheme with these observations. We consider it to be fundamentally correct, but it is still possible for the components of the first missionary speeches to appear earlier in the history of the tradition than Wilckens is ready to allow and hence not to be composed completely by Luke. We admit that we have to do with different types of sermons when preaching to Jews and to Gentiles. But we consider that nothing has as yet been determined about their earlier or later date, simply by the fact that no parallels for the first missionary speeches of the same kerygmatic type occur in the whole of the New Testament. This is in my opinion not yet convincing evidence for the fact that Luke himself created this Jewish-Christian pattern of a missionary sermon.

Moreover I consider that the evidence for asserting that there is a traditional Gentile-Christian missionary pattern is too weak. It is true that the relevant parallels in the passages named by Wilckens do exist, but the passage from the Epistle to the Hebrews is convincing only if it is intended to be directed unequivocally to Gentile

Christians. But this is by no means an unequivocal matter. There is much more to be said for the hypothesis of Jewish Christian recipients and of a Jewish Christian author.

Nor is it correct to say, as Wilckens does, that Paul's speech in the synagogue at Pisidian Antioch is the last summons to the Jews to repent. In fact Paul continues to turn each time first to the Jewish synagogue in all the cities in which (according to the account in Acts) he carries on missionary work, and only after that does he turn to the Gentiles. Nevertheless, it is also correct that except in ch. 28 no further missionary *sermons* by Paul to Jews are described in detail, for the speeches in chs. 22 and 26 are not missionary speeches, but apologies with a different range of ideas. In fact, apart from the disowning of the Jews in Pisidian Antioch (Acts 13.46), there are two more formal repudiations addressed to the Jews, namely in Corinth (Acts 18.6) and in Rome (Acts 28.25–28), of which only the last is really final. Here Luke confirms Paul's words Ἰουδαίῳ τε πρῶτον καὶ Ἕλληνι in Rom. 1.16 and describes him correctly, if not indeed theologically, at least as regards his missionary method.

I. Martin Rese *Luke and the Old Testament*

In his traditio-historical investigation of the missionary speeches in Acts, Wilckens paid no attention to the function of the Old Testament scriptural proof within these speeches. In his investigation *Alttestamentliche Motive in der Christologie des Lukas*, Martin Rese, however, has paid special attention to this function, not only in the Acts speeches, but throughout Luke's two books. In so doing he has disregarded the significance of the Old Testament themes for Luke's ecclesiology and has simply limited himself to the christology.

He sees in the text of the quotations (and particularly in the deviations from the LXX text) an important aid towards determining the relation between tradition and composition in a piece of material. The Old Testament quotations in Luke open up the possibility of seeing Luke's attitude to the tradition of the community and his place within the different traditions (p. 40).

In his detailed investigation, Rese first inquires after the text (what is quoted?), then the form of a quotation (how is it quoted?) and then the meaning of a quotation in its context (why is it quoted?). This enables him to fix the place in tradition of the use of the quotations in Luke.

Investigation of the three scriptural quotations in Peter's speech in Acts 2 leads Rese to the conclusion that they are all connected with christological statements. The speech serves to show Jesus definitely as Messiah and Lord, in the proof for which the quotations occupy an important place. Neither the wording nor the original meaning of the text quoted is sacrosanct for Luke, for Luke is not afraid to alter the quotation by deletions or expansions. The reason for alteration is to fit a text to the context or to a larger theological conception (pp. 84f.).

The scriptural quotations in Peter's speech after the healing of the lame man in Acts 3 are also immediately connected with christological statements, though the place of both quotations is primarily that of soteriology, not christology, as they are related more to the call to repentance than to the kerygmatic part of the speech. They are connected with the call to repentance in so far as they show the significance of the end time; i.e., the reference to the end time is the ground for the call to repentance (p. 106). In this chapter the tradition is clearly subordinate to the composition and the reference back to the tradition is a feature of an apologetic attitude which sets out to confront the Jews, on their own presuppositions, with the connection between salvation and condemnation in Jesus (p. 109).

It is unnecessary here to record the detailed results reached in the investigation of Old Testament quotations and other Old Testament images and allusions in the speeches and other passages of Acts (pp. 109–203). All in all, Rese comes to the conclusion that the varied manner of the use of quotations takes *ad absurdum* the view that Luke *only* uses scripture in the pattern of prophecy and fulfilment. Nor is any general verdict possible about the relationship of Luke and his community to the Old Testament (p. 204). Here he agrees with Suhl that the pattern of prophecy and fulfilment is an insufficient basis for assessing the use of the Old Testament, as Suhl asserted in his investigation of the Old Testament quotations and allusions in the gospel of Mark (cf. M. Rese, *op. cit.*, p. 44, n. 122). Rese makes one exception in the use of Ps. 2.7 in Acts 13.33. Here alone is there a quotation in the prophecy-fulfilment pattern (p. 117).

Rese also investigates the Old Testament quotations, allusions and images in the context of the christological statements in the gospel of Luke, as well as the christological designations and titles in Luke, which may possibly derive from the Old Testament (pp. 207–321). He comes to the conclusion that here, too, there are alterations in the quotations which derive from Luke and therefore give a clue to his intention. The quotations and allusions are a good help in the attempt to draw out individual features of Luke's theology. This is equally clear in Luke 1 and 2, in the special material, and in the synoptic material. Thus in Luke 4.18f. (Isa. 61.1f.), Jesus' preaching and working are programmatically represented as belonging to the end time, and in Luke 22.37 (Isa. 53.12), the same is true of the cross, though Luke knows of no atoning significance of the death of Jesus (p. 322). Nor is there any suggestion of an atoning significance in the suffering and death of Jesus in Acts, as the alteration of Isa. 53.7–8 in Acts 8.32–33 shows (p. 206).

Luke 1.76 and 8.27f. show Luke's concern to differentiate between Jesus and the Baptist, to argue that Jesus alone is the prophet of the end time and Christ, whereas John belongs in the series of prophets who point to the end time. Among the titles taken from the tradition he prefers the title Christ, and alongside it the title Kyrios; all other titles are subordinated to these two (p. 323).

Summing up, Rese argues that both Acts and Luke's gospel display no adoptionist christology and no atoning significance of the death of Jesus. In the Lucan use of Old Testament quotations, in most cases we do not find the scheme of prophecy and fulfilment, but in a few passages there is a hermeneutical use of scripture and authoritative proof from it (pp. 324f.).

J. Günter Klein   *The Origin of the Twelve*

Klein's study *Die zwölf Apostel* (The Twelve Apostles) investigates the problem of the historical origin of the apostolate of the Twelve. As it is only in Luke's books that 'twelve apostles' are mentioned with special emphasis, the author devotes his exegetical study mainly to these. He regards his subject as being connected with the problem of a possible theology of Luke,[99] and he starts with von Campenhausen's statement, 'The "apostles" are earlier than the Church, that is to say, earlier than the Church in the sense of a sociologically defined community',[100] but he sets beside it the thesis: 'The twelve apostles . . . are later than the Church, that is to say, wholly a product of the Church's thinking' (p. 13). This means that in most of

[99] Thus in the title of para. 3 of his study.
[100] Thus H. von Campenhausen, *Kirchliches Amt und geistliche Vollmacht in den ersten drei Jahrhunderten*, 1953, p. 15, quoted in G. Klein, *Die zwölf Apostel*, p. 12.

the other New Testament writings apostles are also mentioned; yet the understanding of them as an exclusive circle with definite conditions for belonging to it occurs first in Luke's two books. Acts 1.21f. is considered to be the *Magna Carta* of the apostolate of the Twelve. Here the principle of being an eye-witness since the baptism of John constitutes Luke's concept of an apostle (already hinted at in Luke 6.21f.); thus the apostolate is firmly embedded in the early stage of the *historia Jesu*.[101] Klein starts from the fact that an original apostolate and an apostolate of the Twelve are not the same thing, and that for the latter an empirical bond with Jesus' life is demanded as an intrinsic element (p. 13).

As regards method, Klein proceeds on redaction-critical lines; hence he does not inquire into the tradition utilized in Luke's book, but about its present state (p. 15). In order to work out his thesis that the apostolate of the Twelve was first Luke's conception, he starts with Paul and examines the writings of the Apostolic Fathers in addition to those of the New Testament. Klein decisively rejects the thesis, supported with special emphasis by Rengstorf, that the twelve apostles were called by the historical Jesus and that his was derived from the Jewish institutions of the Shaliah (pp. 22ff. especially p. 37).

In order to determine Paul's concept of an apostle he examines I Cor. 15.5ff. and Gal. 1.18ff. He comes to the conclusion that it was not confined to the Twelve, but included a wider circle, which was not a small one. Its members could be found within the whole Church; for example, according to Rom. 16.7 Andronicus and Junius belonged to it (pp. 41f.). It was not until later that the historical nucleus of the Twelve was endowed with the character of apostleship, whereas at the beginning οἱ ἀπόστολοι and οἱ δώδεκα were different groups (p. 49).

Klein also rejects Harnack's thesis that Paul brought about the gradual restriction of the concept of apostle to the Twelve, although this was originally a wider circle, and similarly the opinion of Fridrichsen, Munck, Mosbeck and Lohse that through Paul's fight for his apostleship the concept of apostle was not limited to the circle of the Twelve, but was transferred to the originally unapostolic circle of the Twelve (p. 53). Klein emphatically denies that a concept of apostleship existed before Paul and in addition to Paul's, and that Paul had any share in developing a concept of

---

[101] *Ibid.*, pp. 204f.; cf. p. 14; see also J. Roloff, *Apostolat—Verkündigung—Kirche*, Gütersloh 1965, pp. 169f., see also p. 181.

the apostolate as an institution. The origin of the subsequent idea of the twelve apostles continues to be an enigma (p. 60).

He rejects Campenhausen's thesis that the association of the Twelve with the concept of an apostle came into being only after the apostolic generation had died out (p. 61), hence in the early post-apostolic era; nor does he accept Schmithals' view that the idea of apostleship had its home in gnostic myth and that it is to be derived from synoptic Christianity and to be located in Ephesus (p. 63, note 277; pp. 64f.). Since the original link between apostolate and the institution of the Twelve is not historical and is not theologically pertinent in the earliest sources, the origin of the close association is to be sought in post-Pauline times; in this case Matthew and Mark would drop out (p. 65). As a result, Klein looks for the inter-mediate links between Paul and Luke's two books.

In the Epistle to the Ephesians, considered to be deutero-Pauline, the apostles and prophets (Eph. 2.20; 3.5; 4.11) do not belong to the past but serve the Church in the present; Christ is the key-stone of the building. A concept of apostleship of this kind cannot be reconciled with a limited number, but is unrestricted on principle (p. 75). Klein is surely right to deny that the concept of the twelve apostles occurs in Rev. 2.2 and 18.20 (pp. 75, 79); this is not, however, true of Rev. 21.14; here his idea can only be read into the text forcibly[102]. Klein disputes that the concept is in the *Didache*, although it occurs in its title; but otherwise in patristic writings there is little evidence for it in this book, so it may possibly be a later addition. Elsewhere in the Didache a completely different concept of an apostle is found (p. 82).

Similarly I Peter, in spite of giving the title apostle to Peter, shows no evidence for a council of twelve; instead the heading is an indirect witness to the unrestricted concept of apostle (p. 84). I Clement knows the apostolate only as a bygone institution which is probably not rooted in the life of Jesus. The limitation of its numbers cannot be proved and there is no contact with the idea of the aposto-late of the Twelve (p. 90). For Ignatius of Antioch, too, the apostolate is a phenomenon of the past and its origins do not lie in the life of Jesus. The appearance of a closed number arises merely because of the typological function of the institution in the framework of Ignatius'

---

[102] *Ibid.*, pp. 76ff.; this tells against Klein's thesis of an identification of the Twelve with the apostles only by Luke. It is certainly not yet there in I Cor. 15.3-7, but it is probably to be found in Matt. 10.1-3, in certain manuscripts at Mark 3.14, and in Mark 6.30—cf. also Mark 6.7 (on this see E. Haenchen, *Der Weg Jesu*, pp. 247-9).

theology, and can be clearly seen to be such (p. 96). On the other hand, the Epistle of Barnabas is the earliest of the documents considered so far in which it is taken for granted explicitly that the apostolate is intimately connected with Jesus' life, though a restriction to the Twelve is most probably not associated with it (p. 97). In the Shepherd of Hermas, too, the idea of the twelve apostles cannot be established, since it does not occur to the author to fix the number in the circle of the apostles and the current concept of apostle is open (p. 99). The Epistle of Jude is indeed aware of a circle of apostles, but not of any limitation of their number (p. 100). II Peter, however, clearly cannot be included in the negative findings worked out by Klein. This epistle perceives the criterion of apostleship to be the witness by eyes and ears to Jesus' life, so it explicitly anchors the apostolate in the period before Easter (II Peter 1.16ff.) and brings out emphatically what is so to speak a by-product in Barnabas (a retrospect to the transfiguration) (pp. 102f.). The author disparages Paul by declaring that his writings are hard to understand (p. 104). He contrasts the fact of the empirical eye-witness of the apostles with Paul's wisdom subsequently; thus he withholds from Paul the title of apostle and gives him merely that of ἀγαπητὸς ἀδελφός. In doing so the author clearly supports the idea of the apostolate of the Twelve (p. 105). Thus not until II Peter is the idea of the twelve apostles the norm for the theological pattern. It becomes a postulate of the first rank to combine the apostle with the life of Jesus in order to safeguard the institution as a factor guaranteeing the tradition. Consequently the apostleship of Paul cannot be recognized. However, the idea was not invented by II Peter; the earliest evidence of it occurs in Luke's books, though not in the pre-Lucan period (p. 113). Klein, however, in his exegesis of II Peter fails to notice that the *concept* of twelve apostles is not found in it.

In Klein's study, as a result of his main thesis the chief emphasis is naturally laid on Acts in order to work out Luke's picture of an apostle and of Paul. He starts from the picture of Saul in the Acts and compares it with the historical Paul's understanding of his pre-Christian past. In Gal. 1.13f. Paul mentions his activity as a persecutor merely in passing. In II Cor. 11.22ff. and Phil. 3.5ff. the mention of what he was before he became a Christian is provoked by his opponents and is intended to be polemical. The historical Paul is concerned to emphasize his Jewishness (according to Gal. 1.14 he was extremely zealous for the Law), Acts is concerned to reduce it (pp. 129ff.). Thus the difference between Luke's image of Saul and the self-understanding of the historical Paul is that Luke tones down the ἀναστροφή ἐν τῷ Ἰουδαισμῷ and emphasizes his activity as a persecutor, whereas the historical Paul does the opposite (p. 132).

I Tim. 1.12–16 shows that the former activity of the subsequent apostle as a persecutor remained a permanent constituent of what Pauline Christianity remembered. Admittedly, the realistic description of what was known was not made for historical reasons, but for the sake of exhortation; yet the heightening of Paul's understanding of himself did not happen on this account (p. 138). In the post-canonical literature the picture of Saul becomes reduced in size and milder in quality (p. 142); hence there are no analogies for the features of Luke's image of Saul. Therefore Luke incorporated this specific bias in order for it to be a foil to the subsequent Paul (p. 143). In Klein's investigation, special emphasis is placed on the exegetical demonstration that the Lucan Paul is legally subordinated to the leading church authorities in Jerusalem. For this purpose Klein starts from the conversion reported three times in Acts. Since Paul is received into the Church by Ananias he has been placed from the outset in a subordinationist relationship to the officials in charge of the mission and of the church who were set over him at any given time (p. 148). But in Acts 22.6ff., the laying on of hands by Ananias is missing and only the physical restoration of Paul is mentioned. In this way the relationship of one-sided dependence of the new convert on the representatives of the Church is glossed over and the dependence is no longer understood, as in ch. 9, as a matter of principle, but only as an interim measure (p. 152). Then in 26.12ff., Paul is described not only as μάρτυς but also as ὑπηρέτης; he is raised to a still higher position, for in Luke 1.2, Luke identifies the ὑπηρέται τοῦ λόγου with the αὐτόπται, the first generation which formed the tradition with the twelve apostles, who, according to Acts 1.21f., are for Luke the real eye-witnesses ἀπ'ἀρχῆς (p. 157).

In all three accounts of the conversion, Luke emphasizes the idea of the mediation in the giving of an office to Paul, in ch. 9 by a man (Ananias), in ch. 22 also by a place (the temple), and in ch. 26 by the time as well. Whereas in chs. 9 and 22 conversion and calling are differentiated, in ch. 26 the idea of the witness is limited by the concept of the servant (p. 159). On Paul's own testimony about his conversion in Gal. 1, Klein writes: 'Paul demonstrates his independence as an apostle by elaborating the fact that his message was not mediated to him' (p. 161). On the other hand, Luke describes the relationship of Paul to the twelve apostles as a difference in rank due to disparity (p. 165). In Acts 9.26–30, he introduced the figure of Barnabas in order to describe Paul's entry into the centre of the Christian community as being mediated. For Luke, Paul's office is valid only because he established contact with the twelve apostles, because for Luke contact with the apostolic tradition is a *conditio sine qua non* of every Christian existence (p. 164). It was not the apostles who sent Paul through Caesarea to Tarsus because he was in danger in Jerusalem (9.30), but 'the brethren'. Thus it is in Luke's idea of an apostolic succession that Paul evidently occupies only a third place after the apostles and 'the brethren'.[103] For Luke, Barnabas was not only an official of the community at Jerusalem but a delegate of this community as *sedes apostolica*. In this capacity he travels to Antioch in order to guarantee the contact of a new Gentile Christian community with the apostolic tradition; and in this capacity, too, he brings Paul from Tarsus to Antioch (Acts 11.22–26). The same subordinate relationship also appears in Acts 11.30 and 12.25 (p. 167). Acts 13.1–3 marks the decisive turning point in the life of the Christian Paul. Paul, who up till then had been completely subordinated to the bearers of the tradition placed over him, thereafter becomes himself a bearer of the apostolic authority of succession with its corresponding rights and duties (p. 170). The order Barnabas-Saul is reversed at the moment when Saul receives the name of Paul, at the instant when he proves himself to be the missionary filled with the Holy Spirit.[104] Thus Luke shows a carefully worked out pattern by which Paul becomes progressively more independent (p. 172). By his description he also succeeds in making Paul's missionary work appear to be not that of a man of the second apostolic generation playing a lone hand, but as being endorsed by apostolic authority. But the passages in Acts 15.1–2 and 21.18ff. show also that Paul's independence is not absolute, but strictly limited with regard to the founding of young churches. Whereas in Acts 15.2 the community in Antioch has still a right to give instructions to Paul, there is in addition to this the superior authority of Jerusalem, although the elders there would also already be representatives of the second generation.

[103] *Ibid.*, p. 166; for the construction of the unbridgeable gulf between the historical and the Lucan Paul, cf. also J. Roloff, *op. cit.*, p. 171.
[104] *Ibid.*, p. 171. In Acts 14.12, 14 and 15.12, 25 the earlier order has purely material reasons: Zeus comes before Hermes.

In Acts 21.18 the leadership of the Church is already completely in the hands of the elders under the monarchic supervision of James. The supervision of Paul by the Jerusalem Council is preserved, for in 21.18ff. he submits an account of his activities (pp. 173f.).

The following facts are therefore established. According to Luke's account, Paul has a relative independence with regard to his communities, yet he is subject in principle to the bearers of the tradition of superior rank, who are not only the apostles, but also their successors at the *sedes apostolica*. Although on the one hand Paul himself appoints elders (Acts 14.23) and equips them with authority as church leaders (Acts 20.17ff.), he is bound to give an account of himself to other elders. Hence in the Acts there is not yet a hierarchic gradation of official positions, since Paul still remains subject to the post-apostolic authorities of the first rank (pp. 175f.). It is noteworthy that in Acts 14.23 the elders of the community were appointed not by the community itself, but by the sovereign decision of Paul and Barnabas, the bearers of the tradition set over them. During their sojourn there both of them still had, according to Luke, the authority of leadership in the community. Consequently Luke is not at all concerned with vertical *gradation* of official position, but wholly with horizontal *succession* of official positions. In this way Luke safeguards the continuity of the apostolic succession in Paul's missionary area (pp. 175f.). The pericope about the disciples of John (Acts 19.1ff.) shows that Paul in his own missionary area was the competent authority for the problems arising with the foundation of young churches, and that his authority was limited only by that of Jerusalem which in practice did not exist in his own area. Since the disciples of John received the Spirit not by baptism but by Paul's laying on of hands, Luke intended to bring out, as he did in Acts 8.14ff., the superiority of the Church's tradition and authority over the sacrament (pp. 177f.). Paul's speech to the elders of Ephesus at Miletus shows (Acts 20.18ff.) that for Paul appointments to an official position are necessary only when the superior authority retires. This is for him a basic condition for the permanence of the subordinate position. Indeed the speech is an indication of Luke's lack of interest in a hierarchy of official positions, but at the same time of his sympathy with an apostolic succession. For Luke, the central problem is how the Church can secure its permanency when the authorized bearers of the tradition belong to the past time in Church history (pp. 179f.). The warning of the Lucan Paul against heresy shows that the period of the beginning without divisions is approaching its end and that thereafter the discussions about orthodoxy and heresy are to start (p. 181). The speech in Miletus places the Pauline heritage in the care of the clergy whose business it is to interpret it authoritatively (p. 184).

Luke's description of Paul raises, of course, in an acute form the question whether Luke knew Paul's epistles. Klein is strongly in favour of the conjecture that Luke did know them, yet probably he did not *want* to use them.[105] Klein conjectures that Justin Martyr, too, deliberately ignored the *Corpus Paulinum* (p. 200). Thus Luke's relationship to Paul is not an unbiassed one; for on the one hand he is the first to attach importance to the idea of the twelve apostles, and on the other his attitude towards Paul is one of deliberate bias (p. 202).

After an examination of the apostolate of the Twelve in Luke's scheme, Klein reaches the conclusion: 'For Luke, the apostolate of the Twelve is distinguished by an uninterrupted empirical bond with the *historia Jesu*, based on its origin'. The arrangement resulting from it and making it the guarantor of a phenomenon of the time of Jesus which had become a thing of the past, shows it to be suitable as a fundamental institution of the Church. It accomplishes this function, on the one hand, directly by the sermon πρὸς τὸν λαόν which founds the Church, on the other, indirectly, by ensuring that the world mission is apostolic by means of tradition and succession (p. 210).

In conclusion, Klein discusses the contrast between the apostolate of the Twelve and the *picture* of Paul in Luke. For Luke the criterion by which a genuine apostle of Jesus Christ is judged is the fact that he was an eye-witness from the beginning and permanently. Since the apostle guarantees the tradition and the succession as a substitute for the end of the world which has failed to appear, the twelve apostles are represented by him to have absolute pre-eminence above every other Christian office-bearer. Hence Paul could not belong to them (p. 211), because in Luke's opinion the candidature for the office of an apostle is linked with the preliminary condition of having been from beginning to end a witness of the whole of Jesus' public ministry from his baptism until his resurrection (p. 207). Luke, by confining the concept of apostle strictly to the Twelve, at the same time brings Paul's rank down to a subordinate level.[106] But the

---

[105] *Ibid.*, p. 192. This is rejected by Kümmel, *Introduction to the New Testament*, p. 133.

[106] *Ibid.*, p. 212. This is disputed by Kümmel, *op. cit.*, p. 114.

reason for this is not a dislike of Paul; it is based on the objective situation of the Church in Luke's time. As the speech in Miletus shows, heresies threatened the Church. Against these Luke framed the idea of the apostolate of the Twelve, and brought Paul into an indissoluble connection with the apostolic succession going back to the historical Jesus, in order to snatch him away from the agnostics who referred to him for their heresies.[107]

Klein disputes the view of Köster (*RGG* III[3], 1959, col. 21) that only the Pastoral Epistles kept Paul away from the heretics. With regard to the development of the Pauline theology, the Pastoral Epistles are certainly a more mature solution than the negative one of Luke, but by linking the succession firmly to the idea of the tradition and by utilizing both of these for a specific understanding of Paul, Luke advanced further than the Pastoral Epistles (p. 216, note 983).

The following points should be made against Klein's approach: although it is indisputable that Luke incorporates Paul in the tradition of the Church, he occupies a quite special position within it. He is even equated with Peter, in so far as he is a miracle worker in the same way: both heal demon-possessed men (Acts 5.16; 16.16–18), get the better of magicians (8.18–24; 13.6–12), raise the dead (9.36–42; 20.7–12), heal lame men (3.6–8; 14.8–10), communicate the Spirit through the laying on of hands (8.16f.; 19.6), both are arrested and miraculously freed (12.3–17; 16.19–40).

Although Paul is not designated as an apostle (except for 14.4, 14), he is even superior to the apostles in that he is in direct association with the exalted Lord.[108] Flender even argues that by his suffering Paul is portrayed in climactic parallelism with the apostles (p. 131). Flender offers instances of a parallelism between the suffering of Jesus and that of Paul in Luke (p. 131, note 3).

By his formulation that Acts 1.21f. is the *Magna Carta* of the apostolate of the twelve (p. 204), Klein has taken the story of the choice of Matthias (Acts 1.15–26) as a starting point for his recon-

---

[107] *Ibid.*, pp. 213f. Kümmel does not feel that Luke wanted to deprive the gnostics of Paul with the words in Acts 20.29f.; for in these Paul was, after all, not obliged to differentiate between himself and the gnostics (*ibid.*, p. 114). Flender also rejects an anti-gnostic tendency in Acts (*St Luke, Theologian of Redemptive History*, p. 129). On the other hand, Roloff largely shares Klein's grounding of the Lucan picture of the apostle on the danger of the gnostic heresy (*op. cit.*, pp. 198f.).

[108] See the instances in H. Flender, *St Luke, Theologian of Redemptive History*, London and Philadelphia 1967, p. 130.

struction of the Lucan picture of an apostle. In so doing he has laid
the main stress on the terms occurring here which seem to give the
whole process an official character, such as ἐπισκοπή (v. 20), τόπος
and ἀποστολή (v. 25) and κλῆρος (v. 26). These concepts also play a
central role in I Clement 40 and 44, whereas in reality the Lucan
picture of the apostle is shaped by the concepts of μάρτυς and διακονία
(for the concept of the witness, cf. Acts 1.8, 22 with Luke 24.48; see
also Acts 2.32; 3.15; 5.32; 10.39, 41; 13.31; 22.15; 26.16; for the
concept of διακονία see Acts 6.4; 20.24; 21.19).

Luke indeed identifies the group of the apostles with the twelve
in the story of the choice of Matthias, as in his view only the twelve
can fulfil the requirements of the apostolate in the full sense, namely
as witnesses of the resurrection and at the same time as commissioned
bearers of the διακονία of Jesus for the Church. In fact, however, as
we shall see, he also designates Paul as an apostle, though he almost
without exception withholds the title from him[109].

Klein considerably overestimates the role of Ananias in the conversion of Paul. He is merely a certain disciple (τις μαθητής) who is not
commissioned and sent by the apostles, but by the Lord himself
(Acts 9.17). So it is not a representative of the Church's tradition
who accepts Paul into the succession of the Church, as his laying on
of hands does not communicate the Holy Spirit (as the apostles in
Acts 8.17) but is merely meant to remove the blindness from him
(Acts 9.12, 18). Ananias does not even communicate the kerygma to
him, like the evangelist Philip to the Ethiopian treasurer when he
interprets Scripture as a preparation for baptism (Acts 8.35). The
place of baptismal instruction is taken in Paul's case by a direct call
from the Exalted One, which Ananias merely confirms again (Acts
9.12, similarly 22.14–16).[110]

All three versions of the Damascus road appearance (chs. 9; 22;
26) have been shaped in such a way that Paul is put on the same
footing as the apostles. He, too, has seen and heard the Lord and has
been commissioned and sent by him in a special way, even if he has
not seen the earthly Jesus but only the exalted Lord. In Acts 26.16
he, too, is described as μάρτυς and ὑπηρέτης (in Acts 22.15 only as
μάρτυς) and thus incorporated in the ranks of the αὐτόπται καὶ ὑπηρέται
of Luke 1.2, that is, in the ranks of the twelve apostles. Luke makes
particular use of the concept of the witness to connect Paul's office

---

[109] Cf. also J. Roloff, *Apostolat—Verkündigung—Kirche*, Gütersloh 1965, p. 198.
[110] Cf. also J. Roloff, *op. cit.*, pp. 200, 206.

with that of the twelve apostles. Thus there can no longer be any question of subordination[111], especially as in Acts 9.28 Paul already appears with the same standing as the first apostles after his meeting with them.[112]

When Paul is brought in safety via Caesarea to Tarsus because of the threat in Jerusalem (Acts 9.30), Luke is not concerned with a sending off by the 'brethren', which would lay stress on his subordinate position, but with a protective guard of honour. Luke even portrays the event in such a way that Paul seems to be concerned about a link with the apostolic college, but in so doing he avoids all official and juridical terms in defining this relationship. At any rate, it is better to speak of a tendency of Luke to set Paul on the same footing as the apostles rather than of his being incorporated into the apostolic succession as a subordinate. In designating Paul as an apostle *de facto*, Luke breaks out at decisive points from the conditions which he had laid down in Acts 1.21f. for membership of the group of the apostles.

Nor can there be any question of a formal, juristic theory of an apostolic succession in the farewell speech of Paul in Miletus to the elders of the community of Ephesus (Acts 20.17–38), for these leaders, too, are not successors of the apostles. They, too, are in an immediate relationship to the exalted Lord through their calling (Acts 20.28); that is, Luke knows nothing of the continuation of the apostolate in the church as it is to be found, say in I Clement (40–44), nor does he attempt to make the gospel controllable by binding it to an institution.[113] Thus the farewell speech in Miletus is at the same time an interpretation of Acts 14.23: in appointing the elders of the community, Paul and Barnabas act to a certain extent only as instruments of the Lord of the Church, to whom they commend the elders with prayer and fasting.

K. Helmut Flender *Criticism of the Unilinear Interpretation of Salvation History in Luke*

In his dissertation *Heil und Geschichte in der Theologie des Lukas* (Salvation and History in the Theology of Luke[114]), Flender seeks to protect the author of the double work especially from the charges

[111] Cf. also J. Roloff, *op. cit.*, p. 200, note 99; p. 202.
[112] Cf. also J. Roloff, *op. cit.*, p. 206.
[113] See also J. Roloff, *op. cit.*, pp. 234f.
[114] ET *St Luke, Theologian of Redemptive History*, London and Philadelphia 1967.

of Vielhauer, Bultmann and Käsemann, that he has fallen away from the climax of Pauline theology, that his theology stands on the periphery of the canon, or that he has already stepped over the boundary of early catholicism.[115]

He begins by arguing that Luke's outline has far more levels than Conzelmann allows for. Conzelmann does not grasp sharply enough Luke's particular conceptual presuppositions and thus forces him into the structure of modern categories of thought. He does not make enough differentiation in the concept of 'salvation history' (pp. 5f.). The understanding of the Lucan testimony must be found in the borderland between tradition and interpretation, and the possibility must always be taken into account that the variety of historical tradition has been modified in favour of a dogmatic scheme (p. 2). Flender is concerned to demonstrate that Luke's account is not in terms of a unilinear salvation history but is a dialectical one, characterized by complementary, climactic and antithetic parallelism. Thus, for example, there is often an unexpressed allusion to previous passages, e.g. in Luke 22.3 to Luke 4.13; 23.2 to 20.25; 19.38 to 13.35; 22.11 to 2.7; 19.38 to 2.14 and 23.51 to 2.38 (p. 9).

Among the complementary parallelisms Flender counts the parallel stories about a man and a woman, especially in the special Lucan material (pp. 9ff.) and the close connection between the destruction of Jerusalem and the crucifixion of Jesus, which is stressed much more strongly than in Mark. Luke 13.34 says that the prophets die not only *in*, but *through* Jerusalem. Luke shifts the crucifixion on to an individualistic level by depicting it as a martyrdom. It is no longer a saving historical event as in Matthew and Mark; the place of the saving historical view of the cross is taken in Luke by the legal historical event of the destruction of Jerusalem, in which the judicial murder by the Jews finds its proper punishment (p. 17).

As examples of the pattern of climactic parallelism, expressing the relationship between the old and the new worlds, Flender gives the stories of John and Jesus in Luke 1–4 (pp. 21ff.) and the two missionary discourses: the mission of the twelve in Luke 9 is only preliminary and earthbound; that of the seventy in Luke 10 is at the same time a sign of the consummation in heaven, as a prefiguration of the universal mission to the Gentiles (p. 26).

<hr />

[115] Cf. R. Bultmann, *Theology of the New Testament* II, pp. 116f.; E. Käsemann, *Essays on New Testament Themes*, London 1964, pp. 28f.

Luke also has an antithetic parallelism, for example between salvation and judgment (Luke 2.34; 6.20–26; 19.1–10; 19.37f.), strict conditions for discipleship (14.25–33), receptivity and unreceptiveness of hearers for the kingdom of God (10.25–37; 16.19–31; 23.39–43), suffering and glorification of Jesus (24.26, also in the predictions of the passion). The place of the messianic secret in Mark is taken by the secret of the suffering of the Messiah in Luke (pp. 31–3). The journey to Jerusalem is not only a journey to suffering, but at the same time a victorious journey towards exaltation (ἀναλήμψεως in Luke 9.51) (pp. 31f.).

Flender agrees with Conzelmann that in 4.16–30 Luke, as a believing historian, believes that salvation history gives the clue to the 'correct' historical sequence. This is important to him in principle, but one should not speak of a 'historization' of the message of the gospel by Luke[116], because this is a modern idea of a closed system of cause and effect which is alien to Luke. However, Luke has the task of depicting the life of Jesus as a piece of past history in the post-apostolic period (p. 36).

Starting from I Tim. 3.16; Rom. 1.3–4 and Mark 12.35–37, Flender demonstrates that there was a primitive christological tradition before and after Paul, which saw Jesus Christ in earthly and heavenly modes of existence according to the pattern of Hellenistic thought. Luke's christology must also be seen in this framework (p. 41), as the acceptance of Mark 12.35–37 in Luke 20.41–44, with only a few alterations, shows that a similar christological structure can be established in Luke 1.26–38 and Luke 22.66–71 (pp. 43f.). The framework of Lucan christology is provided by the Hellenistic pattern of the heavenly and earthly modes of existence of Christ: the man Jesus stands in the same sequence as the Old Testament prophets. But at the same time he is also the true Adam (in the genealogy, Luke 3.1ff., cf. p. 51) as God willed at creation. As such he is the pattern for Christian life in the old aeon (p. 56; cf. pp. 53f. on the commandments of Jesus). Luke does not begin from a historical situation; for him the decisive event is the exaltation of Christ. He looks back on earthly history in the light of this heavenly event. He is concerned with political apologetic in order to protect the Christ event from earthly misinterpretation and to testify to it as salvation (p. 57; cf. also pp. 61f.).

Only the historical aspect is brought out in the prologue, which

[116] Against Bultmann, *Theology of the New Testament* II, pp. 124f., 116f.

makes possible a certain examination of the events by means of profane scholarship. Alongside this, however, the kerygmatic aspect of the story of Jesus is preserved, for the events which are fulfilled in it are also saving facts brought about by God. Nevertheless, the prologue points only to the factuality of the story of Jesus (p. 66).

Flender shows in detail how the Christian message also enters into worldly ordinances. Luke gives special expression to the way in which the message of Christ is related to the world—the beginning of this is evident in the way in which even Mark allots a considerable role to the teaching of Jesus (p. 72)—in his shaping of the journey to Jerusalem, the scenes at table and the pattern of question and answer (p. 73). In the travel narrative, the journey to Jerusalem, the eschatological call of Jesus and the historical response of men stand in tension, especially in the group of sayings in Luke 14.25–35 (p. 75). The character of the description of the journey to Jerusalem (cf. Luke 19.11–27) shows that man has responsibility in the world (pp. 75f.), but that with Christ or through Christ he is on the way through suffering and death to heavenly salvation. This journey to heaven is a concrete, earthly way, in which the Christian follows his Lord. A characteristic of this following is being open for the instructions of Jesus as the exalted Lord and perceiving worldly responsibility in the service of this Lord (p. 80). Flender shows by means of the scenes at table in Luke how the evangelist depicts proper human life together in company with Christ and the conditions of Christian life in a world which has fallen from God (pp. 80–84; cf. also p. 88). The connection between life in the world and the gospel also comes out well in the dialogues with a question and answer of Jesus (pp. 84–7; cf. also pp. 88f.).

Flender comes to the conclusion that an overriding and superficial theory of salvation history in Luke is very improbable, as Luke has a definite dialectical pattern of concepts through which he can see a reality under different aspects or on different levels. His conception must thus be regarded with more differentiation than is usual at the moment (pp. 90f.). Luke has not historized the whole of reality in a positivistic way, and it will be seen later that he has not sacralized the history of the church in a supranaturalistic fashion either. He had a threefold task: to maintain the uniqueness of the Christ even in on-going history, to examine the problem of historical continuity between Israel and the Church, and to describe the presence of salvation in the Christian community as it passes through time (p. 91).

Against Conzelmann, Flender stresses that it is a misconception of the theological work of Luke to assume that Luke simply postponed the parousia along a given time line and substituted the exaltation instead of it. He shapes the form in accordance with the content and transfers theological statements previously associated with the parousia to the exaltation. For him, what is heavenly in a future sense is also heavenly in a transcendent sense. Thus the tension of present and future is kept up in the eschatological realization of salvation which the apostolic age had expressed in terms of the imminent expectation of the parousia (p. 98). The exaltation of Christ is for Luke as it were the parousia realized beforehand in heaven, the saving event that is already completed there. It marks the end of Israelite salvation history and the cosmic shift of the aeons. Eschatological salvation is preserved from being under human control and a false sacralization of history is avoided, but at the same time the earthly world is not surrendered (p. 106).

Conzelmann's division of salvation history into three stages is challenged by Flender. With reference to certain aspects of Morgenthaler's investigation *Die lukanische Geschichtsschreibung als Zeugnis*, he claims that in Luke there is only a division into two stages, for in Luke 16.16 only two periods of time are mentioned, the old age and the new age (p. 124). Conzelmann projects the different Lucan statements on to one level and thus reaches the questionable pattern of salvation history open to human observation (p. 125).

Flender also rejects Käsemann's understanding of the pericope about the disciples of John (Acts 19.1–6), in terms of early Catholicism. This was understood by Käsemann as evidence of Luke's conception of an undivided unity of the apostolic church in the early period.[117] In this way, Käsemann makes Luke simply into a Christian pragmatist, who seeks to demonstrate the legitimacy of present claims by an ideological theology of history. But this does not touch the theological concern of the text, for Luke does not advocate the unity of the church in a pragmatic, church-political sense; he is writing from a knowledge of the connection of the revelation of God to a historical place. Apollos and the disciples of John stand on different sides on the fringes of this church. As in the gospel of Luke, so here the Baptist shows himself a representative of the old world, as his disciples have to become full Christians (p. 127).

Flender makes a thorough investigation of the way in which Luke

[117] *Essays on New Testament Themes*, pp. 136–48.

depicts the presence of salvation in the Church. This is done in two ways: through the presence of Christ and through the gift of the spirit (p. 135). Whereas Conzelmann understands the role of the spirit in the Lucan work as a substitute for the delay of the parousia, Flender puts it that the work of the spirit stands independently alongside the work of the exalted Christ. It is certainly a matter of one saving event, but the spheres of its influence are clearly differentiated (pp. 138f.). As a consequence of the way in which the functions of the spirit and of Christ are made independent, the Church, endowed with the spirit, remains over against its Lord and does not become a *Christus prolongatus*. Were Luke to extend the Pauline kerygma that the Lord is the spirit (II Cor. 3.17) into the continuation of history, there would be a sacralization of history, and he would rightly be designated a representative of early catholicism. But in fact Luke is a theologian, who counters the threatened confusion between salvation and history more than anyone else in the New Testament, for the spirit is given no functions which are detached from Christ (pp. 139f.).

Luke nowhere prolongs the experiences of the past into the future in the manner of modern philosophers of history, but reaches men, like the apostles, to be open to the wonderful new works of the spirit. He thus knows of no salvation history in the sense that the divine salvation can be prolonged into human history, but has the task of testifying to the revelation of God in a time which has now become past. He avoids extending the sacramental conception of the body of Christ into on-going history. He can speak of a present address by the exalted Christ without getting out of touch with history altogether (p. 146).

The gospel of Luke is not only a testimony to events of the past; it is also a witness which speaks directly to the reader in the present (cf. Mark 1.15 with the today = σήμερον in Luke 4.21). Whereas for Mark the καιρός has been fulfilled, in Luke it is the scripture, i.e. he is closely tied to the Old Testament promises (p. 147). In Luke, straightforward narrative and kerygmatic appeal to faith form a dialectical unity. The account of the historical aspect of the saving event protects the kerygmatic promise of the saving presence of Christ from being merged into history and thus becoming a purely human word. Luke combines an objective account of the earthly life of Jesus with testimony to the eschatological salvation in Jesus, the mystery of which is disclosed only to faith.[118]

[118] *Ibid.*, p. 161f. For this problem see also Flender's article 'Lehren und

All in all, for Luke salvation is completed with the exaltation. The Old Testament prophecies have been proleptically fulfilled in heaven and transcended by acquiring universal dimensions. Thus for Luke there is no salvation history extending in time. True, God works through the Holy Spirit for renewal in history, but the saving plan of God never becomes a chain of saving facts detectable by the human eye. The Holy Spirit remains the superhuman reality of God. It shows God's creative action in the old world. The risen and exalted Christ represents the new world of God. He is himself present in the word of grace (Acts 14.3; 20.32) and salvation (Acts 13.26) (p. 162).

Flender sums up the results as follows: whereas for Paul, Jesus the proclaimer had to become the proclaimed, for Luke Jesus is again the proclaimer in so far as the history of the old aeon continues. The post-apostolic community, with Paul, shares in the fundamentally new situation of the world brought about by Jesus' existence, and at the same time it is moving with Jesus toward the final renewal of the world. This 'at the same time' is the independent theme of Luke alongside Paul and John, with whom the eschatological event is already taking place in the present.[119] Whereas for Paul the continuation of history is meaningless, because he is reckoning on an imminent end of the world, John knows all about the continuation of history, but pays no attention to it because he is concentrating entirely on personal decision. In Luke, who is independent, on the other hand, the salvation-historical view of Paul and the individualistic approach of John are related together dialectically. In this way there emerges a theological conception which maintains the created character of the world, which can make statements about the historical form of the church and can provide a theological answer to the problem posed by the fact that the saving event now lies in the past (p. 165).

The message of Jesus penetrates the social structures of the old world and transforms them so as to make them receptive to the word. Despite the certain acknowledgement and the independence of worldly life, the world is never canonized; as a fallen world it stands under the judgment of God. The necessity of detachment from the world is clear from Luke's attitude to possessions and riches.

Verkündigen in den synoptischen Evangelien', *EvTh* 25, 1965, pp. 701–14, esp. pp. 707f.

[119] *Ibid.*, pp. 163f. Cf. R. Bultmann, *Theology of the New Testament* II, p. 7.

Even the earthly form of the church is a worldly place, which is open to God's saving work: in it the exalted one makes himself present and the Holy Spirit carries on the work of the new creation. The apostolic church is open on two sides: the leaders of the community let themselves constantly be corrected by the work of the spirit (Acts 11.17f.; 16.6–10) and are open to Christians with special gifts of grace (Paul, Stephen). Outwardly the community is incomplete, for alongside the disciples stand the people who ask (Luke 12.41) (p. 166).

The saving history effected by God in the past is fulfilled 'today' in the presence of Christ. But for Luke the past is not objectified history; the Christ event, belonging to the past, remains ambivalent, as Luke makes clear. The factuality of the saving event forms only one aspect of the past and is not made absolute in a positivistic way. The Christ event is depicted in profane categories as *vita Jesu* in order to escape the sacralization and mythicization of history. But the life of Jesus is open to faith which accepts the eschatological act of God in Jesus. The saving event thus corrects and opens up the structures of the world, but is not to hand in them. The shift of the aeons is hidden in heaven until 'the restoration of all things' (Acts 3.21). Thus Luke finds the solution between gnostic denial and early catholic glorification of history. It is to express the supernatural mystery and the earthly visibility of Christ and his history 'at the same time' (p. 167).

L. William C. Robinson   *The Orientation of Luke's Work in Terms of Mission*

Like Flender, W. C. Robinson in his work *Der Weg des Herrn* (The Way of the Lord) is principally concerned to challenge Conzelmann's interpretation of Luke. Above all, he questions Conzelmann's thesis that the emphasis which Luke puts on the geographical framework is primarily governed by the significance which he attaches to particular geographical places and areas. The special significance of Lucan geography does not lie in the fixed significance of limited localities; it is a series of places as a means of showing the growth of the word, the expansion of the Gospel through the world. Luke saw the significance of geography in linking space and time, showing the manner of the extension of Christianity, the way of the Lord, as a journey (p. 8). Luke wishes to describe the continuity of God's guidance in history and not to stamp particular periods or areas with a saving historical significance (Acts 1.7–8). Robinson is concerned especially with the problems of the Lucan account of the beginning and the three periods of the activity of Jesus as Conzelmann interprets them (p. 9).

Referring to Conzelmann, Robinson first investigates the Lucan account of the relationship between the Baptist and Jesus. The Lucan writings give no indication that Luke wants to draw a clear line of division between John and Jesus (p. 13). The reasons advanced for the assumption that Luke has drawn a dividing line between Jesus and John are not compelling. This view might indeed be suggested by Luke 3.19–22, but in Luke's work there is no stress on a caesura between Jesus and John, and there is no interest in a precise definition of the beginning of the activity of Jesus. All signs of an actual and deliberate differentiation between Luke and his immediate predecessors are therefore lacking (p. 16).

Conzelmann's thesis that Luke eliminated the references to Elijah in order to exclude these eschatological allusions can be challenged (the descent from the mount of transfiguration). Each individual omission seems to be more strongly tied up with other considerations. The Lucan account of the Baptist is directed more towards an anti-Baptist apologetic than to a de-eschatologizing, as is clear from the infancy narratives, for here Luke even tolerates the application of the eschatological prophecy of Malachi to the Baptist (Luke 1.17, 76 = Elijah as forerunner of the Lord) (p. 19).

In the account of the beginning of the activity of Jesus, Luke apparently continues the lines which were already indicated in his sources. The Lucan alterations were made *after* a development from an eschatological approach to one in terms of salvation history, but it does not follow from this that Luke understood his account of the Baptist on the basis of this development. At this point, Luke understood his work more in terms of a christological apologetic directed against the Baptist, which he already found in his sources. His ideas in this respect are thus more synoptic and less Lucan than is usually assumed (p. 21).

Instead of dividing the gospel of Luke into three, with Conzelmann, Robinson argues with K. L. Schmidt for a division into four: 1. Activity in Galilee (4.14–9.50); 2. Journey to Jerusalem (9.51–19.27); 3. Last appearance in Jerusalem (19.28–21.38); 4. Passion, death and resurrection (22.1–24.53). Above all, it is difficult to determine where the time of the Church has to begin. Robinson also considers the possibility of dividing the Gospel of Luke into two parts: 4.14–9.50 and 9.51–24.53 (pp. 23f.; cf. also p. 29).

The three epiphany scenes, baptism, transfiguration and entry into Jerusalem, play a decisive role in Conzelmann's division of the Gospel of Luke into three. On the other hand, Robinson feels that Conzelmann's attempt to depict a three stage development of the inner history of Jesus is not successful, even if one concedes that there were already the beginnings of a biography of Jesus in Luke (p. 27).

In support of his assertion that the Gospel of Luke is divided into two parts, Robinson refers above all to the formula in Luke 23.5 which the evangelist himself conceived and thus understood as a summary of the geographical framework of the Gospel of Mark (p. 30). He attacks Conzelmann's interpretation of the travel account and writes that in a certain sense the journey has no geographical details, but is constructed by its function as a transition between the two important stages in the pattern, Galilee and Jerusalem. The interpretation of the travel account goes wrong when it presupposes the view that Luke was interested in specific details of a static geography, that he had intended to localize the journey in a non-Jewish area and in this way to hint by anticipation at the missionary work among non-Jews (p. 34).

The retreat of the problem of the imminent expectation as a consequence of the delay of the end brought about a change in the practical problem of world mission; a transformation of temporal eschatology into a historical geography gave the impression of the fulfilment of a travel plan appointed by God (Acts 1.7), a fulfilment which was realized as a journey made by the missionary testimony of the Christian Church (Acts 1.8) and leading to the end of the earth, in order to reach all people (Luke 3.6; Acts 28.28) (p. 36).

By expanding the quotation from Isa. 40.1ff. in 3.4–5 by two verses, in comparison with Mark 1.3, Luke brings out emphatically that the way of the Lord leads to the Gentiles, for all flesh shall see the salvation of God. In Acts 28.28, too, Isa. 40.5 is the closing word in the Lucan account of the way. Luke thus begins and ends his account with the same Old Testament text which stresses the way of the Lord to the Gentiles (p. 39).

Luke also renders salvation history in the terminology of the way in the speech at Pisidian Antioch (Acts 13.24f.; cf. Luke 13.33, where the work of Jesus is described as a way). Acts describes the Christian teaching as ἡ ὁδός and defines the apostolate as a journey (Acts 1.21f.). The work of Paul is also described as a completion of his δρόμος (Acts 20.24) (p. 40: for further traces of a ὁδός conception of salvation history see the examples on pp. 40f.).

Thus, according to Luke's specific conception, salvation history is a course of events which follows a time scale laid down by God and leads in the form of a 'way' to the Gentiles. This Lucan conception is matched by the expression from the Septuagint which Luke found in Mark 1.2f. and used with added emphasis: 'the way of the Lord' (p. 43).

In his account of Lucan eschatology, Robinson largely follows Conzelmann's remarks (pp. 46–66). He concludes from the exegetical evidence that while Luke awaits a coming of the kingdom of God in the future, he does not lay the chief emphasis on this. It is an over-simplification to assert that Luke added further sayings to those about the delay, for Luke 19.11 and 21.7 are not simply meant to confirm the delay, but belong to the Lucan solution of the eschato-logical problems which were partly worked out by Luke in connection with the theological interpretation of the events in Jerusalem. Luke attempts to solve the problem of an on-going history, but not to put off controversy with this problem. His solution is to work out a theology of salvation history. The Lucan translation of the imminent expectation understood in temporal terms is his view of a spatial approach of the kingdom. Luke delineates this coming of the kingdom of God in the work of Jesus (10.9, 11), above all in the extended and emphatically worked out report of the coming of Jesus to Jerusalem (Luke 9.51ff.) (p. 66).

The leading idea which determines Luke's conception of spatial nearness is that the people to whom the kingdom of God draws near are summoned to decision in the face of the kingdom. For Luke, the work of Jesus, characterized as a way which Jesus travels, is an example of the course of the Christian mission. Lucan geography is not primarily tied to certain places in static terms, even if special places have a particular significance; it is geography in movement. It describes a journey which follows a time scale, corresponds to God's plan and continues under God's guidance, a way of the Lord which leads to the Gentiles, until the time of the Gentiles is fulfilled (p. 67).

VI

MORE GENERAL
REDACTION-CRITICAL STUDIES

Preliminary note

IN THIS LAST section we consider two studies which are not
confined to the redaction-critical examination of a single synoptic
gospel, but which pursue a particular problem in all three synoptic
gospels. For lack of space I can refer here merely to pages 482–502
of the unprinted version of my dissertation for E. Grässer's investigation into the problem of the delay of the parousia in the synoptic
gospels and Acts. We must also mention here A. Strobel's studies of
this problem, especially his book, *Untersuchungen zum synoptischen
Verzögerungsproblem auf Grund der spätjüdisch-urchristlichen Geschichte von
Hab. 2.2ff.*, Leiden/Köln 1961.

A. Günther Baumbach *The Understanding of Evil in the Synoptic Gospels*

Baumbach's study *Das Verständnis des Bösen in den synoptischen
Evangelien* seeks to examine the understanding of evil within the whole
theology of the gospels in question and for this purpose it makes use,
like the other redaction-critical studies, of comparisons between the
synoptists in order to trace the theological purpose of the individual
evangelist by means of the context and peculiarities of each of them.
In so doing, it endeavours to determine the historical place, the *Sitz
im Leben*, for the understanding of evil in the individual evangelists.[1]
  Baumbach makes use of what has already been achieved by redaction-critical research hitherto. He examines each synoptic gospel
by itself and questions each one in six respects: (1) for evil denoted
by the concept πονηρός; (2) for evil denoted by κακός; (3) for the use

---

[1] G. Baumbach, *Das Verständnis des Bösen in den synoptischen Evangelien*, Berlin
1963, pp. 10f.

of the concept ἁμαρτωλός; (4) for the understanding of sin; (5) for statements about Satan and (6) for statements about demons. His examination leads to the conclusion that the understanding of evil in the individual synoptic gospels fits well into their whole theology and is a part of it.

In Mark, three lines of understanding evil are present and these run somewhat loosely beside each other: (1) Evil in the shape of Satan who is considered as *the* adversary of the Son of God, though the approaching rule of God indicates the conquest of Satan. Thus satanology in Mark is strictly related to messianology and has no contact with cosmology, anthropology or ethics. (2) Evil in the form of demons belongs to the rule of Satan. As spirits which torment mankind the demons endeavour to destroy life. (3) Evil as sin is embedded in the evil desire. Here we can feel the dualism of the Old Testament between the holy God and sinful man. Evil as sin is never connected in Mark with Satan or the demons.

In all three forms, evil in Mark is only the dark background against which what is new in the gospel shines all the more brightly. These statements are not yet made into an independent doctrine (pp. 49–51). All three lines are only intended in Mark to serve the kerygma. In this connection, Baumbach rightly rejects Robinson's thesis of the continuous cosmic struggle in history between spirit and Satan in Mark's gospel. Mark himself has given no systematic form to this idea because he has no independent satanology to confront his christology; Robinson gives it an importance of its own which it did not have in Mark at all. Jesus' disputes with Jewish theologians are not a continuation of the cosmic struggle, for Satan is never mentioned in them (pp. 51f.).

In the statements about evil in Matthew's gospel, Baumbach believes that he can recognize discussions within the community represented by Matthew. His opinion is marked by a combination of views of Schlatter, Gerhard Barth and some individual remarks of Trilling. Baumbach sees how evil is understood in Matthew within the shift of emphasis which can be observed in this gospel from kerygma to didache, from Gospel to divine law, from eschatology to ethics (p. 55). In Matthew, ὁ πονηρός is Satan, a transcendent personage for evil. Here a fundamentally changed situation compared with Mark is reflected (p. 56). The fact that the word occurs more often in Matthew than in Mark shows an increased interest. This appears in the didactic consideration of evil and Matthew's use of it for exhortation in church. The evil which must be conceived in terms of morality is very closely connected with Satan as 'the evil one'. In Matthew, the dualism of the two ways is symptomatic of the church and refers to two groups or parties (pp. 92f. cf. p. 120). In the dualism between the good seed and the weeds sown by Satan as the seducers and workers of lawlessness, a very bitter conflict within the community is reflected, with the problem of the right understanding of the Law at its centre (p. 93; cf. pp. 82f., 121). For Matthew, opposition to the divine law is the substance of his understanding of sin; that is to say: in Matthew alone is the name for sin ἀνομία. 'The evil thing' (πονηρός) is practised by opposing the Torah and can therefore also be denoted by ἀνομία. In 7.23, Matthew has ἀνομία, while Luke in the parallel passage in 13.27 has ἀδικία (after Ps. 69.). The different versions of this citation demonstrate what is typical of the two evangelists (pp. 103f.).

Hence Baumbach sees that the variation of the understanding of sin in Matthew compared with Mark has as its background the division into parties throughout Matthew's church between a true and a false interpretation of the Law, between true and false prophets (pp. 63f.). A movement directing its course strictly by the Law is fighting a lawless movement represented by lying prophets, and both claim the Spirit for themselves and turn themselves into heretics under the influence of Satan (p. 121).

It seems to us, however, open to question whether this contrast between the parties can in fact be substantiated from Matthew's gospel and whether it does not perhaps carry interpretation too far. The comment we made on the libertine movement, posited by Barth and attacked by the first evangelist, applies also to Baumbach's thesis. Besides, we might ask: what is the relationship of the unconditional universality of the missionary command to the orthodox separatism, postulated by Baumbach, of that party which is supposed to be fighting against a lawless movement represented by lying prophets? In that case Baumbach would have to make a distinction in terms of method between a Jewish-Christian stage of Matthew's gospel and a later universalist Gentile-Christian final redaction. We refer here to the comments by Trilling and Strecker on this question, namely that Baumbach's thesis about Matthew's community can be correct at most for the stage of the traditional material revised by Matthew, and not for the stage of its final redaction. (For criticism and discussion see also G. Strecker, *Weg der Gerechtigkeit*, p. 250).

The understanding of evil in Luke's writings is considered by

Baumbach in connection with the missionary-theological trend in Luke's books. Luke has used the concepts πονηρός and πονηρία as part of his ethical-soteriological dualism of decision determined by a missionary context. Hence for Luke these concepts are connected with the shifting of the theological centre to the mission directed outwards, with its demand for conversion, and they serve to mark a dualism between evil deeds before conversion and the condition, completely separated from the evil, after conversion (p. 138). The workers of iniquity (Luke 13.27) are here not a group of heretics within the community, but the multitude of the unconverted standing outside the gates. The word ἀδικία in Luke expresses the dualism between God and the world, the concept ἀνομία in Matthew expresses the dualism between a lawful and an unlawful community of God (pp. 159f.).

In Luke, we can note a great increase of the concepts related to πονηρός and πονηρία which denote sinning. Luke has fitted the concepts, which have a moral meaning in Matthew and Mark, into a context which is of service to a missionary sermon and he has given them their typical stamp with this in mind. They served to underline the demand for penitence by describing the condition surmounted in conversion. For sin is the mark of being unconverted, the Holy Spirit is a sign of the community's realm of salvation, and these two are mutually exclusive (p. 163).

Conzelmann had maintained that the middle of time, the time of Jesus, between Luke 4.13 and 22.3, was free from the activity of Satan.[2] But Baumbach proves that this is by no means the case; on the contrary, there are the largest number of statements about Satan in the section devoted to Jesus' time in Luke's historical work (8.12; 10.18; 11.14–23; 13.10–17). Mission in Luke 10.1–20 and in Acts must in fact be understood as a victorious struggle with Satan, as a victory over Satan of the Holy Spirit at work in the missionaries and in the community (pp. 182f., cf. pp. 188f., 206f.). Satan appears in Luke with a significance for missionary theology. His fall is not a unique act at the end of the days, but happens wherever missionary preaching grips men and snatches them out of the realm of Satan (p. 179).

Baumbach comes to the conclusion that the understanding of evil in all three synoptic gospels is associated with the particular character of the individual evangelist and therefore bears a different stamp in each one. In Mark, Satan and demons are the foes of the Messiah.

[2] H. Conzelmann, *The Theology of St Luke*, p. 170.

In his gospel the missionary kerygma expressed in terms of the Messiah is central. In Matthew evil is lawlessness. In his gospel, the Torah expounded correctly as authorized by the Church occupies a pivotal position. In Luke, on the other hand, Satan, demons and sin belonged to the unconverted world and display Luke's theology of conversion with its pietistic and missionary trend (p. 208).

The synoptic statements about evil are not meant to be speculative, but historical; their function is to serve the special kerygmatic and didactic purposes of the individual evangelists and the communities behind them. In all the gospels, evil is the dark background necessary to understanding the work of salvation, and against it Jesus' victory over all the powers of darkness shines all the brighter (p. 208). Since the evangelists wished to proclaim not evil, but its conqueror, they did not deny its existence on principle, but as a result of their experiences they conceded that it had again an effective power and a present significance for the community in their day. The dualism between the good God and sinful men which determines Mark's gospel was later given up in favour of a division of mankind into two parts, and at the same time the eschatological view of Mark was replaced by an ethical outlook. Luke has not only devoted the most thorough theological meditation to his books, but they are the most strongly marked in terms of dualism and represent a transition towards the Gospel of John (p. 209).

B. Joachim Gnilka   *The Hardening of Israel*

Gnilka's study, *Die Verstockung Israels—Isa. 6.9–10 in der Theologie der Synoptiker* is very closely related in terms of method to the work of Baumbach. For he, too, raises a particular theological question by pursuing the redaction-critical method through all three synoptic gospels and including Acts. He, too, takes the broadest possible view of the 'framework' (referring to Conzelmann, Marxsen and Trilling); by this he understands the choice, arrangement and sorting out of the synoptic material and the handing down of the Lord's sayings. He distinguishes between the last revision of the material and the pre-synoptic collectors and transmitters.[3]

It is characteristic that the citation from Isa. 6.9–10 appears in all three synoptic gospels in the same place in the chapter of parables, and in addition it is placed by Luke on the lips of Paul at the end of

[3] J. Gnilka, *Die Verstockung Israels*, Munich 1961, p. 19.

his two books (Acts 28.26f.). In Gnilka's words, Luke is by this means drawing a final line under the activity of Jesus and the apostles, so far as winning over the Jewish people is concerned. In the view of all three evangelists, the judgment of hardening is effected by means of the teaching by parables. In the case of Luke in Acts 28, the thought is prominent that owing to the hardness of Israel, the Gospel passes over to the Gentiles (p. 17). But because all three synoptists have interpreted the scandal of Israel's hardness differently, Gnilka examines the understanding of this hardness in connection with the understanding of parables in the gospel concerned.

In Mark, the communication of the parables represents a special instruction of the disciples in which Mark had a particular interest, for its recipients are the group of disciples including the Twelve. As it is given to these alone, it is not intended for uninitiated persons (pp. 29f.). Mark in particular lays stress on the lack of understanding (p. 31), yet the reproach for this comes only *before* Peter's confession, whereas *after it* the picture of a suffering Messiah is disclosed without any reproof (p. 39).

Mark is acquainted with two kinds of statements about hardening; (1) in remarks like explanatory notes (Mark 6.52; 9.32) and (2) in sayings of Jesus (Mark 4.13, 40, 41; 7.18; 8.17–21). The comments of the evangelist are more critical and reproachful; Jesus' sayings, on the contrary, are expressed as questions (p. 33). Gnilka emphatically argues that the parables were intended to provoke a lack of understanding, for in ch. 4.12 ἵνα and μήποτε exclusively signify purpose. Moreover, the lack of understanding is limited in time, as it is in Isaiah (p. 49).

Gnilka presupposes that in ch. 4 Mark has worked up a parables' source (p. 53), and is trying to grasp its trend and meaning (p. 62). The parables are discourses which are hard to understand and in need of explanation. The evangelist has a different understanding of parables from his source (pp. 63f.). Mark's parables, except those in ch. 4, on the contrary contained the idea of the proclamation that the Messianic salvation is present and that the dawn of God's kingdom is imminent (p. 74). Mark shows a uniform conception of parables in his gospel. The parables addressed to the opponents suggest that in the understanding of the evangelist the veiled effect is a punishment; this is what God has ordained (4.11), but the Jews have deserved it. By interpolating ch. 4.11, 12 (originally a detached logion) Mark has given the parables an important function in salvation history, which is that they should make it impossible for the multitude to understand (pp. 81f.).

Matthew, on the other hand, goes his own way in interpreting Israel's hardness. In Mark, Jesus as the teacher and master of the disciples entrusts the secret of God's kingdom only to a small circle of his adherents, and the people outside are only allowed to hear the veiled and pictorial language of parables. In Matthew, however, the contrast between the disciples who understand and the people who are obdurate is of great importance throughout (p. 89). Here, too, the disciples receive a teaching appropriate to them alone, but for the people it does not mean the last step in their hardness if this special teaching is denied to them. The final cause of the hardness in Matthew lies in God's hands. In Matthew, the essential task of the parables is not to conceal; but they themselves are the means of sorting out mankind; thus those who had understanding would be enlightened by them, but the others would remain without understanding in spite of the instruction (p. 91). Matthew 13.12 signifies that God has not taken his measures in an arbitrary manner. By using the modified saying of Isaiah (assimilated to Ezek. 12.2 and Jer. 5.21), Matthew is underlining the contrast between disciples and people and is thereby emphasizing the preferential position of the disciples (pp. 92f.).

Matthew brings out the contrast between the disciples who understand and the hardened people not only in the parables chapter, but also in the scheme of his whole gospel. This appears, for example, in the series of pericopes in Matt. 11.2–29 (different from Luke 7.36–50) and in Matt. 12.31–50. He underlines the fact that the disciples are open to the things of the kingdom of heaven and understand them. In Matthew, the reproach of lack of understanding is never addressed to the disciples, except in 15.16 (see especially ch. 13.51) (pp. 94f.).

The fundamental difference between Matthew and Mark in their conception of the parables appears in Matt. 13.13 = Mark 4.12 by the particles used; Matthew has ὅτι (because), Mark has ἵνα (in order that). Hence in Matthew the hardness is the starting-point, in Mark it is the object of speaking in parables. It is part of Matthew's peculiarity that he draws special attention to Israel's lack of faith, because he is obliged to justify the fact that Israel would be superseded in the history of salvation (Matt. 8.11–12; 11.16–19; 12.41–42; 43–45; 16.2–4; 22.7–9; 23.29–36; 37–39) (p. 97). For Matthew, the use of parables is a punishment which the people receives for its hardness. Therefore the parables lead only to a still deeper hardness (p. 103).

For the purpose of his interpretation, Matthew extracts from the parables especially that aspect whose significance is limited to the group of the disciples and hence to the subsequent Christian community (p. 109). For Mark, Jesus nearly always spoke to the people in parables, but for Matthew he spoke to them without parables as well (chs. 5–7, *et passim*). For Mark, Jesus is the teacher who is forming a school and entrusting to it the secret of God's kingdom. But Matthew devotes plenty of space also to Jesus as the great teacher *of the people*. The commands to be silent in his gospel are addressed only to the disciples and to those who have been healed, not to the demons too (p. 110).

In Luke the citation from Isaiah speaks of the people's lack of understanding brought about by the use of parables, and the God-given understanding of the disciples is contrasted with it. But in other respects Luke removes the barriers which Mark had raised between disciples and people (p. 124). For he does not lay stress on Jesus being alone with the disciples. In Luke Jesus does indeed often speak to the disciples, but the people are standing round and listening (Luke 6.20; 16.1, 14; 20.45) (p. 120). Luke sees that the end of his two books is an appropriate place at which to bring out the whole significance of the Old Testament prophecy of Isa. 6. This already appears in the introductory words of the quotation. The hardness of the Jews foretold by Isaiah, which was fulfilled during Luke's lifetime, had (Luke thought) finally opened up the road of the gospel to the Gentiles (p. 130).

Luke has held back as long as possible his verdict of rejection on Israel and emphasizes how imminent is the hour of crisis. For Matthew, Israel had already let its time of respite slip by (p. 132). It follows from numerous examples in his gospel that Luke gave the Jewish people at least one more opportunity (p. 132ff.). For him the turning point for the fate of Judaism was Jesus' death in Jerusalem. His activity there is at the same time the climax of his mission and the sealing of the fate of the nation and the city (p. 137). Luke has expounded the crucifixion, which destroyed Israel's election, by means of his idea that Jesus' life was a progress towards Jerusalem. The respite given to the people of Israel lasts as far as the walls of the city (p. 139).

There the significance of Israel and Jerusalem for salvation history is at an end. 'If Luke's gospel is describing a happening which from the outset aims at reaching the Jewish metropolis and there experiences its climax, in Acts the events take place further and further away from Jerusalem.' The city is no longer a centre, but only a starting-point from which the saving event goes out (p. 140). After Whitsuntide a fresh situation arises. An excusable failure to understand the scriptures after the resurrection is no longer possible (p. 141). By means of Paul's missionary work, Luke does indeed display the fact that the Jews have the first claim to salvation, but Stephen's speech, as part of the whole structure of the Acts, is already the demonstration both in history and in theology that the word of God is now turning away from Jerusalem and toward the Gentiles (pp. 143f.). The way to the Church still remains open to the individual Jew, but no longer to all Jews as a nation, for in Luke's view a fresh people of God has already been formed (p. 146). So at the end of his two books Luke rejects the Judaism of his day, because in his view the God of the Old Testament has already rejected the unbelieving and obdurate Jews (p. 154). Gnilka concludes that each of the synoptists interpreted the problem of Israel's hardness in his own way; each of them indeed keep to the traditional material, but use the possibility of giving it a shape of its own through the editorial revision of the framework (p. 187). Thus Mark often transfers the disciples with Jesus into a house or into a lonely place, where they receive teaching which applies to them alone. The instruction of the people consists almost entirely of discourses ἐν παραβολαῖς and is intended to lead the people into hardness (p. 187). Luke takes the disciples together as a group in contrast with the people and understands by 'parable' primarily exemplary stories and short maxims (p. 188). Matthew underlines the open-mindedness of the disciples to Jesus' teaching and the lack of understanding and obduracy of the people; thus he sets two groups with hostile feelings opposite each other (p. 158). The parables of Mark spoke of the nature of God's kingdom; Luke groups pericopes in which the urgency of the present time is brought to the fore, and the critical pronouncements are not addressed to the crowd, but to the individual opponents; Matthew underlines the hardness of the people and makes Jesus express his most severe reproaches in public utterances (p. 185).

However, we consider it to be extremely doubtful whether it is possible to arrive at Jesus' understanding of the parables from that of the synoptists and to determine a historical place in Jesus' life for the logion in Mark 4.11f. Gnilka (with Schnackenburg) would like to assign it to the end of Jesus' Galilean ministry, i.e. Jesus is still endeavouring, though fruitlessly, to make the people understand, for they were obdurate (pp. 204f.). It was not Jesus' intention that the parables should be a veiled means of speaking, but he adapted himself to his hearers, who were filled with prejudices. Parables belong to the context of his preaching on the kingdom of God, in which an image is set before his listeners and is left with them to think over (pp. 193ff.).

C. Heinz Eduard Tödt and Ferdinand Hahn   *Investigations of Christological Titles in the Synoptic Gospels*

Both investigations by the above authors, *The Son of Man in the Synoptic Tradition* and *The Titles of Jesus in Christology*, are characterized by the fact that they concentrate on the titles which are applied to Jesus in the synoptic gospels. Their difference is not in method (both are dissertations under the supervision of Günther Bornkamm, dating from 1956 and 1961 respectively), but in the delimitation of their themes. Whereas Tödt limits himself to the sayings about the Son of man in the synoptic gospels and discusses other investigations (Sjöberg, Wellhausen, Cullmann and Vielhauer) of these logia in excursuses, Hahn also includes other titles in his investigation: Kyrios, Christ, son of David and son of God. In the excursuses, he also goes into some related problems like that of the representatively suffering servant of God, the exaltation of Jesus, the high-priestly Messiah and finally the eschatological prophet. Common to both investigations is the fact that they begin with Wrede's attempt to discover methodically a traditio-historical stratification of the synoptic material, an attempt taken up by Wilhelm Bousset and later also by Bultmann.

Tödt follows Bultmann in his classification of the Son of man sayings. Only the sayings about the coming Son of man are attributed to the earliest tradition; the sayings about the suffering and risen Son of man and the present work of the Son of man are regarded as later constructions[4], which come from the Hellenistic community.

Tödt first investigates the sayings about the coming Son of man in Mark, then those in the source Q and finally those in Matthew and Luke. He also investigates the two other groups of Son of man sayings

---

[4] See Bultmann, *Theology of the New Testament* I, pp. 29ff.; cf. *History of the Synoptic Tradition*, pp. 151–9.

in the same sequence. Among the sayings about the coming Son of man in Mark and Q, Tödt regards the following as authentic: Mark 8.38 (p. 40); Matt. 24.27, 37, 39 par.; Luke 11.30; Matt. 24.44 par.; Luke 12.8f. par. (pp. 59ff.); he counts Mark 13.26f.; 14.62; Luke 12.28–30; Matt. 10.23; 19.28 as later constructions (pp. 47f., 65).

He sees as characteristics of the authentic sayings about the coming Son of man in Q the themes of the threat of judgment and the promise of salvation; the interest is not focussed on apocalyptic elaboration – the direct claim of proclamation on men is the dominant factor (p. 65). Jesus' Son of man sayings offer a radical reduction of all tendencies towards apocalyptic elaboration. All embellishments with their colourful imagery have vanished. True, salvation and condemnation are promised to the hearers, but neither is presented in elaborate form. The traditional features only increase with increasing distance from the proclamation of Jesus, as can be seen in Matt. 19.28; Mark 8.38; 13.26f.; 14.62 (p. 66). The Son of man sayings mentioned earlier show no relation to christology, i.e. they express no identity of Jesus with the coming Son of man (p. 67, cf. also p. 225).

In the Son of man sayings which Matthew has taken over from Mark and Q, there is a predominant interest in the activity of the coming Son of man in judgment (p. 69). In Matthew, Tödt pays particular attention to the sayings about the coming Son of man in 10.23; 19.28; 13.41 and 25.31, which have no parallel in Mark, but belong to the special material. In the two Son of man sayings formulated by Matthew in 13.41 and 25.31, the concept does not appear in short logia as in Q, but the picture of the Son of man there is appropriate for use in preaching. Apocalyptic breadth has taken the place of brief description. For Matthew, the coming Son of man and judge of the world is never anyone but Jesus, but Jesus as proclaimer on earth is also ready to be designated Son of man (pp. 77f.). There is no trace of ideas of lowliness in either passage, but they show a clear picture of the development of the Son of man idea in the Gospel of Matthew (p. 79).

In Matt. 24.30f., the coming of the Son of man is the occasion for a lament in the face of the judgment, but in Mark 13.26f., on the other hand, it is a sign of joy (pp. 80f.). The addition 'from now on' in Matt. 26.64 (cf. Mark 14.62) is meant, on the one hand, to give the present moment a definite conclusion, and, on the other, to give a promising prospect for the new community in the βασιλεία of the

Father. In Luke 22.69, on the other hand, the same phrase describes the beginning of the church (pp. 84f.). The other alterations to the sayings about the coming Son of man may be left out of account here.

With reference to Conzelmann, Tödt points out that in Luke the eschatological material does not have the importance it does in Matthew, as a comparison with the parallels to Matt. 24f. shows. In place of the imminent expectation, Luke offers a sketch of a continuation of salvation history in stages according to God's plan. The kingdom of God is given a purely transcendent character; in the present period of the church the only concern is with the *picture* of the kingdom. These altered eschatological conceptions are not without consequences for the Lucan understanding of the Son of man (pp. 94f.).

Luke combines a view of his own with the concept of the Son of man. There is a planned usage within his larger compositions (Luke 17.22–18.8b) and a planned conclusion to the apocalyptic discourse with a Son of man saying (21.36). The alteration of Son of man sayings in 21.36, 18.8b and 17.22, 25 shows that Luke attached considerable importance to the designation Son of man and not only took it over, but developed it further along the lines of his theological understanding (pp. 108f.). A movement like that in Matthew, who through the Son of man sayings in Mark and Q often went back to traditional material from late Jewish apocalyptic, does not take place in Luke; Luke offers a further development by his association of the sayings with Hellenistic Christian terms and by using them for his own eschatological conception. Here he has reduced the stereotyped features to a minimum and has often put them at the service of primitive Christian paraenesis (21.36; 18.1, 8b; 21.27f.) (p. 109).

Nowhere is the Son of man in Luke the judge or executor of the judgment of the world as he is in Matthew; before the judgment he is rather the intercessor, advocate or guarantor for Christians (12.8f.). True, for Luke the Son of man is also the traditional exponent of the coming rule of God. But as for him the kingdom of God is not only a future entity but is already present now in the time of the *ecclesia pressa*, in the upper transcendent world, so too the Son of man is not only one who is to come but also the exponent of this kingdom who now sits at the right hand of God (Luke 22.69). In Luke, the Son of man is not the object of the imminent expectation; men have to watch and pray at all times.

In Luke, the saving significance of the passion of Jesus retreats because in Jesus' own presence salvation has already appeared on earth. In the saving time of the activity of Jesus, proclamation is given an important role. True, teaching does not play the same part as in Matthew, but it is still an inalienable part of his work (pp. 190f.).

As Tödt presupposes that Jesus spoke only of the coming Son of man as another and future figure, he does not regard the sayings about the present Son of man as authentic sayings of Jesus, but as formulations by the post-Easter community (p. 124), despite their deep roots in the history of the tradition, for they occur both in Q and Mark as well as in the secondary material. As they even occur in Q, they did not first arise in the Hellenistic community (p. 139). For Bultmann, these sayings are merely a misunderstanding: in this group of sayings Son of man would merely be a periphrasis for 'I'.[5] Tödt rejects this view, as in all the sayings in this group the term Son of man designates Jesus in the authority of his work on earth, and this corresponds to the recognition of the community after Easter (pp. 138f., cf. p. 207).

The sayings about the suffering and resurrection of the Son of man were derived by Bousset from the primitive Palestinian community,[6] whereas for Bultmann they are formations of the Hellenistic community.[7] There are no sayings of this sort in Q; they first occur in Mark. According to Tödt, Mark uses these sayings in his composition to lead up to the passion story as the central part of his gospel; the sayings act as a preparation towards the meaning of the passion event (p. 148). In the Gospel of Matthew, their importance in the general structure is less than in Mark. This is a result of the altered conception of the total significance of Jesus, which shows itself in the stress on the Easter and post-Easter accounts, which are lacking in this sense in Mark (p. 150). As sayings like Mark 9.31; 14.21; 14.41 are rooted in the Palestinian milieu, this tells against Bultmann's assumption that the sayings about the suffering and resurrection of the Son of man were only formed in the Hellenistic community (p. 215).

In a concluding chapter, Tödt goes on to investigate the relationship of the three groups of sayings to each other as they can be seen

[5] *History of the Synoptic Tradition*, pp. 152f., note 1; *Theology of the New Testament* I, p. 30.
[6] W. Bousset, *Kyrios Christos*, Göttingen 1913, p. 9.
[7] R. Bultmann, *History of the Synoptic Tradition*, p. 156; *Theology of the New Testament* I, p. 35.

in the synoptic gospels. Here he works out the different understandings in the individual gospels. In Mark, the sayings about the suffering Son of man come only after Peter's confession. True, there were already Son of man sayings in Mark 2.10 and 2.28 (about the earthly work of the Son of man), but the real meaning of the designation Son of man is first revealed for Mark in the prophecies of the passion, which are directed towards the passion. Although Mark offers sayings from all three groups, his real interest lies in the sayings about the handing over, killing and raising of the Son of man (p. 280).

Matthew preserves the sayings in Mark, but has transferred their focal point, for in his writings the sayings about the parousia of the Son of man are given considerable weight and have been strengthened by further sayings of the Son of man shaped by redactional activity (Matt. 13.41; 25.31) (p. 280). This is connected not only with his use of sources but is also to be explained from his theological conception, for in Matthew Jesus, the consummate preacher (according to Q) who issues a sovereign call to discipleship, has become the authenticated teacher. His message is thus understood above all as teaching (p. 281).

The passion also stands in the centre of the Son of man sayings for Luke, as for Mark, for Luke has understood the earthly work of Jesus as a particular period of salvation and has expressed this in his pattern of salvation history. Luke takes over sayings of Jesus because they have their origin in the time of salvation when Jesus was present on earth and therefore can claim validity as a supra-temporal norm. For Luke, the delay of the parousia does not rob Jesus' proclamation and his eschatological message of their force, for Luke also takes over sayings about the parousia of the Son of man. But he does not understand these in the sense of an imminent expectation; he applies them to the time which will come after the *ecclesia pressa* (p. 282). For him, access to salvation is given not only in the passion of Jesus, but also in the teaching and wonders by authority (Luke 4.16–22). True, he has taken over sayings from all three groups, but he has omitted Mark 10.45 (the surrender of the life of the Son of man as a ransom for many), while further strengthening the groups of sayings about the coming of the Son of man and his work on earth by the insertion of Luke 18.8b; 19.10 and 21.36 (p. 283).

Vielhauer has challenged Tödt's investigation in his article 'Jesus and the Son of Man'.[8] He is concerned to defend the thesis which he

[8] P. Vielhauer, 'Jesus und der Menschensohn', *ZThK* 60, 1963, pp. 133–77.

put forward in his article 'Kingdom of God and Son of Man in the Proclamation of Jesus',[9] that all three groups of Son of man sayings are spurious and do not go back to the historical Jesus. He regards even the sayings which Tödt takes to be authentic as interpretations of the risen one by the community (p. 152), whereas for Tödt the coming of the Son of man and the dawn of the kingdom of God are alternative concepts which refer to the same event (pp. 136, 153). Vielhauer bases his view, among other things, on the fact that in Jewish eschatology, the historical presupposition of Jesus' preaching, there is no combination of kingdom of God and Son of man (p. 134). In the second part of his article, Vielhauer rejects Schweizer's view[10] that the sayings about the present activity of the Son of man are the oldest and most authentic words of Jesus (pp. 166f., cf. p. 170).

Like Tödt, Ferdinand Hahn also regards as authentic those of the Son of man sayings in which Jesus and the Son of man are not identified, but clearly distinguished from each other, e.g. Mark 8.38; Luke 12.8f., etc. (pp. 33–42), whereas he understands, as does Tödt, sayings about the coming Son of man with an apocalyptic shaping to be constructions of the community (cf. p. 33).

The two other groups, about the earthly activity and the suffering and resurrection of the Son of man, are also said to be constructions by the community. Hahn, however, differs from Todt in distinguishing two different types of sayings about the suffering Son of man, depending on whether or not there is a reference to the Old Testament. Tödt, on the other hand (Tödt, pp. 151f.), traces them back to one basic structure. Where the motive of the necessity of Scripture is present, they have been influenced by the passion tradition (Mark 14.21, mixed form in Mark 10.45). Both types go back to a Palestinian community tradition, but have undergone substantial development in a Hellenistic milieu (Mark 8.31; 9.12b) (Hahn, pp. 52f.).

The stress in Hahn's investigation of the individual christological titles of honour is not laid on tracing the different interpretations of the sayings in Mark, Q, Matthew and Luke, as in Tödt's book, but on their development by the primitive Palestinian community, Hellenistic Jewish Christianity and Hellenistic Gentile Christianity.

---

[9] Id., 'Gottesreich und Menschensohn in der Verkündigung Jesu', in: Festschrift für Günther Dehn.

[10] 'Der Menschensohn', ZNW 50, 1959, pp. 185–209.

Hahn identifies this chronological extension of Christianity with stages of christological tradition, which leads to a rigid schematism.[11] Only in the paragraphs about the title 'Son of God' does he make any detailed remarks about the different understanding of this concept in the individual synoptic gospels (pp. 318f.), as about the understanding of John the Baptist as the eschatological Elijah in particular gospels (pp. 379f.) and the understanding of Jesus as the new Moses (pp. 400–4).

D. Siegfried Schulz   *A General Redaction-Critical Survey of the Gospels*

As a redaction-critical study which works over the results of all previous redaction-critical investigations in a most judicious way, S. Schulz's book *Die Stunde der Botschaft – Einführung in die Theologie der vier Evangelien* (Hamburg 1967) calls for attention. The special characteristic of this book is the way in which it includes the gospel of John, despite the difficulties of method which that involves. Indeed, it is hardly possible to come to a reasonable decision about the character of the Jesus tradition on which the author of the fourth gospel relies, whether it has points of contact or is even identical with the tradition standing behind the synoptic gospels.

Schulz supposes that the author of the fourth gospel probably knew none of the synoptic gospels, though he was acquainted with the tradition that they used (p. 305, cf. p. 311). He also rejects the thesis that there was a basic source at the beginning of the fourth gospel. The unity of the whole work goes back to the evangelist himself, who shows considerable control and artistic ability in shaping the traditions (p. 315).

It is his view that the tradition of the community before John and the gospel of John itself in the end go back to a syncretistic and gnosticizing Jewish Christianity. This is where the roots of the characteristic soteriological 'I am' sayings lie; the source of the invitations of promise and threat to unbelievers and the dualistic concepts (p. 321). All in all, the gospel of John represents, critically and independently, the theological position of gnosticizing Christianity in the third generation (p. 359).

---

[11] For criticism see P. Vielhauer, 'Ein Weg zur neutestamentlichen Christologie?', *EvTh* 25, 1965, pp. 24–72 (esp. p. 71).

E. Final Assessment of Redaction Criticism

We began this study by describing redaction criticism and distinguishing it from form criticism, and we then proceeded to summarize the existing redaction-critical works; from this we were able to conclude that redaction criticism raises a fresh claim in terms of method compared with form criticism. It is not intended to be understood as in antithesis to, but as a continuation of form criticism, proceeding from its methodological foundation. We would, therefore, be wrong to wish to degrade redaction criticism to an 'addendum to a programme formulated long ago', as Schille tries to do.[12]

Redaction criticism's own methodological claim has been called in question similarly[13] by Strecker, although, as we have seen, he does in fact work according to this method. In opposition to Marxsen,[14] he has defended the thesis that the traditional material was not broken up more and more; instead, he argues that during the pre-literary oral tradition there was only a change in the structure of *individual* pericopes, whilst in other respects a trend towards synthesis can be identified even here. It is to be seen, for example, in the handing down of the account of the Passion or in the sayings tradition. In this way, even before Mark the material was gathered and fixed in writing to form the sayings source and the parable source. The editorial redaction by the evangelists thus only continued the line started in the history of the oral tradition.[15]

It is evident that Strecker's review is written from the point of view of form criticism. But we doubt whether Marxsen would feel Strecker's position to be in such contrast with his own. The fact that the redaction of the gospels had proceeded on the lines already set by oral tradition was, after all, among the presuppositions accepted by redaction criticism. But this argument is not able to contradict the fact that in the oral tradition a tendency for the tradition to dissolve is nevertheless to be seen. How else could the apocryphal gospels and acts of the apostles have come into existence? Marxsen, too, could join Strecker in arguing that the redactors of the gospels framed the

---

[12] G. Schille, 'Der Mangel eines kritischen Geschichtsbildes in der neutestamentlichen Formgeschichte', *ThLZ* 88, 1963.

[13] Col. 492.

[14] Marxsen, *Evangelist Markus*, p. 8.

[15] G. Strecker, 'Besprechung von W. Marxsen', *Der Evangelist Markus*, 1959², *ZKG* 72, 161, pp. 143f.

traditional material not in complete freedom, but in close association with the community's tradition and with the needs of its life (p. 144); for nowhere in redaction-critical studies does there appear, even merely by way of a suggestion, the view that the evangelists dealt in an arbitrary way with the shaping of the tradition. On the contrary, it is the explicit opinion of the scholars using redaction-critical methods that the evangelists had fashioned their material to correspond to the needs of their time, and after all, this means the time of the life of the community. In redaction criticism, what has hitherto often been understood under the misleading concept of 'community theology' has now been defined more precisely and identified as the theology of the author of a gospel who was in touch with the community and in association with it. In consequence, account is taken of the justifiable indication that what deserves the name of theology is not created by the aggregate of anonymous members of the community, but by creative personalities who are, of course, in every way associated with the community. What originates among the anonymous mass should be called 'popular piety'; but this does not exclude the possibility that creative religious personalities can arise out of it.

A good deal also depends on the slogan under which New Testament studies in general are pursued. In the case of 'community theology' in particular, should not the question be: 'What sayings has the exalted Lord placed on the lips of his community?' rather than: 'What sayings did the post-Easter community place on the lips of the historical Jesus of history?'

Nor do the doubts cast by Strecker (p. 144) on the justification for distinguishing a second and a third *Sitz im Leben* affect the true nature of the question, for the second *Sitz im Leben* means the individual pericopes of the tradition before they were fixed in writing, and the third *Sitz im Leben* means the whole of the gospels as we have them. At the same time, this means that each evangelist put the message differently in his own time, although he was bearing witness to one and the same Christ. The individual gospels are thus canonical examples of the way in which the problem of how the message of Christ is to be interpreted was answered in a new situation.[16] To this extent, redaction criticism is of supreme importance for practical theology today, and especially for homiletics, for the more

[16] See also H. Flender, *St Luke, Theologian of Redemptive History*, p. 3.

successful it is in determining the setting of a gospel in the life and history of the earliest church, the more contemporary practical theology can learn how the message of Christ is to be presented in a new situation. The connection between New Testament scholarship and practical theology is thus very close in redaction criticism, in so far as the gospels can be understood as the record and expression of the preaching of the early church.

In my opinion, criticism should not start with the methodological theses on which redaction criticism is based; these are in fact a continuation of the work done hitherto on the synoptists. Nor should the charge be levelled that redaction criticism excludes the problem of the historicity of what is reported. It does this quite deliberately,[17] in order to be able first of all to grasp fully the evangelists' purpose in producing their account and what they intended it to impart. Thus redaction criticism examines how the traditional material was shaped within the setting of the post-Easter church (p. 4).

In any case, we must not fail to note the fact that the problem of the historical Jesus, and consequently that of the historicity of what has been reported, is being taken up again and stimulated, especially by scholars who come from Bultmann's school and are influenced by both form-critical and redaction-critical work. As Bornkamm's book on Jesus in particular shows, this work has achieved conclusions which make the possibility of discovering the historical Jesus much more definite than was the case, for example, in Bultmann's book about Jesus.[18] Whereas Bultmann thought that he might be able to reconstruct something of Jesus' teaching simply out of the *logia* which had been handed down, Bornkamm goes much further and is much less sceptical than Bultmann. But this is not a resumption of the old liberal question of the historical Jesus.

Redaction criticism is, however, to be criticized on detailed points and for its excessive subtlety. We have attempted to draw attention to this again and again in our description of the individual works.

[17] W. Trilling, *Das wahre Israel*, pp. 3f., has exhaustively substantiated this. This limitation of the redaction-critical method is evidently infringed by G. Klein when on the basis of a redaction-critical investigation of the story of Peter's denial he pronounces it unhistorical (see 'Die Verleugnung des Petrus', *ZThK* 58, 1961, pp. 285–328, esp. p. 311; cf. the answer by E. Linnemann, 'Die Verleugnung des Petrus', *ZThK* 63, 1966, pp. 1–32).

[18] On this see pages 523–45 in the unprinted version of my dissertation.

BIBLIOGRAPHY

ALBERTZ, MARTIN, *Die synoptischen Streitgespräche—Ein Beitrag zur Formengeschichte des Urchristentums*, Berlin 1921.

BALTENSWEILER, HEINRICH, 'Die Ehebruchsklauseln bei Matthäus', *ThZ* 15, 1959, pp. 340–56.
'Das Gleichnis von der selbstwachsenden Saat (Mark. 4, 26–9), und die theologische Konzeption des Markusevangelisten', in: *Oikonomia, O. Cullmannzum 65, Geburtstag*, Hamburg-Bergstedt 1967, pp. 69–75.

BARTH, GERHARD, 'Das Gesetzesverständnis des Evangelisten Matthäus', in: G. Bornkamm/G. Barth/H. J. Held, *Überlieferung und Auslegung im Matthäusevangelium*, WMANT 1, Neukirchen 1960, pp. 54–154: ET: 'Matthew's Understanding of the Law' in *ibid., Tradition and Interpretation in Matthew*, London and New York 1963.

BARTSCH, HANS-WERNER, 'Feldrede und Bergpredigt—Redaktionsarbeit in Lukas 6', *ThZ* 16, 1960, pp. 5–18.
'Die theologischen Konsequenzen der formgeschichtlichen Betrachtung der Evangelien', *ThBl* 19, 1940, cols. 301–6, reprinted in: *Entmythologisierende Auslegung—Gesammelte Aufsätze*, Theologische Forschung, XXVI. Veröffentlichung, Hamburg-Bergstedt 1962, pp. 11–15.
'Parusieerwartung und Osterbotschaft', *EvTh* 7, 1947/48, pp. 115–26, reprinted in: *Entmythologisierende Auslegung*, pp. 61–9.
'Zum Problem der Parusieverzögerung bei den Synoptikern', *EvTh* 19, 1959, pp. 116–31, reprinted in: *Entmythologisierende Auslegung*, pp. 69–80.
'Die Passions- und Ostergeschichten bei Matthäus', in: *Basileia, Walter Freytag zum 60. Geburtstag*, Stuttgart 1959, pp. 27–42, reprinted in: *Entmythologisierende Auslegung*, pp. 80–92.
Wachet aber zu jeder Zeit! Entwurf einer Auslegung des Lukasevangeliums, Hamburg-Bergstedt 1963.

BAUERNFEIND, OTTO, 'Zur Frage nach der Entscheidung zwischen Paulus und Lukas', *ZSTh* 23, 1954, pp. 59–88.

BAUMBACH, GÜNTHER, *Das Verständnis des Bösen in den synoptischen Evangelien*, Theologische Arbeiten, Band XIX, Berlin 1963.

BERTRAM, GEORG, 'Die Bedeutung der kultgeschichtlichen Methode für die neutestamentliche Forschung', *ThBl* 2, 1923, cols. 25–36.
'Die Geschichte der synoptischen Tradition', *ThBl* 1, 1922, cols. 32–4.
Die Leidensgeschichte Jesu und der Christuskult—Eine formgeschichtliche Untersuchung, FRLANT 32, Göttingen 1922.

BOOBYER, H. G., 'The secrecy motif in St Mark's Gospel', *NTS* 6, 1959/60, pp. 225–35.

BORNKAMM, GUNTHER, 'Der Auferstandene und der Irdische', in: *Zeit und Geschichte, Dankesgabe an R. Bultmann zum 80. Geburtstag*, Tübingen 1964, pp. 171–91.

'Enderwartung und Kirche in Matthäusevangelium', in: G. Bornkamm/ G. Barth/H. J. Held, *Überlieferung und Auslegung im Matthäusevangelium*, WMANT 1, Neukirchen 1960, pp. 13–47: ET: 'End-Expectation and Church in Matthew' in: *ibid.*, *Tradition and Interpretation in Matthew*, London and New York 1963.

'Evangelien, formgeschichtlich—Evangelien, synoptische', *RGG* II, 1958³, cols. 749–66.

'Formen und Gattungen im Neuen Testament', *RGG* II, 1958³, pp. 999–1005.

Jesus von Nazareth, Urban-Bücher 19, Stuttgart 1959³: ET *Jesus of Nazareth*, London and New York 1960.

'Matthäus als Interpret der Herrenworte', *ThLZ* 79, 1954, cols. 341–6.

'Die Sturmstillung im Matthäusevangelium', in: *Wort und Dienst, Jahrbuch der Theologischen Schule Bethel* NF 1, 1948, pp. 49–54: ET in *Tradition and Interpretation in Matthew*.

'Die Verzögerung der Parusie', in: *In memoriam Ernst Lohmeyer*, Stuttgart 1951, pp. 116–26.

BOUSSET, WILHELM, *Kyrios Christos*, Göttingen 1921².

BRAUMANN, GEORG, 'Der theologische Hintergrund des Jakobusbriefes', *ThZ* 18, 1962, pp. 401–10.

'Das Mittel der Zeit—Erwägungen zur Theologie des Lukasevangeliums', *ZNW* 54, 1963, pp. 117–45.

BULTMANN, RUDOLF, 'Besprechung von E. Fascher, *Die formgeschichtliche Methode*', *ThLZ* 50, 1925, cols. 313–18.

Die Erforschung der synoptischen Evangelien, WR NtlR 1, Giessen 1930², Berlin 1960³: ET: in R. Bultmann and K. Kundsin, *Form Criticism*, New York 1934, pp. 7–78.

Die Geschichte der synoptischen Tradition, fourth edition with supplement, Berlin 1961: ET: *History of the Synoptic Tradition*, London and New York 1963.

Glauben und Verstehen—Gesammelte Aufsätze, Band 1, Tübingen 1933, Band 2, Tübingen 1952: ET: Vol. 1. *Faith and Understanding*, London and New York 1969; Vol. 2. *Essays*, London and New York 1955.

Jesus, Tübingen 1951³: ET: *Jesus and the Word*, London 1958.

Theologie des Neuen Testaments, Tübingen 1954²: ET in 2 vols.: *Theology of the New Testament*, London and New York 1952 and 1955.

BUSCH, FRIEDRICH, *Zum Verständnis der synoptischen Eschatologie, Markus 13 neu untersucht*, NTF IV, 2, Gütersloh 1938.

BUSSMANN, WALTER, *Synoptische Studien*, Band 1, Halle 1925; Band 2, Halle 1929; Band 3, Halle 1931.

CONZELMANN, HANS, *Die Apostelgeschichte*, HNT 7, Tübingen 1963.
'Gegenwart und Zukunft in der synoptischen Tradition', *ZThK* 54, 1957, pp. 277–96.
'Geschichte und Eschaton nach Markus 13', *ZNW* 50, 1959, pp. 210–21.
'Geschichte, Geschichtsbild und Geschichtsdarstellung bei Lukas', *ThLZ* 85, 1960, cols. 241–50.
'Zur Lukasanalyse', *ZThK* 49, 1952, pp. 16–33.
Die Mitte der Zeit—Studien zur Theologie des Lukas, BHTh 17, Tübingen 1954, 1960[3]: ET: *The Theology of St Luke*, London and New York 1960.
'Randbemerkungen zur "Lage" im Neuen Testament', *EvTh* 22, 1962, pp. 225–33.

CULLMANN, OSCAR, 'Das wahre durch die ausgebliebene Parusie gestellte neutestamentliche Problem', *ThZ* 3, 1947, pp. 177–91.
Petrus, Berlin 1961[2]: ET: *Peter. Disciple, Apostle, Martyr*, London and Philadelphia 1962.
'Parusieverzögerung und Urchristentum—Der gegenwärtige Stand der Diskussion', *ThLZ* 83, 1958, cols. 1–12.

DAHL, NILS ALSTRUP, 'Formgeschichtliche Beobachtungen zur Christusverkündigung in der Gemeindepredigt', in: *Neutestamentliche Studien für R. Bultmann*, BZNW 21, Berlin 1954, pp. 3–9.
'Der historische Jesus als geschichtswissenschaftliches und theologisches Problem', *KuD* 1, Berlin 1956, pp. 109–37.
'Die Passionsgeschichte bei Matthäus', *NTS* 2, 1956, pp. 17–32.

DELLING, GERHARD, 'Besprechung von G. Bornkamm/G. Barth/H. J. Held, *Überlieferung und Auslegung im Matthäusevangelium*', *ThLZ* 85, 1960, cols. 925–8.

DESCAMPS, ALBERT, 'Essai d'interprétation de Mt. 5, 17–48: "Formgeschichte" ou "Redaktionsgeschichte" ', in: *Studia Evangelica*, TU 73, Berlin 1959, pp. 156–73.

DIBELIUS, MARTIN, *Aufsätze zur Apostelgeschichte*, Berlin 1956[3]: ET: *Studies in the Acts of the Apostles*, London 1956.
Die Formgeschichte des Evangeliums, Tübingen 1919, 1959[3]: ET: *From Tradition to Gospel*, London 1934.
'Zur Formgeschichte der Evangelien', *ThR NF* 1, 1929, pp. 185–216.
'Zur Formgeschichte des Neuen Testaments (ausserhalb der Evangelien)', *ThR NF* 3, 1931, pp. 207–42.
Die urchristliche Überlieferung von Johannes dem Täufer, FRLANT 15, Göttingen 1911.

DINKLER, ERICH, 'Geschichte und Geschichtsauffassung, II A Neutestamentlich', *RGG* II, 1958[3], cols. 1476–82.

DOBSCHÜTZ, ERNST VON, 'Matthäus als Rabbi und Katechet', *ZNW* 27, 1928, pp. 338–48.
'Zur Erzählkunst des Markus', *ZNW* 27, 1928, pp. 193–8.

DODD, CHARLES HAROLD, *The Parables of the Kingdom*, Welwyn 1958[15].

EBELING, HANS-JÜRGEN, *Das Messiasgeheimnis und die Botschaft des Markus-Evangelisten*, BZNW 19, Berlin 1939.

ELLIGER, KARL, 'Der Jakobskampf am Jabbok', *ZThK* 48, 1951, pp. 1–31.

ELTESTER, WALTER, 'Lukas und Paulus', in: *Eranion, Festschrift für Hildebrecht Hommel*, Tübingen 1961, pp. 1–17.
'Gott und die Natur in der Areopagrede', in: *Neutestamentliche Studien für R. Bultmann*, BZNW 21, Berlin 1954, pp. 202–27.

FASCHER, ERICH, *Die formgeschichtliche Methode*, BZNW 2, Giessen 1924.

FEINE, PAUL/BEHM, JOHANNES, *Einleitung in das Neue Testament*, Heidelberg 1950[9].

FEINE, PAUL/BEHM, JOHANNES/KÜMMEL, WERNER GEORG, *Einleitung in das Neue Testament*, Berlin 1965[13]: ET: Kümmel, W. G., *Introduction to the New Testament*, London and New York 1966.

FIEDLER, MARTIN JOHANNES, *Der Begriff DIKAIOSYNE im Matthäus-Evangelium, ungedruckte theologische Dissertation* (typescript), Halle 1957.

FLENDER, HELMUT, *Heil und Geschichte in der Theologie des Lukas*, BEvTh 41, Munich 1965: ET: *St Luke, Theologian of Redemptive History*, London and Philadelphia 1967.
'Lehren und Verkündigen in den synoptischen Evangelien', *EvTh* 25, 1965, pp. 701–14.

FUCHS, ERNST, 'Jesu Selbstzeugnis nach Matthäus 5', *ZThK* 51, 1954, pp. 14–34.

GLOMBITZA, OTTO, 'Acta 13, 15–41—Analyse einer lukanischen Predigt vor Juden', *NTS* 5, 1958/59, pp. 306–17.
'Die Titel διδάσκαλος und ἐπιστάτης für Jesus bei Lukas', ZNW 49, 1958, pp. 275–8.
'Das Zeichen des Jona—Zum Verständnis von Matth. 12, 38–42', *NTS* 8, 1961/62, pp. 359–66.

GNILKA, JOACHIM, '"Parusieverzögerung" und Naherwartung in den synoptischen Evangelien und in der Apostelgeschichte', *Catholica* 13, 1959, pp. 277–90.
Die Verstockung Israels—Jes. 6. 9–10 in der Theologie der Synoptiker, StANT 3, München 1961.
'Die Kirche des Matthäus und die Gemeinde von Qumran', *BZ NF* 7, 1963, pp. 43–63.

GRÄSSER, ERICH, 'Die Apostelgeschichte in der Forschung der Gegenwart', *ThR NF* 26, 1960, pp. 93–167.

Das Problem der Parusieverzögerung in den synoptischen Evangelien und in der Apostelgeschichte, BZNW 22, Berlin 1957.

GREEVEN, HEINRICH, 'Die Heilung des Gelähmten nach Matthäus', in: *Wort und Dienst, Jahrbuch der Theologischen Schule Bethel NF* 4, 1955, pp. 65–78.

GRUNDMANN, WALTER, 'Die Bergpredigt nach der Lukasfassung', in: *Studia Evangelica*, TU 73, Berlin 1959, pp. 180–89.

Das Evangelium nach Markus, ThHKNT 2, Berlin 1959.

Das Evangelium nach Lukas, ThHKNT 3, Berlin 1961.

'Fragen der Komposition des lukanischen Reiseberichtes', *ZNW* 50, 1959, pp. 252–70.

Die Geschichte Jesu Christi, 2 Auflage mit Ergänzungsheft, Berlin 1959.

HAENCHEN, ERNST, *Die Apostelgeschichte*, KEKNT III, Göttingen 1956[10], 1959[12], 1961[13].

'Die Komposition von Mark. 8, 27–9, 1', *NovTest* 6, 1963, pp. 81–109.

'Matthäus 23', *ZThK* 48, 1951, pp. 38–63.

'Quellenanalyse und Kompositionsanalyse in Acta 15', in: *Judentum, Urchristentum, Kirche, Festschrift für J. Jeremias*, BZNW 26, Berlin 1960, pp. 151–64.

'Tradition und Komposition in der Apostelgeschichte', *ZThK* 52, 1955, pp. 205–25.

Der Weg Jesu—Eine Erklärung des Markus-Evangeliums und der kanonischen Parallelen, Sammlung Töpelmann, II Reihe, Band 6, Berlin 1966.

'Das "Wir" in der Apostelgeschichte und das Itinerar', *ZThK* 58, 1961, pp. 329–66.

HAHN, FERDINAND, *Christologische Hoheitstitel—Ihre Geschichte im frühen Christentum*, FRLANT 83, Göttingen 1963: ET in preparation.

HARDER, GÜNTHER, 'Das eschatologische Geschichtsbild der sogenannten Kleinen Apokalypse Markus 13', in: *Theologia Viatorum* 4, Jahrbuch der Kirchlichen Hochschule Berlin 1952, Berlin 1953, pp. 71–107.

HASLER, VIKTOR, 'Die königliche Hochzeit Matth. 22, 1–14', *ThZ* 18, 1962, pp. 25–35.

HELD, HEINZ JOACHIM, 'Matthäus als Interpret der Wundergeschichten', in: G. Bornkamm/G. Barth/H. J. Held, *Überlieferung und Auslegung im Matthäusevangelium*, WMANT 1, Neukirchen 1960, pp. 155–287: 'Matthew as Interpreter of the Miracle Stories', in *ibid.*, *Tradition and Interpretation in Matthew*, London and New York 1963.

HILGERT, EARLE, 'Symbolismus und Heilsgeschichte in den Evangelien— Ein Beitrag zu den Seesturm-und Gerasenererzählungen', in: *Oikonomia, O. Cullmann zum 65. Geburtstag*, Hamburg-Bergstedt 1967, pp. 51–6.

HILLMANN, WILHELM, *Aufbau und Deutung der synoptischen Leidensberichte—*

Ein Beitrag zur Kompositionstechnik und Sinndeutung der drei älteren Evangelien (Dissertation Münster), München 1951.

HIRSCH, EMANUEL, 'Fragestellung und Verfahren meiner Frühgeschichte des Evangeliums', *ZNW* 41, 1942, pp. 106–24.
Frühgeschichte des Evangeliums, erstes Buch: *Das Werden des Markus-Evangeliums*, Tübingen 1941; zweites Buch: *Die Vorlagen des Lukas und das Sondergut des Matthäus*, Tübingen 1941.

HOMMEL, HILDEBRECHT, 'Neue Forschungen zur Areopagrede Acta 17', *ZNW* 46, 1955, pp. 145–78.

HUMMEL, REINHART, *Die Auseinandersetzung zwischen Kirche und Judentum im Matthäusevangelium*, BEvTh 33, München 1963.

IBER, GERHARD, 'Zur Formgeschichte der Evangelien', *ThR NF* 24, 1957/58, pp. 283–338.

IERSEL, B. M. F. VAN, *"Der Sohn" in den synoptischen Jesusworten—Christusbezeichnung der Gemeinde oder Selbstbezeichnung Jesu?*, SupplNovTest III, Leiden 1961.

JEREMIAS, JOACHIM, *Die Abendmahlsworte Jesu*, Berlin 1962³; ET: *The Eucharistic Words of Jesus*, London and New York 1966².
Die Gleichnisse Jesu, Berlin 1956³; ET: *The Parables of Jesus*, London and New York 1963².
'Kennzeichen der ipsissima vox Jesu', in: *Synoptische Studien, Alfred Wikenhauser dargebracht*, München 1953, pp. 86–93; ET in: *The Prayers of Jesus*, London 1967.
'Perikopen-Umstellungen bei Lukas?', *NTS* 4, 1957/58, pp. 115–9.
'Die Muttersprache des Evangelisten Matthäus', *ZNW* 50, 1959, pp. 270–4.

JÜLICHER, ADOLF/FASCHER, ERICH, *Einleitung in das Neue Testament*, Tübingen 1931⁷.

JÜNGEL, EBERHARD, *Paulus und Jesus—Eine Untersuchung zur Präzisierung der Frage nach dem Ursprung der Christologie*, Hermeneutische Untersuchungen zur Theologie 2, Tübingen 1962.

KÄHLER, MARTIN, *Der sogenannte historische Jesus und der geschichtliche, biblische Christus*, Leipzig 1896²; ET: *The so-called historical Jesus and the historic, biblical Christ*, Philadelphia 1964.

KÄSEMANN, ERNST, 'Das Problem des historischen Jesus', *ZThK* 51, 1954, pp. 125–53.
'Die Anfänge christlicher Theologie', *ZThK*, 57, 1960, pp. 162–85.
'Begründet der neutestamentliche Kanon die Einheit der Kirche?', *EvTh* 11, 1951/52, pp. 13–21.
Exegetische Versuche und Besinnungen I (Tübingen 1965⁴) and II (Tübingen 1965²): ET (partial) of I: *Essays on New Testament Themes*, London 1968³; ET of II in preparation.

KARNETZKI, MANFRED, 'Die galiläische Redaktion im Markusevangelium', *ZNW* 52, 1961, pp. 228–72.
'Die letzte Redaktion des Markusevangeliums', in: *Zwischenstation, Festschrift für Karl Kupisch zum 60. Geburtstag*, München 1963, pp. 161–74.
Die alttestamentlichen Zitate in der synoptischen Tradition, unpublished (typescript) dissertation, Tübingen 1955.

KLEIN, GÜNTER, *Die zwölf Apostel—Ursprung und Gehalt einer Idee*, FRLANT NF 59 (77), Göttingen 1961.
'Lukas 1, 1–4 als theologisches Programm', in: *Zeit und Geschichte, Dankesgabe an R. Bultmann zum 80. Geburtstag*, Tübingen 1964, pp. 193–216.
'Die Prüfung der Zeit (Lukas 12, 54–56)', *ZThK* 61, 1964, pp. 373–90.
'Die Verleugnung des Petrus', *ZThK* 58, 1961, pp. 285–328.

KNOCH, OTTO, 'Die eschatologische Frage, ihre Entwicklung und ihr gegenwärtiger Stand', *BZ NF* 6, 1962, pp. 112–20.

KOEHLER, LUDWIG, *Das formgeschichtliche Problem des Neuen Testaments*, SgVSThR 127, Tübingen 1927.

KÖSTER, HELMUT, *Synoptische Überlieferung bei den Apostolischen Vätern*, TU 65, Berlin 1957.

KUBY, ALFRED, 'Zur Konzeption des Markus-Evangeliums', *ZNW* 49, 1958, pp. 52–64.

KÜMMEL, WERNER GEORG, 'Futurische und präsentische Eschatologie im ältesten Christentum', *NTS* 5, 1958/59, pp. 113–26.
Verheissung und Erfüllung—Untersuchungen zur eschatologischen Verkündigung Jesu, AThANT 6, Zürich 1956²; ET: *Promise and Fulfilment*, London 1966³.

LERLE, ERNST, 'Die Predigt in Lystra — Acta 14, 15–18', *NTS* 7, 1960/61, pp. 46–55.

LINDESKOG, GÖSTA, 'Christuskerygma und Jesustradition', *NovTest* 5, 1962, pp. 144–56.

LINDSEY, R. L., 'A modified Two-Document Theory of the Synoptic Dependence and Interdependence', *NovTest* 6, 1963, pp. 239–63.

LINNEMANN, ETA, 'Die Verleugnung des Petrus', *ZThK* 63, 1966, pp. 1–32.

LOHMEYER, ERNST, *Galiläa und Jerusalem*, FRLANT NF 34, Göttingen 1936.
Das Evangelium des Markus, KEKNT I, 2, Göttingen 1959¹⁵.
'"Mir ist gegeben alle Gewalt"—Eine Exegese von Matth. 28, 16–20', in: *In memoriam Ernst Lohmeyer*, Stuttgart 1951, pp. 22–49.

LOHMEYER, ERNST/SCHMAUCH, WERNER, *Das Evangelium des Matthäus*, KEKNT, Sonderband, Göttingen 1956.

LOHSE, EDUARD, 'Die Bedeutung des Pfingstberichtes im Rahmen des lukanischen Geschichtswerkes', *EvTh* 13, 1953, pp. 422–36.
'Missionarisches Handeln Jesu nach dem Evangelium des Lukas', *ThZ* 10, 1954, pp. 1–13.
'Lukas als Theologe der Heilsgeschichte', *EvTh* 14, 1954, pp. 256–75.

LUCK, ULRICH, 'Kerygma, Tradition und Geschichte Jesu bei Lukas', *ZThK* 57, 1960, pp. 51–66.

LUZ, ULRICH, 'Das Geheimnismotiv und die markinische Christologie', *ZNW* 56, 1965, pp. 9–30.

MARXSEN, WILLI, 'Bemerkungen zur "Form" der sogenannten synoptischen Evangelien', *ThLZ* 81, 1956, cols. 345–48.
'Redaktionsgeschichtliche Erklärung der sogenannten Parabeltheorie des Markus', *ZThK* 52, 1955, pp. 255–71.
'Erwägungen zum Problem des verkündigten Kreuzes', *NTS* 8, 1961/62, pp. 204–14.
Der Evangelist Markus—Studien zur Redaktionsgeschichte des Evangeliums, FRLANT NF 49, Göttingen 1956.
Einleitung in das Neue Testament, Gütersloh 1964²: ET in preparation.

MAURER, CHRISTIAN, 'Knecht Gottes und Sohn Gottes im Passionsbericht des Markusevangeliums', *ZThK* 50, 1953, pp. 1–38.

MEYE, ROBERT, P., 'Messianic Secret and Messianic Didache in Mark's Gospel', in: *Oikonomia, O. Cullmann zum 65. Geburtstag*, Hamburg-Bergstedt 1967, pp. 57–68.

MICHAELIS, WILHELM, *Einleitung in das Neue Testament—Entstehung, Sammlung und Überlieferung der Schriften des Neuen Testaments*, Bern 1954².
'Kennen die Synoptiker eine Verzögerung der Parusie?', in: *Synoptische Studien, Alfred Wikenhauser dargebracht*, München 1953, pp. 107–23.

MICHEL, OTTO, 'Der Abschluss des Matthäusevangeliums—Ein Beitrag zur Geschichte der Osterbotschaft', *EvTh* 10, 1950/51, pp. 16–26.
'Der "historische" Jesus und das theologische Gewissheitsproblem', *EvTh* 15, 1955, pp. 349–63.

MORGENTHALER, ROBERT, *Die lukanische Geschichtsschreibung als Zeugnis*, Band 1 und 2, AThANT 14/15, Zürich 1949.

MUSSNER, FRANZ, 'Der historische Jesus und der Christus des Glaubens', *BZ NF* 1, 1957, pp. 224–52.

NAUCK, WOLFGANG, 'Die Tradition und Komposition der Areopagrede', *ZThK* 53, 1956, pp. 11–52.

NEUGEBAUER, FRITZ, 'Geistsprüche und Jesuslogien—Erwägungen zu der von der formgeschichtlichen Betrachtungsweise Bultmanns angenommenen grundsätzlichen Möglichkeit einer Identität von prophetischen Geistsprüchen mit Logien des irdischen Jesus', *ZNW* 53, 1962, pp. 218–28.

PROCKSCH, OTTO, *Petrus und Johannes bei Markus und Matthäus*, Gütersloh 1920.

PUNGE, MANFRED, *Endgeschehen und Heilsgeschichte im Matthäus-Evangelium*, unpublished (typescript) dissertation, Greifswald 1962.

RAD, GERHARD VON, *Das formgeschichtliche Problem des Hexateuch*, BWANT IV, 26, Stuttgart 1938: ET: 'The Problem of the Hexateuch', in id., *The Problem of the Hexateuch and other essays*, London 1965.

REHKOPF, FRIEDRICH, *Die lukanische Sonderquelle—Ihr Umfang und Sprachgebrauch*, WUNT 5, Tübingen 1959.

RESE, MARTIN, 'Zur Lukas-Diskussion seit 1950', in: *Wort und Dienst, Jahrbuch der Theologischen Schule Bethel* NF 9, 1967, pp. 62–7.
Alttestamentliche Motive in der Christologie des Lukas, Bonn 1965.

RIESENFELD, HARALD, 'Tradition und Redaktion im Markusevangelium', in: *Neutestamentliche Studien für R. Bultmann*, BZNW 21, Berlin 1954, pp. 157–64.

ROBINSON, JAMES MCCONKEY, *Das Geschichtsverständnis des Markus-Evangeliums*, AThANT 30, Zürich 1956: English version: *The Problem of History in Mark*, London 1956.

ROBINSON, JAMES M., λόγοι σοφῶν. Zur Gattung der Spruchquelle Q', in: *Zeit und Geschichte, Dankesgabe an R. Bultmann zum 80. Geburtstag*, Tübingen 1964, pp. 77–96.

ROBINSON, WILLIAM C., *Der Weg des Herrn—Studien zur Geschichte und Eschatologie im Lukas-Evangelium*, ThF 36, Hamburg-Bergstedt 1964.

ROLOFF, JÜRGEN, *Apostolat—Verkündigung—Kirche, Ursprung, Inhalt und Funktion des kirchlichen Apostelamtes nach Paulus, Lukas und den Pastoralbriefen*, Gütersloh 1965.

SCHELKLE, KARL HERMANN, *Die Passion Jesu in der Verkündigung des Neuen Testaments—Ein Beitrag zur Formgeschichte und zur Theologie des Neuen Testaments*, Heidelberg 1949.

SCHICK, EDUARD, *Formgeschichte und Synoptikerexegese—Eine kritische Untersuchung über die Möglichkeit und Grenzen der formgeschichtlichen Methode*, NTA XVIII, 2/3, Münster 1940.

SCHILLE, GOTTFRIED, '*Anfänge der Kirche—Erwägungen zur apostolischen Frühgeschichte*, BEvTh 43, München 1966.
'Bemerkungen zur Formgeschichte des Evangeliums', *NTS* 4, 1957/8: I 'Rahmen und Aufbau des Markusevangeliums', pp. 1–24.
II 'Das Evangelium des Matthäus als Katechismus', pp. 101–14; *NTS* 5, 1958: III Das Evangelium als Missionsbuch', pp. 1–11.
'Der Mangel eines kritischen Geschichtsbildes in der neutestamentlichen Formgeschichte', *ThLZ* 88, 1963, cols. 491–502.
'Die Topographie des Markusevangeliums, ihre Hintergründe und ihre Einordnung', *ZDPV* 73, 1957, pp. 133–66.

SCHLATTER, ADOLF, *Der Evangelist Matthäus—Seine Sprache, sein Ziel, sein Selbständigkeit*, Stuttgart 1929.

SCHMAUCH, WERNER, 'Die Komposition des Matthäus—Evangeliums in ihrer Bedeutung für seine Interpretation', in: ". . . *zu achten aufs Wort*", *Ausgewählte Arbeiten*, Berlin 1967, pp. 64–86.

SCHMID, JOSEF, *Das Evangelium nach Matthäus*, RNT 1, Regensburg 1948, 1959[4].

SCHMIDT, KARL LUDWIG, 'Das Christuszeugnis der synoptischen Evangelien', BhEvTh2, 1936, pp. 7–33.
Der Rahmen der Geschichte Jesu—Literarkritische Untersuchung zur ältesten Jesusüberlieferung, Berlin 1919.
'Die Stellung der Evangelien in der allgemeinen Literaturgeschichte', in: *Eucharisterion für Hermann Gunkel* II, FRLANT 36, 2, Göttingen 1923, pp. 50–134.
'Formgeschichte', RGG II,[2] cols. 638–40.

SCHNACKENBURG, RUDOLF, *Gottes Herrschaft und Reich*, Freiburg 1961[2].
'Zur formgeschichtlichen Methode in der Evangelienforschung', ZkTh 85, 1963, pp. 16–32.

SCHNEIDER, JOHANNES, 'Zur Analyse des lukanischen Reiseberichtes', in: *Synoptische Studien, Alfred Wikenhauser dargebracht*, München 1953, pp. 207–29.
'Der Beitrag der Urgemeinde zur Jesusüberlieferung im Lichte der neuesten Forschung', ThLZ 87, 1962, cols. 401–12.

SCHNIEWIND, JULIUS, 'Zur Synoptiker-Exegese', ThR NF 2, 1930, 129–89.

SCHOEPS, HANS-JOACHIM, 'Ebionitische Apokalyptik im Neuen Testament', ZNW 51, 1960, pp. 101–11.

SCHREIBER, JOHANNES, 'Die Christologie des Markusevangeliums—Beobachtungen zur Theologie und Komposition des zweiten Evangeliums', ZThK 58, 1961, pp. 154–83.
Theologie des Vertrauens—Eine redaktionsgeschichtliche Untersuchung des Markus evangeliums, Hamburg 1967.

SCHÜRMANN, HEINZ, 'Die vorösterlichen Anfänge der Logientradition—Versuch eines formgeschichtlichen Zuganges zum Leben Jesu', in: *Der historische Jesus und der kerygmatische Christus*, Berlin 1960, pp. 342–70.
Der Paschamahlbericht Lk. 22, (7–14) 15–18. I. Teil einer quellenkritischen Untersuchung des lukanischen Abendmahlsberichtes Lk. 22. 7–38, NTA XIX, 5, Münster 1953.
Der Einsetzungsbericht Lk. 22. 19–20. II. Teil einer quellenkritischen Untersuchung des lukanischen Abendmahlsberichtes Lk. 22, 7–38, NTA XX, 4, Münster 1955.
Jesu Abschiedsrede Lk. 22, 21–38. III. Teil einer quellenkritischen Unter-

suchung des lukanischen Abendmahlsberichtes Lk. 22, 7–38, NTA XX, 5, Münster 1957.

'Zur Traditions-und Redaktionsgeschichte von Mt. 10, 23', *BZ NF* 3, 1959, pp. 82–8.

SCHULZ, SIEGFRIED, 'Die Bedeutung des Markus für die Theologiegeschichte des Urchristentums', in: *Studia Evangelica*, Vol. II, Part I, TU 87, Berlin 1964, pp. 135–45.

'Markus und das Alte Testament', *ZThK* 58, 1961, pp. 184–97.

Die Stunde der Botschaft—Einführung in die Theologie der vier Evangelisten, Hamburg 1967.

'Gottes Vorsehung bei Lukas', *ZNW* 54, 1963, pp. 104–16.

SCHUSTER, HERMANN, 'Die konsequente Eschatologie in der Interpretation des Neuen Testaments, kritisch betrachtet', *ZNW* 47, 1956, pp. 1–25.

SCHWEIZER, EDUARD, 'Anmerkungen zur Theologie des Markus', in: *Neotestamentica et Patristica (O. Cullmann zum 60. Geburtstag)*, SupplNovTest VI, Leiden 1962, pp. 35–46.

'Zur Frage der Messiasgeheimnistheorie bei Markus', *ZNW* 56, 1965, pp. 1–8.

'Der Menschensohn—Zur eschatologischen Erwartung Jesu', *ZNW* 50, 1959, pp. 185–209.

SOIRON, THADDÄUS, *Die Bergpredigt Jesu—Formgeschichtliche, exegetische und theologische Erklärung*, Freiburg 1941.

'Das Evangelium als Lebensform des Menschen', *Der katholische Gedanke*, 11, München/Rom 1925.

Die Logia Jesu—Eine literarkritische und literargeschichtliche Untersuchung zum synoptischen Problem, NTA IV, 4, Münster 1916.

SOUČEK, J. B., 'Zu den Problemen des Jakobusbriefes', *EvTh* 18, 1958, pp. 460–68.

STENDAHL, KRISTER, *The School of St. Matthew*, ASNU XX, Uppsala 1954.

STRECKER, GEORG, 'Besprechung von W. Marxsen, *Der Evangelist Markus* 1959²', *ZKG* 72, 1961, pp. 142–47.

'Das Geschichtsverständnis bei Matthäus', *EvTh* 26, 1966, pp. 57–74.

'Die Leidens-und Auferstehungsvoraussagen im Markusevangelium', *ZThK* 64, 1967, pp. 16–39.

'Zur Messiasgeheimnistheorie im Markusevangelium', in: *Studia Evangelica*, Vol. III, TU 88, Berlin 1964, pp. 87–104.

Der Weg der Gerechtigkeit—Untersuchungen zur Theologie des Matthäus, FRLANT 82, Göttingen 1962, 1966².

STROBEL, AUGUST, 'In dieser Nacht (Lk. 17, 34)—Zu einer älteren Form der Erwartung in Lk. 17, 20–37', *ZThK* 58, 1961, pp. 16–29.

'Die Passa-Erwartung als urchristliches Problem in Lk. 17, 20f.', *ZNW* 49, 1958, pp. 157–96.

Untersuchungen zum synoptischen Verzögerungsproblem auf Grund der spät-jüdisch-urchristlichen Geschichte von Hab. 2, 2ff., SupplNovTest II, Leiden/ Köln 1961.
'Zum Verständnis von Mt. 25, 1–13', *NovTest* 2, 1958, pp. 199–227.

SUHL, ALFRED, *Die Funktion der alttestamentlichen Zitate und Anspielungen im Markusevangelium*, Gütersloh 1965.

TÖDT, HEINZ EDUARD, *Der Menschensohn in der synoptischen Überlieferung*, Gütersloh 1963; ET: *The Son of Man in the Synoptic Tradition*, London and Philadelphia 1965.

TRILLING, WOLFGANG, *Das wahre Israel—Studien zur Theologie des Matthäus-evangeliums*, Erfurter Theologische Studien 7, Leipzig 1959.
'Die Täufertradition bei Matthäus', *BZ NF* 3, 1959, pp. 271–89.

VIELHAUER, PHILIPP, 'Das Benedictus des Zacharias (Lk. 1, 68–79)', *ZThK* 49, 1952, pp. 255–72.
'Erwägungen zur Christologie des Markusevangeliums', in: *Zeit und Geschichte, Dankesgabe an Rudolf Bultmann zum 80. Geburtstag*, Tübingen 1964, pp. 155–69.
'Gottesreich und Menschensohn in der Verkündigung Jesu', in: *Festschrift für Günther Dehn zum 70. Geburtstag*, Neukirchen 1957, pp. 51–79.
'Jesus und der Menschensohn. Zur Diskussion mit H. E. Tödt und E. Schweizer', *ZThK* 60, 1963, pp. 133–77.
'Zum "Paulinismus" der Apostelgeschichte', *EvTh* 10, 1950/51, pp. 1–15.
'Ein Weg zur neutestamentlichen Christologie?', *EvTh* 25, 1965, pp. 24–72.

VÖGTLE, ANTON, 'Das christologische und ekklesiologische Anliegen von Mt. 28, 18–20', in: *Studia Evangelica*, Vol. II, TU 87, Berlin 1964, pp. 266–94.

WALTER, NIKOLAUS, 'Tempelzerstörung und synoptische Apokalypse', *ZNW* 57, 1966, pp. 38–49.

WIKENHAUSER, ALFRED, *Einleitung in das Neue Testament*, Freiburg 1959³.

WILCKENS, ULRICH, 'Kerygma und Evangelium bei Lukas—Beobach-tungen zu Apg. 10, 34–43', *ZNW* 49, 1958, pp. 223–37.
Die Missionsreden der Apostelgeschichte—Form und traditionsgeschichtliche Untersuchungen, WMANT 5, Neukirchen 1961: ET in preparation.

WINTER, PAUL, 'Besprechung von H. Conzelmann, *Die Mitte der Zeit*, 1954,' *ThLZ* 81, 1956, cols. 36–38.

WREDE, WILLIAM, *Das Messiasgeheimnis in den Evangelien—Zugleich ein Beitrag zum Verständnis des Markusevangeliums*, Göttingen 1913², 1963³.

INDEX OF NAMES

Figures in bold type refer to the pages where an author's work is reviewed at length.

INDEX OF BIBLICAL REFERENCES